SUBVERTING EXCLUSION

THE LAMAR SERIES IN WESTERN HISTORY

The Lamar Series in Western History includes scholarly books of general public interest that enhance the understanding of human affairs in the American West and contribute to a wider understanding of the West's significance in the political, social, and cultural life of America. Comprising works of the highest quality, the series aims to increase the range and vitality of Western American history, focusing on frontier places and people, Indian and ethnic communities, the urban West and the environment, and the art and illustrated history of the American West.

RECENT TITLES

Furs and Frontiers in the Far North: The Contest among Native and Foreign Nations for the Bering Strait Fur Trade, by John R. Bockstoce

War of a Thousand Deserts: Indian Raids and the U.S.–Mexican War, by Brian DeLay

Defying the Odds: The Tule River Tribe's Struggle for Sovereignty in Three Centuries, by Gelya Frank and Carole Goldberg

The Bourgeois Frontier: French Towns, French Traders, and American Expansion, by Jay Gitlin

"Liberty to the Downtrodden": Thomas L. Kane, Romantic Reformer, by Matthew J. Grow

The Comanche Empire, by Pekka Hämäläinen

Hell on the Range: A Story of Honor, Conscience, and the American West, by Daniel Herman

William Clark's World: Describing America in an Age of Unknowns, by Peter Kastor

The Jeffersons at Shadwell, by Susan Kern

The American Far West in the Twentieth Century, by Earl Pomeroy

Borderlines in Borderlands: James Madison and the Spanish-American Frontier, 1776–1821, by J. C. A. Stagg

FORTHCOMING TITLES

Welcome to Wonderland: Promoting Tourism in the Rocky Mountain West, by Peter Blodgett

The Shapes of Power: Frontiers, Borderlands, Middle Grounds, and Empires of North America, by Pekka Hämäläinen

Bold Spirits, by Monica Rico

Chosen Land: The Legal Creation of White Manhood on the Eighteenth-Century Kentucky Frontier, by Honor Sachs

Making Los Angeles: Race, Space, and Municipal Power, by David Torres-Rouff

The Cherokee Diaspora, by Gregory Smithers

Geronimo, by Robert Utley

ANDREA GEIGER

Subverting Exclusion

TRANSPACIFIC ENCOUNTERS WITH RACE,
CASTE, AND BORDERS, 1885–1928

Yale UNIVERSITY PRESS

NEW HAVEN AND LONDON

Published with assistance from the Louis Stern Memorial Fund.

Yale University Press books may be purchased in quantity for educational, business, or promotional use. For information, please e-mail sales.press@yale.edu (U.S. office) or sales@yaleup.co.uk (U.K. office).

Set in Scala Roman type by IDS Infotech Ltd., Chandigarh, India.

Printed in the United States of America

Library of Congress Cataloging-in-Publication Data

Geiger, Andrea A. E.

   Subverting exclusion : transpacific encounters with race, caste, and borders, 1885–1928 / Andrea Geiger.

     p. cm.—(The Lamar series in Western history)

   Includes bibliographical references and index.

   ISBN 978-0-300-16963-8 (alk. paper)

   1. Japanese—North America—History—19th century. 2. Japanese—North America—History—20th century. 3. Japanese—North America—Social conditions. 4. Racism—North America—History. 5. Canada—Emigration and immigration—History. 6. United States—Emigration and immigration—History. 7. British Columbia—Emigration and immigration—History. 8. Japan—Emigration and immigration—History. 9. Boundaries—Social aspects—North America—History. 10. North America—Race relations. I. Title.

   E49.2.J3G45 2011

   305.80097—dc22

2011014180

A catalogue record for this book is available from the British Library.

This paper meets the requirements of ANSI/NISO Z39.48-1992 (Permanence of Paper).

10 9 8 7 6 5 4 3 2 1

To my parents

CONTENTS

ACKNOWLEDGMENTS

I owe a debt of gratitude to far more people than I can acknowledge in these few pages. Like many first books, this was a dissertation in its initial incarnation. I will always be grateful to my advisor, Richard White, for taking on the task of transforming this former lawyer into a historian. His longstanding interest in the construction of race and difference in the North American West, his clear vision and incisive critique, and his willingness to challenge conventional narratives shape both his teaching and his scholarship and set the standard to which I aspire as a historian. Other professors at the University of Washington to whom I am also grateful for their sage advice include Charles Bergquist, John Findlay, Moon-ho Jung, and Kenneth B. Pyle.

I benefited from conversations with many others who read or spoke with me about my work, including, in various parts of the United States, Roger Daniels, George De Vos, Andrew Graybill, Benjamin Johnson, Matthew Klingle, Lon Kurashige, Shotaro Frank Miyamoto, Leslie Moch, Seizo Oka, Gary Okihiro, Michael Weiner, K. Scott Wong, and members of my cohort at the University of Washington, especially Connie Chiang, Jennifer Seltz, and Coll-Peter Thrush. A number of scholars, activists and students of Japanese emigration history were kind enough to meet and talk with me during trips to Japan, including Yoshikazu Akisada, David Boggett, Yasuo Endo, Daniel Foote, Mieko Fujioka, Tetsuro Hirano, Masumi Izumi,

Shigeru Kojima, Megumi Komori, Yumiko Konishi, Hisakazu Nishihama, Shinji Okano, Mitsuhiro Sakaguchi, Yasuo Sakata, Toshiji Sasaki, and Atsushi Sato. In British Columbia, fellow academics and students of Japanese immigration history who took the time to discuss various aspects of my research with me include Midge Ayukawa, Jeremy Brown, Luke Clossey, Stan and Masako Fukawa, Keay Homma, Osamu Kasahara, Sonja Luehrmann, Janice Matsumura, Patricia Roy, David Sulz, Tsuneko Takaki, Jay Taylor, Ikuye Uchida, Masaki Watanabe, and Moe Yesaki. I had the opportunity to present parts of my work at history conferences and workshops throughout North America and am thankful to all who attended and shared their insights. I am also grateful to Christopher Rogers, Laura Davulis, and Mary Pasti at Yale University Press for their guidance and warm support and to my anonymous readers for their thoughtful comments.

I owe a deep debt of gratitude to the many archivists and librarians who went out of their way to assist me in places from Japan to California to the British Columbia interior, as well as to the Japanese migrants whose voices are reflected in the many archival collections I consulted. In British Columbia, the Japanese Canadian National Museum and Archives, now located in Burnaby, B.C., deserves special acknowledgment. I am also grateful to the archivists at the B.C. Archives, Victoria; Cumberland Museum and Archives; Courtenay and District Museum; Kelowna Public Archives; Nelson Museum and Archives; New Westminster Archives; Revelstoke Museum and Archives; University of British Columbia Special Collections and Archives; Vancouver Public Library, Special Collections Division; and the Vernon Museum and Archives. In Japan, archivists who gave generously of their time include those at the Buraku Liberation and Human Rights Research Institute, Osaka; Japanese Emigration Museum, Yokohama; National Diet Library, Tokyo; Osaka Human Rights Museum; and Wakayama Civic Library, Emigrant Resources Division. In the United States, they include archivists at the Bancroft Library, University of California, Berkeley; Hoover Institution on War, Revolution and Peace Library and Archives, Stanford University, Palo Alto, California; Japanese American History Archives, San Francisco; Japanese American Research Project, University of California, Los Angeles; Oregon Nikkei Legacy Center, Portland; University of Washington Libraries, Special Collections and Archives, Seattle; and the U.S. National Archives and Records

Administration, San Bruno, California, and Washington, D.C. During the later stages of this process, the library staff at the Simon Fraser University Library in Burnaby, B.C., worked miracles, tracking down original images on both sides of the Pacific that were seemingly impossible to find. Jonathan Fast scanned and prepared the images for submission to the press with meticulous care and artistry, and Bill Nelson created the original maps and Derek Gottlieb the index with the same consummate skill.

I am grateful to Simon Fraser University for its financial support as I revised the manuscript for publication and to my colleagues in the history department for the warm and collegial environment in which I have the good fortune to work.

Parts of this book were previously published and are included here, in revised form, with the permission of the original publishers. Chapter 3 was originally published in abridged form as "Negotiating the Boundaries of Race and Class: Meiji Diplomatic Responses to North American Categories of Exclusion," in *BC Studies* 156/157 (Winter/Spring 2007/2008). Parts of Chapters 5 and 6 were published as "Caught in the Gap: The Transit Privilege and North America's Ambiguous Borders," in Benjamin Johnson and Andrew Graybill, eds., *Bridging National Borders in North America* (Durham, N.C.: Duke University Press, 2010); copyright 2010, Duke University Press; all rights reserved; reprinted by permission of the publisher. Part of Chapter 7 was published in expanded form as "Writing Racial Barriers into Law: Upholding B.C.'s Denial of the Vote to Its Japanese Canadian Citizens, *Homma v. Cunningham*, 1902," in Louis Fiset and Gail M. Nomura, eds., *Nikkei in the Pacific Northwest: Japanese Americans and Japanese Canadians in the Twentieth Century* (Seattle: University of Washington Press, 2005); reprinted by permission of the publisher.

Finally, I would like to thank all those family and friends whose affection and support has sustained me through the years. Solitary though the research and writing of a book such as this is, Lawrence and Sarah, in particular, made sure that I always knew I was not alone in that endeavor. To all, I return their affection in full measure. Although my parents did not live to see this book published, their determination to challenge the Eurocentric views of the societies in which they were raised by the way they lived their own lives took our family to Japan and profoundly affected my understanding of social issues and, in time, my approach to history. It is to them that this book is dedicated.

Nikkei—literally "Japan" and "thread"—is the term generally used in English to refer to people of Japanese ancestry living abroad. I prefer the term *nikkeijin*—which adds *jin,* or "people," to *nikkei*—although I use *nikkei* as an adjective. I do not capitalize Japanese words—including *issei* (first-generation Japanese immigrant) and *nisei* (second-generation Japanese immigrant)—to avoid giving them a level of emphasis or self-consciousness that they do not have in Japanese, which does not distinguish between capital and lowercase letters in any case. I apply the same principle to terms such as *burakumin* and *buraku jūmin,* used to refer to former outcaste groups in Japanese. Other, more derogatory terms used to refer to people in these categories are addressed in historical context in the text. In English, I use "outcaste" to refer to groups identified as such within the context of the Tokugawa status system and "outcast" in more general contexts. I capitalize proper names and list given and family names in the order used by the individual in question. Although it is the custom in Japan to list family name first, many immigrants or Japanese writing for English-speaking audiences have adopted the custom of listing given name first. They also sometimes anglicize their names. Spellings used here are those employed by the original sources.

Such terms as "white racism" and "exclusionist" are used as shorthand for attitudes organized around late nineteenth- and early twentieth-century articulations of race in the North American West. I recognize that a wide range of perspectives and rationales is included in these categories and that racism was not only an attitude of whites. My specific purpose here, however, is to explore its larger impact on Japanese immigrants in North America as it intersected with caste-based ways of understanding difference rooted in Japanese history and culture. Whiteness itself is also a contested category, the contours of which have varied over time and from place to place. Although scholars regard caste and class as conceptually distinct categories, Japanese immigrants did not always differentiate between them when speaking in English, using "class" even where context makes it clear that reference to "caste" was intended and at times conflating the two. These terms should thus be read in context, and the difference between them should be understood as one of emphasis and not rigid definition. The same is true of the word "status," used both to refer to the Tokugawa status categories (*mibun*) and, more generally, to refer to rank or social position in Western societies. Also important to read in context are references to the West as a region in North America that spans parts of the United States, Canada, and northern Mexico. These need to be differentiated from more general references to Western nations.

Finally, I distinguish between emigrants, immigrants, and migrants. Emigrants are people engaged in the act of leaving their home countries; immigrants are those entering a country other than the one in which they were born with the intention of residing there on a permanent basis; and migrants are simply people in motion, whether within the boundaries of their home country or in international space.

SUBVERTING EXCLUSION

Introduction

AFTER LEARNING THAT THE UNITED STATES had passed legislation barring further labor immigration from Japan in 1924, an anonymous Japanese immigrant living "at the base of the Rockies" wrote:

> *Boku wa nihon ni oite wa shinheimin de aru.*
> *Amerika ni atte wa japu to iu shinheimin de aru.*

> In Japan, I am an outcaste.
> In America, I am an outcaste called "Jap."[1]

The author's equation of racial discrimination in North America with the caste-based prejudice he had experienced in Japan suggests the extent to which culturally specific perceptions of difference rooted in Japanese history provided an interpretive framework for the racial hostility he and other Japanese immigrants encountered in the West of the late nineteenth and early twentieth centuries.

Like all immigrants, Japanese immigrants perceived and responded to the new environments they encountered in North America in terms of the social and cultural understandings they brought with them from their countries of origin. These included, in Japan, historical status and caste categories—*mibun* in Japanese—written into law to reinforce the status system of the Tokugawa period (1600–1867). Although these categories

1

were abolished early in the successive Meiji period (1868–1912), before most Japanese emigrants went abroad, social attitudes that were a product of that system persisted and served to frame their responses to the racial barriers they confronted in Canada and the United States. Their experience of white racism, in other words, was refracted through the lens of mibun. With this premise as a beginning point, I examine how social and cultural attitudes rooted in mibun factored into Japanese immigrant negotiations of race, class, and gender in the North American West and consider how people who structured their perceptions of social difference in terms of caste and mibun participated in shaping definitions of nation, race, and empire as they moved through and across the borders of Canada, the United States, and Mexico.

Written large, late nineteenth- and early twentieth-century Japanese emigration to North America parallels that from Europe in significant ways, including underlying motivation and larger demographic pattern. As other historians have also pointed out, migration to North America from both Europe and Asia was integral to the expansion of a world capitalist system. The development of industrial capitalism in the North American West, in turn, created a growing demand for labor. Parallel processes that disrupted existing economic patterns in both Europe and Japan gave rise to new patterns of migration, first to urban centers and, in time, to destinations beyond what were often newly defined national borders. The willingness of increasing numbers of labor migrants to travel to faraway places to find work was itself partly a product of the extension of industrial capitalism to places like the United States and the Canadian West.[2] Capital development on an increasingly global scale also played a key role in shaping Western imperialist strategies in Asia during the nineteenth century, including the United States' interest in extending its commercial influence to Japan.[3] A great majority of the sweeping social, political, and economic changes that followed the Meiji Restoration in 1868, which instated a new government in Japan, were a direct result of Japan's determination to resist Western encroachments by meeting them head on. Japan's efforts to achieve industrial and economic parity with the West and to redefine itself as a modern and civilized nation in Western eyes, helped to create the conditions that led to the emigration of many thousands of Japanese laborers to other parts of the world— including the North American West—in the late nineteenth and early twentieth centuries.[4]

Although European and Asian migrants went abroad with similar objectives in mind, Japanese and other Asian migrants faced a range of race-based legal barriers in both the United States and Canada intended not only to limit their numbers but to direct those who did arrive toward particular industries. All immigrants encountered prejudice of one kind or another, but anti-Asian prejudice was written into law and integrated into the very structure of society to a degree that distinguished it from the challenges that others faced. Had ever more restrictive immigration laws not interfered, migrant streams from Japan and other parts of Asia might well have come to resemble more closely, in terms of relative numbers, those from Europe. Instead, European immigrants—roughly 23 million during the late nineteenth and early twentieth centuries—far outnumbered the 270,000 Japanese who arrived in the United States and Canada during the same period.[5] Partly responsive to hostile immigration policies and attitudes in North America, however, the Meiji government's own approach to emigration also reflected cultural attitudes specific to Japan that were a product of its own historical experience, including a persistent concern with mibun.

Rooted in a system of formal status and caste divisions reinforced by law for most of the preceding two and a half centuries of Tokugawa rule, hierarchical views of society and nation and traditional ways of understanding status and caste difference infused Meiji society. Not only were social tensions a major factor leading to the Meiji Restoration, but historical status categories were a major target of the reforms implemented by the Meiji oligarchs during the early decades of the Meiji period. An integral part of a larger effort to prove to Western nations that Japan was a modern nation deserving of recognition as an equal, the changes instituted by the new Meiji government reverberated throughout Japanese society, affecting all Tokugawa status groups in significant ways and leading, in the case of *samurai* and outcastes, to a complete redefinition of their roles. Embedded in the very framework of Japanese society for well over two centuries, however, mibun was at the core of the way in which people in Japan understood their place in the world, with the result that the perceptions of difference associated with the Tokugawa status system proved remarkably tenacious. Meiji-era Japanese emigrants, as a result, often carried these ideas and associated ways of viewing the world with them went they went abroad decades after the formal abolition of the status system. Culturally distinct ways of understanding difference shaped not just the immigrants' responses to the race-based hostility they encountered in the North American West but also informed both the Meiji government's attitude toward its own emigrants and its responses to the legal barriers that its subjects encountered in the North American West.

Particularly revealing in this context is the idea of outcaste status. Although it was abolished as a matter of law together with other status categories at the beginning of the Meiji period, social taboos associated with outcaste status proved more difficult to eradicate. Because Meiji-era notions of race and caste difference came into sharp focus around the idea of outcaste status, it serves as an especially poignant example of the ways the consideration of status issues internal to particular immigrant groups can illuminate their strategies with respect to the dominant society in the countries to which they traveled. Mibun in general, and perceptions associated with outcaste status in particular, not only shaped relations among Japanese immigrants but mediated their responses to both constraints and opportunities in the North American West. Choices made by Meiji-era Japanese immigrants regarding potential livelihoods, for example, were a product of their own association of certain kinds of occupations with outcaste status, as well as a product of economic restrictions imposed by Canada and the United States. White racism, moreover, was offensive not only because it relegated Japanese to the bottom of the race-based labor hierarchies that ordered social relations in both the United States and the Canadian West but because it rendered all Japanese equivalent to outcastes within the context of North American societies and failed to recognize status and caste differences to which Japanese continued to ascribe meaning.

Because Japanese immigrants in all status categories equated their treatment by white racists with that meted out to outcastes in Tokugawa Japan, the idea of outcaste status figured prominently in strategies developed by Meiji diplomats and immigrants alike to challenge exclusionary measures. As a result, their efforts to respond to white racism cannot be fully understood without taking mibun generally and outcaste status in particular into account. Both the status system and outcaste status factored into arguments regarding the composition of Japanese immigrant communities: how race was to be defined and understood, who should be permitted access across national borders, what the relationship of Japanese immigrant communities was to the larger nation-state, and what the contours of citizenship were. Though not always central to these debates, the idea of outcaste status emerges as a persistent theme in the rhetorical encounters between anti-Japanese exclusionists and the governments of Canada and the United States. It also intersects with the issue of illegality and sheds light on the internal dynamics of prewar immigrant communities. In that context, it enables us to challenge their depiction as homogeneous and devoid of the kinds of racist attitudes that plagued the dominant societies. Communities of Japanese living abroad, specifically, *nikkei* communities in North America, we come to realize, were always more complex and divided along various axes than Japanese community leaders, on the one hand, and white racists, on the other, found it expedient to admit.

A discussion of word usage is important here. Because the official terms used to refer to outcastes during the Tokugawa era were profoundly derogatory, efforts have been made since that time to find ways to discuss the historical experience of people in these categories without invoking the same pejorative connotations. Although the term *burakumin* is not universally accepted, it is the one most widely used by English-language scholars to refer to former outcastes and their descendants. *Burakumin*, a shortened form of *hisabetsu burakumin* (discriminated-against village people), has begun to assume negative connotations in Japan, however. To avoid these connotations, a new term has been coined that is gradually being adopted: *buraku jūmin* (village residents). Expressly intended to avoid labeling the person, it instead emphasizes ancestral links to partic- ular places of residence.[6] For this reason, and because it highlights the centrality of place to the larger narrative here, I use the term *buraku jūmin* to refer both to people categorized as outcastes in Tokugawa Japan and to those who became the objects of prejudice at later times based on their descent from outcaste groups. To faithfully reflect original sources, I make an exception where a particular term appears in a direct quotation or is otherwise germane to the topic under discussion. Retaining the term used in the original situates it in historical context and serves to illustrate the vehement and irrational nature of the prejudice that people in this category faced. The associated imagery also brings into sharp focus the intensity of the immigrant reaction to white racism when, as in the brief poem that introduces this chapter, the two are equated.

Also important to understand are other less formal euphemisms or code words that have been used at various junctures. Code words give us access to gaps between apparent and intended meanings, which provide a basis for better understanding attitudes and subtexts not openly stated. Ambiguity is built into the very structure of the Japanese language. It is entirely possible, for example, to form complete sentences in Japanese without ever identifying the subject of the sentence. The added ambiguity offered by euphemism provides a way to communicate subtexts and hidden meanings while avoiding the discomfort associated with more direct language.[7] Subtexts also make it easier for speakers to deny any prejudice on their part. Euphemism is sometimes used to diffuse negative connotations, but it can also be used to perpetuate them. Meiji-era Japanese immigrants, for example, often used the phrase *saika no kyū*, generally translated into English as "lowest of the low," where reference to buraku jūmin or other outcaste groups was intended. While using the phrase avoided use of the derogatory *eta*, with which Meiji Japanese in North America tended to be most familiar, its intended meaning is clear.[8]

A very loud silence has muffled discussion of the buraku issue not only in Japan but also in the context of Japanese immigration to North America. That silence, I came to realize in the course of my research, obscures not just the presence of buraku jūmin among Japanese immigrants abroad but also the nuanced nature of their reaction to racial bias. Silence also contributes to the prejudice against buraku jūmin that persists to this day in some circles.[9] The abolition of outcaste status in Japan in 1871 has itself, ironically, reinforced the silence that surrounds this issue. There are some who argue that any discussion of outcaste status and its historical consequences only perpetuates a prejudice that would not otherwise continue to exist.[10] But silence is not the same as absence of discrimination. This was made clear to me when a classmate at a Japanese high school showed me a pejorative hand gesture used to signal the identity of others she identified as burakumin, even as she warned me to avoid them on the ground that they were purportedly dangerous.

The silence that surrounds the buraku issue also manifests itself in other ways. More than once I have opened a journal to the pages where an article on this subject was published and have found it cut out of the journal. This proved to be the case, for example, with an article in the

University of Washington's copy of volume 37 of the journal *Sociology and Social Research*. The article had clearly been scissored out, and a note in the margin indicates that the damage was noted by the library in June 1982. The article that was cut out was entitled "The Eta: Japan's Indigenous Minority."[11] It is hard to read such an act as anything but an effort to suppress knowledge about buraku jūmin. Whether it is an act of prejudice or an attempt to resist that prejudice is more difficult to discern. The stark reality of the missing pages, however, is graphic evidence of an effort on someone's part to deny the reader any knowledge of their content.

Silence is also a tool that those descended from people historically classified as outcastes have been able to use to obscure their identity in order to avoid the stigma that still continues to be associated with such status among at least some Japanese. Because the only sure way to identify an individual as buraku jūmin today is to link that person to an ancestral community in a particular geographical location, the ability to obscure ancestral ties to places where outcastes lived during historical times offers the possibility of "passing" and avoiding the prejudice that might otherwise be directed at their descendant. The need to resort to silence and to obscure one's own historical identity to live free of prejudice, however, has also allowed many of the old stereotypes to persist. For buraku jūmin to succeed even during the twentieth century has often been contingent on their ability to draw attention away from their buraku origins.[12] The myth that buraku jūmin were less capable than other Japanese thus goes unchallenged, and the evidence that would expose it as false remains hidden from those who embrace it.

The continuing power of negative stereotypes on both sides of the Pacific well into the twentieth century has made historians reluctant to raise the issue of outcaste status in Japanese emigration histories.[13] Some eight decades after it was abolished in Japan, for example, Robert B. Hall, Sr., reported that "ordinary people, in the parts of Japan where outcasts are numerous, are very much afraid of and repulsed by Buraku people."[14] Even after World War II, George De Vos and Hiroshi Wagatsuma reported in the 1960s, negative attitudes included the perception that buraku jūmin were dangerous, capable of inflicting bodily harm, contagious as bearers of disease, " 'vulgar,' 'dirty,' 'disgusting,' and 'quarrelsome.' "[15] The acute sensitivity that such stereotypes produce led the author of the only study to examine the issue of outcaste status in North America to use a pseudonym to disguise his identity.[16] Even today, the issue of outcaste status continues to create so much discomfort among some *nikkeijin* (people of Japanese ancestry) in Canada and the United States that I have at times been asked to avoid it as a subject of scholarly inquiry. While those who made this request denied any prejudice on their own part, they expressed concern that if the question were raised, people in Japan would think that all Japanese immigrants were buraku jūmin. Implied in their concern is the fear that this would cause Japanese to view all Japanese abroad in a more negative light. What such expressions of fear illustrate is the pervasive and continuing nature of these historical prejudices. As Edward Fowler has pointed out, however, we have an obligation as scholars not to allow such negative stereotypes to shape our own scholarship.[17] In my observation, it is not acknowledgment of the historical experience of buraku jūmin that gives rise to prejudice but the negative characterizations projected onto people in this category by those who do not understand that their prejudice is based not on objective fact but on historically constructed ideas. Like racial discrimination, caste prejudice tells us little of substance about the people against whom it is directed but a great deal about those who accept it.

Widely denied though it is, caste prejudice is still widespread enough to make it impossible to quantify or directly trace the migrations of buraku jūmin in definitive terms.[18] I focus instead on the role that the idea of outcaste status played in shaping the behavior and attitudes of Meiji-era immigrants to North America. Even in this context, the prejudices and negative perceptions associated with outcaste status can be difficult to pin down. In much the same way that popular discourse surrounding racism in post–civil rights America insists on its disappearance through official acts and silence even as it persists in everyday life, caste-based prejudice tends to be "hidden though tacitly practiced."[19] "Racism exists as an object of vehement denial but its positive existence is elusive," and so does prejudice against buraku jūmin. Like the study of race, the study of caste becomes the "study of a submerged phenomenon, consciously hidden and obliquely discussed."[20] Although direct evidence also exists, the oblique and submerged nature of caste-based distinctions makes it necessary to adopt an indirect approach in studying this way of understanding difference. Direct expressions of bias or animus also exist, but to fully appreciate their significance as a force shaping the attitudes of Meiji-era Japanese immigrants in the North American West, it is necessary to construct what lawyers call a "but for" argument: but for the presence of a particular factor, a certain result could not have been obtained.[21] Much as an astronomer might infer the presence of unseen planets from variations in the orbits of those that are visible, I argue that some behaviors and strategies of Meiji Japanese can be fully explained only when the idea of outcaste status, and attitudes regarding mibun more generally, are taken into consideration.

Although I was repeatedly told that the submerged nature of caste-based prejudice made a study involving outcaste status in North America impossible, I realized that there were numerous, if brief, references to outcaste status in a wide variety of primary and secondary sources, from local Japanese-language newspapers to autobiographical accounts, guidebooks, oral histories, poems, and essays written to refute claims made by anti-Japanese exclusionists. Often no more than a few lines in length, these references are frequently worded in ways that made plain the power of the idea of outcaste status and the association with pollution and marginality embedded in it. Taken together, the many separate short references tell a larger story about how status- and caste-based ways of understanding difference contributed to shaping the lives of Meiji-era Japanese emigrants and mediated their attempts to negotiate the racial divides that ordered social relations in the North American West.

Like race, caste is a social and historical construction that lacks any meaningful biological basis.[22] Indeed, the idea of outcaste status is compelling, in part, precisely because those categorized as outcastes in Tokugawa Japan were effectively racialized through sumptuary laws that made social differences visible, even though there was no discernible physical difference between those denoted outcastes and others. Because race and caste are constructed categories, both depend on convoluted rationalizations to justify the differences they purport to describe. George De Vos observes that the rationalizations supporting race- and caste-based distinctions tend to be rooted in different mythological constructs. "Racism," he notes, "is usually based on a secularized pseudo-scientific biological mythology," whereas "caste is often based on a pseudo-historical religious mythology."[23] Given the absence of physical differences to which caste categories can be ascribed, Gerald D. Berreman suggests that caste requires even more "physical and psychic energy" to maintain than does race.[24] Notwithstanding the differences between race and caste, the parallels are such that a closer examination of their intersections and overlaps in Japanese immigrant communities in the North American West has the potential to provide new insights into their deployment.[25] The intersection of race and caste also provides a framework for analyzing and understanding some of the complex ways in which race was experienced by immigrants who organized their own perceptions of difference in terms of caste and status distinctions. Although sociologists distinguish race and caste, the race-based hierarchies established in the U.S. and Canadian West, and the legal mechanisms used to enforce it, paralleled those of the caste system with which Meiji immigrants were more familiar.

As the protracted silence regarding the real experience of slavery in U.S. historiography reveals, nikkei histories are not alone in avoiding topics regarded as likely to undermine the image the community desires to project.[26] Community histories of all ethnic groups are subject to similar kinds of constraints. Like nikkei histories in both Canada and the United States, other ethnic histories are also often circumscribed by efforts to respond to unfair and stereotyped representations of their communities.[27] Standard ethnic histories, Rolf Knight and Maya Koizumi observe, are nothing more than "bowdlerized tales which while seeming to promote an appreciation for cultural diversity mainly tend to denigrate the real vitality and history of the people involved." The components of such histories, they argue, can be readily identified as "early settlers, initial hardships overcome by hard work and frugality, an invariable commitment to political quiescence and conservatism, eventual payoff in modest financial security, unique cultural values and an ethos never fully understandable to outsiders, warm and strong family ties, and the mention of a few Horatio Algers and 'contributions to [North American] culture.' " Most ethnic histories, they conclude, "are primarily reflective of the views and interests of political brokers or of certain elements of an ethnic bourgeoisie." Few topics are "more taboo than internal class division," with the result that most authentic ethnic histories are untranslated.[28]

This book is an attempt to challenge the taboo to which Knight and Koizumi refer as it pertains to Japanese immigration history, in order to tell a larger story about the ways in which two culturally distinct ways of understanding difference—one focused on caste and mibun and the other on race—overlapped and intersected in the North American West. The inclusion of buraku jūmin in particular, and the consideration of outcaste status more generally, illuminates aspects of that history that are otherwise obscured and sheds new light on how Japanese immigrants understood and responded to white racism, infusing their efforts to position Japanese within the racial hierarchies of both the United States and Canada with new meaning. Acknowledging the presence of buraku jūmin among those who emigrated may also contribute to a deeper and more nuanced understanding of Japanese immigration history itself.

Buraku jūmin are important in their own right, as entitled to acknowledgment as any other human beings. Their presence in the story of immigration, as well, makes it possible to begin to raise questions regarding the extent to which Japanese emigrated to avoid social constraints that persisted in Meiji Japan. The fact that some Japanese emigrated for social reasons makes it possible, in turn, to challenge the convention that Meiji-era emigration was fundamentally different in character from European emigration. As Sucheng Chan and others have observed, there is a longstanding tendency in the literature "to dichotomize Asians and Europeans who have come to America as 'sojourners' and 'immigrants' respectively."[29] Although historians have increasingly recognized this distinction as false, characterizations of Japanese migrants as interested primarily in economic gain continue to go largely unchallenged and remain imbedded in the popular imagination, as they are in older immigration histories.

Place, space, and migration—and movement from place to place— are central to this narrative. Because ancestry, occupation, and geography combined to fix outcastes in social space, place was integral to the maintenance of outcaste status during the Tokugawa period, and knowledge of an individual's place of origin had the potential—even after the abolition of outcaste status—to reveal ancestral ties to locations where those categorized as outcastes had lived. By providing access to new social landscapes and distancing individuals from the places to which outcaste status was historically linked, migration offered the possibility of reconfigured social relationships.[30] It was because the Japanese "geographies of status" could not be exactly reproduced in North America that migration had the potential to undermine social categories rooted in place.[31] To illu-minate this dynamic, I begin by describing the social contexts in which Meiji emigrants lived and worked in Japan. I then follow them across the Pacific Ocean and across the borders of the United States, Canada, and Mexico to the various parts of the North American West to which they traveled.

Space, place, and movement are also important in the context of understanding conditions in the regions to which the emigrants traveled. Because the power of national governments is also bounded and linked to space, new geographies of status structured around racial categories written into law by each nation differed from place to place. For that reason, movement through and across the borders of the physical and jurisdictional spaces represented by the United States, Canada, and Mexico enabled emigrants to position themselves in different ways in relation to each nation and, in so doing, to rearticulate their legal status to reach their intended destinations.

The regional focus of this study is broad. Like European emigrants, Japanese emigrants, more often than not, traveled to a series of linked regions and not to a single destination. Japanese emigrants settled throughout the North American West, from British Columbia to northern Mexico, including the Pacific coast and the intermountain regions on both sides of the international borders that transect North America. Here, then, "North American West" is broadly defined to include the United States west of the Mississippi River, western Canada, and northern Mexico. Although many Japanese emigrants traveled to North America through Hawaii, the primary focus here is on the mainland. The world in which the immigrants lived was nevertheless always also a transpacific world. For all immigrants, as Gunther Peck has explained, the "bound-aries of local community" were always understood "in close connection with the imagined communities of race and nation."[32] Not only did Japanese and Europeans retain ties to the old country, but—in the case of Japanese—those ties were often reinforced by exclusionary laws to a degree that has not always been recognized. Both Japanese and Europeans made multiple crossings, with the result that distinctions between settler and sojourner remained fluid and unstable. Migrants who intended to stay returned to their home countries, and others who intended to return put down permanent roots. Japanese in North America, moreover, were continuously in conversation with one another across the U.S.-Canada and U.S.-Mexico borders and with supporters and critics alike on both sides of the Pacific Ocean.

Partly a work of transnational history that traces the persistence of Tokugawa status categories in new social and geographical contexts, this book is also a comparative study of the legal constraints faced by Japanese immigrants in both Canada and the United States. Although the international borders are largely irrelevant to a discussion of perceptions of social difference, the borders become crucial in comparing the various categories of exclusion imposed on immigrants by both nations. Differences in the constitutional structure of Canada and the United States forced each nation to adopt different kinds of legal mechanisms to give form to a shared anti-Japanese bias. Comparing the two illuminates parallels and differences in the ways the United States and Canada used law to establish and maintain racial boundaries. It also serves to isolate rhetorical strategies developed by Meiji diplomats to challenge exclusionary laws as specific to one nation or the other and makes clear the extent to which Japanese immigrants used their ability to migrate from one jurisdiction to another to facilitate the realization of their own individual goals.

Within the context of this larger discussion about the legal environment that Meiji-era immigrants confronted in the North American West, I argue for a more complicated understanding of illegality and what it represented in the context of Meiji immigrant society. Despite the persistent efforts of Meiji officials to discourage any activity that marked Japanese as illegal or undesirable, the determination of certain immigrants to subvert or avoid race-based legal constraints put them at odds not only with U.S. and Canadian officials but with their own government. Some believed that evading racially motivated entry requirements was a legitimate form of resistance to growing webs of exclusionary law in both countries that unfairly targeted Japanese. Their actions, however, raised for others fears that such challenges would serve only to render all Japanese subjects the functional equivalent of outcastes in U.S. and Canadian society. Illegality loomed as a particular threat because it appeared to tarnish the reputation not only of individuals who defied such laws but the reputation of Japan as a nation and nikkeijin as a whole, such that it could be used by exclusionists to justify the relegation of all nikkeijin to the lowest levels of society in both countries. Regardless of migrants' own intentions, however, they were at times rendered illegal simply because they were caught between the different bodies of law generated by the nations to whose jurisdiction they were subject—the United States, Canada, Mexico, and Japan.

By the end of the nineteenth century, efforts to create the United States and Canada as racialized spaces had resulted in a complex, cross-Pacific dialogue about race, caste, status, and gender in which Meiji immigrants and diplomats, anti-Japanese exclusionists, and the governments of Japan, Canada, the United States, and Mexico all participated. The debates occurred both at the intersection of race and caste and at the intersection of nation and empire. While mibun retained its importance well into the early decades of the twentieth century, what defined social status was modified and complicated both by immigrant interaction with conditions in the North American West and by evolving understandings of identity and citizenship that were themselves a product of that interaction. Meiji-era Japanese immigrants were never simply victims of others' efforts to define them as outsiders. Rather, they contested and avoided the legal barriers erected by the governments of Canada and the United States, and they imposed exclusionary categories of their own in the process of defining who "belonged" within their own communities. In the North American West, two separate and distinct cultures of exclusion and ways of understanding difference—both in flux—overlapped, reinforcing or undermining one another to shape new kinds of Japanese identities. The result was a far more complex and dynamic process of negotiation and adaptation to conditions in North America than the simpler paradigms of heritage or assimilation that have framed so much of prior immigration history can comprehend.

CHAPTER ONE

Caste, Status, *Mibun*

IN 1905, AS THE MEIJI ERA was drawing to a close, Japanese novelist Shimazaki Tōson published a novel that raised the question of whether emigration to the North American West offered those descended from outcaste groups in Japan a chance to leave behind the stigma still associated with their status. Natsume Sōseki, one of Japan's foremost novelists of the twentieth century, later called Shimazaki's work the "only genuine novel of the Meiji era." *Hakai* (The Broken Commandment) immediately became a best seller and has never been out of print.[1] In *Hakai,* Shimazaki tells the story of a schoolteacher who had long been able to hide his outcaste descent in accordance with his father's proscription that he never disclose his identity. In time, however, he is forced by his own anxiety about his ancestry to reveal it in the wake of his father's death, resulting in his dismissal from the school at which he had taught for some years. The novel ends with another character's proposal that he emigrate to Texas because there his descent from an outcaste family would be irrelevant.[2] Implicit in this suggestion was the assumption that emigration to the North American West offered a way to avoid caste-based discrimination because in North America, one need only identify oneself as a Japanese subject. Emigration, in other words, held out the promise that one could shed a stigma that continued to confront former outcastes and their children even in rapidly modernizing Japan during the early decades of the twentieth century.

The prejudice that Shimazaki proposed his protagonist escape by emigrating to North America was rooted in a status system established during the early seventeenth century as part of an effort by the Tokugawa shogunate (*bakufu*) to ensure the stability both of Japan and of its own rule. To that end, it imposed severe restrictions on travel within Japan and barred foreigners and Japanese subjects alike from entering or leaving Japan. The failure to comply with the prohibition was punishable by death, a sanction that remained in place through 1854, when Commodore Matthew Perry's intrusion on behalf of the United States helped to set in motion the processes that led Japan to begin to open its borders to the West.[3] Constraints on physical mobility within Japan and beyond its coastal boundaries were intended to work with parallel restraints on social mobility to fix members of Japanese society in place both geographically and in terms of social hierarchy.

The Tokugawa status system comprised four major status categories, or mibun; in descending order, they were samurai, farmers, artisans, and merchants. Not included in these official status categories but also integral to the functioning of the Tokugawa system were outcaste groups, who provided the labor needed for tasks regarded as polluting by other Japanese. Although some scholars have argued that outcastes were essentially unclassified people, they were subject to strict legal constraints in many parts of Japan throughout the Tokugawa period. As David L. Howell and others have noted, the boundary between the four major status groups and the outcaste groups was qualitatively far more significant than that which existed between the four major status categories.[4] Caste difference was regarded as immutable and adherent in blood, so the prohibition against marriage to members of outcaste groups was far more rigidly enforced than the prohibition against marriage between members of other status categories.[5]

The social and legal position of outcastes as outside the four official categories was justified by reference to their engagement in forms of work regarded as polluting, which meant that they were regarded as polluted in turn. This projection was reflected in the official terms used to identify the two largest and most significant outcaste groups under Tokugawa law—*eta* and *hinin*. Generally translated into English as "full of filth" and "nonhuman," both terms are extremely pejorative.[6] *Hinin* was the more fluid category, comprising not only beggars and people born into this category but also individuals who had been sentenced to hinin status as a result of conviction for certain crimes. As well, hinin included commoners who had committed certain kinds of civil infractions, including "family desertion, drunkenness, debauchery, making threats, juvenile delinquency, child abuse, and petty thievery." Those who married individuals in this category—knowingly or not—became hinin, as did some who divorced. Hinin also included samurai who had dishonored their families by failing to commit ritual suicide (*seppuku*) when that was viewed as the required response to a given situation.[7] Those relegated to hinin status because they had dishonored their families or committed civil infractions could, if certain limited conditions were met, be read-mitted to society over time, but readmission did not allow them to escape entirely the stigma of having once been hinin. In most areas, hinin, also regarded as outcastes, were considered higher in status than eta, which was the more inflexible of the two categories.[8]

Eta status was inherited and was often tied to occupations regarded as polluting. It could not be shed by pursuing a different occupation or in any other way. Occupations associated with eta status varied to some degree from one region of Japan to another, but those involving the slaughter of animals or the handling of leather were relegated to people in this category in all parts of Japan. People categorized as eta included tanners, butchers, undertakers, executioners, and grave watchers. "Well diggers, palanquin bearers, gardeners, and toilet cleaners"—all of whom engaged in work regarded as defiling by others in Japan—were also included in this category in many areas.[9] In some regions, textile dyers and craftspeople who produced bamboo articles such as baskets, tea whisks, umbrellas and writing brushes or straw products such as straw mats (*tatami*), sandals, clogs, rain capes, and baskets were also classified as outcastes.[10] Other "dishonorable occupations" associated with eta or hinin status, according to one contemporary observer, were those held by "fortune tellers; dancers; beggars; actors; street singers; prostitutes; jailers; dealers in horse; pilgrims; story tellers; [and] jugglers." Elsewhere, drum makers, bathhouse atten-dants, sweepers, riverboat men, brothel keepers, ironworkers, and black-smiths were included in these categories.[11] The digging and selling of coal was also an occupation dominated by members of outcaste groups in certain areas, including parts of Fukuoka prefecture, on the island of Kyushu.[12] And midwifery and fishing were occupations associated with outcaste status in still other parts of Japan.[13]

Village blacksmith in Japan, circa 1920. (*The Trans-Pacific*, January 1921.)

Strict sumptuary laws dictating allowable clothing and hairstyles made social and legal barriers between different status groups visible, effectively racializing them.[14] Difference was also graphically inscribed onto the bodies of people relegated to outcaste status through the propagation of popular myths that invoked animal imagery and suggested that outcastes were anatomically different from other people. According to Shigesaki Ninomiya, rumors of this kind included allegations that the skeletons of "eta" lacked a rib bone or included a dog bone, that their necks did not cast shadows in moonlight, and that dirt did not adhere to their bare feet, because they were less human than animal.[15] Yet another common myth—still perpetuated today even though scholars have shown it to be untrue—is that buraku jūmin are descended not from Japanese but from Koreans or other foreigners brought to Japan at an earlier stage of its history.[16]

While people in outcaste groups used words such as *kawata* (leather-worker) to describe themselves, expressions used by other Japanese, like the official terms *eta* and *hinin*, were often deeply pejorative and suggested, in accordance with popular myths and rumors, that members of outcaste groups were not fully human.[17] Hugh H. Smythe and Yoshimasa Naitoh reported as late as 1953 that buraku jūmin were also often referred to by the numbers four, eight and nine (*yotsu, yatsu,* and *kokonotsu*), "all of which ... represent imperfection" in Japanese numerology. Implicit in the use of such terms, they argue, is the inference that eta were " 'deformed' (despised) people." The numerical classifier historically used in official documents during the Tokugawa era to count members of outcaste groups reflected a similar perception. Whereas the classifier normally used to count human beings was *nin,* the one used to count outcastes was the same as that used to count animals—*hiki.*[18] The vehement nature of the prejudices projected onto people in outcaste categories was such that they were regarded not only as defiled but also as defiling. "Bow once to an Eta," a Tokugawa-era proverb declared, "and you must not lift your head again for seven generations."[19]

Negative attitudes were further reinforced through the spatial organization of difference, which found expression not only in terms of where those categorized as outcastes were required to live but in the way space itself was depicted on Tokugawa maps.[20] Members of outcaste groups were often required to reside on marginal lands along rivers or at the edges of the towns and villages, one reason that some outcaste groups were often referred to as *kawaramono* or "river people."[21] Nor did official Tokugawa government maps record the location of eta villages, and they excluded portions of any road that passed through an outcaste village from distance calculations.[22] Bakufu policy, in short, sought quite literally to erase those categorized as outcastes from the social landscape, at least as it was imagined on official maps. Although hinin were also relegated to the periphery of society, the hinin population was generally more mobile, since they were permitted under Tokugawa law to move from one domain to another as long as they did not disguise their status and registered as hinin in each domain.[23]

In addition to dictating where outcastes were permitted to live and travel, local sumptuary laws specified what kind of clothing and hairstyles people in different status categories were permitted to wear. Although rules of this kind applied to people at all levels of society, the weight of such proscriptions fell most heavily on outcaste groups. Harsh regulations combined with strict social taboos to define people classified as outcastes as "other" and made their status visible so that those in other categories could both identify and shun them.[24] Marriage between members of outcaste groups and other Japanese was not only avoided as a matter of social custom but prohibited by law.[25] Other edicts issued during the Tokugawa era restricted the kinds of work outcastes were permitted to do, forbade them to enter districts where higher status groups lived, and specified the architectural details of their houses so that their status would be immediately apparent to anyone approaching their homes.[26] Smythe and Naitoh summarize the range of legal prohibitions enforced against members of outcaste groups under Tokugawa law as follows:

> [Eta] were forbidden to live in the same house or eat with other Japanese. They could not enter castle farms or the homes of non-Eta, or even the front gates of the latter's yards ... The Shōgunate in 1723 decreed that either the Eta had to shave their heads or wear their hair in a special style to distinguish them from other Japanese, while women Eta were prohibited from tying the *obi* (kimono sash) as other Japanese women. They were forced to go barefooted and not allowed to wear the wooden clogs, *geta,* or wear headgear even in inclement weather. An ordinance in 1778 provided severe punishment for any Eta caught wearing the costume of farmers or merchants ...
>
> Further, the severity of Tokugawa regulations restricted the Eta to certain sections of cities and towns. Only in these areas were they allowed to beg for food, clothes, and money; and their personal movements without official permission were limited. Crimes against them by non-Eta were not recognized as criminal acts, since the Eta were considered as having practically non-human status.[27]

By the early nineteenth century, the legal reinforcement of caste categories for over two centuries had resulted in a deep social divide between those categorized as *heimin* (commoners) and outcaste groups. The institutionalization of the caste system during the Tokugawa period, in Cullen Tadao Hayashida's words, effectively locked the "ritually polluted pariah ... in place both territorially and hierarchically." "Occupational specialization, residential segregation, and enforced endogamy," he adds, acted together to create an "impassable barrier."[28] As the Tokugawa era entered its final decades, however, people at every level of society began to chafe at the status restrictions that bound them. Even among samurai, restrictions of rank had become a source of significant tension, to the point where historians have identified the frustration of lower-level samurai as a major factor leading to the Meiji Restoration.[29] Restrictions on travel broke down as increasing numbers of *dekasegi* laborers (temporary labor migrants) traveled to such growing urban centers as Osaka and Edo.[30] By the end of the Tokugawa period, the rigid social system created to ensure the regime's stability had begun to break down, largely as a result of social tensions and economic developments produced by the system's codifiers themselves.

Tokugawa authorities responded to the growing social unrest by imposing still stricter sumptuary laws and rigorously enforcing existing laws. Various domains also implemented legal measures to prevent the erosion of the social barrier maintained between outcastes and commoners. In 1819 and 1820, for example, the *daimyō* of Tosa on the island of Shikoku issued edicts proscribing the sale of land to "eta" and forbidding them to walk down the middle of the street or enter commoners' homes.[31] Even after the Meiji Restoration in 1868, the newly reconstituted "modern" government of Wakayama prefecture viewed the regulation of those classified as outcastes as key to maintaining the continued stability of society in Japan and promulgated a series of regulations in December 1870 to reinforce the subordinate position of outcaste groups:

1. In using public thoroughfares, Eta must walk at the extreme sides of the road and move out of the way of other Japanese at all times, and they must never be discourteous to other Japanese at any time, either in their own communities or in the cities and villages.
2. Between sunset and dawn Eta are prohibited from entering and moving about in any non-Eta community, and they must refrain from such movement even on the outskirts of such communities during this curfew period. Except at festival times, they are prohibited from moving about after nightfall within their own communities.
3. They are forbidden to eat or drink in non-Eta communities.
4. Eta are forbidden to wear headgear, except during inclement weather.
5. They are forbidden to wear any kind of footgear except *zori* [straw sandals].[32]

Edicts such as these may well be evidence that people categorized as eta or hinin had begun to challenge the legal constraints imposed on them during the Tokugawa period and that domain officials feared that existing social barriers between outcastes and others might erode. Domain governments that adopted such oppressive solutions, however, soon found themselves at odds with the new Meiji leaders.

MEIJI SOCIAL REFORMS

The unwelcome advent of Perry's ships off Yokohama in 1854 and the imposition of semicolonial status on Japan via a series of unequal treaties with the United States and others combined with growing social and political tensions to bring about the Meiji Restoration fourteen years later. Recognizing that Japan lacked the technological ability to resist American or European pressure, the Meiji government embarked almost immediately on a comprehensive effort to develop Japan's industrial capacity. Meiji leaders also quickly concluded that modernization—understood as the importation of Western technology, culture, and civic institutions— was critical to meeting Japan's goals of resisting Western encroachment and securing recognition as a nation equal in status to those of the West. In Hayashida's words, the Meiji government was determined that Japanese stop "being treated as an uncivilized people" and that Japan "regain control over its own destiny."[33] Advocates of rapid industrialization viewed the West, by virtue of its advanced technologies, as—at least temporarily—higher on the scale of scientific achievement in the hierarchy of nations and civilization in the modern world. Both the commitment to technological advancement and Japan's adoption of *bunmei kaika,* "civilization and enlightenment," were also key elements of its larger quest to win acceptance as an equal by the West and to secure the removal of the unequal treaties imposed by Western nations.

The importation of Western legal forms and the elimination of what a majority of the new Meiji oligarchs (*genrō*) perceived to be archaic social structures—representing the antithesis of the modern and civilized nation they were determined that Japan should become—were also seen as integral to Japan's quest for status and recognition. In addition to implementing policy changes designed to foster rapid economic and industrial growth, the genrō moved quickly to eradicate the legal status categories that, they believed, marked Japan as backward and uncivilized.

The elimination of historical status and caste boundaries, together with the constraints on spatial and occupational mobility that they entailed, was also key to facilitating the creation of the mobile labor force needed to advance industrialization. Equally of concern to the new Meiji leaders was the creation of a strong sense of national identity; they hoped to foster a commitment on the part of the Japanese people to Japan's newly articulated goals of economic and industrial development, goals that the elimination of historical status barriers also served.[34]

In April 1868, just a few short months after the Meiji Restoration, the Meiji emperor issued an Imperial Charter Oath, at the behest of the genrō, which articulated Japan's new course and announced to the Japanese people some of the changes that lay ahead. In the Imperial Charter Oath, the emperor promised to unify "all classes high and low" and declared that "base customs of former times shall be abandoned and all actions shall conform to the principles of international justice." The oath also decreed that knowledge be "sought around the world" and used to strengthen the "foundations of Imperial polity."[35] Both the notion that Japan should turn to the West for knowledge and that Japanese should travel abroad to acquire that knowledge were thus formally incorporated into the new Meiji government's articulation of its vision for the future. The same was true of the formal abolition of the historical status categories now associated with Japan's feudal past.[36]

Major concerns of the Meiji government included the elimination of the old feudal domains and the dismantling of samurai privilege. Because identity in Tokugawa Japan was rooted not only in mibun but also in residence in a particular domain, the rearticulation of both structures was regarded as important to the creation of a nation-based sense of identity. The restrictions on travel within Japan for more than two centuries, together with the difficulty inherent in traveling through Japan's mountainous terrain, had led to the evolution of local customs and regional dialects so distinctive that some were virtually incomprehensible to people from other areas. Shotaro Frank Miyamoto, whose parents immigrated to Seattle in the late nineteenth century, reports, for example, that variations in dialect continued to be so pronounced that they divided Japanese immigrant communities even in the 1930s.[37] While this did not mean that travelers could not make themselves understood, it fostered the perception that those from other parts of Japan were as foreign as those from outside the country.[38] One of the Meiji government's priorities was thus fostering a uniform sense of national identity. Among the first steps in that process was the reorganization of the administrative units into which Japan was divided: in 1871, just three years after the Meiji Restoration, it issued an edict abolishing the clans and replacing their domains with prefectures.[39]

The Meiji government acted almost immediately to disassemble the sources of samurai privilege. In 1870 it issued an edict allowing commoners to take surnames, something that, with limited exceptions, only samurai had been permitted to do before.[40] A year later, the long-standing ban on marriage between commoners and samurai was lifted. Sumptuary laws regulating personal dress and appearance were systematically rescinded, and people at all levels of society were permitted to dress as they pleased and to build any kind of house they could afford. By 1876 all remaining samurai privileges, including receipt of the stipends to which samurai had been entitled for more than two centuries, had been officially terminated.[41]

A majority of the genrō regarded the emancipation of Tokugawa-era outcastes as another critical step toward putting Japan on a modern footing and establishing it as a civilized nation.[42] The new Meiji leaders were well aware that slavery had been abolished in the United States just a few years earlier.[43] Even before the Meiji Restoration, several bakufu officials had proposed that the categories *eta* and *hinin* be abolished together with the constraints under which people in those groups were forced to live and work. During the first years of the Meiji period, officials who made similar proposals emphasized the potential utility of the occupational skills of "eta" to Japan's industrializing economy and suggested that they migrate to the northernmost large island of Hokkaido or to unsettled parts of the other main islands.[44] One official linked this proposal directly to Japan's quest for status as a civilized nation equal to those of the West, observing that eta did not exist in Western nations and urging Japan to immediately eliminate "this flaw" in its own society.[45] In April 1869, just one year after the Meiji Restoration, another Meiji official proposed that the *ri*—the official measure of distance—be standardized to include outcaste villages in distance compilations. In March 1871 the Meiji government proclaimed that the owners of cattle were to dispose of their carcasses themselves.[46] And on October 12, 1871, it issued an edict abolishing the distinction between commoners and outcastes that had long been written into Tokugawa law: "The names *eta, hinin,* and so forth are hereby abolished. Henceforth in their status and occupation [former outcastes] shall be treated as commoners [*heimin*]."[47] As Howell notes, although this edict is often referred to as an "emancipation edict," it in fact makes no reference to emancipation. As a practical matter, however, it freed those formerly categorized as eta or hinin from the obligations imposed on them under Tokugawa law and allowed them to pursue new lines of work.[48]

An American visitor in Japan during the early Meiji period celebrated the abolition of outcaste status as equivalent to the abolition of slavery in the United States.[49] As in the U.S. South, however, the rescission of formal legal constraints did little to eradicate the social prejudices built up over the years. Though not required to do so, local and prefectural administrators often denoted newly emancipated outcastes as *shinheimin* (new commoners), which made their descent from those categorized as outcastes under Tokugawa law readily apparent to those with access to government records. Because use of the term *shinheimin* allowed the distinction between people in this category and heimin to be maintained, it rapidly acquired derogatory connotations even though it was intended as a more neutral referent than the profoundly offensive terms it replaced.[50]

In the absence of any discernible difference in physical appearance, the removal of restrictions on social and occupational mobility made it considerably more difficult for those without access to government documents to identify a given individual as descended from a former outcaste group. Japan's rigid family registration system, however, provided for the transfer of family registration records (*koseki*) when individuals moved to other parts of Japan, allowing historical caste distinctions to be perpetuated and effectively preventing the absorption of former outcastes into the Japanese population as a whole. Even after 1882, when the practice of noting status on registration records was formally ended, koseki remained important in part because they also listed the original area of domicile (*genseki*) of a family. It was because mibun was no longer recorded that place of origin became important, since it could still be used—in at least some cases—to determine whether an individual had ancestral ties to an outcaste community.[51]

While former hinin were more readily absorbed into Meiji society than former eta, the latter found it far harder to cross historical social and occupational boundaries.[52] When former eta invoked the 1871 edict to refuse defiling work that they had been required to do under Tokugawa law, other Japanese resented what they regarded as their newfound arrogance and retaliated in various ways, denying access to communal resources and even resorting to violence.[53] During the years following the abolition of outcaste status, *eta seibatsu* (eta chastisements) by other commoners—including riots and other violent outbursts—erupted in various parts of Japan.[54] Even in Meiji government circles, attitudes were slow to change. As late as 1880, George O. Totten and Hiroshi Wagatsuma note, an official Ministry of Justice publication defined eta and hinin as "the lowliest of all the people, almost resembling animals."[55]

The tension engendered by the elimination of historical class and caste barriers came to a head in another context, motivating some Japanese to emigrate to Canada and the United States. The Meiji government's determined efforts to remake Japan on a Western model and to dismantle the sources of samurai privilege included the establishment of a modern, conscript army. On January 10, 1873, the Meiji government issued a compulsory military service edict requiring every adult male between the ages of twenty and thirty-two who passed the requisite examination to serve for three years in the newly established military. Conscription was also an integral element in the Meiji government's efforts to reform the status system and to replace institutions that marked Japan as backward or uncivilized. Because this edict challenged the idea that military service was the exclusive responsibility of an elite warrior class, the Meiji government tried to make the change palatable to former samurai by presenting it as a return to conditions that had existed in Japan prior to the establishment of Tokugawa rule, when no formal legal distinction between soldiers and farmers existed. The Meiji government had similarly characterized the overthrow of the Tokugawa bakufu itself as a restoration of imperial rule and not just a coup by competing clans.[56]

Although conscription was intended to contribute to the erosion of samurai privilege, its implementation angered other commoners, even though it ostensibly placed them on the same level as former samurai. Universal conscription erased not just the historical status barrier between farmers and samurai but also the barrier between farmers and outcastes.

Farmers bitterly resented having to serve as equals to former eta and hinin and were also concerned that conscription, which they characterized as a "blood tax," would deny them needed labor on family farms.[57] So deeply did farmers resent universal conscription that historians regard it as a major cause of the peasant uprisings that swept through Japan in the 1870s.[58] It also, in time, became an important motivation for the emigration of young Japanese men to the North American West.

CONTOURS OF MEIJI-ERA EMIGRATION

Farmers in Japan, like those in Europe, were those most affected by modern conscription laws, and they and other rural residents were also the ones on whom the cost of industrialization fell most heavily. Early Japanese labor emigrants left a nation "reeling under the impact of Western imperialism and the first sprouts of industrial capitalism."[59] Although industry developed later in Japan than in many parts of Europe, its impact on Japan's agricultural base was much the same. During the first decades of the Meiji era, Japanese farmers and artisans were exposed to a range of economic pressures that paralleled those endured by European farmers earlier in the nineteenth century. In Japan, as in Europe during earlier decades, the shift from a still largely feudal to a capitalist economic system meant that artisans and farmers who depended on handicraft manufacture for supplemental income were severely affected by the increasing availability of cheaper factory-produced goods.[60] Railroads replaced existing transportation systems in Japan, undermining the economic foundation of villages located along the old trunk roads and rivers. Much as improved transportation networks between inland and coastal areas had facilitated emigration in Europe just a few decades earlier, newly built railway lines in Japan carried rural laborers away from the countryside and carried mass-produced goods in. As in Europe, these changes resulted in new agricultural patterns and practices that produced a dramatic increase in population: estimated at thirty-one million in 1868, the population of Japan increased to forty-four million by the end of the century—an increase of 30 percent in just three decades.[61]

The pressure on rural economies in Japan was exacerbated by land tax reform, one of the earliest measures instituted by the new Meiji government to create the economic foundation necessary to facilitate industrialization. The new tax law substituted fixed payments based on the assessed value of a farmer's land for payments in kind based on a percentage of the annual rice harvest. Although fixed payments allowed the Meiji government to accurately predict its annual revenues, it placed the risk associated with poor harvests squarely on the farmers. The Meiji government relied heavily on taxes paid by the agricultural sector to finance industrialization; in 1880, for example, taxes paid by farmers comprised 80 percent of the tax revenue.[62] In 1881 the stringent fiscal measures imposed by Finance Minister Matsukata Masayoshi to stabilize the Japanese economy only added to their burden, forcing the growing number of farm owners unable to pay their taxes to sell their farms. Tenancy rates rose rapidly as land ownership came to be concentrated in the hands of an ever smaller number of rural landlords.[63]

Changes in rural economies and in landholding patterns combined with rapid population growth to create an expanding body of rural laborers willing to migrate first to cities and, later, abroad to find work. Although dekasegi laborers, who worked away from home on a temporary basis, had appeared before the end of the Tokugawa period, their number increased dramatically after the Meiji Restoration. Indeed, dekasegi labor networks eventually extended across the Pacific to North and South America.[64] Although the concept of dekasegi labor has come to be associated in particular with Asian laborers in the North American West and the suggestion that as "sojourners" there, Asian migrants were less interested in permanent settlement than those from Europe, dekasegi labor was never as singular as it has sometimes been made out to be. In Europe as in Japan, temporary rural labor migration to urban areas predated industrialization and expanded dramatically in its wake: Belgians, Germans, Hungarians, Swedes, Slovaks, Italians, and Poles traveled first within their own countries and later to other parts of Europe to find work throughout the nineteenth century.[65] Although the term *dekasegi* is Japanese, the concept and practice of dekasegi labor would have been familiar to European migrants of the same period.

Rates of return migration bear this statement out. Although return migration has received far greater emphasis in Asian than European migration histories, return migration rates for Japanese and European migrants were in fact similar. During the late nineteenth and early twentieth centuries, when return rates were over 40 percent for some European countries, return rates to Japan were about 33 percent—roughly the same as those for British migrants.[66] Figures like these show that return migration rates are not a meaningful basis for differentiating between immigration from Europe and from Asia.[67] Permanent settlement, John Bodnar notes, was rarely the intention of any emigrant, and the choice of some to stay abroad "should not obscure the fact that a return was usually every emigrant's goal." Many migrants made multiple crossings, and both Japanese and Europeans were aptly described as birds of passage, or *wataridori*.[68]

Migrants' reasons for traveling to North America, wherever their point of origin, reflect many common elements: "America fever" struck the towns and cities of both Europe and Japan, and European migrants shared "dreams of gold" with Chinese and Japanese migrants. There is no question that economic goals were one major reason why people left Europe and Japan.[69] In Japan, as in northern Italy, the largest number of emigrants came from areas where mountainous or marginal land prevented the growing of cash crops or where fishing was the main livelihood.[70] Mio in Wakayama prefecture, for example, often identified as the village that sent the largest number of emigrants from Japan to Canada, is on a peninsula that juts into Osaka Bay, where the Inland Sea meets the Pacific. Clinging to cliffs that rise from the water's edge or squeezed into narrow mountain valleys, the villagers' homes occupy almost every inch of buildable land. Rice fields are scattered and few, making villagers in Mio and its adjacent communities dependent on the vicissitudes of the local fishing industry, which collapsed in the late nineteenth century.[71] Not all people in areas affected by economic hardship chose to emigrate, however.

In Japan, as in Europe, emigrants came predominantly from some regions and not from others; emigration was concentrated in particular areas at both the local and the provincial level. A disproportionate number of German emigrants to the United States during the mid-nineteenth century came from the provinces of Baden and Württemberg, for example, and a large majority of Japanese emigrants to the North American West prior to 1924 came from just eight of Japan's forty-seven prefectures.[72] Three of those prefectures—Fukuoka, Kumamoto, and Kagoshima—are in western Kyushu, the southernmost of Japan's four main islands. The five remaining prefectures—Hiroshima, Wakayama,

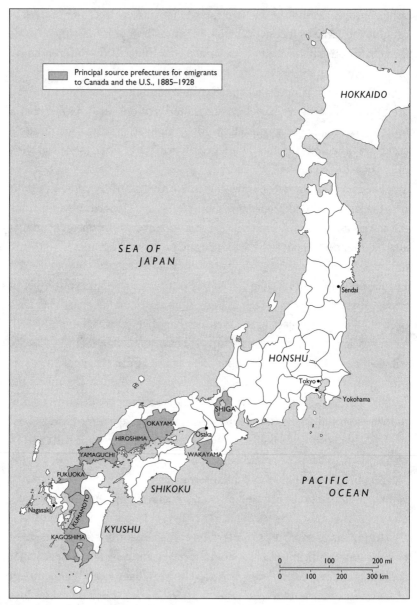

Principal prefectures from which Japanese emigrants to Canada and the United States came, 1885–1928. (Map by Bill Nelson.)

Shiga, Okayama and Yamaguchi—are in southern Honshu, the main island. With the exception of Shiga, which is in the mountains, all the prefectures have access either to the Inland Sea or to the Pacific Ocean.

What the uneven distribution of emigration reveals, Bodnar has explained, is that economic exigency and population pressure alone do not fully explain the emigration patterns of the period.[73] As in Europe, the regions in Japan that sent the largest number of people abroad were neither the poorest nor the most densely populated, and migration rates varied from one district to the next in both timing and demographic distribution.[74] Although the wage differential between Japan and North America was important, Yuzo Murayama and others have pointed out that it was also a factor for the majority who did not emigrate and, again, cannot explain why some but not others left to work abroad.[75]

It is the failure of economic considerations to adequately explain variations in regional migration patterns that makes clear the need to take other social and historical factors into account.[76] Chain migration, which is based on information about destination countries provided by earlier emigrants, has been identified as one factor that explains variations in regional migration patterns, to the point where it rapidly made the labor contractors who facilitated early emigration from both Europe and Japan largely irrelevant. The single most important factor in explaining variations in regional emigration patterns, however, is found in what Bodnar calls a "persistent pattern of selectivity" rooted in the social structure of the emigrants' home countries.[77] As Mark Wyman has explained, "striving for status—to hold onto a vanishing position, or even to climb higher—emerges as one of the main forces behind ... emigration." British, German, and Norwegian migrants were motivated in part by a wish to avoid a decline in social status; so, too, Japanese emigrants were often motivated by a concern that the social position of their families not deteriorate because they were no longer able to command the resources needed to maintain it in a rapidly changing Japan.[78] Also of importance was the opportunity that migration offered to enhance the family's status in an emigrant's home village.[79] In both Europe and Japan, emigration and return migration rates were highest in areas where status was a function of land ownership and where land was available for purchase.[80] But because economic advantage was often invested with social meaning that transcended mere financial gain, migrants' stated economic goals can be fully understood only within the larger social context of their home towns and villages.

Social and cultural factors, including status issues, are important in explaining not only what migrants hoped to achieve by going abroad but also what going abroad gave them the opportunity to avoid. Emigration, for example, offered some Japanese women a way to overcome culturally specific social impediments to marriage.[81] As Shimazaki Tōson suggests in his novel *Hakai,* it also offered a way to obscure other sources of stigma, including outcaste ancestry. Because the ability to identify individuals as buraku jūmin depended in part on knowledge of their place of origin, emigration offered one possible way to conceal outcaste descent and avoid the still "brutal and unyielding" stigma associated with such status in Meiji-era Japan.[82]

Although Meiji officials were frequently ambivalent about allowing those they deemed low status to emigrate to North America for fear that they would undermine perceptions of Japan as a modern and civilized nation, authorities in some prefectures advocated emigration as a solution to the problem they believed that former outcastes posed by their very presence.[83] In 1890, for example, officers of the Kyushu Heiminkai (Kyushu Commoners' Association) in Fukuoka prefecture advised local buraku jūmin that in North America they would be able to define themselves simply as Japanese subjects: "Foreigners do not distinguish between heimin and shinheimin. When you encounter foreigners abroad, you simply present yourselves as subjects of the Japanese empire in the same way we do. If you work patiently, save your money, and return with riches, then no one will shun you anymore."[84] That former outcastes were also aware of the opportunity that emigration offered is suggested by the statement of one self-identified burakumin based in the United States who wrote in 1924 that many shinheimin had emigrated in previous decades because they had believed that North America offered an opportunity to live free of the economic and social discrimination they continued to face in Japan.[85]

The stigma associated with outcaste status even today has made it impossible to arrive at any concrete estimate of the number of buraku jūmin who emigrated to the United States and Canada during the late nineteenth and early twentieth centuries. Like emigration figures, population estimates for outcaste groups in Japan at the beginning of the Meiji period vary according to source. A government census conducted in 1871, the same year that outcaste status was abolished, counted 280,311 eta, 23,480 hinin, and 79,095 people in other outcaste categories, giving a total of 382,886. By 1924, Japanese government sources estimated that between 700,000 and 1,500,000 people were living in buraku communities. Sources within those communities, in contrast, cited substantially higher figures, estimating that there were 3,000,000 burakumin living in approximately six thousand buraku villages in Japan.[86]

Historians of emigration generally suggest that even though outcaste groups composed roughly 2.5 percent of Japan's population during the Meiji period, they made up just 1 percent of the Japanese immigrant population in North America.[87] These estimates, however, are based on what one author admits are guesses on the part of his informants as to the number of buraku jūmin who emigrated—guesses that themselves almost certainly reflect a reluctance to admit that people in this category emigrated to North America in any number.[88] The sources that cite this figure, moreover, do not appear to take into account the extent to which immigrants in this category may have been successful in obscuring their buraku origins. That the actual number of buraku jūmin who emigrated may have been disproportionately high, as John Lie has suggested, is supported by the report of one self-identified burakumin, who says that as many as 20 to 30 percent of the Japanese immigrants he encountered when he traveled in the United States in the 1920s confided that they were buraku jūmin. Although the estimates of this reporter may be overly high, the reluctance of those he did encounter to openly identify themselves as buraku jūmin is arguably evidence that the opportunity to rearticulate their identity was a motivating factor in their decision to go abroad. It also suggests that outcaste ancestry continued to make people the object of discrimination within Japanese immigrant communities.[89]

Because the number of buraku communities varied from one part of Japan to another, discrimination was not inevitably an issue of which all emigrants were aware. But the prefectures that sent the largest number of emigrants abroad during the late nineteenth and early twentieth centuries—including Wakayama, Okayama, Fukuoka, Hiroshima, and Shiga prefectures—were also those where the largest number of outcaste villages were located during the Tokugawa era, which makes it unlikely that migrants in the North American West, a majority of whom were

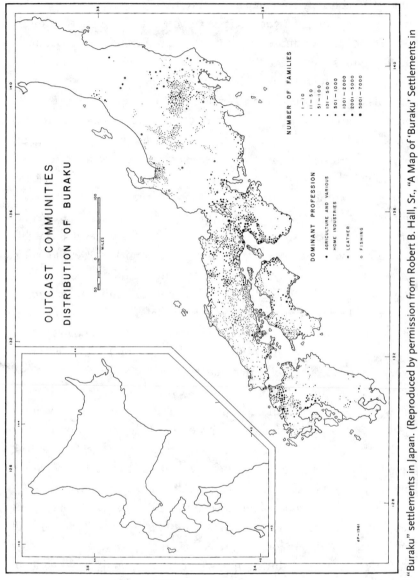

"Buraku" settlements in Japan. (Reproduced by permission from Robert B. Hall, Sr., "A Map of 'Buraku' Settlements in Japan," *Papers of the Michigan Academy of Science, Arts, and Letters 47* [1962]: 523.)

from these areas, were unacquainted with the idea of outcaste status. Although the correlation is not so perfect that it can be identified as a factor that was necessarily determinative, the fact that the prefectures that sent emigrants abroad are the same ones where buraku communities were historically located increases the likelihood that buraku jūmin were among those who availed themselves of the opportunities that emigration appeared to offer.[90]

Japan was not alone in differentiating among people based on social status. As Bodnar notes, the societies from which all emigrants came had "ranks and hierarchies based on wealth and skill," and many immigrant groups remained conscious of home-country status distinctions.[91] What was distinctive about Meiji-era ways of understanding difference was that in Japan, social standing was a function not just of ancestry or economic resources but also of caste-based categories that were historically justified by reference to ideas about purity and pollution. While financial gain might serve to enhance one's status within one's own status group, it was not sufficient to break down caste barriers or to erase the stigma associated with descent from former outcaste groups. Movement from one social and cultural space to another, as a result, might well have appeared to offer an opportunity to avoid a stigma increasingly rooted in place.

CHAPTER TWO

Emigration from Meiji Japan

IN EARLY 1908, JUST AS THE Gentlemen's Agreements into which Japan had entered with both the United States and Canada were about to go into effect, a new question about the veracity of the information provided on Japanese passports threatened to upset the delicate diplomatic balance that Japan had achieved by agreeing to restrict labor emigration to North America to forestall passage of anti-Japanese legislation. Now growing irritation on the part of U.S. immigration officials regarding discrepancies between occupations listed on the passports of Japanese labor immigrants and the occupations they named as their intended occupations when they arrived brought the issue of veracity to a head. Immigration officers were convinced that Meiji passport authorities were dishonest in recording the immigrants' real occupations in order to avoid the limitations recently agreed to under the terms of the Gentlemen's Agreement.[1] The arrival of the *Tosa Maru* in Seattle on February 20, 1908, appeared to confirm their suspicions: although 106 of the Japanese migrants on board told immigration officers that they intended to work as laborers in the United States, only eight passports stated that this was their intention, and just one passport indicated that the bearer himself was a laborer.[2]

On March 9, 1908, the U.S. ambassador to Japan raised the U.S. government's concern about the repeated discrepancies with Vice Minister of Foreign Affairs Ishii Kikujirō and questioned his

Japanese passengers on board ship, circa 1905. (Cumberland Museum and Archives, C140.28.)

government's compliance with the Gentlemen's Agreement. Ishii hastened to assure the U.S. ambassador that the passports in question must have been issued prior to December 1907, when the agreement was finalized. Occupations recorded on passports were not intended to indicate the bearer's intended occupation in the United States, Ishii told the ambassador, but to denote the "bearer's social status" (mibun) based on the official categories utilized during the Tokugawa period. In Ishii's words, these "designations ... were merely formal and referred to the old classification of Japanese society under the heads of soldier, farmer, artisan and merchant." A case in point was that of tatami makers, who were listed as such, not because they proposed to make straw mats in North America, but because that was the traditional occupation of their family in Japan. The same was true of other designations, Ishii explained, including herder, shoemaker, bathhouse attendant, dyer, weaver, and blacksmith.[3]

On April 17, 1908, the U.S. immigration commissioner-general asked immigration officers posted in various North American port cities, including Montreal and Vancouver, whether their experience bore out Ishii's claims as to what the occupational designations were intended to convey.[4] Inspectors in the field confirmed Ishii's veracity but expressed irritation about the vagueness of the occupational designations, which often failed to indicate even the occupation of the bearer's immediate family.[5] A case in point, one inspector grumbled, was the category "artisan." Though a meaningful status category and class referent under Tokugawa law, it provided no information about an immigrant's family that the inspector regarded as currently useful. In his own interviews with Japanese migrants, he had found out that the "family may be engaged in embroidering; they may be painters, weavers, furniture makers, wood carvers; or ... any one of a thousand or more differing occupations in the line of art in the home."[6] Much the same was true of the designation nō (farming). As with the category "artisan," it was not intended to indicate that the immigrant planned to do farmwork in the United States; rather, it indicated the historical status of his family in Japan—in this instance, that the passport holder was a member of a "family belonging to the farming class."[7]

A more detailed response to the immigration commissioner's query regarding the weight to be assigned the occupational designations listed on Japanese passports was provided by Barnabas C. Haworth, an interpreter for the U.S. Immigration Service in Vancouver, British Columbia (B.C.), who had lived in Japan for many years. Based on his examination of passports of immigrants applying to enter the United States after landing in Canada, Haworth advised his superiors that Ishii's explanation was sound. The occupations on Meiji passports, he confirmed, were intended not to describe the kind of work the bearers intended to do in North America, but to flag the bearer's mibun for Japanese consular officials. Haworth provided his superiors with a short history of the Japanese status system, noting that it had included outcaste classes but that older status distinctions were gradually being replaced by new designations: "Formerly there existed in Japan a clear line of demarcation, amounting almost to a rigid caste system, between the Aristocracy or Nobles, the Military, the Farmer, the Artisan and the *Eta* (outcast) classes. These distinctions have been largely obliterated or displaced by the simpler classification into Nobility and Common People, the latter ('Heimin') now including all but the royal family and the nobility. In the older passports we can trace the influence of the old system of records by social class. More recent passports, however, either omit all reference to social class or insert simply the word 'Heimin' for all sorts of people below the noble class."[8] Haworth assured his superiors that Japanese passport officials intended no deception in recording occupation on Japanese passports.[9] Their purpose, rather, was limited to providing information that continued to be regarded as meaningful in Meiji society.

Although Ishii's candor and Haworth's familiarity with Japan helped to avoid a more serious diplomatic incident, the brief furor over the supposed discrepancies on Meiji passports highlights the kinds of misunderstandings that could result from the failure of each side to recognize culturally distinct ways of understanding difference and defining social status. Meiji passport officials did not deliberately misrepresent the bearers' occupations on the passports. Rather, U.S. immigration officials failed to recognize the real significance of the designations. After their purpose was revealed, U.S. officials noted that the status categories in question had no significance in the context of U.S. immigration law, and they considered the matter resolved. Curiously, however, when the short history of the Japanese status system provided by Haworth to his superiors in the U.S. Immigration Bureau reached the U.S. secretary of state, all reference to the existence of "Eta" had been erased.[10] Just why this happened as the report worked its way up the chain of authority is not revealed in the relevant correspondence, but its absence raises questions about the meaning of the erasure: Was it a product of interaction with Meiji officials? If so, were the officials anxious to avoid creating the impression that Japan had not succeeded in erasing the remnants of a feudal past, or were they more interested in upgrading the perceived quality of the migrants to whom passports were being issued? Both reasons—as this and subsequent chapters reveal—are possibilities.

MEIJI EMIGRATION LAW AND POLICY

Although the Meiji government had moved quickly to eliminate Tokugawa-era status barriers, it was more hesitant to ease restrictions on travel abroad and to lift the bar on labor emigration. Meiji-era emigration policy initially evolved within the context of the Meiji oligarchs' major foreign policy objective of negotiating an end to the unequal treaties imposed on Japan by Western powers during the waning years of the Tokugawa period. On May 17, 1868, the first organized group of labor emigrants left for Hawaii under the auspices of Eugene Van Reed to work on plantations at the request of the Hawaiian government.[11] Among the 150 laborers recruited by Van Reed were several who identified them-selves as leather workers—individuals who would have been classified as eta under Tokugawa law by virtue of occupation alone. The severe hard-ships that these early migrants encountered in Hawaii led Meiji authori-ties to regard this first experiment as a failure. Forty-two returned to Japan in 1870, before their three-year contract expired; eleven returned after completing it; seven died; and ninety remained in Hawaii. The perceived failure of this experiment contributed to the Meiji government's reluc-tance to allow labor emigration for another two decades, even as it sent students abroad to acquire the knowledge that it had identified as critical to Japan's modernization.[12] Other factors that contributed to its decision not to permit Japanese laborers to travel abroad included its interest in directing rural labor migrants to Japan's urban centers to ensure an adequate labor supply for new industry. The Meiji government also encouraged emigration to Hokkaido to shore up Japan's claim to that island against Russian encroachment, in much the same way that the United States and Canada had encouraged settlement in newly acquired western lands in order to perfect their claims to title.[13]

Because the Meiji government did not relax the bar on labor emigration until 1884, most Japanese who traveled to Europe or the United States during the early decades of the Meiji period were classified as students. Although that category always included some individuals whose real intention was to find work, those people had to characterize the purpose of their trip as "study" in order to obtain a passport that allowed them to leave Japan.[14] Labor emigration began in earnest only after Meiji authorities eased restrictions in 1884 to allow all its subjects—at least in theory—to travel abroad regardless of social status as of 1885. The Meiji government's decision was partly a response to ongoing requests on the part of the Hawaiian government for Japanese laborers. Another factor, Yasuo Wakatsuki argues, was the depression that followed Finance Minister Matsukata's determined effort to stabilize the Japanese economy in the early 1880s. Also important was the view of Meiji officials that emigration itself was a marker of a country's status as a modern, civilized nation.[15]

Although the Meiji government's tolerance for labor emigration increased after 1884, it continued to have serious reservations about permitting unchecked emigration to Canada and the United States and exercised a significant degree of control over who was permitted to leave, issuing instructions to prefectural governors on the classes of persons permitted to emigrate and under what conditions. As Mitziko Sawada observes, prefectural governments were instructed not to issue passports to individuals regarded as "low class" or "densely ignorant."[16] Because prefectural governors were assigned responsibility for issuing passports, differences in prefectural emigration policy determined who could travel to North America. Emigrants later reported that they sometimes moved from one prefecture to another to take advantage of variations. As one emigrant explained, "Prefectures such as Hiroshima, Okayama, and Wakayama issued passports without asking troublesome questions," in contrast to Kanagawa prefecture, which emphasized "domestic development rather than ... emigration."[17]

After the promulgation of the Meiji Constitution in 1889 and establishment of a National Diet in 1890, the Meiji oligarchs issued an Order Protecting Emigrants, codified in 1896 as the Emigrant Protection Law. Although the Meiji government's concern in issuing the order was ostensibly to protect would-be emigrants from being taken advantage of by unscrupulous agents and labor contractors, historians generally agree that the government was less concerned about ensuring the welfare of its emigrants abroad than ensuring that those who were recruited were not likely to undermine its international prestige.[18] The Emigrant Protection Law required those applying for passports to undergo an investigation by local police and to submit a certified copy of their koseki, which enabled passport officials to ascertain mibun. Passports restricted emigrants to particular destinations, and the Meiji government retained the authority to cancel permission to emigrate, a power that it invoked in 1900 and again in 1907 to limit emigration to North America.[19]

Concerned that Japanese subjects not become the object of exclusionary legislation like that directed at Chinese immigrants in the United States in 1882 or a poll tax like that imposed on Chinese immigrants by Canada in 1885, the Meiji government acted in 1900 to restrict the number of passports issued for travel to both countries.[20] Although that number, in Canada's case, was already as low as fifty per month, the Meiji government directed prefectural governors to issue no new passports for either Canada or the United States.[21] The primary concern underlying this prohibition, as Sawada has explained, was the fear that those emigrating would undermine Japan's status as a nation in Western eyes.[22] The effect of the prohibition was quickly apparent in Canada. At the end of 1901, Canadian authorities reported that only fifty-six Japanese immigrants had arrived during the previous six months.[23] Although just eighty-three passports were issued to individuals identified as laborers in 1901, however, the number of Japanese emigrants applying to enter the United States increased. Some were able to avoid the restrictions on travel to the United States by going first to Hawaii and then to the mainland, since there were no restraints on travel between Hawaii and the mainland after its annexation by the United States. Others tried to avoid passport restrictions by citing occupations that they believed passport officials would regard as more acceptable; some were aided in this regard by passport officials themselves. One immigrant later reported, for example, that rather than being listed as the peddler he once was—a peddler would probably have been categorized as hinin under the old Tokugawa status system—his occupation was listed as "merchant."[24]

The Meiji government's voluntary restriction of the number of passports issued for travel to Canada and the United States in 1900 established a pattern that culminated eight years later in Gentlemen's Agreements with both nations.[25] Although this pattern of voluntary restriction succeeded in forestalling immediate action by the U.S. and Canadian governments to bar Japanese immigration, both agreements functioned as articulations of the humiliation that Meiji officials had worked so hard to avoid, and both were regarded as an affront to Japan's national honor and a derogation of its status within the community of nations.[26]

PREWAR IMMIGRATION HISTORIES

Despite the possibilities that emigration to North America offered people at all levels of society to redefine themselves in ways that made mibun irrelevant, histories of Japanese migration have been marked by a distinct reluctance to consider status issues generally and the emigration of buraku jūmin in particular. There is evidence that North America was idealized in the minds of at least some migrants at all levels of society as a place where Japan's historical caste differences were absent and where opportunity was available to all regardless of mibun. One advocate of emigration directed his appeal to members of the lowest of the four former status categories into which most Japanese fell. America, he declared, had much to offer not only merchants and artisans—no matter how tenuous their skills—but any who sought to acquire new skills after they arrived: "Come, merchants! America is a veritable human paradise, the number one mine in the world. Gold, silver, and gems are scattered on her streets … Come, artisans! Sculptors, lacquerers, carpenters, painters—anyone skilled in the least in the Japanese arts—can earn a lot of money by making fans, ceramics, and lacquerware. Come, students! Working during the daytime, you'll have time to attend night school in the evening."[27]

Although autobiographical accounts of Japanese emigrants hint that status considerations were indeed a factor in their decision to go abroad, such references are almost always obscured by the use of oblique language that makes the specific nature of the status issue difficult to discern. In a 1993 book, *Stubborn Twig,* Laura Kessler describes one character as someone who saw in emigration to the United States an opportunity to escape the social constraints that would have bound him in Japan. "Masuo was a bright and ambitious boy whose future was severely circumscribed by his environment," Kessler writes, adding that changes in the law notwithstanding, Japan's rigidly stratified social structure had remained largely intact.[28] Yet another immigrant, who agreed to marry a man twenty-two years older than herself in 1921, explained that she did so in order to go abroad because she was a member of a poor family "treated as small in the village"; she and her siblings were ostracized and bullied in school no matter what they achieved. She left for the United States, she told the interviewer, determined never to return to her home village.[29] Although the precise social constraints are not clear, both emigrants clearly saw in travel abroad an opportunity to avoid status-based prejudice.

Rather than address the issue directly, historians have, for the most part, dismissed the possibility that former outcastes emigrated in substantial numbers. To the extent that they insist, however, that buraku jūmin could not have emigrated because they were so "base and poor" that they could not have afforded the cost of overseas passage and lacked the capacity to realize their goals, the historians themselves reflect the prejudice against former outcastes that still exists in some circles. Yamato Ichihashi, a Stanford professor, made precisely this argument about emigration by buraku jūmin in his 1932 book, *Japanese in the United States,* and later historians have often relied on it for that point. In the book, Ichihashi expressly asks whether the "submerged classes of Japan" emigrated to North America, only to conclude that they did not, based on his own assertion that "they could not and would not, for they lacked both the means and the ambition to do so." Only the "upper layer of the working classes and middle classes" emigrated to the North American West. The two hundred yen needed to take a ship to the United States or Canada "was not possessed by a member of the poorest class, nor was he able to borrow it from anybody." Besides, Ichihashi adds, "the ambitious and adventurous ones are not commonly found in such a class."[30] The "scums of Japan" lacked both the means and the initiative to follow through on any impulse to go abroad, Ichihashi declares, so they did not emigrate to North America.[31]

Ichihashi's conclusions as to the status of the immigrants' ancestors were deeply flawed by his own deeply entrenched class and caste biases. Arguments like his improperly conflate character and social status. They also fail to take into account the financial situation of buraku jūmin: not all were necessarily too poor to take advantage of the opportunity that emigration to the United States or Canada offered. Villages where former outcastes lived were among those hardest hit by the economic upheavals that followed the Meiji Restoration, in part because they lost their monopolies on specialties such as leatherwork, but the same monopolies had also allowed some families to accumulate sufficient resources to give them access to alternatives that included emigration.[32]

Although many categorized as outcastes during the Tokugawa period were forced to live in marginal conditions, the "baseness" of their communities was often exaggerated by popular prejudice. Foreign visitors to Japan in the late nineteenth century discovered that reports from other Japanese about the squalid conditions in which buraku jūmin lived were not always borne out, notwithstanding the impoverished conditions in some communities. One contemporary historian described a visit to a buraku community: "Even complete social ostracism did not lower their self-respect so far as to make them less regardful of cleanliness than their persecutors. [The visitor], instead of encountering ugliness and filth, found 'a multitude of neat dwellings, with pretty gardens around them, and pictures on the walls of the rooms.' A large public bath-house and laundry, also showed that the instinct for personal cleanliness had survived through all the centuries of their degradation."[33] Also important to keep in mind when considering the question of buraku jūmin finances is the possibility that they pooled their resources. Families and villagers at all levels of society who were not initially able to afford the cost of emigration sometimes banded together to form rotating credit associations to cover travel costs.[34] There is no reason to assume that buraku jūmin would not also have cooperated in similar ways.

An increasing tendency to conflate the question of whether former outcastes emigrated with the question of whether Japan's poorest laborers emigrated—and to use "class" when translating mibun into English—also confused the historical record. Defenders of Japanese immigrants in North America made a strategic effort to rebut claims by white exclusionists and government entities that those arriving from Japan were drawn from its lowest classes, whether "class" was defined in economic terms or whether it referred to mibun. In 1899, for example, a report prepared by U.S. Immigration Commissioner W. M. Rice—which was also appended to Canada's 1902 Royal Commission report on Asian immigration—included the statement that Japan's "immigrating class" was drawn "largely from the lower order." Rice added that there was a "wide line of demarcation between this class and the better people." Questions posed to witnesses appearing before the 1902 Royal Commission included inquiries regarding the social classes from which Chinese and Japanese immigrants were drawn, "their condition before coming," and their "habits and standard of living" in their home countries. American witnesses invited to appear before the Canadian commission included San Francisco immigration inspector R. Ecclestone, who said that Japanese migrants arriving in San Francisco were drawn from the "very lowest class" in Japan, and T. M. Crawford, who testified that Japanese arriving in Oregon were drawn from the "worst class of the Japanese." The class from which they were drawn, Crawford added, was a "low type and an ignorant class" that "may be called the coolie class."[35] If caste biases played a part in shaping the questions about Japanese immigrants, so did their early defenders' desire to prove to a hostile white public that those who actually immigrated were not base and ignorant. The result, as Stefan Akio Tanaka argued, was that nearly every study of Japanese migration up to the late 1970s endeavored to prove to anti-Japanese exclusionists that Japanese immigrants were not drawn from "the lowest classes or social misfits."[36]

Although early histories of Japanese immigration were shaped by a steadfast determination to counter the negative claims of anti-Japanese exclusionists about the quality of Japanese immigrants, they also served the second purpose of countering the popular notion in Japan that emigrants were, in effect, *kimin,* "discardable or discarded people." An aphorism succinctly expressed the sentiment: *imin wa kimin,* "emigrants are discarded people."[37] Although the reference is to the perceived abandonment of Japanese abroad by the Meiji government, Japanese immigrants also regarded it as offensive because it invoked historical associations with hinin, who included those with no fixed home—*ryūmin,* or "drifting people." The character *ryū* suggests "floating, wandering, vagrancy, transmigration, and exile." Like hinin, people characterized as ryūmin had no formal place in organized society during the Tokugawa era. The association between ryūmin and emigrants was further reinforced by the etymological relationship between *ryūmin* and *imin,* the term used to refer to emigrants during the Meiji period. So objectionable are these associations that *imin* continues to this day to be considered an offensive term because of its pairing with *kimin* in the expression *imin wa kimin,* with the result that alternative terms continue to be preferred by people of Japanese ancestry in North America.[38]

In Japan, negative characterizations of emigrants were a product not only of traditional ideas associated with rootlessness and migration but also of a heightened sense of nationalism, the product of intensive efforts by the Meiji oligarchs to bind the Japanese people to the state. During the Meiji period and the following Taishō period (1912–1926), many Japanese assigned selfish motives to those who emigrated, assuming that they went abroad for ignoble reasons—to avoid shame, for example, or because they were unable to succeed in a rapidly modernizing Japan. In Paul R. Spickard's words, most Japanese viewed emigrants "as trash, as cowards, as people who had failed to make it in Japan and so were forced to go abroad."[39] After the Russo-Japanese War began in 1904, those who emigrated were also frequently characterized as unpatriotic; it was assumed that they had emigrated to avoid conscription.[40]

Non-emigrants projected qualities historically associated with Japan's lower status groups, including both merchants and outcastes, onto those who emigrated. When Wakatsuki compared reasons for emigration cited by emigrants with reasons cited by others from their home villages, he found that the non-emigrants tended to assign more mercenary objectives to the emigrants than they themselves gave. During the Meiji era, Wakatsuki concluded, many Japanese believed that those who went abroad were mostly people motivated by greed or failure who did not reflect the true values of Japanese.[41] The notion that emigrants were drawn largely from the lower reaches of Japanese society and that they left Japan primarily to avoid poverty or for other shameful reasons—including low-caste status—was reflected in the response of one Japanese newspaperman to the question of whether emigration companies relied on newspaper advertisements to recruit emigrants. Intent on defending newspapers like his own against any claim that they facilitated emigration, he dismissed that possibility out of hand. Emigration companies and labor contractors did not bother to advertise in newspapers, he declared, because emigrants were drawn "in all cases" from "the lowest class of people ... too ignorant to enable themselves to understand newspapers."[42]

Given the dual concern with proving the quality of emigrants both to white exclusionists and to Japanese at home, defenders of Japanese immigrant communities in North America continued to define status in ways that were culturally specific to Japan. Not only did mibun serve as a general frame of reference for identifying an individual's position in society in the minds of those who wrote, but it also provided a language comprehensible to North Americans and Japanese alike. Japanese writers' tendency to conflate "caste" and "class" when writing in English, using "class" even where their argument makes it clear that they are referring to historical status categories (mibun), also contributed to a growing lack of clarity in historical discussions regarding status of immigrants. In addition to writing descendants of former outcastes out of histories of Japanese immigration to North America, North American defenders of Japanese immigrants also endeavored to use the conceptual framework provided by Tokugawa status categories to bolster their assertions about the high quality of those who settled in Canada and the United States. The precise nature of their arguments varied, ranging from claims that Japanese immigrants in North America were predominantly drawn from the samurai class to reluctant concessions that even if most were drawn from Japan's lower classes, they at least were not drawn from Japan's very lowest status groups.

As early as 1891, Inazo Nitobe lamented the decline in the status of emigrants after the bar on labor emigration was lifted in 1884. Those who had gone abroad before, Nitobe declared, were "by no means" members of the "laboring classes"; most were "sons of old *samurai*, full of ambition and energy, yet without means to obtain a liberal education."[43] Nitobe's placement of "laboring classes" on the same continuum as samurai, the highest of the four formal status groups in the Tokugawa status system, suggests that he did not have just economic status but mibun in mind. His was a two-pronged appeal: the purported samurai ancestry of Japan's earliest immigrants was a marker of high status in Japanese society, and the immigrants' stated determination to acquire a liberal education marked status within the social and cultural framework of North America.

In 1909, Yoshida Yosaburo echoed Nitobe's claim that the status of Japanese immigrants had declined after 1884, but he adopted a new strategy to explain their circumstances, hoping to set the minds of white Americans at ease. To counter the claim of anti-Japanese exclusionists that Japanese were competing with European immigrants and Canadian and American settlers for land and resources, Yoshida asserted that Japanese migrants did not intend to settle permanently in Canada or the United

States. Instead, he insisted, they were interested only in temporary economic gain and hence posed no long-term threat to the racial composition of the North American West. Japanese labor migrants, according to Yoshida, were drawn from "the lower classes of the Japanese community, if not the lowest of all"; their "sole motive" was to "make money, and nothing more." Ironically, by tailoring his argument this way to refute the claims of white exclusionists, Yoshida played directly into their hands, allowing them to turn the same argument against Japanese immigrants. They claimed that because Japanese migrants were only interested in making money the migrants did not have the same stake in North America as those from Europe but sought only to take economic advantage during their stay.[44]

Although Yoshida insisted that Japanese who emigrated after 1884 were of low status, others relied on Nitobe to reach the opposite conclusion. In 1906, for example, S. K. Kanda insisted in an article published in English in *Washington Magazine* that the seven thousand Japanese living in Washington State "represent by no means the laboring classes" and included very few who were "mere drudges." Kanda, ironically, borrowed words that Nitobe had used fifteen years earlier to describe an entirely different group of migrants. Many of the Japanese living in Washington State, he declared, were "the sons of old Samurai, full of ambition and energy, yet without means to obtain a liberal education."[45] Where Nitobe had been describing the students who had been the first to go abroad during the early decades of the Meiji period and contrasting them with the labor emigrants who left later, Kanda used the same words—and the reference to mibun embedded in them—to entreat Washingtonians not to discriminate against Japanese who settled in Washington.

Because fewer than 7 percent of all Japanese were classified as samurai during the Tokugawa period, it is unlikely that Kanda was correct in stating that most Japanese immigrants in Washington were former samurai. Ironically, however, some who did have a legitimate claim to samurai ancestry may well have been individuals whose ancestors were categorized as hinin during the Tokugawa period, since samurai who violated certain tenets of the samurai code could be relegated to hinin status. Those who had been defeated in battle were sometimes absorbed into farming communities, too.[46] In many such cases, their descendants remained acutely conscious of their samurai ancestry. One immigrant who migrated to North

America during the early years of the twentieth century told an interviewer that her family was descended from a samurai retainer who, after being defeated in battle, took refuge in the mountains "in such a starved condition that they had to learn farming."[47] A similar understanding of the origins of at least some outcaste families is reflected in Shimazaki Tōson's novel *Hakai*, where the main character's father makes a point of telling his son that their family was descended "from samurai bloodlines, so that they are not aliens (*ihōjin*), unlike other *eta* whose ancestors, he says, came from Russia, China, Korea, and other foreign places."[48]

Still other prewar defenders of Japanese immigration, also preoccupied with delineating the historical social status of the immigrants, gave an alternative origin. Even if Japanese immigrants were not primarily of samurai origin, they argued, they were at least not drawn from Japan's lowest classes but from its farming class. To be a farmer in Japan, they explained, indicated status as well as occupation. In endeavoring to educate white North Americans about the significance of this distinction, Kiyoshi K. Kawakami described the status of farmers during the Tokugawa period as "exalted." "The farmer," he declared, "ranked next only to the *samurai* in the social scale."[49]

Prewar strategies intended to counter the claims of anti-Japanese exclusionists distorted the work of postwar historians who relied on earlier texts without carefully examining the basis on which their authors arrived at their conclusions. Consequently, the earlier paradigms came to be deeply embedded in the historiography of Japanese immigration. In 1978, for example, Howard Hiroshi Sugimoto relied heavily on Kawakami and Ichihashi to argue that Japanese immigrants in Canada were drawn primarily from the "farming class." Like Kawakami, Sugimoto noted the relatively high status of farmers in Japanese society during the Tokugawa period and emphasized that those who immigrated were not "coolies." Those whom he characterized as coolies purportedly lacked both the means and the initiative to emigrate. In Sugimoto's words, most Japanese in Canada "came from the relatively well-to-do farming class ... Few, if any, *coolies* migrated to Canada for two main reasons. First, they did not possess the money or the means to make the costly arrangements and to pay for the voyage across the Pacific. Second, they belonged to the very depressed class which did not enjoy any of the cultural, social, or economic amenities likely to have given rise to desires for emigrating." Sugimoto added that the "intensive investigation and rigid scrutiny that prospective emigrants were subjected to at the municipal and prefectural level" by officials familiar with their family background ensured that no one who might be from a coolie "class" or group emigrated to Canada.[50] Implicit in his argument is the claim that descendants of those once designated as outcastes did not settle there.

The question of whether buraku jūmin emigrated to North America was raised, without resorting to euphemism, in a far more nuanced analysis of Japanese immigration in 1979, but even its author, Yasuo Wakatsuki, concluded that it was unlikely that they did so in any number. Although Wakatsuki does not acknowledge Ichihashi as his source, his reasoning is all but indistinguishable: the "factors which militated against their emigrating included (1) insufficient economic means, (2) lack of 'intrepid spirit' to migrate overseas, and (3) the policy of the Japanese government to withhold passports from this class."[51] That this view continues to shape Japanese immigration histories is suggested by Masakazu Iwata's *Planted in Good Soil: The History of the Issei in United States Agriculture*, published in 1992. The social oppression that former eta faced in Meiji Japan, the author candidly observes, "would obviously have compelled a larger percentage" to look to North America with considerable hope. In considering whether they acted on that hope, however, Iwata also adopts Wakatsuki's rationale—derived in turn from Ichihashi's flawed reasoning—to conclude that it was unlikely that they were able to act on that motivation. Echoing Ichihashi's words almost verbatim three-quarters of a century later, Iwata also concludes that most people in this category would have lacked either the means or the initiative to act on that impulse.[52]

That these kinds of cultural attitudes regarding the significance of the historical status categories rooted in the thinking of the Meiji period continue to be reflected in the work of recent authors reveals the extent to which they are accepted as true. Because they are so embedded in the historiography of Japanese emigration, they continue to shape current interpretations of Japanese immigration history in North America. If we reject, as I do, Ichihashi's problematic argument that buraku jūmin lacked the character or initiative to go abroad, it follows that people in this category—at the confluence of the economic pressures that resulted from Japan's rapid industrialization and historical status biases—may well have taken advantage of the opportunity represented by emigration. The North American West, as Richard White has noted, offered people from all parts of the world the chance to transform themselves.[53] To argue categorically that buraku jūmin would not have availed themselves of this option is to accept Ichihashi's deeply flawed claim that descendants of those most harshly classified in Japan's historical status hierarchy did not have the same capacity for initiative as other Japanese.

The historiographical habit of denying the presence of buraku jūmin by erasing any reference to them in the historical record—including, as we saw, in the report on the Tokugawa status system sent to the U.S. secretary of state in 1908—played into the hands of anti-Japanese exclusionists who suggested that Japanese emigrated only for economic reasons and that they were less committed to permanent settlement than Europeans were. As I discuss in subsequent chapters, the writing-out of outcaste status, and the ways of understanding difference that the writing-out exemplifies, has also obscured key elements of the strategies developed by both Meiji diplomats and immigrants in their efforts to negotiate entrenched racial divides in Canada and the United States.

The vantage point offered by North America also reveals just how tenacious perceptions of difference rooted in mibun proved to be even when removed from their original historical and geographical context. Although the Meiji government believed that the elimination of formal status barriers was a key to establishing Japan as a modern and civilized nation, the culturally distinct ways of understanding difference that Tokugawa-era status barriers had produced reinforced the fears of Japan's elite that Japan's position in the hierarchy of nations might be undermined if those who were historically members of lower status groups represented Japan abroad. The tension between these two imperatives is reflected in the use of a modern legal mechanism—intended to facilitate emigration—to monitor the mibun of emigrants. This tension illustrates a larger conundrum that the Meiji government created for itself. On the one hand, Meiji officials were concerned about preserving a set of distinctions based in part on spatial organization and the control of movement across the social and geographical boundaries that defined it, and, on the other hand, they reorganized space to allow for a greater degree of social and spatial mobility, which they believed was critical to achieving their goal of remaking Japan as a modern, industrial nation.

CHAPTER THREE

Negotiating Status and Contesting Race in North America

WHEN NAKAHARA HADATARO, a young labor emigrant from the coal-mining region in northern Fukuoka prefecture, obtained his passport permitting him to travel to North America in 1906, he also received an official notice from the governor of his prefecture admonishing him not to forget that he was a subject of the Japanese empire and not to leave anyone in any foreign nation to which he traveled with a "shameful impression" of Japan. His purpose in "traveling ten thousand *ri* across the rough waves to a distant foreign land," said the notice, was to work hard and to earn enough to ensure the welfare of his family in Japan. Like others categorized as dekasegi laborers by the Meiji government, Nakahara was also instructed to be honest with his employer, to suppress all impulses to be rude or to gamble, to obey the laws of any country he visited, and to carry the notice with his passport.[1]

Acutely conscious of perceptions of Japanese in North America at a time when both Canada and the United States were increasingly engaged in efforts to racialize their borders, Meiji leaders were particularly concerned that Japanese emigrants not behave in any way that might undermine Japan's status as a modern and civilized nation equal to the nations of Europe and North America. Meiji officials were convinced that the tremendous effort that Japan had made to use Western models in restructuring its economic, social, and political institutions set Japan apart from other Asian nations. Britain's rescission of its unequal treaty with Japan in 1894 and Japan's victories in the Sino-Japanese War in 1895 and the Russo-Japanese War in 1905 were proof, in their view, of the progress that Japan had made, and demonstrated that Japanese subjects should be treated in the same way as the citizens of any Western nation when they were traveling abroad. Japan was the "co-equal of the most civilized nations of Europe and America," K. T. Takahashi, one of four hundred Japanese immigrants then living in British Columbia, declared in 1897, "hence, Japan, as a power, should receive, and is entitled to, all the international courtesies as observed by the civilized nations of the world."[2] In 1902 a lawyer retained by the Meiji government to represent Japan's interests before the Royal Commission on Chinese and Japanese Immigration in Canada, articulated Japan's position as follows: "As a people the Japanese have made great strides in civilization; or rather, they have always been a civilized people, but have improved their civilization; ... they have adopted the methods of European powers; their course in the last few years has been one of extraordinary and gratifying progress; they are accredited to all civilized powers."[3]

Meiji diplomatic efforts to counter negative perceptions of Japanese migrants did not just emphasize the progress Japan had made, however, but also became entangled with officials' own historical status biases in ways that led them to conflate failure to modernize with low-caste status. Meiji government leaders had viewed the abolition of historical status and caste categories as a crucial element in redefining Japan as a modern, nonfeudal nation. The same was true of their 1884 decision to relax the bar on labor emigration. But persistent assumptions about the meaning of status and caste differences meant that to Meiji diplomats, labor emigrants often appeared to pose a threat to Japan's modern image. Drawn largely from rural areas that had yet to embrace new cultural forms imported from the West, labor emigrants, unlike Japanese living in larger cities, were often unacquainted with Western ways. Meiji diplomats viewed them with concern both because they were not sufficiently "modern" and because they perceived them as deriving, at least in part, from lower status groups. The persistent conflation of economic class and mibun meant that the qualities associated with one came to be associated with the other.

As early as 1884, for example, Meiji consular officials had linked concerns about how Japanese were viewed in the United States to the status of emigrants. In February of that year, the Japanese consul in New York City asked his government to take immediate steps "to control the passage of sailors, lower-class servants, and the like to the United States." He characterized the emigrants to whom he referred as low in status both because they were entertainers—many of whom would have been classified as hinin under Tokugawa law—and because they wore the same clothing they would have worn in Japan even in public. Their clothing, the consul declared, made them the "object of public scorn and ridicule wherever they went."[4] In 1891 the Shokumin Kyōkai (Colonization Society) similarly described a group of emigrants who had just arrived in Vancouver as belonging to the "lowest classes of laborers." Worse, they were "grotesque" in appearance—an assessment that was in part an expression of historical status-based biases and in part a reaction to the newcomers' lack of familiarity with Western clothing.[5] The same year, the Japanese consul in San Francisco expressly linked the perceived status of those arriving in North America with the issue of Japan's standing in the world. "The continuation of the mass migration of lower class Japanese," he warned his government, "will undoubtedly create a grave situation in the relationship between Japanese and Americans in this country which, sooner or later, will adversely affect the honor and reputation not only of the Japanese in this country but also of those in Japan."[6]

Accounts that appeared in the North American press seemed only to confirm the worst fears of Meiji consular officials. A group of clippings sent to Tokyo by the consul in San Francisco with his 1891 dispatch, for example, included several that blamed a recent group of arrivals for the unsanitary conditions on board the ship on which they had traveled. "Dirty Japanese," one headline blared, "Filthy State of Steamer's Passengers." The migrants' clothes, its author declared, were "a fearful and wonderful mixture of male and female attire." One man "was arrayed in an American necktie tied around a Japanese skin free of any shirt [and] over his bare skin was an old vest several sizes too large for him." One woman "wore a corset reaching to her neck and strutted about the commissioners with a gravity becoming an alien just initiated into the mysteries and responsibilities of American fashions."[7] Deeply concerned about the negative impact that depictions like these might have on Japan's image as a modern nation, the consul urged his government to prevent the emigration of "low class and densely ignorant" people who might tarnish Japan's reputation abroad.[8] Not only was their lack of familiarity with Western ways attributed to low status, but negative depictions such as these were later used to admonish migrants not to behave in the same "animal-like" way as those who had arrived in the 1890s—an admonishment that expressly invoked imagery historically associated with outcaste status in Japan.[9]

The Meiji government instituted a range of strategies to counter negative perceptions of Japanese migrants among North Americans. In addition to monitoring the historical status (mibun) of those who received passports and admonishing passport recipients to behave in ways that would not undermine Japan's image as a modern imperial nation, Meiji leaders developed a series of rhetorical arguments to reposition Japanese in American and Canadian society. Determined to defend Japan's status among Western nations, the Meiji government was particularly concerned that its subjects not become the object of anti-Japanese legislation like that first imposed on Chinese immigrants in 1882.[10] Embedded in the remarks of Meiji diplomats and others, however, was the persistent notion that those who were the object of prejudice were themselves primarily responsible for it. Partly an extension of traditional attitudes rooted in mibun toward those who were members of low status groups and partly a consequence of accepting Western culture as the model of civilization, Meiji officials criticized not white racism but the appearance and behavior of Japanese emigrants, which Japanese officials claimed gave rise to that prejudice.

The notion that the emigrants themselves were the primary cause of anti-Japanese prejudice in the North American West and that status-based differences between "lower class" and other Japanese explained white racism informed the attitudes of Japanese leaders for decades. As late as 1914, for example, Baron Rempei Kondo, a peer and president of a leading transpacific shipping company with ports of call in Seattle and Vancouver, declared that the "Japanese who go to America generally belong to the lower classes. When they suddenly make their appearance in America, it is no wonder that they do things the Americans do not like." Kahei Otani, a former member of the House of Peers, likewise attributed anti-Asian prejudice in North America to those at whom he believed it was really directed: "Only the lowest section of the Japanese are being discriminated against or excluded in America. The more respectable classes of Japanese are well treated and respected by the Americans. It is a striking illustration of this fact that there has been no anti-Japanese movement in Chicago or New York. In California and other Pacific coast states only has unfriendliness been shown toward our people. This is because many Japanese in those regions are unworthy."[11]

What Meiji officials did not initially realize was the extent to which anti-Japanese elements understood and would be able to turn to their own purposes both Meiji government concerns that their own labor emigrants did not adequately represent a newly modernized Japan and the caste- and status-based distinctions that Meiji officials drew between themselves and dekasegi laborers. Vancouver's *Daily News-Advertiser* embraced precisely this distinction when it told its readers in 1893 that "lower class Japanese are by no means ... desirable settlers ... They stand in a wholly different position from that occupied by the intelligent Japanese of the middle and higher classes."[12] Failure to restrict the emigration of Japanese deemed low class, consular officials warned the Meiji government, threatened to bring down upon Japan the same kinds of exclusionary laws that had been imposed on Chinese migrants—laws they attributed less to white racism than to the Chinese themselves. In 1884, for example, the Japanese consul in New York harshly criticized not the U.S. Congress but the Chinese immigrants for passage of the Chinese Exclusion Act: "In seeking ... an answer to the question of why these undesirable Japanese began to arrive suddenly in increasing numbers since two years ago, I have come to a conclusion that these Japanese laborers must have been recruited in Japan and brought to this country to replace the Chinese laborers whose passage to this country was stopped in 1882. It is indeed the ignominious conduct and behavior of indigent Chinese of inferior character, however, that brought upon the Chinese as a whole the contempt of the Westerners and resulted in an enactment of the legislature to exclude them."[13]

Newspaper accounts in the North American press that equated Japanese and Chinese exacerbated fears of Meiji diplomats that North Americans would fail to distinguish between Japanese and Chinese. The latter were the object not only of the Chinese Exclusion Act in the United States but, after 1885, a head tax in British Columbia that required each migrant to whom it applied to pay $50 as a condition of entry.[14] In May

1892, for example, the *San Francisco Call* published an article declaring that Japanese immigrants were "little better than Chinamen in regard to customs, uses and habits." Californians, it added, would soon recognize that Japanese laborers were "not the kind of immigrants that California requires for the development of its resources."[15] "Immigration is increasing steadily," the *San Francisco Chronicle* reported in 1905, "and, as in the case of the Chinese, it is the worst she had that Japan sends to us."[16]

The cultural lens through which Meiji diplomats abroad viewed their own country's emigrants also deepened their fears that North Americans would fail to distinguish between themselves and the emigrants they described in such negative terms in their dispatches home to their own government. To persuade North Americans to differentiate between Japanese and Chinese, on the one hand, and among Japanese, on the other, the Meiji government developed a two-pronged argument. Rather than attacking racism in the North American West directly, Japanese consular officials invoked historical status differences and appealed to North Americans to distinguish between the officials and the "low class" immigrants who were, they believed, the real focus of white hostility. They argued, in effect, that Japanese labor migrants were not the object of prejudice because they were Japanese but because they purportedly came from what were historically Japan's lower classes. Having drawn that distinction based on both class and status, consular officials went on to argue that even though Japanese emigrant laborers were of low status relative to Japanese like themselves, the same emigrants—as subjects of a modern, imperial nation—should be deemed higher in status than emigrants from nations like China that had not made the same commitment to modernization that Japan had. Rather than reject anti-Asian prejudice out of hand, then, Meiji officials attempted to bridge the racial divide by recasting anti-Japanese sentiment in terms they regarded as more acceptable by invoking both historical status distinctions and Japan's place in the hierarchy of modern nations.[17]

The dual nature of the Meiji government's response to white racism is apparent in remarks made by Shimizu Seizaburo, Japanese consul in Vancouver, during his visit to the coal mining community of Cumberland, B.C., in 1899. Even as Shimizu urged white Canadians not to discriminate against Japanese laborers working in the coal mines in Cumberland, he was at pains to distinguish himself from the coal miners whose working conditions he had come to inspect. "It is generally the lower class of my countrymen who immigrate into this country," Shimizu told a reporter, "and it is hardly fair to judge all of us from a single type."[18] Although Shimizu was willing to concede that white prejudice against Japanese labor migrants who worked in the mines was essentially justified, he also argued that the miners whom he characterized as low in status relative to himself were of a higher class and more advanced than migrant laborers from other countries. Shimizu pointed, in particular, to the eight years of compulsory education required in Japan, a policy instituted early in the Meiji period as part of Japan's quest to reconstruct itself as a modern nation. Given the focus on education in Japan, he told the reporter, even its lowest classes of laborers were literate, in contrast to those from other countries and particularly China. Canada's upper classes, Shimizu declared, had recognized Japan's achievements—he had been gratified to learn that "all classes of Canadians [were] unanimous in the opinion that Japanese labourers are far ahead of Chinese."[19]

Shimizu repeatedly emphasized Japan's progress in remaking itself as an industrial nation, contrasting it with China's failure to adopt "modern" institutions. It was Japan's success in this regard, Shimizu argued, that made its citizens better labor migrants than those from China. Others associated with the Japanese consulate in Vancouver had made similar arguments. In 1897, for example, K. T. Takahashi had also contrasted Japan with China to argue against the proposed extension of the head tax to Japanese, invoking white stereotypes of the Chinese to defend Japan's "lower classes" against those of China. That a newly modernized Japan had "no outcast and no pauper class" in contrast not only to China but also to Western nations was further evidence that Japanese should not be equated with Chinese. He added:

> In China they have a large, floating population that have no
> home, no citizenship, but live, simply live, from day to day,
> upon the dregs and refuse of the street, and are ever pining even
> for slavery abroad rather than continue their native life under
> the incessant pressure of hunger and inhumanity.
> With these people, frugality verging upon starvation is
> inevitable, and low living becomes a habit. Japan, however, is
> not China, and is absolutely free from those execrable features

so characteristic of the latter. Not only that, but even what is commonly known in the great cities of Europe and America as the "pauper class" is an unknown quantity and practically has never existed in Japan. In other words, even the lowest class of people in Japan have no opportunity to become habituated to what may be termed a "low standard of living."

The disingenuous nature of the head-tax advocates, in Takahashi's view, was evident in their failure to distinguish Japanese and Chinese, which he regarded as a deliberate strategy used by exclusionists to inflame anti-Japanese sentiment. "Their tactics have always been to speak of 'Chinese and Japanese' in one breath and one phrase, as if the two were one and same people with identical traits and characters."[20]

Arguing against proposed exclusionary measures in 1899, Shimizu also invoked imperial politics in defense of Japanese immigrants, pointing to Canada's status as a British dominion and contrasting its subordinate role within the British empire with Japan's own position as an imperial power that had begun to acquire colonies of its own. If British Columbia adopted anti-Japanese legislation, he reminded Canadians, his own government retained the option of appealing to the "Imperial authorities" to which the province was subject. Great Britain, he noted, had recognized Japan as a nation equal in status when it rescinded its unequal treaty with Japan in 1894.[21] Canada, as a dominion that remained subject to British imperial authority, was thus precluded from treating Japan as less than equal.

Shimizu also pointed to Japan's 1895 victory over China as evidence that Japan was both the equal of European nations and superior to China. "Japan made wonderful progress before that," he declared, "but the Chinese war demonstrated to other peoples that we have taken our place among the great nations of the world, and our government is determined to uphold that honour." Given Japan's achievements, Shimizu concluded, it "would be an insult to our national dignity" to exclude Japanese from Canada in the same way that Chinese—who, in his view, had not made equivalent progress—had been excluded.[22] Shimizu had made much the same point in a letter to Sir Wilfrid Laurier one year earlier: "It is unfair and unjust to legislate, or even attempt to legislate, discriminately against the subject[s] of the country which I have the honour to represent here, whose progress in civilization has excited the admiration of the world, and who has been internationally recognized as the equal of any country, in the same way as against the Chinese."[23]

Shimizu's approach extended an argument made by his predecessor, Nosse Tatsugoro, in response to efforts by members of the B.C. legislature to persuade the Canadian government to raise the head tax that applied to Chinese immigrants to $500 per person and to extend it to Japanese immigrants in 1898. Like Shimizu, Nosse had also urged Canadians to draw a distinction between Chinese and Japanese immigrants. The failure to distinguish the two, Nosse declared, "was a mistake which only extreme ignorance could make." The Chinese who came to Canada were, in his words, "the lowest on the scale" and essentially amounted to a "species of slavery."[24] In an apparent effort to invoke white stereotypes about Chinese in order to position Japanese migrants more favorably, Nosse also argued that the low status of Chinese immigrants was demonstrated by their behavior: "they smoke opium; they start gambling dens; they are unclean; they never assimilated with the population; [and] they take all they earn to China." In contrast, Nosse declared, Japanese were representatives of a "modern, civilized" nation and "highly civilized people." Nosse also pointed to the growing presence of women within Japanese immigrant communities as evidence of both the stability and the civilized nature of Japanese immigrant society. A majority of the eight hundred Japanese then living in British Columbia were Christians, Nosse claimed, and at least sixty of that number were women who were also wives: "they are clean and frugal; they set up the family; they open churches."[25] In short, it was Japan's successful quest for modernity, together with the willingness of Japanese immigrants to embrace what Meiji officials identified as markers of Western civilization, such as Christianity, that made the Japanese more desirable immigrants than the Chinese. In 1903, Nosse expanded this argument to insist that Chinese immigrants themselves recognized that difference, claiming that after China's 1895 defeat in the Sino-Japanese War some Chinese in North America began to wear Western clothing and pretended to be Japanese.[26]

Interviewed in Montreal at a time when there were few Japanese migrants in eastern Canada, Nosse—described by the reporter as "modern to his fingertips"—apparently felt no need to call attention to any distinction among Japanese based on historical status-based distinctions. In addition to urging North Americans generally to distinguish between Japanese and Chinese migrants, however, Nosse also adopted several rhetorical strategies specific to Canada. Like Shimizu one year later, Nosse underscored Canada's status as a British dominion, contrasting its subordinate role within the British empire with Japan's position as an imperial nation. Because Britain had recognized Japan as an equal, Nosse argued, Canada had no justifiable basis for discriminating against Japanese subjects: "Now why should we be discriminated against? England was the first to recognize Japan as a modern, civilized nation. England gave to Japan, in the new treaty, which was made with her two years ago, the benefit of the most favored nation clause. We are in the East what England is in Europe ... Canada is the greatest colony in the British Empire. Why should this colony discriminate against that people the progress and civilization of which England was the first to recognize. Thirty years ago I would not have complained if an attempt had been made to keep us out. We had no status then in the civilized world; but to discriminate against us now is most unfair."[27]

Meiji diplomats, in short, argued against white racism in North America not by attacking it directly but by endeavoring to recast it in terms of class difference and by drawing on the language of modernity. By distinguishing between modern Japan and "tradition-bound" China, Meiji officials sought to explain anti-Asian prejudice not on the basis of race but as a result of "backwardness" or the failure to modernize, whether on the part of individuals or on the part of entire nations. In doing so, they embraced a hierarchical view of national progress that mirrored in significant ways the hierarchical social structure around which difference was organized in Meiji Japan.

Meiji officials undermined their own contention that race should not be regarded as a meaningful basis on which to determine admissibility to the United States and Canada, however, by simultaneously invoking race in other contexts to argue for the inclusion of Japanese. Aware that Canada was actively recruiting European immigrants to populate its western provinces, for example, Meiji diplomats argued that immigrants from northern Japan were racially better adapted to conditions in the Canadian prairies than European immigrants were. In 1897, Nosse declared that "Canada needs a thrifty, hardy population, which Japan can supply." Japanese from northern Japan, he argued, were especially well suited to settle Canada's Northwest based on physical characteristics that were a product of their lives in areas of Japan where they had had to deal with harsh weather and tidal waves. In Nosse's words, they were "hardy; they have strong bodies and a high stature; and they are accustomed to hardship ... they are thrifty; they are strong; they are peaceable; and they can endure both cold and heat."[28] Japanese were racially better suited to Canada, Nosse argued, than Europeans from more temperate climes, who had not had to endure equivalent hardships.

Astute observers of the complex relationship between Canada and the United States, Meiji officials also devised arguments tailored to political conditions in North America not directly related to their own objectives. Meiji officials in both countries, for example, emphasized the transient nature of dekasegi migrants to argue that they did not pose a threat to the dominant society because they did not intend to establish permanent homes. Meiji diplomats in Canada, however, added another component to this argument in an effort to position the United States as a negative example that Canada should not emulate in its approach to the issue of race. Comparing dekasegi laborers to the Africans forcibly transported to the Americas to provide slave labor, whose descendants had settled permanently in the United States, Meiji diplomats argued that because dekasegi laborers had no interest in settling down, Canada could avoid the development of a "race" question like the one that plagued the United States. Just as Nosse had invoked negative white stereotypes of Chinese to position Japanese immigrants in a more favorable light, the lawyer hired by the Meiji government to represent its interests before the Royal Commission on Chinese and Japanese Immigration in 1902 invoked white stereotypes of African Americans to suggest that Canada could avoid the creation of a racial divide like that in the United States by admitting dekasegi laborers: they would not stay in Canada, nor would they have children.

> Now, it is said that it is important to consider whether we are not laying up for ourselves a race question. In the United States there is the race question with the negro in that country. The reason of that is the negro settles down on the land; they are a prolific people, and their numbers are growing more rapidly than those of the white people alongside of them. But the very thing that is charged against the oriental is the very thing that

may be alluded to as preventing any such thing in this country. I grant you if they came here and settled on the land with their families, and increased, it would be a serious matter for the white man; but they come here and give us the advantage of their labour at a reasonable rate; the results of their labours are left with us; but that they go back to their country again seems to me to be a great advantage instead of a disadvantage.[29]

Meiji diplomats also attempted to negotiate favorable conditions for Japanese migrants in Canada by invoking Canadian fears that the United States might seek to incorporate parts of British Columbia into its own West.[30] Nosse's argument that the head tax should not be extended to Japanese, for example, included the point that it would not be genuinely "Canadian" to pass such a tax, because the proposal was, "to a great extent, fathered by men who are not even British subjects." "Do you know," Nosse asked, "that in [B.C.'s] Kootenay district and the Fraser river district the country is flooded with Americans, who want all for themselves, and who would prevent any other people from participating in benefits which are all the time increasing in value?"[31]

Takahashi had likewise invoked Canadian stereotypes of Americans to bolster his own argument against extending the head tax to Japanese. It was the Americans and not the Japanese, he insisted, who posed the greatest threat to Canadian interests. Americans were also the more transient: "The real and most serious enemy to the bread-winners of British Columbia are today as it had always been, those predatory aliens other than Japanese who freely cross and recross the boundary line and carry all their earnings away into the American side. When prospects are better and wages rise on our side they promptly come swarming in and at once make themselves the competitors of the sons and daughters of our soil. As promptly they depart when the tide changes, leaving our own workers poorer by what they take away with them."[32]

Like Nosse and Shimizu, Takahashi offered two separate frameworks for a hierarchy of nations in North America within which Canada could position itself. On the one hand, Takahashi appealed to Canada's vision of itself as unlike the United States in its embodiment of British virtues. In this context, he argued that the passage of anti-Japanese legislation would "be an act of undignified petulancy toward a friendly power—an act unworthy of British fair play and Canadian dignity." Canada, he urged, was principled in ways the United States was not. On the other hand, he held the United States up as an example that Canada should emulate. Even though there were several thousand Japanese immigrants in the United States by 1897, it had passed no laws excluding Japanese from that country. Surely, Takahashi declared, the fact that the United States "had longer and larger experience with the Japanese" but had "not found any cause to object to the latter's immigration" made it clear that there was no reason to extend the head tax to Japanese. British Columbians had no reason to find fault with the Japanese when the Americans did not.[33]

Concerns about the implications of status and mibun not unlike those evident in the rhetoric of Meiji officials were reflected in the attitudes and behavior of Japanese immigrants themselves. Although the redefining of status categories was just as important to immigrants, differences between their own personal objectives and those of Japanese consular officials meant that their efforts to renegotiate categories such as race and mibun sometimes assumed distinct forms. On the one hand, North America offered emigrants of low status—including buraku jūmin—an opportunity to obscure their historical status or caste origins, which meant that they had an interest in concealing the very kinds of status designations that Meiji officials had sought to preserve by noting family occupation and origin on their passports. On the other hand, Meiji officials emphasized emigrants' common identity as citizens of a modern imperial nation, which was consistent with the immigrants' own goals of erasing historical status and caste barriers between themselves and other Japanese.

One area of common ground was consular officials' and immigrants' shared attitude toward Chinese laborers. Both were, in Yasuo Wakatsuki's words, "appalled by the idea that they should be compared to Chinese immigrants."[34] Although Meiji-era immigrants in the North American West regarded themselves as subjects of a modern imperial nation, they found themselves relegated to the bottom of race-based labor hierarchies in Canada and the United States, treated as indistinguishable from the Chinese immigrants they looked down on as subjects of a nation that had failed to make the same kind of progress as Japan had. Payment structures in the industries in which they worked expressed that equation. The Union Coal Company in Cumberland, B.C., for example, paid Japanese and Chinese laborers alike half the daily wage paid white laborers for the same job.[35] Determined to challenge this perception, Japanese laborers took what steps they could to distinguish themselves from Chinese laborers. Inota Tawa, for example, reported that the Japanese boss of the railroad gang he worked for during the early years of the twentieth century refused to allow his crew to bring soy sauce or *miso* soup into his camp and insisted that they wear shirts and dungarees like those the American laborers wore. "Since you are different from Chinese," his boss reportedly told his workers, "live like Americans."[36]

Traditional status biases among Japanese immigrants were reflected in efforts either to avoid certain kinds of occupations historically associated with outcaste status in Japan or, where such occupations could not be avoided, to hide or to explain away their involvement in them. The aversion of Meiji-era immigrant laborers to work they regarded as stigmatizing was most clearly evident in their attitudes toward coal mining. Coal mining, directly identified in certain parts of Japan with outcaste status, was one occupation for which Japanese laborers were recruited after the Meiji government eased its bar on labor emigration in 1884.[37] More than five hundred Japanese immigrants found work in British Columbia coal mines between 1884 and 1900, for example, beginning with a group of 24 miners brought to Canada in 1889 to work in the Union Coal Mines near Cumberland, B.C., followed by a second group of about 130 in December 1891. A third group of experienced coal miners recruited in Fukuoka and Kumamoto prefectures, on the island of Kyushu, arrived in August 1892 and were followed by others brought over by various emigration companies over the next two decades.[38] That many in this line of work moved on as quickly as they could is suggested by the Royal Commission finding that just 102 Japanese immigrants were "employed at the Union Mines, as miners, helpers, runners, drivers, labourers, timbering, blacksmiths, and labourers above ground, 77 being employed underground and 25 above ground."[39]

Given the association of coal mining with outcaste status in some parts of Japan, the occupation provoked intense concern about its impact on the perceived status of those who engaged in it. Masato Uyeda of Seattle, for one, later told Kazuo Ito that when he was asked what kinds of work he had done in North America by the Japanese crown prince during his visit to Seattle in 1960, he could not bring himself to admit that he had worked as a coal miner when he first arrived. "For us 'Meiji men,' " he told Ito, coal mining was a "job for criminals or the lowest of the low."[40]

Four Japanese coal miners with lunch buckets in Cumberland, B.C., circa 1915. (Cumberland Museum and Archives, C140.66. Hayashi/Kitamura/Matsubuchi Studio.)

Evidence also suggests that when Meiji-era Japanese immigrants believed that others had ties to outcaste groups, they were unwilling to associate with them. In April 1893, for example, Cumberland's *Weekly News* reported on a group of Japanese laborers who had recently arrived to work in the local coal mines but who refused to accept aid from another group of Japanese migrants who had arrived the previous year, even though the new arrivals were unaccustomed to mine work and lacked both food and adequate clothing for a colder climate, to the point where several were close to death. "Why they did not apply to their countrymen in the camp who were able to help them is a mystery," the reporter declared.[41] What the reporter did not realize was that the earlier group was composed of experienced miners, brought to Canada from Fukuoka prefecture, one of the regions where coal mining was an occupation associated with outcaste status.[42] Whether the miners in question actually had ties to former outcaste communities or not, the fact that they had worked as coal miners in an area where a significant percentage of such laborers were former outcastes appears to have been enough to trigger caste-based concerns on the part of the new arrivals.

The antipathy to coal mining meant that the labor contractors often had to struggle to meet contractual obligations to mining companies. Men hired as miners in Japan were anxious to pursue new lines of employment when they arrived in Canada, and many deserted or left as soon as they could negotiate an end to their contracts.[43] S. Gotoh, a labor contractor and head of the Canadian Nippon Supply Company informed members of Canada's Royal Commission on Asian immigration in 1908 that although he had recruited 135 miners who had come to Canada to work as miners, he had, in the end, "been unable to supply more than forty, as the men when they landed on this side of the Pacific declared that they preferred to work on the railways and he had no way of compelling them to go into the mines." Given their reluctance to accept jobs as coal miners once they arrived, Gotoh had been unable to fulfill the conditions of his contract and had cancelled it. By the time he testified before the Royal Commission, he had given up on trying to recruit miners in Japan altogether. Records submitted to the Japanese consulate in Vancouver by Japanese employment agents who differentiated between "common immigrants" and "miners" and tallied each separately provide further evidence of the significance ascribed to that difference.[44] That Meiji officials continued to regard it as important to monitor the mibun of its subjects in Canada and the United States is also reflected in a report prepared by the Japanese consul in Tacoma, Washington, in 1899, in which "lowest class" and "ordinary class" Japanese immigrants in Seattle were tallied separately.[45]

The stigma associated with coal mining among Meiji-era Japanese immigrants in North America and the power it had to define an individual's place in society found expression in the efforts that Japanese who had mined coal in North America made to hide their occupation or, when that was not feasible, to distinguish their own situation from that of those whose family occupation in Japan was coal mining. Even when Japanese immigrants later had no choice but to admit that they had worked as coal miners, many were quick to point out that they had done so reluctantly because that was the only kind of work available to them as Japanese in a highly race-conscious society and not because their families had mined coal in Japan. Implicit in these explanations was the fear that the failure to make that distinction would lead others to conclude that their families might have historical ties to low-status or outcaste communities in Japan. Gohachi Yoshida, who eventually settled in Tacoma, explained that he left Japan for North America based on the assurance of representatives of the Kyushu Immigration Company that many jobs were available in Victoria, B.C. Only after he arrived in October 1898 did he learn that the only jobs available to Japanese laborers were in the coal mines on Vancouver Island. "Desolate" at the prospect of having to mine coal but with no alternatives available, Yoshida worked for the Union Coal Mine in Cumberland, B.C., for just four months. Once he had saved the $50 or $60 needed to travel to Seattle, he, like others, broke his contract and left for the United States, where he arrived on March 5, 1899.[46]

The same insistence on explaining that jobs mining coal were accepted only because other avenues of employment were foreclosed by white racism and not because coal mining was a family occupation in Japan is reflected in interviews with children of Cumberland coal miners conducted by Cheryl Maeva Thomas in the 1980s. One coal miner's daughter told Thomas that her father knew nothing about mining and had never been underground until after he arrived in Cumberland in 1910. He had even had to work for a while without pay in order to learn to how to do the job. The son of another coal miner also emphasized that his father had taken a job mining coal as a last resort because that was "the only way he could come." These social divides, as well as the racial divide, were reflected in the geography of the small town of Cumberland. Whites lived in the main village, Japanese immigrants in the two areas known as No. 1 and No. 5 "Jap" Towns. The men brought from the mining regions in Fukuoka and Kumamoto prefectures to work as coal miners in the late nineteenth century largely settled in No. 1 Town; others from Japan tended to settle in No. 5 Town.[47]

Another strategy used by Japanese immigrants to avoid the stigma associated with work regarded as low class or unclean was to use names that were not their own. False names were taken both by those who feared that they might be stigmatized as being of low status in origin and by those of higher status who sought to avoid the possibility that their family would be shamed by their having accepted jobs as common laborers in Canada or the United States. A consensus existed among Meiji-era immigrants in the North American West to avoid any topic of conversation that touched on personal identity. No one "asked anyone where he was from or any other personal questions," said one elderly immigrant in the 1960s.[48] "Lots of immigrant people changed their real names to cover up their origins," said another immigrant many years later.[49] Some names, particularly those intended to be used only temporarily or in a particular context, are readily identifiable as false.[50] The name Tosayama, cited as the false name of a Japanese mining boss whose real name was Yamamoto Sadai, is one such example—Tosa is the name of a Tokugawa-era domain on the island of Shikoku and *yama* means "mountain."[51] Names of historical figures were also sometimes used. According to one elderly immigrant, in the wake of Japan's 1905 victory in the Russo-Japanese War an inordinate number of men gave their name as "Heihachi Togo," a garbled anglicized version of the name of the admiral who won the decisive battle of that war.[52]

When immigrants learned that their names suggested to others that they had historical ties to former outcaste communities, less obvious and more permanent changes were made to family names. Some name changes involved changing a character in the family name but retaining the same pronunciation, or retaining the same characters but changing the pronunciation. A family whose name included the character for "up," for example, might change the way in that character was pronounced from *ue* to *kami*, or vice versa.[53]

Immigrants who sought to obscure their identity did not rely solely on Japanese names. On January 15, 1901, for example, the *Victoria Daily Colonist* reported the arrival of the first Japanese immigrant required to comply with the requirements of a new Immigration Act, which directed that Japanese immigrants to fill out an application for admission upon arrival in Canada. He did so promptly and in English, the newspaper reported, even signing his name to the application. He was a naturalized British subject and a blacksmith by trade—in an occupation historically associated with outcaste status in at least some parts of Japan.[54] Curiously, though not remarked on by the paper, the immigrant provided not a Japanese but an English name—Y. Charles. Names, as Charles himself clearly realized, had the power both to obscure difference and to provide the basis for a claim to a new identity. Here, the name change would have accomplished two objectives: it would have served to obscure Charles's Asian origins from the ready view of white society and to obscure his place of origin in Japan from others in the Japanese immigrant community.

Inadvertent name changes that were a product of the failure of immigration officials to understand Japanese names, on the other hand, could lead to claims that migrants were not properly registered and were in Canada or the United States illegally. It is not hard to imagine that the Japanese immigrants whose names were incorrectly recorded as "Ka Je Ka Wa" or "Hari Sawa" in Canadian immigration records might later have found it difficult to prove that they had entered Canada legally.[55]

As we have seen, Meiji diplomats and immigrants alike remained acutely conscious of mibun and associated status issues, shaping both occupational and rhetorical strategies in response to the racial animus they encountered in North America. Monitoring mibun on passports and in other kinds of consular records to preserve status distinctions, Meiji government officials relied on a series of equivocal and internally contradictory arguments that ultimately served only to reinforce claims made by anti-Japanese exclusionists. Migrants, in contrast, often had a stake in obscuring the same kinds of distinctions that Meiji authorities found important to maintain. Some believed their families would be shamed because they had worked as laborers in the North American West, and some wanted to obscure ties to groups regarded as low in status in Japanese society. Although the goals of officials and migrants did not always coincide, their interests overlapped to the extent that migration allowed them to assert their newly articulated status as subjects of a modern imperial nation. The strategies of both diplomats and immigrants reveal that the process of negotiating identity in the North American West was never just the result of simple confrontations with white racism but involved far more complicated acts of positioning that made reference as well to historical ways of understanding status in Japan.

CHAPTER FOUR

Confronting White Racism

THE RESPONSES OF JAPANESE LABOR IMMIGRANTS to coal mines and other aspects of the North American West reflected traditional attitudes combined with the values of a westernizing Japan. In this context, the United States and Canada represented modernity—nations where the goals that Japan had set for itself were already realized in terms of both technological development and social ideals. Viewed in this light, the two countries appeared to offer Japanese an alternative to the social and economic constraints that circumscribed their lives at home. The alternative seemed to be reflected in the very landscape itself. Compared to the narrow mountain valleys and tight social and geographical ties that bound them in ancestral villages in Japan, the vast undeveloped expanses of the North American West offered not just financial opportunities but freedom from the traditional status and gender roles that continued to order much of Japanese society.

Although Japanese immigrants' perceptions were complicated upon their arrival by their encounters with white racism, for those who had yet to leave Japan, the sparsely settled vistas of the imagined landscape of the West embodied the social ideals and personal liberty that both the United States and Canada represented. One immigrant later reported that he had chosen the "rich, vast Western plains" where "one could see a thousand miles at a glance" to be his destination after seeing a movie called *Rodeo* in

Okayama in the first years of the twentieth century. That broad terrain, in his mind, was evidence not only of the size of the North American continent but also of "respect for freedom and equality." A soldier returned from the Russo-Japanese War recalled that the North American West appeared to offer the space for him to choose his own way in the world, whereas Japan's mountains seemed to hamper his ability to move.[1] A vision of the foreign landscape as uncultivated and replete with possibility also found expression in a short story written by Nagai Kafū, who arrived in the United States in 1903 and lived in Washington State for a time before moving east. "In Japan, where even in remote mountain villages land is almost everywhere cultivated, one feels the din and bustle of the world," Kafū wrote, "but, as can be expected, in the vast American continent, everywhere there is such an uninhabited area just two miles outside a town."[2]

To many Japanese immigrants Canada also appeared to be an enormous country with great stretches of land presenting a broad range of opportunities and a level of social equality and self-determination unavailable in Japan. The Canadian landscape, a Japanese-language newspaper based in Vancouver suggested in 1909, embodied limitless promise. "Spread before us are fertile plains and dense forests stretching far and wide for thousands of miles and blessed with an abundance of natural resources, more than half of which have not been cultivated or even fully explored."[3] The driftwood piled along the edges of Vancouver's harbors alone was enough to suggest to one young immigrant the wealth and promise Canada appeared to offer.[4]

Canadian and U.S. missionaries working in Japan and guidebooks written by Japanese advocates of emigration both played a role in shaping this idealized vision of the two countries. In the words of one immigrant, American missionaries in Japan had given him the impression that the United States was "the ideal country" offering a degree of "personal freedom and independence" not yet available in Japan.[5] But where the United States benefited from the popular perception, shared by many during the Meiji period, that it was a benefactor to which Japan owed a debt of gratitude for its role in opening Japan to modern development, Canada profited from its ties to Great Britain, the first Western nation to renegotiate its unequal treaty with Japan in 1894—a gesture that seemingly exemplified notions of British justice and fair play.[6]

Political opponents of the Meiji government saw in the United States in particular a genuinely democratic alternative. Rigid constraints were imposed on political debate in Meiji Japan, and a lawyer imprisoned for a decade by Meiji authorities later explained that he left for the United States after his release because he believed that he would learn "more of democratic ways of living and thinking" there than in Japan.[7] Travel to America, one Japanese advocate for emigration explained in 1906, had become popular because it was the "land of freedom."[8] Another one wrote, after living abroad for years, that Abraham Lincoln and the Declaration of Independence defined the "inner vision of the United States ... at once momentous and enduring."[9] Canada also represented freedom and independence. Privacy and the ability to move freely about, one immigrant later told her son, were the two most important considerations in her decision to emigrate to Canada.[10]

The United States and Canada also represented the modern because they offered freedom from the gendered social constraints that bound both men and women in Meiji society, including intricate webs of duty and obligation owed by a wife not just to her husband but to his family.[11] Women also believed that their status as women would be enhanced in North America, based on their impression that men in "civilized countries" like Canada and the United States were more likely to treat them as equals. One reason that Mary Kiyoshi Kiyooka agreed to marry an emigrant farmer lower in status than herself was that both she and her father, a former samurai, believed that she would be better treated as a woman in Canada than in Japan.[12] Yamada Waka, who arrived in Seattle in the late nineteenth century and later became a well-known feminist in Japan, likewise identified this as a factor that women going abroad considered. In one of her short stories a character declares, "In Japan I was despised for being a woman, but I'll be cared for and well treated in America."[13]

Although some Japanese men were confused by North Americans' respect for women in light of the racial animus they themselves faced on a daily basis, others saw in North America an opportunity to redefine gender roles in ways that appealed to them. One immigrant later recalled that he first began to think about emigrating the day he saw a Japanese Christian minister walking down the street carrying his child while his wife walked alongside. To see the minister, rather than his wife, carrying their child, he explained to an interviewer, struck him both as "new and rare" and as "very modern, and very Western" and caused him to long for that kind of freedom "at the same time that it was something very strange."[14]

Most importantly, however, Canada and the United States represented the modern because they were places where historical status and caste distinctions that retained their significance in Japan had no meaning. As early as 1884, Fukuzawa Yukichi, one of Japan's foremost advocates of westernization during the early Meiji period, had written, "America is a country of elites!" In nations committed to democratic principles, Fukuzawa explained, all citizens had access to opportunities historically reserved to the elite in Japan.[15] Even in 1914, Kiyoshi Kawakami continued to celebrate the absence of historical status and caste categories in North America. The United States is "a great Republic of brothers," he wrote, where "nobody is called upon to sacrifice the best years of his life for military duties" and "social caste has never been established." In the United States, "all the blessings of modern civilization— schools, libraries, museums"—are "placed at the disposal of every one," and "officials are in the true sense of the term servants of the people."[16] North America, as imagined by Meiji-era Japanese who believed its democratic claims, offered opportunities to people at all levels of society that rendered mibun irrelevant.

The goals of at least some immigrants were realized in the United States and Canada, if only for a time. Those who emigrated with an eye toward loosening the status- or gender-based constraints that had bound them in Meiji Japan often viewed conditions in North America as less harsh than those that they had faced in Japan. Ai Miyasaki, for example, reported how impressed she was that men "all tipped their hats to show the women respect, even to us Japanese." Their actions convinced her that the United States was indeed "free and democratic" and respectful of women. Shoichi Fukuda was likewise satisfied with the changes that emigration had produced in his life. A pickle maker's apprentice who was later apprenticed to a blacksmith, his duties in Japan had required him to deliver heavy barrels of pickles on a hand-drawn cart in summer and to plunge his arms into icy saltwater in winter. No matter how harsh the conditions he faced after he emigrated, he was convinced that North America had provided him with options that his family's historical status and occupation would have foreclosed in Japan.[17]

Japanese migrants' idealized images of Canada and the United States were complicated, however, by their reactions to conditions they encountered after they arrived in the North American West, including their aversion, springing from Japanese cultural attitudes, to such Euroamerican customs as the slaughter and eating of animals. Because meat eating and leatherworking were historically associated with outcastes in Japan, *hakujin* (white people) represented not only the modern but also the polluted in the minds of many Meiji-era Japanese, resulting in an ambivalence that added yet another dimension to their responses to white racism.

Reactions of Meiji-era immigrants to hakujin in North America paralleled those of Tokugawa-era Japanese to the Europeans and Americans who had arrived in Japan in the mid-nineteenth century. Although hakujin represented a level of technological achievement that Japan had yet to achieve, they were initially regarded with revulsion in Japan because they engaged in cultural practices regarded as polluting. When hakujin first landed in Japan in 1854, T. Yasuda later wrote, Japanese "were disgusted at the presence of persons wearing shoes of oxhide, which were regarded as polluting the sacred soil of Nippon [Japan]." Meiji government officials were not permitted to wear foreign boots and shoes made of leather until 1871, three years after the Meiji Restoration and the year in which outcaste status was abolished as a matter of law. Even in 1871, Yasuda argued, public sentiment against the wearing of leather was still so strong that the Meiji government's lifting of the ban on the wearing of leather boots should be understood as profoundly radical.[18] Beef eating, historically restricted to outcaste groups in Japan, was equally regarded with revulsion, notwithstanding its identification as a marker of "civilization" by those who advocated the adoption of Western customs during the early decades of the Meiji era.[19]

The contradiction inherent in this association of beef with civilization was not lost on representatives of outcaste communities in Japan. In 1867 and again in 1870, individuals classified as eta and hinin in the Kyoto and Osaka areas petitioned first the Tokugawa shogunate and then the Meiji government for emancipation on the ground that the government had established cordial ties with foreigners who also ate meat but whom it did not subject to the same constraints imposed on outcaste communities: "We are discriminated against as unclean people because we eat animal meat," but "those foreigners with whom Japan has recently entered into friendly relations also eat meat." If government officials were willing to associate with foreigners, outcastes also deserved to be integrated into the newly evolving society.[20]

Beef eating continued to be regarded with abhorrence in Japan even after the turn of the twentieth century despite the efforts of advocates of westernization to promote it. Yasuo Wakatsuki notes that as late as 1900, "ordinary people" in Fukuoka prefecture—one of the regions that sent a large number of emigrants to North America—did not eat beef or horse-meat, implying that only descendants of former outcaste groups continued to eat them.[21] An elderly immigrant born in Hiroshima prefecture later told her daughter, the anthropologist Akemi Kikumura, how distasteful she had found the sight of sausages hanging in a store window when she arrived in 1923, more than fifty years after the categories of eta and hinin were abolished in Japan. "It was unheard of to eat meat," she declared. "Meat was for *yotsu*." *Yotsu*, explains Kikumura, was a pejorative term meaning "four-legged" and intended to imply the "subhuman attributes of this outcaste group."[22]

As beef eating became a marker of civilization in early Meiji Japan, emigrant guidebooks took up the cause. They included cooking sections where Japanese immigrants could learn how to prepare meals such as roast beef or stew. Knowing how to cook meat would allow them both to respond to the needs of North American employers and to demonstrate their own civilized status to Westerners with whom they came in contact—a contradiction that reflects the ambiguity of their position as Japanese immigrants in a Western world.[23]

Hakujin smelled odd to Japanese, based in part on their habit of eating beef and other animal products; Westerners' odor had served to distinguish them from the time they first arrived in Japan.[24] So ubiquitous was this perception that in 1906, even an eastern American newspaper, the *New York Daily Tribune,* observed that "Japanese do not like the smell of white men."[25] Hakujin also looked outlandish to Japanese seeing them for the first time in North America. One young immigrant's description of the immigration inspector who spoke with him when he arrived in the United States suggests how bizarre a Caucasian could appear. The inspector looked like a *tengu*, a "long-nosed demon": he was "a huge creature with red fur upon its face ... the pale skin of a ghost and eyes so light they seemed to be transparent."[26] A Japanese traveler described his revulsion at watching a hakujin woman chop off the head of a chicken and at seeing the ease with which she wielded the hatchet. He described it as a barbaric and inhuman scene. The chicken's blood spattered up and down her arms, he wrote, is what must have made the lipstick of this animal-like woman so red.[27]

Throughout the late nineteenth and early twentieth centuries, then, hakujin represented progress and modernity, on the one hand, and barbarity, on the other—at once deserving of admiration and disdain. Kinya Tsuruta, who has explored the reflection of this paradoxical reaction in modern Japanese literature, observes that portrayals of *gaijin*—the term means "outside people" or "foreigners" and is also used to refer to hakujin—tend to fall into either of two categories: idealization or debasement. Hakujin are "elevated to the status of goddess-like beauties or lowered to the subhuman level of animals."[28] Interestingly, the tension parallels the contradictory ways in which "eta" were historically characterized in Japan: they were the "lowliest of all the people, almost resembling animals," on the one hand, and, at the same time, a group that included individuals of uncommon beauty, implicitly all the more dangerous as sources of impurity.[29]

Anti-Japanese prejudice—the antithesis of the democratic ideals that both the United States and Canada purported to exemplify—often came as a profound shock to immigrants who had idealized both nations. As late as 1919, one man immigrated to the United States to escape the strict hierarchical order that defined Japanese colonial society in Manchuria because he had been led to believe that in America, "a peaceful and intimate relationship" existed between Japanese and Caucasians, only to be startled to discover instead that Japanese were the object of endemic racial prejudice.[30] Relegated for the first time to the lowest strata in societies where race was the dominant factor in defining difference, Japanese immigrants who had not been exposed to social prejudice in Japan found the anti-Japanese sentiment especially galling. In the words of one immigrant, even "those who had never been insulted before in their life back in Japan had to take such insults"; all Japanese "were insulted indiscriminately in this country."[31]

White racism was offensive not only because it consigned Japanese to the bottom tier of the race-based labor hierarchies that ordered social status in the North American West but also because it appeared to render all Japanese equivalent to outcastes within the context of North American societies, failing to distinguish among them on grounds to which they continued to ascribe meaning. In Canada and the United States, buraku jūmin, long regarded as uncompromisingly "other" in Japanese society, were treated as indistinguishable from other Japanese. Instead, race was the dominant factor in defining difference. White racism was particularly degrading to those who regarded themselves as members of Japan's upper classes, both because white racists failed to differentiate them from Japanese they regarded as low caste and because they were convinced that the hakujin who looked down on them were themselves members of what they deemed Europe's lower classes. Inazo Nitobe declared as early as 1891 that in America, "social oppression" prevents even former samurai "from free movement—where to be an oriental 'heathen,' is to be generally despised by more heathenish (uncultured) masses."[32]

The extent to which Japanese immigrants equated their treatment by white racists with that historically directed at buraku jūmin in Japan is also revealed by their language and their use of animal imagery to describe their own reactions to white racism. One immigrant who arrived in the United States in 1919 at the age of seventeen later explained feeling that those who used the epithet "Jap" "must have thought of us as something like dogs."[33] The Japanese-language newspaper *Shin Sekai* (New World) was still more graphic, making explicit the perception that white racism rendered all those from Japan equivalent to outcastes: "Though we have been treated like *burakumin* (outcasts), our legal rights were still undecided [until recently]. Now, we are clearly branded as *burakumin* [in America]. Yet ... even if [America] dealt with us as pigs, or perceived us as dogs or cats, we must focus on our work obstinately."[34]

The equation of white racism with the prejudice historically directed against outcastes in Japan was also reflected in Nagai Kafū's use of the same kind of animal imagery to depict the way he thought Americans regarded Chinese, adding still another dimension to the concern that North Americans not treat Japanese the same way they treated Chinese. Americans, Kafū wrote, perceived the Chinese as "not so much an inferior race as animals—the same way they consider a certain class of Japanese—as objects."[35]

The bitterness engendered by white racism and the perception that it rendered Japanese the equivalent of outcastes found expression, among some Japanese immigrants, in the use of the word *ketō* in lieu of the word *hakujin*.[36] First coined when hakujin arrived in Japan during the mid-sixteenth century and written with the characters for "hair" and "Tang," the latter a reference to an early Chinese dynasty, it is usually translated into English as "hairy barbarian."[37] Some Japanese immigrants regarded the word *ketō*—which invoked images of hairy animals—as equivalent to the use of the term "Jap" to refer to Japanese. In the early years of the twentieth century, the author of a pseudo-advice column in Seattle's *Taihoku Nippō* (Great Northern Daily News), which parodied white stereotypes of Japanese, noted with some irony the contrast between the treatment of Japanese in the North American West and the romanticized image of old Japan popular in North America at the time. "White people should be called 'Ketō,' " the author declared, "not in revenge for being called 'Jap,' but [because] the word 'Ketō' has been handed down from the Nagasaki period."[38]

Japanese immigrants' reaction to white prejudice was compounded by their understanding that anti-Asian prejudice was located along the same continuum as that against *kokujin* (blacks), whose position in American society they identified, not inaccurately, as equivalent to that of outcastes in Japan. One reason that Japanese were so concerned about anti-Asian prejudice, David Starr Jordan explained in a 1907 article, was the Meiji government's concern that its subjects not be placed in the " 'Jim Crow' position of the Chinese and Africans."[39]

That kokujin were also the object of racist stereotypes in a Japanese cultural context added yet another dimension of meaning. Partly an expression of Meiji-era ideas about racial purity and partly a result of contact with white attitudes about race and racial difference to which Japanese were exposed after they arrived in North America, Japanese immigrants' attitudes toward kokujin clearly equated African Americans with historically denoted outcastes.[40] When foreigners arrived in Japan in the mid-nineteenth century, some Japanese tried to explain the position of outcastes by comparing them to kokujin. One Western visitor was told that "*Eta*" were "isolated and kept out of the nation" because they were "curly-haired negroids."[41] Animal imagery similar to that historically used to depict outcastes in Japan was also used to describe kokujin. Nagai Kafū, for example, refers to a black woman in one of his short stories as having "more animal than human blood."[42]

Parallels drawn between blacks and outcastes were also entangled with perceptions that white racism had its origin in the history of African slavery. Together the two biases provided a vocabulary to describe the Japanese experience of white racism. Hakujin, one immigrant told an interviewer, believed that "Japanese were like slaves ... they thought of us as cows or horses.[43] Another elderly immigrant drew on a mixture of images to explain his experience of white prejudice. Hakujin, he declared, "treated Japanese as animals," citing as evidence their mandatory seating at the theater: in the same seats where African Americans were forced to sit, "highest and farthest back in the gallery."[44]

An even more explicit equation of race- and caste-based characterizations of difference is reflected in a story reported by Hugh and Mabel Smythe in 1956 about a young Japanese man who was warned by his father not to accept a scholarship that he had been offered to study at an African American college in the United States. Based on his own experience in the United States during the early decades of the twentieth century, the father told his son that he would disown him if he accepted the scholarship because his association with African Americans would shame the entire family. Although the father's attitude was partly a function of his own prejudice against African Americans, implicit in his remarks is also a concern that no one in his family be treated like outcastes: "If you go to live among Negroes, you will be an outcast. You will be lonely—there will be no Japanese near you to help you. You will be in physical danger. Worst of all, you will live with bowed head. *That* no member of this family has ever done. I will not say that you may not go; you must make your own decision. But if you go, it must be on your own responsibility; I will no longer be able to call you my son."[45] The young man's acceptance of the scholarship would have rendered him twice an outcaste, then, for associating with people his father identified as equivalent to outcastes and for being cast out of his own family.

That this young man's father was not alone in equating African Americans with outcastes is reflected in the comment of another Japanese visitor, one who passed through Chicago as he traveled across the United States. Because the "bloody work" of the stockyards—the "gory spectacles of killing, skinning and chopping up of cattle ... was performed almost exclusively by negroes," it reminded him of the "unclean and defiled creatures," the "*eta*" in Japan, to whom the "slaughtering of beasts" had once been relegated.[46]

Just as Meiji-era Japanese immigrants viewed white racism through the lens of status and caste differences, their strategic responses were also shaped by ways of understanding prejudice rooted in Japanese history and culture. As anti-Japanese rhetoric intensified during the waning years of the nineteenth century, Meiji consular officials urged local community leaders along the Pacific coast to "clean up" their communities and to eradicate those elements believed to be responsible for encouraging racist attitudes against Japanese. By advocating reforms intended to counter negative allegations grounded in racial bias, their actions reflected the assumption—also embedded in attitudes toward outcastes in Japan—that those who were the object of prejudice were primarily responsible for it.

Their strategy, ironically, paralleled that of some former outcastes in Japan who had internalized the caste-based prejudice directed at them there. Although all buraku jūmin did not turn prejudice inward, there were those, as John Donoghue reported in the 1960s, who believed that they continued to be the object of caste-based prejudice because they had not yet done enough to eradicate the "most obvious 'trace' features of their status." These they identified as "special occupations, obnoxious behavior, and heavy drinking and pugnacity." For that reason, Donoghue observed, they made a special effort to promote such Japanese family values as maintenance of family obligations, honesty in business dealings, and moderate drinking. They also considered it their responsibility to demonstrate that they were not "immoral, criminal, irresponsible and alcoholic."[47]

Japanese immigrant leaders demonstrated a similar understanding of the sources and causes of discrimination. Rather than attacking white racism directly, they focused on eradicating behaviors that they believed produced anti-Japanese prejudice. One example is the effort they made to eradicate prostitution among Japanese immigrants.[48] Meiji consular officials had expressed concern about the impact of prostitution on the reputation of both Japanese immigrants and the nation itself since at least the 1880s. In 1891 the Japanese consul in San Francisco noted that a number of his predecessors had already informed the Japanese Foreign Ministry

about the existence of Japanese prostitutes and expressed his own concern
that their presence would undermine the standing of all Japanese in the
eyes of North Americans: "As the number of Japanese prostitutes and
operators of houses of pleasure in this city have, in recent years, steadily
increased, their ignominious conduct has begun attracting public attention and often resulted in scandalous publicity in local newspapers. It is
indeed a deplorable situation that their being the cause of public scandals
must cause unnecessary hardship in our endeavor to maintain the reputation of the Japanese as a whole."[49] When the Japanese consul sent his aide
to inspect conditions in cities along the north Pacific coast later that year,
the aide reported that prostitution appeared to be a source of livelihood for
a significant number of Japanese immigrants in the Pacific Northwest,
including Portland, Oregon, and Seattle and Spokane, Washington.[50] The
same year, Inazo Nitobe expressed concern about some of the women who
had entered the United States at San Francisco in 1889. Although port
arrival records showed that the eighty-eight women migrants included
thirty-three maids or domestics, thirty tourists or students, three seam-
stresses, and one teacher, Nitobe insisted that there was a "strong suspicion as to the real vocation of some of these women."[51]

As the turn of the century neared, an increasing number of reports in
the North American press regarding Japanese prostitutes appeared to
confirm the fears of Meiji officials about the impact they would have on
the reputation of all Japanese. As early as 1892 the *San Francisco Bulletin*
suggested that Japanese women were likely to be associated with prostitution and equated them with the lowest classes of European women.[52] The
Meiji government's determination to see that the issue of prostitution
was addressed only deepened when the United States passed legislation
in 1907 and again in 1910 excluding those involved in prostitution.[53]
Ignoring the unfair singling out of Japanese in this regard by anti-
Japanese exclusionists, Meiji consular officials urged Japanese community leaders in both Canada and the United States to do what they could to
eradicate prostitution, convinced that this would also help to solve the
larger problem posed by racial prejudice. Japanese immigrants themselves embraced that attitude. As one said, those engaged in prostitution
and gambling were the "worst class of Japanese immigrants" who did
"injury to Japanese immigrants in general ... They dirty our faces and
make Americans think less of all the Japanese."[54]

Women who were or became prostitutes were often among the first Japanese to reach a number of remote locations in the North American West. When Japanese men first arrived in Nevada in 1872 seeking rail-road work, they discovered Japanese prostitutes already there, who told them that officers on American ships had helped them to stow away. Women were also the first Japanese to arrive in other U.S. cities, including Denver, Colorado; Butte, Montana; and Ogden, Utah, as well as in Canadian towns ranging from Kaslo, Revelstoke, Nelson, Cranbrook, and Slocan in British Columbia to Edmonton and Medicine Hat in Alberta.[55] Some women appear to have been intrepid adventurers who traveled widely. One woman from Shiga prefecture who had worked as a prosti-tute in Seattle later traveled to Vancouver, where she worked for a time as a cook and then went on to live in Medicine Hat, MacLeod, and Cranbrook.[56]

Other women were kidnapped or smuggled aboard vessels bound for North America and locked in cabins or trunks until the ship left port. In 1894, for example, *The Japan Mail* reported that four women between the ages of seventeen and twenty-one had been found locked in trunks on board the steamship *Tacoma* as it was about to sail from Yokohama.[57] When they reached Canada or the United States, the women were smug-gled ashore or sometimes just thrown overboard.[58] Traffickers, *The Japan Mail* reported, estimated that they would be able to sell each for between $400 and $500 in gold. Although the Meiji government endeavored to remedy the situation by passing the Emigrant Protection Law in 1896, providing for the imposition of fines of 80 to 120 yen on smugglers of this kind, the editors of *The Japan Gazette* regarded this as far too lenient a sanction to be an effective deterrent.[59]

As in Europe, other women, many of whom were reportedly fisher-men's and farmers' daughters from Hiroshima, Kumamoto, and Shizuoka prefectures, among others, were duped into going abroad by procurers who invoked the same idealized vision of the United States and Canada that motivated other emigrants, and assured the young women that the North American West offered opportunities to them not yet avail-able in Japan.[60] Instead, they were forced into prostitution after they arrived. Unable to speak English and unfamiliar with the geography and the terrain, there was no practical way to escape. One example is that of a *sake* shop owner's daughter in Shizuoka prefecture who had long dreamed of studying abroad. Her father was eager to give his daughter every advantage in a rapidly modernizing Japan and entrusted her to a couple who told him that they lived in Seattle and promised that they would find her a place in a school where she could study English. Instead, they sent her to Calgary, where she was forced to work as a prostitute in a brothel with iron bars on the doors and windows that made escape virtually impossible. According to the *Tairiku Nippō*, she eventually moved to Nelson, B.C., where she continued to work as a prostitute because she no longer believed she had any other alternative. That magazines with titles such as *Jōgaku Sekai* (Schoolgirl World), sent by her parents from Japan, continued to arrive at the brothel in Calgary every month for a period of many years suggested, at least to the reporter, that she had never told her parents about her fate.[61]

As this story suggests, the stigma associated with prostitution was such that even prostitutes regarded it as ineradicable, an attitude that mirrored the way they were regarded by others. Regardless of how prostitutes were drawn into the business, all prostitutes were illiterate and careless of speech, and not one untainted heart could be found among them—or so declared the editors of the *Tairiku Nippō* in 1909. Prostitutes, in their words, were little better than slaves.[62] A woman was ostracized even if it was public knowledge that she had been forced into prostitution, Tomoko Yamazaki notes; she had no chance of reestablishing herself in society, either through marriage or by obtaining a respectable job.[63] The shame of prostitution, in Mikiso Hane's words, "reduced [prostitutes], in effect, to the status of outcastes."[64]

Much as some buraku jūmin reacted to caste-based prejudice by internalizing others' negative projections, women who were prostitutes tended to internalize the shame associated with prostitution. The voice of one woman from Mie prefecture who had worked as a prostitute was "barely audible," writes Yamazaki; it reflected the "permanent stigma she carried in her heart."[65] The feeling of shame was also reflected in the efforts that prostitutes made to hide their real names and their prefectures of origin. A Japanese woman named Koma, for example, told others that her real Japanese name was Masu and used the name Mabel professionally.[66] As Yamazaki notes, however, such ruses rarely succeeded: although names could be changed and backgrounds falsified, distinctive regional dialects made it difficult to obscure actual places of origin.[67]

ANTI-PROSTITUTION CAMPAIGN

In 1909 the editors of the *Tairiku Nippō* launched a campaign to eradicate prostitution in Vancouver by publishing a book entitled *Kanada no Makutsu* (Brothels of Canada), which comprised a series of articles that had previously appeared in its pages condemning all who participated in the prostitution business. The only way to eradicate anti-Japanese prejudice, the editors argued, was for all Japanese living abroad to work together to eliminate any reason for their communities to be subject to criticism. The base and irresponsible "animal-like" behavior of all those associated with prostitution, the editors declared, not only undermined the reputation of Japanese immigrants engaged in legitimate business but also "eroded the prestige and dignity of the nation." Only by excising these bad elements from their community would it be possible to redeem the reputation of Japanese immigrants and Japan as a nation; this alone would resolve the problem of anti-Japanese prejudice. The method adopted by the editors was twofold. First, they intended to make public the names of all women who had been prostitutes, regardless of whether they were still in the business, to shame them into leaving Vancouver, a sanction reminiscent of the historical Japanese village practice of *mura hachibu*—ostracism and banishment as a punishment for social transgression. Second, they offered their readers a series of cautionary tales to warn them of the dire consequences of prostitution. These stories, based on what appear to be largely secondhand accounts, suggest the extent to which gossip was also used to punish those who violated social mores— again, a practice not unfamiliar in village Japan.[68]

Determined though the editors were to facilitate reform, however, they were unwilling to concede Japan's place in the hierarchy of nations. Although their primary purpose was to expose Japanese involved in prostitution in Canada, they were at pains to remind their readers that prostitution was a worldwide issue. No one should forget, they wrote, that the winds of prostitution blew not just through Japan but also through European countries, including France, Spain, Italy, Russia, and Norway, and across the Asian mainland to places like Manchuria and Siberia. It existed in cities around the world, including Berlin, Paris, London, Rome, Moscow, Singapore, New York, and Chicago. Shameful as it was to have to admit that there were also Japanese prostitutes in such cities as San Francisco, Seattle, Portland, Sacramento, and Los Angeles, some of whom

Two women publicly identified as prostitutes in 1909. (Osada Shohei, comp., *Kanada no Makutsu* [Vancouver, B.C.: Tairiku Nippō-sha, 1909]).

catered solely to white men and others only to Japanese, they were not alone in engaging in prostitution.[69]

Prominent among the morality tales included in *Kanada no Makutsu* to illustrate the dire personal consequences of a life of prostitution was the story of the murder of a Japanese prostitute named Jennie on April 5, 1905, in Revelstoke, B.C., described by the *Revelstoke Herald and Railway Men's Journal* as the "most blood-thirsty and awful crime in the history of the city or the west" and a threat to the "good name of this city and of

British law and order."[70] Differences in the reporting of the story in the Japanese and non-Japanese press illustrate the ways Japanese immigrants sought to locate themselves in relation to both whites and Chinese. The *Tairiku Nippō*'s reporter, Osada Shohei, wrote that the white man who was initially suspected by police was later cleared and that the case remained unsolved, but added that he had it on good authority that a Chinese man to whom Jennie had entrusted $2,000 in savings, money she had planned to use to return to Japan, had murdered her to steal it.[71] Revelstoke's English-language newspapers, in contrast, reported that police had arrested two Japanese on suspicion of murder but released the men after local Japanese refused to help police because of their lack of sympathy for the victim. The *Kootenay Mail* reported that "the Japanese say the woman was no good and not worth hanging a man for."[72]

Clearly determined to use Jennie's murder as an object lesson, the reporter for the *Tairiku Nippō*, Osada Shohei, described the crime in gruesome detail. A photograph taken by police, he wrote, showed that her throat been cut from ear to ear and that the skin of her face had been pulled back, leaving the blood vessels exposed. Her life must have been a pitiable and miserable existence, he declared, for it to come to such an end. Osada concluded his account with a graphic and ominous warning: those still involved in prostitution might become a Jennie at any time and end their lives with their skin pulled back from their faces. If only for that reason, they should resolve to leave the business of prostitution. Even when prostitutes did not end their lives as murder victims, Osada added for good measure, many died of disease.[73]

Although Osada argued that prostitutes must find new lines of work for their own sake as well as for the sake of the Japanese immigrant community, he made clear in another story, "The Prostitute Who Became a Christian," that in his view those who had once worked as prostitutes had no real chance of redemption. The prostitute described in this story was a woman who had come to Canada with her husband and operated a restaurant in Three Valley, B.C., before returning to Hokkaido for a time. A few years later, she came back to Canada alone to join her older brother, who worked on the railroad in the British Columbia interior. After her return, Osada reported, she became a prostitute to support herself. Although the woman had since left the business, Osada felt no compunction about exposing her in order to warn his readers that former prostitutes could be found even among those who appeared to be upstanding Christian women. The woman's real name was Omaki, Osada told his readers, but she used the name Fanny in her new life. Fanny had dreamed of returning to Japan to marry an engineer—arguably a symbol of a new kind of status in a Japan committed to rapid industrialization—but she had married a black (kokujin) barber instead. The extent to which this itself constituted a transgression is suggested by the editors' use of *furigana* (superscript phonetic characters) the first time the characters for *kokujin* appear in the text to indicate that they are to be pronounced not "kokujin" but "kurombo"; *kurombo* is a profoundly derogatory term also used to refer to African Americans. Osada went so far as to insinuate that Omaki was not an authentic Christian; he mocked answers she gave to questions put to her about her faith by a reporter sent to interrogate her on its doctrinal foundation, and challenged her claim to being Christian, saying that her beliefs incorporated Buddhist elements.[74]

Although the primary concern of the publishers of *Kanada no Makutsu* was to warn Japanese immigrants of the personal consequences of engaging in prostitution, their concurrent desire to align their community with white authority was reflected by the inclusion of an English-language endorsement of the book by Vancouver's chief constable, R. G. Chamberlain.[75] It was largely through the efforts of Chamberlain, the editors explained approvingly, that Japanese prostitutes had been forced to abandon Vancouver during the decade prior to publication of *Kanada no Makutsu*. Many, they noted, had followed the Canadian Pacific Railway into the B.C. interior and beyond the Rockies to places like Banff, Winnipeg, and Fort Williams. The editors hoped that the publication of *Kanada no Makutsu* would complete the job by encouraging the eradication of prostitution among Japanese in all parts of Canada.[76]

Confident though the editors were of the contribution that they had made to that end, their approach ultimately played into the hands of white exclusionists, who did not hesitate to use their admissions against the very communities that they sought to defend. Although the editors believed that they could effectively purge their communities of undesirable elements by publically shaming those involved in prostitution, thereby reconstituting and redefining them along lines that would render them invulnerable to the negative claims of white racists, anti-Japanese agitators used the same disclosures to label Japanese immigrant communities as flawed in their entirety. Japanese community members themselves apparently realized as much. Because the publication of *Kanada no Makutsu* drew attention to the participation of Japanese immigrants in the prostitution business, its publisher was ostracized by the rest of the Japanese immigrant community, or so Katsuyoshi Morita later reported in *Powell Street Monogatari* (Tales of Powell Street).[77] Shaming and gossip, tools effectively used in Tokugawa Japan to sanction those who transgressed, had unintended consequences in early twentieth-century North American society, where those hostile to Japanese immigrants were all too willing to apply criticism against certain status groups or individuals to the entire community. What the editors of the *Tairiku Nippō* failed to see because they viewed anti-Japanese prejudice through the lens of caste difference was that the singling out of Japanese prostitutes in the North American press was a product of white racism, not its cause.

JAPANESE SHOEMAKERS ASSOCIATION

A far more direct and successful challenge to white racism was launched in San Francisco by a group that included many who would have been categorized as eta by Meiji-era Japanese by virtue of their occupation alone: leather working. Racial tensions in San Francisco, one of the first cities in the United States where Japanese immigrants had settled in sizable numbers, reportedly ran higher than in other North American cities.[78] A 1906 article published in New York's *Japanese-American Commercial Weekly,* for example, drew on images associated with historical status categories to describe the vehemence of the racial tension that existed between hakujin and Japanese immigrants in San Francisco. "San Francisco elicits hatred, as when a samurai enters an *eta* [outcast] village ... New York is a mature and discreet adult compared to San Francisco which is a demon brat."[79] White San Franciscans, the writer argued in effect, hated Japanese immigrants because they recognized them as higher in status and ability than themselves—like the samurai who occupied the top tier of the Tokugawa class hierarchy. By equating white racists with "*eta,*" it was clearly his intention to imply that they existed at the lowest levels of human society.

Ironically, the Japanese immigrants who mounted the first organized effort to challenge white racism in San Francisco were shoemakers and shoe repairers. The writer of the article would almost certainly have regarded them as eta. They had established the Nihonjin Kakō Dōmeikai (Japanese Shoemakers Association) in 1893 in response to a boycott organized by white shoemakers to force all Japanese cobblers out of business after fifteen were hired to break a strike at a local shoe factory.[80] Many of the Japanese shoemakers reportedly emigrated to San Francisco after a Japanese immigrant named Shiro, who had arrived in 1889, notified friends and colleagues back in Japan that the city offered substantial opportunities to leatherworkers and shoemakers.[81] When the Nihonjin Kakō Dōmeikai was organized, its leaders later wrote, Japanese cobblers were the object of both racial prejudice and caste-based prejudice. Their own countrymen subjected them to insults and indignities because they regarded leatherworkers as the most "base and inferior of all laborers." Even if the leatherworkers in San Francisco were not descended from families engaged in leatherwork, they were still treated like outcastes because they worked with leather.[82] Members of the association, however, saw in the racial conflict that erupted with white shoemakers an opportunity to assert their common identity as Japanese subjects and, in so doing, to challenge the traditional caste prejudices of other Japanese immigrants. Their purpose was not only to establish a base for organizing against white racism but also, through their effective resistance to white racism, to prove themselves to fellow immigrants who disparaged them because of their ancestry or their work.

The leaders of the Nihonjin Kakō Dōmeikai carefully negotiated the issue of status within the Japanese immigrant community, cognizant of the critical gaze of others and careful not to overstep their bounds. They made clear that in organizing the Nihonjin Kakō Dōmeikai they did not intend to make any claim to status as Japanese immigrant leaders in the United States. Forced by the nature of their work to emigrate thousands of miles from home, they wrote, they had expected simply to take their place among other similar businesses in the United States. But after arriving in California, they realized that Japanese generally were the object of racial prejudice and hostility.[83] Although they themselves were of the "yellow race" and spoke little English, they did not regard themselves as inferior to whites. Rather, they considered themselves fortunate to be members of the Japanese race.[84] There was no point, in their view, in dwelling on the unanticipated disadvantages encountered in the

Japanese shoemaker living and working in San Francisco, 1913. (National Archives and Records Administration, San Francisco, RG 85, File 13137/12–04.)

United States because they were not white. Instead, they were determined to use the power of cooperation to address the problems that all Japanese faced in this country. Just as "a single hair was too weak to bear much weight but many hairs tied together could lift a thousand pounds," it was the purpose of the Nihonjin Kakō Dōmeikai to provide a framework within which its members would be able to ensure one another's success by mutual support and aid in the event of illness or unexpected calamity.[85]

Although a majority of members would historically have been classified as eta by birth or by occupation, the public face of the Nihonjin Kakō Dōmeikai was a former samurai named Jō Tsunetarō.[86] Originally from Kumamoto prefecture, Jō was an associate of Nishimura Katsuzō, another former samurai who became a prominent shoe manufacturer in Japan after the Meiji Restoration. Like other samurai left jobless by the Meiji reforms, Nishimura was forced to redefine his role in a rapidly industrializing nation. Certain occupations also began to undergo redefinition during the Meiji period, including shoemaking and commerce generally, which Japan's elite disdained as a parasitic endeavor; it involved, after all, the handling of money and had been the exclusive province of the lowly merchant class. Central to the process of redefinition was the demand for leather footwear for Japan's newly established conscript army, itself emblematic of Japan's determination to stand up to the West.[87] The army connection enabled former samurai to argue that they had stepped into the leatherworking field and engaged in commerce—occupations once limited to outcastes and merchants—to fulfill their traditional warrior duties and further national goals, notwithstanding the personal cost to themselves.[88]

Nishimura entered into the manufacture of the leather boots, which he contracted to supply to the Meiji government, only reluctantly.[89] Even toward the end of the Meiji period, an individual's being engaged in leatherwork would have suggested ties to former outcaste communities.[90] Because outcaste status was a function not only of descent but of occupation, moreover, those not descended from eta families who adopted occupations historically associated with outcaste status ran some risk that the stigma of outcaste status might attach to them. Thus, Nihonjin Kakō Dōmeikai members who were not descendants of former outcastes were arguably willing to challenge prevailing ways of defining difference rooted in Japanese tradition. That historical sensitivities about the meaning of leatherwork had not yet been eradicated, however, is further suggested by the decision made within the Nihonjin Kakō Dōmeikai to avoid using the word "shoemaker" (*kakō*) when translating the association's name into English. Instead, its name was translated as "Japanese Shoe Repairers Association"; shoe repair was regarded as a less polluting job since repairers were not directly involved in processing leather.[91]

The establishment of the Nihonjin Kakō Dōmeikai in 1893 was vigorously opposed by some elements within the Japanese immigrant community, including the Oriental Trading Company, which played a key role in providing railroad labor in the Pacific Northwest and elsewhere in North America.[92] Its fiercest opponent, however, was the largely white Boot and Shoe Repairers' Union, whose cause was quickly adopted and widely circulated by the *San Francisco Chronicle*. In 1905 the *Chronicle* published an article attributing the success of the Nihonjin Kakō Dōmeikai to the "extraordinary cohesion" that existed among the "Japanese invaders." The Japanese Shoe Repairers Association was successful only because it was undemocratic and was governed from Japan by a single "boss," who functioned as a "slave driver in the case of the coolie laborers" and as a "capitalist in the case of ... skilled workmen."[93] In fact, the association's constitution and bylaws would have made it difficult for any single person to dominate it: members of its board of directors were elected for six-month terms at general meetings held in the spring and fall each year. By providing that no member of the board of directors could be elected to more than one term, the constitution and bylaws guaranteed that the positions would circulate widely among its membership.[94]

The *Chronicle* did not stop with criticism of the structure of the Nihonjin Kakō Dōmeikai. It also invoked the specter of disease, reprinting allegations made in 1903 by a representative of the Boot and Shoe Repairers' Union, who claimed that because many Japanese shoe repairers lived in the back of their shops, the shops were "liable to become disease-producing spots equally as bad as those established by the Chinese."[95] The *Chronicle* article concluded with an appeal issued by the Boot and Shoe Repairers' Union to San Francisco's white residents: "We appeal to you, if you have been patronizing the Japanese, to in the future refrain from doing so and patronize those of your own race. By complying with this request you are protecting your own interests as well as those of the white shoemakers, because if the Japanese are encouraged they will soon enter other branches of trade and perhaps be in direct competition with yourself." According to the *Chronicle,* there were nearly two hundred shoe repair and shoemakers' shops in San Francisco run by Japanese immigrants, which meant that "a precisely corresponding number of American skilled workmen have been disposed [and] that wages have been lowered throughout the whole industry."[96] The *Chronicle*'s warning and the Boot and Shoe Repairers' Union appeal appear to have gone largely unheeded, however.

Although some sources cite lower figures for the number of shoe shops run by Japanese immigrants in San Francisco, the success of the Nihonjin Kakō Dōmeikai is evident in the number of Japanese cobblers in San Francisco compared to the number in other cities on the West Coast. The *Japanese American Yearbook* published in 1905, just a few months before the April 1906 earthquake, lists 131 shoemakers and repairers in San Francisco, 119 of whom were adults and 12 of whom were still minors.[97] In contrast, there were just two shoemakers and one shoe store among the Japanese businesses in Seattle in 1907.[98] A U.S. Immigration Commission report of 1911 lists five shoemakers in Seattle, one in Portland, three in Sacramento, two in Fresno, seventeen in Los Angeles (where the Nihonjin Kakō Dōmeikai established a branch), and seventy-six in San Francisco.[99] A 1909 report issued by the Nihonjin Kakō Dōmeikai stated that its total membership in California, from San Diego in the south to Chico in the north, was three hundred. The combined revenue was no less than $250,000.[100]

The Nihonjin Kakō Dōmeikai achieved its success, H. A. Millis argued in 1920, by implementing a carefully coordinated effort. It helped newcomers get set up in business by advancing supplies at 10 percent over cost, provided aid to those who encountered unanticipated difficulties either in business or in their personal lives, and ensured that members' shops were spaced far enough apart that they were not in direct competition with one another.[101] Nihonjin Kakō Dōmeikai leaders themselves cited three policies as primarily responsible for their success: (1) treating white customers kindly and being meticulous about meeting completion dates, (2) charging prices just a fraction lower than those of the Boot and Shoe Repairers' Union, and (3) establishing an apprenticeship program that ensured that the skills of the average Japanese cobbler were superior to those of their white competitors.[102]

The efforts of the Nihonjin Kakō Dōmeikai were not restricted to ensuring the economic well-being of its members. It also sought to ensure that its members were well-informed citizens of the world. In January 1911 it published the first issue of a newsletter intended to tell members not only about matters related to their employment but also to bring them news of Japan and other countries. Its features included a list of those who had provided the most leather to others in the organization (the designations were borrowed from those used to denote the rank of *sumo* wrestlers); humorous stories (*kokkei banashi*); poems (*haiku*); and news stories, among them reports about a new railway being built through the Alps, on efforts to rebuild after the San Francisco earthquake, on sales of *sake* in America, on the cost of forest fires in New York State, on a painting bought by the British Museum for five million pounds, on the number of people persecuted in Russia (876 in six months), and about the most popular breeds of cat in England. Other features were a drawing of a frog leaping into a pond to illustrate Bashō's famous haiku; instructions for reconstituting dried cement and for putting an old knife to good use; and a list of members' "hidden" talents, including making dolls, telling stories, singing Japanese folk songs, playing the *shamisen* (Japanese lute), engaging in mimicry, drawing, performing humorous skits (*kyōgen*), and composing amusing or erotic poems.[103] There were advertisements of businesses in the San Francisco area as well as inns in Japanese cities, such as Yokohama, where members of the association were encouraged to stay when they returned to Japan.[104] In much the same way that Meiji consular officials and immigrant leaders urged all Japanese immigrants to moderate their behavior so as not to draw criticism, in the newsletter the leaders of the Nihonjin Kakō Dōmeikai also advised their members to put their own houses in order and live exemplary lives.[105]

Notwithstanding the success of association members during the first two decades of the twentieth century, by 1929 there were just twenty-three Japanese shoemakers in San Francisco, a decrease that one author attributes to the increase in the number of chain shops.[106] New forms of transportation reduced the wear and tear on leather shoes, and the growing availability of ready-made shoes also made it easier to replace them when they wore out. The 1920 decision of the Boot and Shoe

Repairers Association to accept Japanese immigrants as members, however, stands as one measure of the success of the Nihonjin Kakō Dōmeikai.[107]

Able though the Japanese association was in providing a solid foundation for organizing against white racism, however, it was less successful in eroding historical caste-based prejudice. The number of Japanese shoemakers and repairers also dwindled because many chose to leave shoemaking when they could afford to do so to avoid the stigma that continued to be associated with leatherworking. Some returned to Japan or moved to other parts of the United States or Canada.[108] It may well be that providing members a way to stand up to caste-based prejudice directed at them by other Japanese, as well as the means to effect transitions that allowed them to distance themselves from the stigma associated with leatherwork, should itself be understood as a second measure of the success of the Nihonjin Kakō Dōmeikai. With its support, at least some of its members appear to have been able to realize the promise of the North American West and to remake themselves in ways that allowed them to take advantage of opportunities not yet available to them in their home country.

The willingness of the Nihonjin Kakō Dōmeikai to take a direct stand against white racism stands in contrast to the approach adopted by both Meiji diplomats and a majority of Japanese community leaders to counter racist allegations. In the course of asserting their equality with whites, members of the association simultaneously asserted their status as fully participating members in the Japanese immigrant community in California. Although its leaders endeavored to elide the historical association between leatherwork and "eta" by emphasizing shoe repair over shoemaking in the organization's name and putting up a samurai for its public face, members were drawn largely from the two social groups at the center of the clash of old and new values during the Meiji period—former samurai and former outcastes—which may well be why the group maintained its focus on white racism instead of debating the historical status origins of Japanese immigrants. The more ambivalent response of Japanese community leaders to racist claims, and particularly their conviction that "low-class" individuals were primarily responsible for white racism, played directly into the hands of white exclusionists. By failing to see that critiques of Japanese immigrants in North America were largely a product—and not the cause—of white racism, they inadvertently reinforced the white exclusionists' claims. As long as Japanese immigrant leaders conflated caste- and race-based ways of understanding difference, their efforts avoided—and thus could not resolve—the real issue.

CHAPTER FIVE

The U.S.-Canada Border

DURING THE LATE NINETEENTH AND EARLY TWENTIETH CENTU-
ries, legislators in both the United States and Canada turned their attention
to the development of legal measures intended to restrict Asian immigration. Japanese migrants, careful students of exclusionary law and policy,
found ways to challenge or avoid the growing webs of legal constraints.
Some turned to the courts to contest unjust laws, and others resorted to
direct defiance of discriminatory provisions.[1] Still others invoked their privilege under international law to travel across the territory of other civilized
nations, forcing the governments of both countries to allow border crossings
they would have preferred to prevent. Japanese who were unable to obtain a
passport from their own government permitting them to travel to the United
States, for example, might instead buy a ticket to London and exercise their
privilege of transit across Canada to access the U.S. land border directly.[2]

Despite efforts by both the United States and Canada to abrogate the
transit privilege, it remained a point of vulnerability for both nations that
neither was able to negate in its entirety. Extended under international
law to the citizens of allied or friendly nations and recognized in treaties
between those nations, the transit privilege demonstrated the civilized
status not only of those granting the privilege but also of those to whom it
was granted. Because the rationale for barring Japanese migrants
depended in part on each nation's characterizing itself as more civilized

than Japan, to deny the transit privilege not only would have contravened each nation's obligations under international law but would also have undermined the rationale put forward for excluding Japanese migrants to begin with; both nations premised their exclusion of Japanese immigrants in part on the assumption that the immigrants were less civilized than those of Western nations.[3] Because the Meiji government also understood the transit privilege as a marker of Japan's civilized status, it vigorously defended the right of its nationals to travel across both the United States and Canada, regardless of its efforts elsewhere to curb illegal immigration.

Canadian efforts to use law to exclude Japanese coalesced around repeated attempts by the British Columbia legislature to impose a literacy requirement on prospective immigrants. In contrast to the U.S. Congress, which was considering legislation that would require immigrants from all countries to show that they were able to read a short passage in any language, drafters of B.C.'s Natal Acts between 1898 and 1908 repeatedly defined literacy to exclude Asian languages.[4] Determined to effect the exclusion of Japanese immigrants, the authors of the Natal Acts—so named because they were modeled after legislation first adopted in the British Colony of Natal—required all immigrants to demonstrate the ability to read and write in English or another European language. By providing for a penalty of up to twelve months' incarceration, the B.C. legislature effectively made the inability to speak English a jailable offense.[5]

Although Canada's Dominion government disallowed each act as it was passed on the instructions of the British Colonial Office, the implicit support of the British Colonial Office for British Columbia's efforts to pass a literacy requirement is suggested by the fact that it was the British colonial secretary, Joseph Chamberlain, who recommended to B.C. legislators that they use the original Natal Act as a model, based on his belief that the Meiji government could be persuaded not to object to an educational test.[6] The British Privy Council also supported his recommendation, tacitly acknowledging the racializing intent of the act's purportedly neutral language and clearly conscious of its implications for the rest of the British empire: "It is in the interest of the Empire," the Privy Council said in a 1900 report, that British Columbia "be occupied by a large and thoroughly British population rather than by one in which the number of aliens would form a large proportion."[7]

Notwithstanding Chamberlain's belief that the Meiji government would not object to an educational test, Meiji diplomats immediately saw through the purported neutrality of the acts. After the first of the Natal Acts was passed by the B.C. legislature in 1898, the Japanese minister to the Court of St. James made clear his government's conviction that it was unfriendly to Japan as a nation and unfairly discriminated against Japanese subjects.[8] Shimizu Seizaburo, Japan's consul in Vancouver, declared in 1900 that obviously the real purpose of the Natal Act was not simply to ensure that immigrants who proposed to settle in British Columbia were literate, because even those highly proficient in the Japanese language would not be able to pass the test, since Japanese was not one of the tested languages. Nor, he pointed out, could the test fairly be described as "a test of the vernacular language of this province, because other European languages than the English are admitted for the test."[9] Most offensive, however, was not that the direct entry of migrant laborers into Canada was restricted but that "these obnoxious bills" threatened to "most injuriously interfere with the free movement of all classes" by also preventing higher-status Japanese from exercising the transit privilege in the territories of a treaty partner. "These high-handed measures totally deprived [all Japanese subjects of] their treaty right of free entry into Canada," wrote Nosse Tatsugoro, arguing that Canada should be understood as part of "an international highway" comprised of "both ... land and water."[10]

The Natal Acts were particularly problematic, in short, because they called into question the civilized status not only of migrant laborers but also of members of Japan's upper classes. This was a distinction that the British government well understood. It was because the Natal Act was "discriminatory in effect," British Minister of Justice David Mills conceded in 1898, that it was "extremely repugnant to the sentiments of the people and government of Japan," an ally of Great Britain.[11] It was not "the practical exclusion of Japanese to which the government of the Mikado objects," Chamberlain admitted in turn, "but their exclusion *ad nominatim*, which specifically stamps the whole nation as undesirable persons."[12] Chamberlain nevertheless made it clear to British Columbians that as long as the wording of any such law appeared racially neutral on its face, he supported them in their efforts to pass anti-Japanese legislation. Even after Canada's Dominion government disallowed the first Natal Act in 1898, he reassured them that he remained committed to "guarding against the possibility of the white labour in the province being swamped by the wholesale immigration of persons of Asiatic origin." There was no reason, in his view, "why a more stringent and effective Act of a similar character should not be adopted so long as the disqualification is not based specifically on distinction of race or colour."[13]

Despite Chamberlain's assurances, resentment in British Columbia grew as each version of the Natal Act was disallowed by the Dominion government. In 1903 the *Rosland Courier* protested that British Columbians should not be required to "sacrifice [their own] prosperity for the shibboleth of 'Imperial Reasons,' " and in 1907 proponents of the Natal Acts went so far as to burn the lieutenant governor—the king's representative in British Columbia—in effigy for his refusal to intervene on their behalf.[14] The restrictions imposed on British Columbia's ability to make its borders impermeable to Asian immigration, its leaders suggested, called into question the incorporation of British Columbia into the Canadian nation-state in the first instance. Had B.C. residents realized the extent to which their power to pass exclusionary legislation could be limited by the Dominion government, B.C.'s attorney general declared in 1905, they would never have agreed to enter confederation.[15] B.C. officials also demonstrated their resistance to the will of the Dominion government by being slow to comply when a Natal Act was disallowed. After nineteen Japanese laborers employed by the Great Northern Railway to erect a fence on the Canadian side of the border near Blaine, Washington, were arrested in 1902, for example, B.C. government officials refused to release the eighteen who could not pass the literacy test even after they learned that the Natal Act under which the arrest was made had been disallowed several days earlier.[16] This, the *Vancouver Daily Province* noted wryly, left B.C. authorities in the awkward position of prosecuting the Japanese they had arrested under an act that no longer existed. The disallowance of the Natal Act, the *Victoria Daily Colonist*'s editors added, had left "a large hole in the provincial government's case."[17]

During the time that the Natal Acts were in force, B.C. officials also struggled with the practical question of how they were to be applied. Officials were uncertain, for example, just how much English an immigrant was required to know. The first Japanese immigrant required to take an educational test pursuant to a Natal Act had presented no problem.

Y. Charles, a former blacksmith who had adopted an anglicized name, was a naturalized British subject who had no trouble reading the required declaration. A group of Japanese immigrants who arrived in January 1901, however, included one man who was able to read the questions posed to him but unable to write his occupation—photographer—in English. Immigration officials ultimately relented, allowing him to use the word "artist," which he was able to write in English, to describe his occupation.[18]

Others denied permission to land in Canada because they could not read the English-language form that confronted them remained on board the ships on which they had arrived until they were able to disembark at U.S. ports, where there was no literacy test.[19] This, in turn, raised the delicate question of whether the Natal Acts applied to Japanese migrants who sought to enter Canada on their way to the United States. Given the Meiji government's fervent protests against interference with its subjects' right of transit, B.C. authorities reluctantly agreed that it did not. Japanese who did not intend to remain in Canada, the B.C. legislature conceded, were required only to say so and to pay a fee to avoid the educational test. It granted this exception in the face of intense local opposition. To allow Japanese migrants to invoke the transit privilege to avoid the act, the *Vancouver Daily Province* declared in 1903, undermined its very purpose and rendered the entire act "worthless" and "farcical in application."[20]

Ultimately, it was not the Dominion government's repeated disallowance of the Natal Acts that brought to an end the B.C. government's efforts to pass legislation that would effectively bar Asian immigrants from the province, but the determination of two Japanese migrants arriving at the Canada-U.S. border to mount a deliberate challenge to the Natal Acts in B.C.'s courts. On February 17, 1908, M. Nakane and T. Okazake were jailed after they arrived at the Canada-U.S. border by rail from Portland, Oregon, and refused either to take the literacy test or to return to Portland.[21] Determined to force the courts to rule on the validity of the Natal Act then in force, Nakane and Okazake filed writs of habeus corpus. Four days after their arrest, the chief justice of the B.C. Supreme Court ordered their release, noting that the recent Treaty of Commerce and Navigation between Japan and Great Britain, like the treaties that preceded it, provided that the subjects of both parties had "full liberty to enter, travel or reside in any part of the dominions and possessions of the

Four young immigrant women on board a ship at sea, circa 1905. (Japanese Canadian National Museum and Archives, File 1997.200.)

other." British Columbia, the chief justice noted, lacked the power to interfere with privileges afforded to Japanese nationals under the treaty. Because only the Dominion government had the power to restrict immigration, the passage of the Natal Acts was ultra vires of any Canadian province.[22] On February 25, 1907, the full court affirmed the chief justice's decision and ordered that the two prisoners be released, effectively putting an end to the B.C. legislature's efforts to pass a Natal Act.[23]

The difficulties faced by British Columbia in denying the transit privilege, together with an increase in the number of Japanese migrants arriving in the United States after its annexation of Hawaii in 1898, gave rise to considerable anxiety among U.S. officials, who were just as determined as B.C. officials to exclude Japanese and other Asian migrants, even though the U.S. Congress had yet to pass any legislation that expressly targeted Japanese. During the two years following the United States' annexation of Hawaii, thirty thousand Japanese laborers had migrated to Hawaii to work on its sugar cane plantations. The organization of Hawaii as a U.S. territory in 1900 opened the door to travel to the U.S. mainland.[24] According to Hawaiian sources, fifty-seven thousand Japanese migrants left Hawaii for the mainland between 1898 and 1908.[25] Though partly instigated by the outbreak of the bubonic plague in Honolulu in December 1906, the migration had an even more significant impetus: the growing demand for labor in British Columbia and the U.S. Pacific Northwest. Both nations were seeking to tap the natural resources and develop the industrial capacity of their respective regions.[26] Although Meiji officials directed Japanese not to travel to any destination not identified on their passports, in crossing the Pacific they traveled far beyond its jurisdiction, which compromised its ability to enforce its proscriptions on travel abroad. Concerned that its subjects not be rendered illegal, which it feared would undermine Japan's status as a nation, the Meiji government instead adopted a strategy of encouraging U.S. and Canadian authorities to strictly enforce the conditions that it imposed on its subjects.[27]

The determination of the United States to count Japanese among those it excluded on racial grounds first found expression in the Act of February 20, 1907, which authorized the president to bar Japanese migrants traveling with passports that did not expressly designate the United States as a destination to which their own government permitted them to travel. The act was part of a compromise reached between President Roosevelt and California school board officials to resolve the San Francisco school crisis that followed its 1906 decision to segregate Japanese students. Although the crisis was purportedly a response to the discovery that grown Japanese men were attending classes with young children in order to learn English, H. A. Millis describes it as an overreaction, noting that just twelve of the ninety-three Japanese students in San Francisco's schools were eighteen or older.[28]

Just one week before the Act of February 20 was passed, a U.S. immigration inspector, Marcus Braun, submitted a report to Congress based on his investigation of conditions along both the northern and southern borders of the United States. Braun advocated the implementation of "modern" immigration laws—laws that required immigrants entering a nation's territory to undergo physical examinations and excluded any who had trachoma or who were contract laborers.[29] Braun was particularly concerned that immigration officers stationed along both the northern and the southern borders of the United States maintain a "zealous vigilance" to keep out migrants of the "wrong kind." That category included all those who would make the United States the "dumping ground of the scum of European and Oriental society," as well as all who crossed U.S. borders clandestinely and who evaded inspection. The U.S.-Canada border was relatively secure, in Braun's opinion, since Canada had recently adopted immigration laws patterned after those of the United States, even if they were not quite as stringent.[30] Because Mexico had yet to adopt laws excluding contract laborers and those afflicted with trachoma, however, Braun regarded the U.S.-Mexico border as at risk. On March 14, 1907, President Roosevelt invoked his authority under the Act of February 20 to issue an executive order barring Japanese and Korean migrants holding passports for Mexico, Hawaii, or Canada from the United States.[31]

Determined though the Meiji government was to find a mutually agreeable solution to the problem of transmigration from Hawaii, it regarded the restrictions imposed on its subjects by the U.S. government in the spring of 1907 as discriminatory—as unfairly targeting Japan and calling into question its status as a nation.[32] The issue was not, in its view, whether the U.S. government was entitled to exclude any general categories of immigrants that it wanted to exclude, but whether Japan should be treated in the same way as any other civilized country. All along the Pacific coast, Braun reported, "prominent Japanese businessmen, bankers, officials and visitors" expressed concern that Japanese were "discriminated against and are not treated like aliens of other races." It was apparent even to Braun, however, that their concerns were limited to those deemed upper class. As he noted, "These men claim there can be no objection to the rigid exclusion of undesirable Japanese, but seem to think that the question of undesirability should be decided upon the same basis as that observed in excluding other aliens."[33]

To facilitate the U.S. government's efforts to restrict labor immigration while protecting the ability of Japan's upper classes to travel freely abroad, the Meiji government proposed a change in the way it classified its own subjects on the passports it issued. To make this status distinction clear, it would cease designating occupation and mibun and instead use the terms *imin* (emigrant) or *hi-imin* (non-emigrant). *Imin* would refer to those who left Japan to "reside abroad for the purpose of earning a living by engaging in some form of labor"; *hi-imin* would refer to "professionals, agents, bankers and manufacturers, and merchants and dealers"—those, in Mitziko Sawada's words, "whose class background, education, and status ostensibly precluded any confusion with *imin*."[34]

Combined with the general bar against contract labor that had been in place since 1885, the executive order redirected a substantial number of Japanese migrants north to British Columbia.[35] In the autumn of 1907, Canadian immigration authorities estimated that just one-third of the 4,811 Japanese who had arrived in Canada during the first eight months of that year had come straight from Japan; the other two-thirds had gone to Hawaii before traveling to British Columbia.[36] Canadians attributed the number of Japanese immigrants arriving in British Columbia to the refusal of U.S. immigration officials to admit migrants with passports for Hawaii to the continental United States in the wake of Roosevelt's executive order. In July 1907, for example, the *Ottawa Free Press* warned its readers that the "Mikado's subjects who were refused admittance to the United States may land at Vancouver"; "thousands of Japanese were anxious to find employment in Canada."[37]

Also a factor in explaining the increased migration to British Columbia from Honolulu, U.S. and Canadian officials agreed, were steamship companies, boardinghouse keepers, and employment agencies. All encouraged Japanese labor migrants to seek work on the mainland in order to maximize their own profits. So high was the demand for labor on both sides of the U.S.-Canada border, however, that the U.S. consul in Victoria was able to report that most arrivals quickly found work. Many of the three hundred Japanese immigrants who arrived in Vancouver on August 18, 1907, he noted, had found work on the Great Northern Railway, and the Japanese Boardinghouse Union was quickly finding jobs for those still in Vancouver.[38]

Travel to the United States by way of Canada was a sound strategic choice both for migrants coming from Hawaii and for those coming directly from Japan. In the absence of laws expressly barring migration directly from Japan, U.S. and Canadian officials relied heavily on medical examinations to exclude those who could be characterized as undesirable. By 1906 both Canada and the United States had enacted immigration laws that barred individuals "afflicted with a loathsome disease" or deemed "likely to become a public charge."[39] Where literacy tests had failed, medical examinations promised to provide an effective tool for excluding Asian immigrants, given the association of disease with "Oriental" immigration in the popular imagination and in the minds of many immigration officers.[40] U.S. officials regarded medical examinations as a practical way to reduce the number of immigrants admitted to the United States. In October 1906, for example, an immigration officer based in Hawaii suggested to the U.S. immigration commissioner that stricter medical examinations were one way to limit travel from Hawaii to the mainland; he estimated that as many as one in ten could be detained as carriers of contagious disease or at least held for further observation.[41]

The medical examinations required of immigrants were unpleasant for all who were subjected to them, Asians and Europeans alike.[42] Because the granular lesions that were a major symptom of trachoma occurred under the upper eyelid, inspectors turned it up to examine its under surface.[43] Language barriers and racist assumptions that Asian migrants were more likely to be diseased, however, made the medical examination all the more distressing for them. One U.S. official gave voice to these assumptions when he declared that "aliens arriving from the Orient are more frequently afflicted with dangerous contagious diseases (trachoma in particular) than those arriving from Europe."[44] What conclusions of this kind failed to take into account was the extent to which this result was dictated by the examination process itself, structured as it was by a race-based belief system that "conflated fears of immigrants, particularly from Asia, with anxiety about disease."[45] In other words, if Asians were the ones who were examined most or most closely, they were likely to account for most of the discovered cases of disease.

For Meiji Japanese, the medical examinations also invoked historical associations between disease and impurity, which were linked in turn to the idea of outcaste status.[46] The Japanese found the medical examinations objectionable, then, not only because they racialized the Japanese but also because they appeared to mark Japanese as diseased and thus equivalent to outcastes as that category was historically understood in Japan. Moreover, to the extent that the imposition of medical examinations implied that hygiene in Japan fell short of modern standards, the medical examinations called into question Japan's status as a modern nation.[47] In this context, as in others, the ongoing failure of U.S. and Canadian immigration officers to differentiate between Japanese and Chinese also remained deeply problematic in the eyes of Meiji government officials.

Concerned that Japanese subjects not be rejected as diseased when they arrived in North America, the Meiji government began to require its citizens to undergo medical examinations by Japanese physicians before granting them permission to leave.[48] Medical examiners were charged with ensuring that those suffering from syphilis, heart disease, colic, consumption, gonorrhea, any chronic disease, or even a large bladder did not emigrate. Those who were crippled or otherwise "deformed" were also to be prevented from going abroad.[49]

In addition to undergoing medical examinations before leaving Japan, emigrants were required to undergo oral examinations by port police, who ascertained their mibun, occupation, purpose in traveling abroad, and financial circumstances (whether they had sufficient funds to take along). Status distinctions were not only noted at the time of departure but reflected in administrative procedures related to issuing passports. Meiji government regulations required that passports issued to laborers (imin) be forwarded to the port of departure to ensure that they did not leave Japan until they had passed the medical examination. The higher-status, better-educated hi-imin, in contrast, were permitted to pick up their passports at the places where they were issued—generally an individual's hometown. They were presumed to be both more trustworthy and less likely to be diseased. A further distinction was drawn between hi-imin traveling second or third class, who were required to undergo medical examinations before leaving Japan, and hi-imin traveling first class, who were not, because the risk that authorities would embarrass individuals in the latter category was deemed greater than the risk that individuals in this category would embarrass Japan.[50] Because U.S. immigration officials attributed far more significance to race than to mibun in identifying health risk, they disliked this approach, but they reluctantly conceded that it was necessary to treat first-class passengers with more regard than those traveling second or third class, given the importance ascribed to that distinction by Japanese. A failure to treat them respectfully would also reflect poorly on the U.S. officials themselves.[51]

Guidebooks available in Japan warned emigrants that even if they passed the medical examinations required in Japan, there was no guarantee that they would pass those in Canada or the United States. Japanese travelers, even those who had been successfully treated for trachoma or hookworm in Japan and who had passed the medical examinations there, should exercise great care on board ship to ensure that they were not reinfected.[52] Emigrants who failed the medical examinations were sometimes able to obtain passports after undergoing further treatment. One eleven-year-old child who failed the eye examination in Kobe remained behind on her own receiving daily treatments until she was able to pass the examination and join her family in Canada. Others whose eyes were permanently scarred were denied that option.[53]

Not all of those who failed the medical examinations in Japan were willing to accept exclusion from the United States and Canada. When denied passports to North America, some chose alternative destinations within Japan's own growing empire, including, in time, Formosa (Taiwan), Korea, and Manchuria.[54] Others found alternative ways to reach their intended destinations in North America—for example, by stowing away along with those who were denied passports for other reasons.[55] Like European migrants crossing another ocean, still other Japanese resorted to the use of passports not their own, assuming the names of those to whom they had been issued. Japanese immigrants in Canada and the United States also sometimes sent passports back to friends or relatives in Japan for reuse.[56] Strategies such as this, however, put immigrants at odds with the Japanese government as well as both the U.S. and the Canadian governments. The possibility that Japanese subjects might be branded as illegal not only evoked historical images associated with outcaste status in Japan but undermined the Meiji government's efforts to establish Japan as a nation equal to those of the West.[57] To discourage illegal immigration into the United States or Canada, the Meiji government imposed severe penalties on those who helped smuggle them and imposed a forty-yen penalty on migrants who traveled to destinations other than those listed in their passports, payable by their guarantors in Japan.[58]

Ironically, Japanese immigrants were sometimes rendered illegal not only by U.S. or Canadian law but by the very measures instituted by the Meiji government to avoid that outcome. By restricting travel by its subjects to destinations denoted on passports and encouraging Canada and the United States to strictly enforce those limitations, it provided both countries with a mechanism they could use to mark Japanese immigrants as illegal;

the U.S. Congress took full advantage of the mechanism when it passed the Act of February 20, 1907. Even if Japanese were denied passports in Japan, those arriving in the United States or Canada without documentation before 1907 may well have been admissible under U.S. or Canadian law as long as they passed the medical examination. As U.S. authorities themselves later recognized, stowing away was not illegal, but crossing the border without undergoing the required medical inspection was.[59]

Much the same was true in Canada. When Oikawa Jinzaburo and eighty-three other migrants left Miyagi prefecture for Canada in 1906 in a fishing boat that they chartered after being denied passports, they landed on the coast of Vancouver Island, not at a port, because they feared that without passports, they would be treated as pirates. Canadian authorities noted that Japanese migrants were admissible under Canadian law even if they did not have passports or permission to leave Japan as long as they passed the required medical examinations.[60] The Miyagi migrants faced deportation precisely because they had not submitted to the required medical examinations. Japanese consular officials intervened, however, negotiating an agreement that granted them immigrant status in exchange for two years' work on a branch of the Canadian Pacific Railway being built across the Canadian Rockies.[61]

For Oikawa, who reportedly smuggled several more Japanese groups into Canada in the years that followed, helping those who were denied passports enter Canada was an act of protest, both against social and economic conditions in Japan and against hostile immigration policies in Canada. Japanese, he believed, were entitled to leave Japan at will for any destination they chose and entitled as well to avail themselves of economic opportunities in Canada on the same basis as immigrants from European nations.

A similar desire to protest restrictive laws appears to have motivated Yoshie Saburo, a clerk at the Japanese consulate who helped negotiate a solution for the Miyagi immigrants. He was convicted of immigration fraud in the 1930s for helping others avoid Canadian restrictions on Japanese immigration. Although Yoshie may have acted in part because aiding immigrants could be a lucrative business, he also believed that emigration offered Japanese a way "to prove their equality" and "demonstrate their value and excellence" to people around the world who were unfamiliar with their abilities.[62]

Being smuggled directly into the United States or Canada from Japan was not the only option open to migrants who were refused passports to their intended destination for medical reasons. Differences in each country's administration of medical examinations provided an alternative to migrants otherwise subject to exclusion. Although both the United States and Canada excluded those who suffered from contagious diseases, Canada permitted migrants suffering from excludable diseases that were deemed treatable to remain in Canada to undergo treatment. By agreement between the Canadian and the U.S. governments, Japanese migrants arriving in Canada with passports for the United States were first examined by U.S. immigration officials stationed at Canadian ports. Those refused entry to the United States by U.S. officials were turned over to Canadian officials, who permitted those with treatable conditions to stay in Canada. Only those regarded as very seriously ill by both U.S. and Canadian officials were required to return to Japan.

U.S. and Canadian officials were both suspicious of the others' reasons for administering the medical examinations required by both countries. Canadian government officials grumbled that the United States avoided responsibility for the health of its immigrants by shifting the burden of treating them to Canada.[63] U.S. government authorities, in turn, accused Canadian officials of undermining their efforts to seal the border they shared against those who were diseased and admitting migrants who only appeared to be well.[64] Notwithstanding the magnitude of U.S. officials' fears about disease, however, relatively few of those who applied to enter the United States after arriving at a Canadian port proved to be ill. Of the 1,191 Japanese migrants who arrived in Vancouver from Honolulu on the S.S. *Kumeric* in July 1907, for example, just nine were debarred on grounds of illness—eight because they had trachoma and one because he had beriberi.[65] Only ninety-one Japanese were refused entry to the United States across the British Columbia border in 1907 on the ground that they were "afflicted with dangerous contagious diseases or ... likely to become public charges."[66]

Suspicious though they were of one another, U.S. and Canadian officials agreed that steamship companies played a key role in encouraging Japanese migrants to travel through Canada regardless of their final destinations. U.S. Commissioner of Immigration John Clark complained in 1907 that steamship companies encouraged immigrants bound for the

United States to disembark at Canadian ports not only to avoid the risk of carrying any who were denied entry back to Japan but also to avoid paying the four-dollar head tax imposed on steamship companies for each alien landed at a U.S. port.[67] U.S. and Canadian officials alike accused the steamship lines of making Victoria, B.C., a "dumping ground for diseased immigrants."[68] U.S. officials were also convinced that many of those who entered the country via Canada were in fact contract laborers, even though labor arrangements were less formal than they once had been. According to one official, many of the Japanese migrants arriving in Canada en route to the United States were "subject to a regular *padrone* system" that required laborers to give boardinghouse keepers or others a percentage of the wages they earned on a continuing basis.[69]

Steamship companies stood to benefit from increased transpacific migration and were not inclined to cooperate with immigration officials. Determined to force them to comply with its efforts to control the number of Asian migrants seeking to enter the United States, the U.S. government enacted new rules making a steamship line responsible for returning to the port of origin any migrants arriving on its vessels who were refused entry into the United States, and returning them, moreover, at the company's expense. U.S. steamship companies endeavored to undermine implementation of the new rules by arguing that U.S. officials lacked the authority to enforce them while the ships were in Canadian ports. As long as the ships had no passengers on board when they entered U.S. waters, the shipmasters had no obligation to provide the passenger lists demanded by U.S. officials, or so the company officers insisted.[70] Efforts by the United States to monitor U.S. ships in Canadian waters interfered not only with their ability to compete on equal terms with the Canadian Pacific Railway's steamship line but with Canadian sovereignty itself—an argument, ironically, that the companies made but that the Canadian government declined to make on its own behalf.[71]

Steamship lines also responded to the new constraints imposed by the United States by encouraging Japanese labor migrants to travel to the United States through Canada. This became clear when U.S. immigration officers asked Japanese migrants disembarking in Victoria who held passports for the United States why they had not traveled directly to the United States. More than half of those surveyed during the last six months of 1907–that is, 642 of the 1,156 questioned—reported that steamship companies had refused to sell them tickets to any North American destination other than Victoria or Vancouver and that they had been forced to disembark at Victoria by ship's officers giving them ticket vouchers for a U.S. port. Another 123 said that boardinghouse keepers or steamship company agents had advised them to buy a ticket to Victoria, and 90 said either that they had traveled aboard a ship not licensed to travel to the United States or that they intended to continue their journey down the coast to San Francisco by steamer. A smaller number, 20, had been told that it was easier to enter the United States via Canada, and 9 said that they had disembarked in Canada because they were concerned about eye disease or because they were otherwise ill. Three said that they had left their ship when it arrived in Victoria because they "thought it was all 'America.' "[72]

In contrast to the United States, Canada did not require the "transoceanic deportation" of migrants who arrived in Canada en route to the United States but who were refused entry at the U.S.-Canada border; and once the primacy of the transit privilege had been affirmed in connection with the Natal Acts, Canada no longer tried to stop migrants who did not intend to stay in Canada from landing at Canadian ports on their way to other destinations.[73] U.S. policy providing for the return of excluded migrants to the country where their trip had originated combined with the transit privilege to give migrants arriving at the U.S. border en route from Canada the option of remaining in Canada and not being returned to Japan. Japanese migrants bound for the United States thus increasingly made the strategic choice to travel to the United States via Canada in order to reduce the risk that they would be deported to Japan if they were refused entry into the United States on medical grounds.

Meiji consular officials were quick to assure the Canadian government that its medical examinations were every bit as strict as those of the United States and claimed that Japanese migrants preferred Canadian ports only because of the 1906 San Francisco earthquake. They also pointed out that the exercise of the transit privilege through Canada was of economic benefit to British Columbians.[74] U.S. officials suspected, however, that instead of remaining in Canada, Japanese denied entry into the United States at the U.S.-Canada border simply reapplied to enter the United States after they had undergone treatment in Canada.[75] In the words of one U.S. official, Japanese migrants were well aware that by entering the United States from Canada they could "secure a double opportunity of entering the United States"—that is, "if rejected, they will not immediately be deported to Japan."[76] U.S. officials were particularly concerned that some migrants might apply a second time to enter the United States after receiving treatment.[77] Even if the migrants no longer showed any signs of disease, the officials continued to view them as implicitly tainted by having been diseased.

In the fall of 1907, continuing disquiet on the part of U.S. Immigration Bureau officials about the use that Japanese migrants were able to make of the international border led Braun to urge the U.S. government to enter into a "treaty with Canada under which rejections by United States officers will be regarded as rejections under Canadian law, or, if this cannot be done, [to] abrogate the agreement and withdraw all United States officers from Canada, make the examinations on American soil, and deport to the trans-oceanic country of origin all aliens rejected under this system." Not all U.S. authorities agreed with Braun's proposal. The U.S. commissioner general of immigration, among others, dismissed Braun's allegations, insisting that there was no evidence that Japanese migrants who remained in Canada for treatment entered the United States illegally, as Braun and other lower-level officials claimed. Instead, the commissioner general maintained that Canada was as anxious as the United States to deport those who were diseased or who were likely to become public charges. Canada, he said, differed only in being "glad to have men, when rejected by the United States officials, stay in her territory." It was enough that railroad companies returned those denied entry to "points remote from the Canadian border, so as to discourage their clandestine entry after having been rejected." The measures that Braun had proposed, the commissioner added, would only interfere with commerce.[78] He understood, as Braun did not, that the real goal of the United States was not to construct an impenetrable barrier at its borders but to establish a racialized filter. The United States wanted to allow entry to needed goods and laborers even as it excluded those who posed a threat to the race-based hierarchy that ordered social relations in the West.

Lower-level officials remained convinced that those turned away on medical grounds did not have just a second opportunity to enter the United States but multiple opportunities, particularly migrants willing to cross that boundary covertly.[79] Over 50 percent of those caught trying to cross the border clandestinely had trachoma, declared one U.S. official in October 1907.[80] And Braun insisted that Canada's deporting of just two of the ninety-one Japanese labor migrants refused entry into the United States at the B.C. border on medical grounds in 1907 could only mean that the other eighty-nine had entered the United States illegally.[81] Immigration officials complained that the forests along the Washington State–British Columbia border were so dense with new foliage in springtime that it was all but impossible to see more than twenty feet in any direction, offering countless opportunities to cross the border clandestinely.[82] Most such crossings, U.S. immigration officers believed, occurred along the fifty-mile stretch between Blaine, Washington, and the foothills of the Cascade Mountains, where there was a "vast forest with numerous roads" and a series of railway bridges across the fast-running Nooksack River.[83] Islands dotted the waters between Canada and the United States in the Puget Sound and the Gulf of Georgia, along the westernmost stretch of the boundary. As one immigration inspector sent to investigate conditions in the area in 1907 reported, "No other place in the United States furnishes as many advantages for smuggling as the Puget Sound with its multitude of small islands."[84]

The danger inherent in the local landscape that undetected border crossings might occur was compounded by the indifference of local residents on both sides of the border. To them, the international border appears to have signified far less than it did to immigration officials. U.S. inspectors complained that Blaine residents were "exceedingly unwilling" to provide information on Japanese and other migrants who arrived in their small border town after crossing the border illegally.[85] Canadian officials grumbled that B.C. residents living just north of the border turned a blind eye on illegal migration and instead made a tidy profit guiding Japanese and European migrants into the United States along one or another of the fifteen or so trails in the immediate area not guarded by immigration officials.[86]

In November 1907, U.S. authorities succeeded in persuading Canadian officials to comply with a change in policy intended to prevent U.S.-bound passengers from invoking the transit privilege upon arrival at Canadian ports. Although U.S. immigration officers stationed at B.C. ports had been willing up to that time to examine U.S.-bound passengers when they landed there, releasing them to Canadian officials only if they

Groups of immigrants on board a ship in Vancouver Harbour, circa 1906. (Vancouver Public Library, Special Collections, VPL 3027.)

failed the medical examinations, they now refused to inspect U.S.-bound Japanese passengers. Consequently, Canadian officials also refused to allow U.S.-bound Japanese to land; those passengers had to remain on board until they could be inspected at a U.S. port. Particularly offensive to the Meiji government was the singling out of Japanese passengers: European immigrants arriving at Atlantic ports en route to the United States continued to be permitted to transit Canada as before.[87] In protest, the Japanese consul in Vancouver adopted the argument in defense of Canadian sovereignty first made by U.S. steamship lines: that the United States had no jurisdiction in Canada and could not insist that U.S.-bound passengers remain on board ship in B.C. ports. The consul insisted that in the absence of a treaty between Japan and Canada that restricted landing in Canada to those who held passports for Canada, Japanese nationals were entitled to leave the ship and transit Canada regardless of their final destination.[88] But he protested in vain.

The first vessel to which the new policy was applied was the S.S. *Kumeric*, which arrived in Victoria, B.C., on November 23, 1907. Of the 146 Japanese on board, 107 held passports for the United States. Although the Dominion immigration agent had previously insisted on the right of transit passengers to land, he now refused to allow those going to the United States to disembark; they had to remain on board until the ship arrived at Port Townsend, Washington. U.S. officials believed that the Dominion agent's change in attitude was partly explained by the Canadian government's recent decision to negotiate an agreement to restrict Japanese migration to Canada in ways consistent with U.S. policy. Britain's ambassador to Japan also assured his U.S. counterpart that Britain fully supported Canada's desire to restrict Japanese immigration. Given these developments, U.S. authorities decided to make no further effort "to interfere" with Canadian immigration policy.[89]

U.S. officials were further reassured by William Lyon Mackenzie King, who had been appointed to investigate Japanese immigration to Canada in the wake of the September 1907 Vancouver Riot.[90] At a dinner meeting on November 16, he promised U.S. Immigration Commissioner John H. Clark that his government would amend its immigration laws to "restrict the landing of these people in Canada" once his investigation was complete. Although hearings were still under way, Mackenzie King assured Clark that his investigation would "result not only in bringing about the deportation of those who are found to be diseased upon arrival at this port, but will also result in preventing any alien landing for treatment." His confidence was founded in part on documents that had been forcibly seized from Japanese employment agencies in Vancouver; agents had even broken into desks. Though unwilling to disclose the documents' contents, Mackenzie King told Clark that they would help "put a stop to Japanese immigration in this end of the country."[91] True to his word, the recommendations made by Mackenzie King in the report of the Royal Commission submitted in 1908 were entirely in accord with the wishes of U.S. authorities. Canada was advised to continue to offer medical treatment to migrants arriving on the Atlantic coast but to stop offering medical treatment to those arriving on the Pacific coast. If Japanese with passports for the United States were rejected by U.S. officers, "they should be declared *ipso facto* undesirables, so far as Canada is concerned, and not allowed to land."[92]

In the face of growing anti-Asian sentiment in California and British Columbia and the apparent failure of its policy of limiting the number of passports issued for travel to the United States and Canada, Japan agreed in 1908 to impose a new series of restrictions on the emigration of its citizens in exchange for the U.S. government's assurance that it would not pass legislation specifically targeting Japanese immigrants similar to the Chinese Exclusion Act passed in 1882. U.S. diplomats had first raised the possibility of entering into such an agreement early in 1907, but the Meiji government was initially reluctant to proceed, recognizing that its subjects would see it as the substitute for discriminatory legislation that it was.[93] Within a matter of months, however, the same officials concluded that it was in Japan's best interests to agree voluntarily to restrict emigration to the United States. The result came to be known as the Gentlemen's Agreement. Under its provisions, Japan agreed to stop issuing passports to imin bound for the United States and instead to limit passports for the United States to former residents, their immediate relatives, and "settled agriculturalists." Vice Foreign Minister Ishii Kikujirō assured his U.S. counterpart that the "departure of fresh emigrants" would be "absolutely forbidden."[94]

Rodolphe Lemieux, sent to Japan by Canada's Dominion government in the fall of 1907, reached a similar accord with the Meiji government authorities in 1908, one that all but cut off new Japanese immigration to Canada. Under the terms of the Gentlemen's Agreement that he negotiated, Canada agreed to strictly honor travel restrictions imposed by the Meiji government on its subjects. Japan, in turn, agreed not to object to Canada's limiting new immigrants from Japan to just four hundred per year.[95] It also agreed to permit Canada to deny its subjects the right to transit its territory. "Although the existing treaty between Japan and Canada absolutely guarantees to Japanese subjects full liberty to enter, travel and reside in any part of the Dominion of Canada," Meiji officials reluctantly observed, "it is not the intention of the Imperial Government to insist upon the complete enjoyment of the rights and privileges guaranteed by those stipulations when that would involve disregard of special conditions which may prevail in Canada from time to time."[96]

Given the nature of the Gentlemen's Agreements, each of which comprised a series of diplomatic notes and memoranda that were confidential in nature, enforcement proved to be a problem for U.S. and Canadian officials alike. Asked to prepare an outline of the basic terms of the U.S. Gentlemen's Agreement for the immigration inspectors charged with enforcing it, an Immigration Bureau lawyer described the task as virtually impossible. The various memoranda, he explained with some frustration, involved "such a maze of intricacies, of propositions, counter propositions, exceptions, counter exceptions, and unexpressed or illy-expressed exceptions, that it has been almost impossible to reduce it to a workable basis."[97]

Similar uncertainty about the precise meaning of Canada's Gentlemen's Agreement—also often referred to as the Hayashi-Lemieux Agreement—was reflected in the difficulties that it created for Japanese already resident in Canada. When S. Kuroda, general manager of Awaya, Ikeda and Company in Vancouver, returned from a business trip on September 5, 1909, for example, he was ordered off the train at White Rock, B.C. Canadian border officials insisted that because his passport indicated that the Meiji government permitted him to travel to Europe and America, he was excluded from Canada under the terms of the agreement. The reference to America, Kuroda explained, referred to travel anywhere in Europe and North America. The Canadian border officials were not persuaded. Even if America included Canada, they told him, he would still be denied admission by virtue of the continuous passage rule, a newly instituted provision that required persons entering Canada to travel directly to Canada from their country of origin without transiting any other nation's territory or interrupting their journey along the way.[98]

When Japan's consul general contacted Canada's minister of the interior about Kuroda's exclusion, he explained that his government had not intended that the Hayashi-Lemieux Agreement apply to all Japanese regardless of status, but had assumed that the practice of differentiating among Japanese based on status would continue. "I cannot think even a moment that the Canadian Government has instructed their immigration officers to treat all Japanese coming to Canada as immigrants, irrespectively of their classes."[99] In December 1909, Canada acceded to the Japanese government's request that it differentiate among Japanese based on status, clarifying that the purpose of the Hayashi-Lemieux Agreement was to exclude Japanese labor migrants, and it instructed its immigration inspectors "not to prevent other classes of Japanese travelers [from] coming into Canada."[100]

Notwithstanding this clarification, the broad impact of the Hayashi-Lemieux Agreement was quickly apparent. In 1909, Canadian immigration officials informed their U.S. counterparts that just 851 Japanese were admitted to Canada at Pacific coast ports in 1908, plus 7 at Atlantic ports, and 11 at ports along the Canada-U.S. border.[101] The number of Japanese entering the United States did not drop as quickly as expected, however. On the contrary, Japanese immigration to the United States peaked in 1907 and 1908—a direct result of efforts by individual Japanese to emigrate to the United States before the new restrictions provided for in the Gentlemen's Agreement made that all but impossible. In 1907, the number of Japanese immigrants admitted to the United States was 30,824, more than double the number—14,243—who were admitted in 1906. Another 16,418 were admitted in 1908 before the Gentlemen's Agreement went into effect that summer.[102]

During a July 1908 meeting with the U.S. ambassador to Japan, Vice Foreign Minister Ishii assured him that despite the U.S. government's perception that the Gentlemen's Agreement was a failure, just 1,053 passports had been issued that year to emigrants bound for the United States.[103] The impact of the agreement became apparent one year later. In 1909 only 3,275 Japanese immigrants were admitted to the United States—less than a fifth of the number admitted in 1908 and barely a tenth of the number admitted in 1907.[104] In April 1909 the *Vancouver Daily Province* reported with some satisfaction that "even persons belonging to the upper classes" in Japan were finding it difficult to obtain passports.[105]

The tightening web of exclusionary policies along the U.S.-Canada border and the Pacific coast complicated travel for Japanese migrants. Increasingly, they had to choose between the two countries. A decade earlier they had traveled back and forth across the international boundary with relative ease in response to cross-border calls for labor.[106] For a brief period just after the turn of the century, British Columbia's efforts to exclude them had persuaded some Japanese that the United States was the more welcoming destination. In 1903, Nosse informed Prime Minister Wilfrid Laurier that hundreds of Japanese migrants intended to leave British Columbia for the United States "on account of the local agitation and oppressive measures adopted against our people by both the provincial and municipal authorities."[107] Migrants denied entry to Canada because they were unable to pass the literacy test required by the Natal Acts could still be admitted to the United States, and although the question of whether *issei*—first-generation Japanese immigrants—were entitled to U.S. citizenship was increasingly subject to debate, the courts had yet to rule on whether nikkeijin had to be born in the United States to be citizens. By 1907 migrants' perceptions had changed. Japanese who might have opted to go to the United States traveled to or through Canada instead.[108]

By the end of 1908 the legal landscape had shifted again. The U.S. executive order of March 14, 1907, taken together with the Gentlemen's Agreements that Japan had been persuaded to enter with the United States and Canada, ensured that the barriers against Japanese immigration erected by the two nations were mutually reinforcing. Although the U.S. government pressured the Dominion government to align its policy with that of the United States, it was a province that took the lead in developing anti-Japanese law and policy in Canada. Britain was complicit in that process; it made its sympathy and support for British Columbia's restrictive legislation clear, notwithstanding its alliance and treaty of friendship with Japan. The parallel provisions of the two Gentlemen's Agreements not only reduced the number of Japanese immigrants admitted to the United States and Canada to a trickle but redefined the migrant stream from Japan. First, the emphasis placed by both agreements on prior residence in Canada or the United States or family ties to immigrants already in residence tended to limit further emigration from Japan to places where earlier migrations had originated; only they were sources of new emigrants.[109] The growing number of legal obstacles erected by both Canada and the United States along the Pacific coast and the international border that they shared also forced emigrants and emigration companies to reconsider other opportunities; specifically, their efforts were redirected southward to the U.S.-Mexico border and beyond.

CHAPTER SIX

The U.S.-Mexico Border

THE EXECUTIVE ORDER OF MARCH 14, 1907, which redirected some Japanese migrants north to Canada, encouraged others to go south to Mexico. Although the Meiji government had begun to restrict the number of passports issued for Canada and the United States as early as 1900, it made no parallel effort during the first years of the twentieth century to restrict the number issued for other North American destinations.[1] As Meiji government restrictions on emigration to Canada and the United States tightened further in the wake of the Gentlemen's Agreements, emigration to Mexico offered many Japanese emigrants the only chance they had to obtain a passport to any North American destination. To obtain a passport for Mexico, emigrants had to show that they were guaranteed work when they arrived, which generally required them to have entered into a labor contract. They were able to enter into labor contracts to work in Mexico because, in contrast to the United States and Canada, Mexico had yet to adopt what the immigration inspector Marcus Braun called "modern" immigration laws—laws that excluded contract laborers from the country and made undergoing a medical inspection mandatory for all labor immigrants. Mexico even encouraged the recruitment of contract laborers by emigration companies on behalf of private companies to facilitate the development of its agricultural and industrial infrastructure.[2]

As in Canada, the transit privilege, in particular, again emerged as a mechanism that Japanese and other migrants were able to use to challenge the power of the United States to exclude them. Just as migrants arriving at Canadian ports had been able to invoke the transit privilege across Canada to access the U.S.-Canada border, migrants arriving at Mexican ports retained the option of invoking the transit privilege at the U.S.-Mexico border to enter the United States in transit to Canada. Once in the United States, migrants could either complete their journey or discontinue it, remaining in the United States temporarily or permanently. Yet another strategy employed by Japanese migrants after March 14, 1907, was to obtain passports for Peru and then travel north to Mexico and apply for admission to the United States from there, since those with passports for Mexico were excludable under the March 14 Executive Order but not those with passports for Peru, which was not specifically named in that order.[3] As at the U.S.-Canada border, this was an effective strategy; migrants denied admission to the United States at the U.S.-Mexico border were required only to return to Mexico, not to Japan. Japanese migrants who arrived at Mexican ports also retained other options, including settling in Mexico as immigrants, covertly crossing its northern border into the United States, or traveling south to Peru, Brazil, or another country on the southern continent.

For all these reasons, Mexico increasingly became the destination that offered the greatest number of alternatives to emigrants bound for all parts of North America. U.S. immigration officials ultimately concluded that more Japanese entered the United States through Mexico during the first decade of the twentieth century than through Canada.

So concerned were U.S. immigration officials about illegal entry across the U.S.-Mexico boundary that Braun predicted in his February 1907 report to Congress that northward migration through Mexico was likely "to bring about more friction and unpleasantness" than the San Francisco school incident had. Braun reassured Congress, however, that the government of Mexico fully supported U.S. efforts to reinforce the border between them based on its own interest in preventing Mexican rebels from escaping the reach of Mexican authorities by crossing into the United States.[4] Steamship lines and emigration companies, on the other hand, anxious to retain as much of the cross-Pacific transport business as possible despite the tightening restrictions on migration to North America, took the lead in recruiting Japanese laborers to work in Mexico.[5]

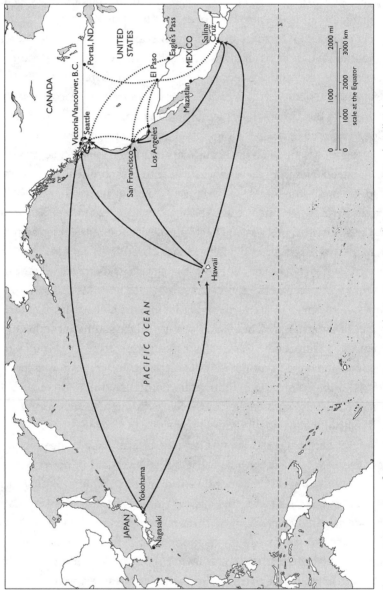

Representative routes of Japanese immigrants to various destinations in North America. (Map by Bill Nelson.)

Although Japanese laborers generally preferred work on cotton plantations, they also agreed to work in coal mines in order to get to Mexico. The journey to Mexico in itself provided an opportunity to reach the United States or Canada to those willing to jump ship at north Pacific ports of call. When a ship carrying fifty-nine Japanese labor migrants recruited to work at a coal mine in Las Esperanzas, Mexico, stopped at Seattle, Washington, in October 1906, for example, Meiji consular officials reported to their government that thirty-seven jumped ship while it was in port and that eighteen of the twenty-two who remained departed for Mexico's northern border soon after they arrived in Mexico. Most of the eighteen, they added, were readily able to cross into the United States.[6] This was a pattern on which the Canadian press also kept an eye, particularly after four other migrants bound for Mexican ports on a Mexican vessel docked at New Westminster, B.C., attempted to slide down the ship's bowline to the pier, only to fall into the icy waters of the Fraser River, where one drowned.[7]

Those who reached the coal mines in Mexico faced extremely harsh conditions. Although Braun remained convinced that the real goal of most Japanese was the United States, many Japanese migrants in Mexico abandoned their contracts only after efforts to address the conditions in the mines had failed. Even then, many did not go on to the United States. When, in 1904, a group of 500 Japanese laborers sent to Mexico by the Tokyo-based Tōyō Imin Gaisha to work at El Boleo, a coal mine run by the Mexican Coal and Coke Company, refused to work under conditions that included dangerous mineshafts and daily temperatures in excess of 100 degrees Fahrenheit, 450 simply returned to Japan.[8] Conditions at other coal mines were similar to those at El Boleo, including difficult and dangerous work environments, salaries much lower than those promised by emigration companies, inadequate food, lack of fresh water, and accommodations so dismal that the migrants and consular officials alike regarded them as suitable only for cattle.[9]

In a secret report to Foreign Minister Komura Jutarō regarding the conditions in which Japanese migrants lived along the Mexico-U.S. border in 1908, Baron Takahira Kotaro wrote that wages were so low that many were barely able to eke out a living and that they were always hungry and thirsty. Takahira described the shacks in which the migrants lived as even worse than those in Mannen-cho—regarded as the worst of Tokyo's slums, an area to which outcastes had been relegated in historical times. In Takahira's words: "Their houses are miserable; the walls are worn through, doors broken, there are no floor boards and no toilets ... They live like cattle on the mud floors, eating pieces of moldy bread, barely hanging onto their frail lives. I don't have any words in my vocabulary to describe their misery."[10] The Japanese migrants with whom he spoke were unwilling to return to their jobs in the coal mines, Takahira reported, because they could no longer bear the cruel punishment meted out by Mexican bosses, who, they felt, treated them like slaves; instead, they preferred to die of hunger. The deaths of twenty-two Japanese coal miners in an explosion at the Las Esperanzas coal mine in February 1907 reconfirmed the dangers of working in the mines.[11]

Notwithstanding the conditions that labor migrants faced in Mexico's coal mines, some emigration companies went so far as to use the proximity of Mexico to the United States as a recruitment tool in Japan, telling potential recruits that they could easily enter the United States from Mexico.[12] Labor emigration companies also sometimes actively encouraged migrants to break their contracts and migrate to the United States. This allowed the emigration companies not only to recruit new groups of migrants who would require passage to Mexico but also to demand payment of the 100–150 yen penalty that was imposed in Japan when migrants abrogated their labor contracts. In 1909, for example, a Japanese newspaper reported that Tokyo District Court prosecutors were conducting an investigation into such practices by the Dairiku Emigration Company, which had sent more than thirty-eight hundred emigrants to Mexico in recent years.[13]

Although some Japanese migrants arrived in Mexico intending to complete their contracts, others went to Mexico with the express intention of immigrating to the United States. Kusakabe Dengo, who had twice failed the trachoma examination required in Japan of migrants traveling to the United States or Canada, admitted to U.S. immigration officers in 1906 that he had answered a call for coal miners in Mexico put out by an emigration company because traveling to Mexico provided an alternative way to reach the United States.[14] When Tomida Tetsujiro was caught covertly crossing the border near San Antonio in 1907, he likewise admitted that he had agreed to work the coal mines in Las Esperanzas because he had been informed that he would be able to access the many jobs available just beyond Mexico's northern border.[15] In February 1907, Braun estimated that just 2,000 of the 8,000 Japanese laborers who had arrived in Mexico during the previous year and a half remained there.[16] The Mexican Coal and Coke Company, which ran the Las Esperanzas mine, had lost 1,400 of 1,500 laborers recruited during that time, all of whom, Braun insisted, had made their way north into the United States either on foot or by train.[17]

Before the March 14 Executive Order most Japanese immigrants who arrived at the U.S.-Mexico border first attempted to enter the United States legally. Prior to that date, Japanese migrants who had passports for Mexico or for Peru could legally immigrate to the United States; only those who were excludable on medical grounds or who were deemed likely to become public charges had any reason to turn to clandestine means.[18] Because contract laborers had been barred for several decades, Japanese immigrants recognized that it was necessary to avoid the impression that they had come to Mexico as contract laborers; instead, they took care to present themselves as students or businessmen.[19] Only if Japanese migrants were denied entry to the United States by U.S. officials did they try to circumvent legal entry procedures. Most made the journey north by rail, often traveling in the oil or water tanks of locomotives and then on foot, wading across the Rio Grande at night.[20] Because they knew that U.S. immigration inspectors watched trains closely at the last stations before the border, Japanese migrants left the trains short of the border, some walking along the railroad tracks for days to reach a point where they could cross into the United States.[21] Then, as now, some who tried to cross the border covertly died in the desert short of their goal.[22]

Whatever the law-abiding intentions of migrants, the March 14 Executive Order drove virtually all Japanese migration at the U.S.-Mexico border underground. In Braun's words, Japanese migrants had crossed that boundary northward legally "in a continuous stream" prior to March 14, and they had crossed it "surreptitiously ever since."[23] Whereas the thick foliage along the Canadian border aided migrants' passage because of what it obscured, along the Mexican border the desert gave aid because of what it revealed: enforcement was made more difficult along the southern boundary by the ease with which immigration inspectors in their dark blue uniforms could be spotted miles away.[24]

Most Japanese who were able to avoid the inspectors did not remain in Texas but left for the Pacific coast. They wished not to be identified as contract breakers or as immigrants who had entered the country without undergoing inspection. Another factor was the apparent lack of welcome from the relatively small Japanese immigrant community in Texas, reportedly comprised largely of hi-imin who had succeeded in rice cultivation there.[25] Although some scholars have concluded that in Texas "discrimination was directed at the blacks and Hispanos," so "Japanese found themselves classified with the whites," individual narratives tell a different story.[26] A Japanese woman who later served as a matron and interpreter at Angel Island in San Francisco Bay, for example, reported that members of the American Legion had told one family to get out of town within hours of its arrival in Texas and that the Ku Klux Klan had driven Japanese melon pickers at a Japanese-run hotel in Tulare County from their beds.[27]

After March 14, Japanese migrants who had been denied passports for the United States by the Meiji government turned to a new strategy: asserting their right under international law to enter the United States from Mexico in transit to Canada. In addition to using the right to transit Mexico to minimize the risk that they would be deported to Japan if they were not admitted to the United States, Japanese migrants in Mexico realized that they could use their ability to enter the United States in transit to Canada to remain in the United States. Migrants who used this strategy discontinued their journey en route, leaving the train at some predetermined point where they redeemed the unused portion of their tickets.[28] In December 1907, for example, four Japanese migrants who had applied to transit the United States to Canada but left the train in Denver, admitted to U.S. immigration officers that for one hundred Mexican dollars, a Mexican man had provided them with railway tickets and instructions to leave the train at Denver because that station was not closely monitored by immigration officials. Their determination to remain in the United States is reflected in the effort two of them made to escape as they were being returned to Mexico: they jumped from the window of the moving train as the officer assigned to guard them took a nap. Despite the serious injuries one sustained, he avoided capture for two days by hiding in the bushes along the railway tracks.[29]

Ironically, although the March 14 Executive Order expressly barred Japanese migrants with passports for Canada, Mexico, or Hawaii from entering the United States, the power of the United States to deny them the right to transit its territory remained in doubt. Although U.S. border officials indignantly described the invocation of the transit privilege by Japanese migrants bound for Canada as a "mere subterfuge to get into the United States," they could do little to deny them without contravening international law.[30] As U.S. Immigration Bureau attorneys reluctantly concluded, even under the authority of the March 14 Executive Order, the bureau could not prevent Japanese migrants from passing through U.S. ports or traveling across the United States by rail in transit to Canada, even if their passports did not designate the United States as a destination.[31] In 1908, U.S. officials briefly considered requiring migrants to transit the United States in special barred railroad cars. They soon concluded that this was not feasible, however, since it would have required at least thirty migrants to travel at a time, and it would also have required the U.S. government to authorize railroad companies to use force to prevent escape, something the government was unwilling to do.[32] Instead, the bureau directed border officials to make careful note of the physical characteristics of all Japanese migrants who applied to transit the United States, including height and "patent physical peculiarities."[33] To reassure the Meiji government that its nationals were not unfairly singled out, immigration inspectors were further directed to conduct their inquiries "without inconveniencing or annoying the passenger" and were reminded to avoid any action that, "in fact or in appearance, could be construed as a discrimination against such aliens."[34] Inspectors were to err on the side of caution: "if, in following this policy with regard to Japanese residents who desire to cross and recross the boundary, the surreptitious entry of laborers is assisted, that could not be helped."[35]

Although Meiji government representatives endeavored to ensure that Japanese subjects were not singled out for investigation or otherwise discriminated against by U.S. officials, Japanese associations in the United States shunned those who used the transit privilege to enter the country and remain there. According to reports in a Japanese-language paper in San Francisco, when a group of Japanese migrants in transit to Canada left their train in Los Angeles on May 3, 1907, and turned to a local Japanese association for assistance, the association refused to grant them any aid.[36]

Migrants who invoked the transit privilege to enter and remain in the United States often saw their actions as a justified act of defiance against laws that unfairly discriminated against them. R. L. Pruett, an interpreter for the Immigration Service in El Paso, Texas, who was fluent in Japanese and had lived in Japan for many years, reported in June 1907 that hundreds of Japanese migrants had told him that "the Executive order which discriminates against us was meant [only] to satisfy a few people in San Francisco."[37] Other Japanese deliberately challenged U.S. officials' assumptions that seeking to transit the United States to Canada was illegal. Two Japanese migrants who sought to cross the border at El Paso on April 9, 1907, for example, stated that they were fishermen with suffi-cient funds to transit the United States to Vancouver and made it clear that they considered theirs a test case, triggering a quick telegram from local border officials to Washington, D.C., seeking instructions.[38] Another Japanese migrant who was admitted to the United States at El Paso on February 26, 1908, made sure that U.S. officials noted that he left the United States at Portal, North Dakota, a few days afterward so that he would not later be branded as an illegal.[39]

U.S. officials, nevertheless, remained convinced that the United States was the real destination of most Japanese migrants who invoked the transit privilege at the U.S.-Mexico border. To determine whether an individual's real reason for traveling to Mexico was to enter and remain in the United States, U.S. border officials examined maps and guidebooks found in a migrant's possession to determine what his intentions were. "Many" Japanese laborers arriving in Mexico had slips of paper with the names and addresses of Japanese contacts in the United States in their possession, which was "conclusive evidence," Braun concluded, that they had intended to go on to the United States even before they arrived in Mexico.[40] More persuasive were the maps recovered from some migrants showing railroad routes across the border into the United States and on to California, but not through to Canada. Even R. L. Pruett, who was gener-ally sympathetic to the Japanese migrants he examined, reported that a number of the immigrants he spoke with arrived carrying compasses and Japanese-English conversation books along with their maps of the United States.[41]

Some Japanese migrants no doubt had such materials in their posses-sion, but descriptions of the evidence obtained by U.S. border officials tend to exaggerate the significance of the items seized. According to Braun, for example, many migrants had a copy of a Japanese-language

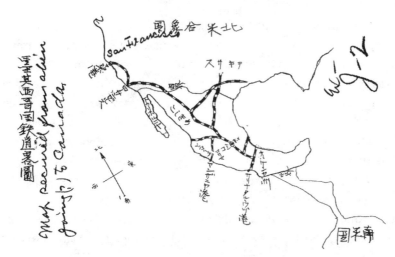

Map found in the possession of a Japanese migrant, 1907. (National Archives and Records Administration, San Francisco, RG 85, Report of Marcus Braun, U.S. Immigrant Inspector, 12 February 1907, exhibit J-2.)

pamphlet published by the Tōyō Imin Gaisha with them when they arrived in Mexico. According to Braun, although it was "ostensibly a 'Guidebook for Immigrants to Mexico,' " it was really a "guide book in a rough way to points within the Continental United States."[42] A copy of the guidebook in question still exists in U.S. immigration records; nothing in the Japanese-language original reflects that it was intended as a guide to the United States. It is just what it purports to be—a guide to travel in Mexico. A similar tendency to exaggerate evidence was reflected in the discrepancy between Braun's estimate that thousands of Japanese migrants were making their way north across the U.S.-Mexico border in violation of the March 14 Executive Order and the number of those actually arrested during the ten weeks after the executive order went into effect—just thirty-one.[43] In December 1907, even the U.S. ambassador to Japan objected to the tendency of U.S. border officials to exaggerate the number of illegal immigrants, complaining that the estimates were inconsistent with Meiji government statistics showing that far fewer people had been permitted to leave Japan for Mexico during the relevant period.[44]

Ironically, illegal entry, to the extent that it did occur, was a function not only of the actions of the migrants themselves but also of U.S. immigration officers, including medical examiners, who on more than one occasion accepted bribes to change previously made determinations that certain migrants were excludable. In June 1907, for example, R. L. Pruett reported that Warren Garrett, an employee of the Trans-Oceanic Emigration Company, had invited a doctor to come on board a company ship that had just arrived carrying 423 Japanese migrants, 223 of whom the doctor had refused to admit on medical grounds. Once the doctor was on board, Garrett "made rich presents to him of silks and curios and Japanese wines and also the free use of a Geisha." The following day, the doctor agreed to allow all 423 migrants to land in return for $4,000.[45]

Although some migrants defied the increasingly restrictive immigration laws and became illegal immigrants as a result of their own decisions, others were caught in the gap between the shifting sets of legal regulations developed by Canada and the United States to counter the effects of the transit privilege. Migrants sometimes became illegal immigrants not because it was their intention to violate the transit privilege and to evade the immigration laws of either the United States or Canada, but because they found themselves trapped between two systems of law that overlapped or contradicted one another in unanticipated ways. In June 1908, for example, Tatsumi Mitsutaro was caught in such a bind when he entered the United States at Eagle Pass, Texas, in transit to Canada. Unable to deny the privilege of transit to Japanese migrants altogether, the United States had acted in October 1907 to require that certain categories of migrants seeking to exercise the transit privilege post a $500 bond that was forfeited if they did not leave the United States within twenty days.[46] Tatsumi had posted a bond. When he reached the U.S.-Canada border at Blaine, Washington, however, he was turned back because of a recent Order in Council issued by the Dominion government that prohibited the entry of immigrants into Canada "unless arriving by a continuous journey from the country of their birth or citizenship on tickets purchased before leaving that country."[47] That order, originally issued in 1906, was incorporated into Canada's Immigration Act in 1908 partly to cut off Japanese immigration to Canada through Hawaii.[48] Consequently, any immigrant arriving in Canada in transit through the United States—bonded or not under U.S. law—was, by definition, "debarred and ... rejected on arrival at the Canadian frontier."[49] By virtue of Tatsumi's failure to leave the United States, however, he was also immediately in violation of U.S. law and illegally in the United States. Lacking the funds to travel by railroad all the way back to the U.S.-Mexico border, Tatsumi instead traveled from Blaine to Seattle to try to obtain funds to prevent forfeiture of the bond. In Seattle, already an illegal immigrant and unable to obtain the travel money he needed to return to Mexico, Tatsumi disappeared.[50] Only by first becoming a Mexican citizen, U.S. immigration officials themselves noted with some irony, could Tatsumi legally have entered Canada in transit through the United States, but only if he did not interrupt his railway journey along the way.[51]

Unable to attack the transit privilege directly, both Canada and the United States had found ways to make it impractical for most migrants to utilize—the United States by requiring the posting of a $500 bond and Canada by implementing the continuous passage rule. Resort to an indirect approach allowed both countries to maintain their claim to status as "civilized" nations that honored the terms of the international treaties that bound them. Until that time, however, Japanese and other migrants were able to use inconsistencies in the laws of the United States, Canada, and Mexico, together with the transit privilege, to subvert efforts by Canada and the United States to exclude them. Taken together with the Gentlemen's Agreements into which Japan had entered with both the United States and Canada by 1908, the measures adopted by both countries forced Japanese labor migrants once again to consider alternative destinations.

In November 1907, Canadian authorities received a report from a confidential informant in Brazil stating that Brazil had begun to recruit Japanese laborers. This was, in their eyes, a welcome development and the key to avoiding further racial conflict of the kind that had occurred during the Vancouver Riot earlier that fall.[52] One month later, U.S. government officials expressed similar satisfaction when they obtained a copy of a contract between the Brazilian state of São Paulo and the Imperial Emigration Company in Tokyo for the recruitment of three thousand immigrants, including laborers and their families, over a period of three years. They were also pleased to learn that a similar agreement had been concluded with the state of Rio de Janeiro and that the Meiji government had started negotiations with the states of Rio Grande do Sul and Paraná.[53] Meiji government representatives regarded Brazil as an ideal destination, noting that it offered not only "land suitable for rice cultivation" but also market opportunities for artisans who produced "Japanese silks, pottery, bamboo and lacquerware, fans and fireworks, etc."[54]

When, in 1908, the Meiji government agreed to restrict passports to Mexico as it had restricted them to Canada and the United States several years earlier, partly as a result of pressure brought to bear on both Mexico and Japan by the United States, the trend toward migration to Brazil was again reinforced.[55] In 1909, British Columbians were pleased to hear that both Brazil and Peru had contacted emigration companies in Japan in order to recruit labor immigrants; echoing rationalizations often applied in the context of African slavery, they opined that "climatic conditions" there would be "much more congenial to Japanese" than those in North America.[56] In 1910 the Meiji government's minister in Brazil declared that Japanese immigration to Brazil had only just begun. By 1920 more than twenty thousand Japanese immigrants had settled in Brazil.[57]

The impact of U.S. and Canadian exclusion laws was literally sketched across the landscape, reflected in the alternative routes that Japanese migrants took. Exclusionary law and policy also forced many migrants underground, rendering illegal migrants who would have been admissible just a few years earlier. Ironically, the Meiji government's conciliatory policy of accommodating and even anticipating the racially discriminatory demands of the U.S. and Canadian government, allowed both nations to mark Japanese subjects as excludable or illegal in some of the very ways that the Japanese government had tried to avoid. But the fact that the United States shared a border with both Canada and Mexico created opportunities for Japanese migrants to negotiate both in ways that would not have existed but for the presence of the other. As the migrants themselves realized, the power of both borders to exclude depended in part on how they positioned themselves in relation to them. The determination of Japanese migrants to pursue their individual goals regardless of the dictates of their own government, together with the surprising power of the transit privilege to force the governments of Canada and the United States to allow border crossings they would otherwise have chosen to impede, ensured that the exclusionary measures devised by both countries during the first decade of the twentieth century were never perfectly implemented.

CHAPTER SEVEN

Debating the Contours of Citizenship

THE EFFORTS OF BOTH CANADA AND THE UNITED STATES to create the territories defined by their borders as racialized spaces that excluded Japanese and other Asians focused on not only regulating their entry through the use of immigration law but passing other exclusionary laws intended to limit their meaningful participation in U.S. and Canadian society. Key among these constraints were laws intended to restrict access to the full rights of citizenship—laws that directly raised questions about what qualified an individual to become a U.S. citizen or a British subject. Although the full rights of citizenship were denied to Japanese immigrants in both Canada and the United States, the different sets of constitutional constraints by which the two governments were bound forced them to employ different legal mechanisms to achieve that objective. Although the United States was able to bar first-generation Japanese immigrants (*issei*) from citizenship, the Fourteenth and Fifteenth Amendments to the U.S. Constitution, which made it unconstitutional to deny the full rights of citizenship to anyone born in the United States based on race or color, prevented it from doing the same to the second generation. To remedy what he saw as a problem, California senator James D. Phelan proposed to a committee of the House of Representatives in 1920 that the U.S. Constitution be amended to deny citizenship to the children of those ineligible for citizenship even if they were born in the United States, but he failed in this endeavor.[1]

Canada, in contrast to the United States, did not exclude issei from citizenship. Although some members of the B.C. legislature argued that Canada should emulate the United States and Australia by denying citizenship to issei, the Dominion government was unwilling to risk jeopardizing imperial relations with Japan, which it feared might be compromised if Canada acted to contravene the Anglo-Japanese Alliance of 1902.[2] British Columbia, however, was able to use the absence of any constitutional constraint equivalent to the Fourteenth and Fifteenth Amendments to deny the vote to naturalized British subjects of Japanese and other Asian ancestry in that province.[3] Its "right" to exclude Japanese immigrants from the franchise, according to one local newspaper, was grounded in British Columbia's geographical contiguity to Japan, which made it especially vulnerable to the effects of unchecked immigration, or so it was argued.[4]

Anti-Japanese exclusionists in the United States and Canada borrowed freely from one another to make a series of internally contradictory arguments to support their respective positions. On the one hand, anti-Japanese elements in British Columbia, like their U.S. counterparts, characterized Japanese immigrants as a special threat precisely because the immigrants understood the significance of the right to vote and would use its power to further the immigrants' cause; on the other hand, they insisted on the purported inability of the same immigrants to appreciate the significance of the franchise and to exercise it responsibly. At times exclusionists argued that if Japanese immigrants were permitted to vote, they would "overwhelm" the polls; at others, they insisted that "Japanese care little ... for the authority to vote" and that "few (if indeed any) would seek to exercise the franchise" even if it were extended to them.[5] Japanese were to be excluded from voting, in short, both because they might exercise their power as voters and because they might not vote.

B.C.'s attorney general D. M. Eberts also abandoned consistency. He declared that Japanese immigrants had no real interest in Canada and no knowledge of its political institutions. He was willing, however, to accommodate his argument to the possibility that they would exercise the franchise as responsibly as any other citizen. If that were the case, they should still be excluded, he said, because they were not assimilable.[6] Eberts ignored that voting responsibly was itself evidence that the immigrants had successfully adapted to their new environment. The Royal

Commission appointed by the Dominion government in 1902 to investigate Chinese and Japanese immigration nevertheless agreed, declaring that Asian immigrants should not be allowed to vote "as they are not and will not become citizens in the proper sense of the term or an integral part of the nation."[7]

Japanese and other defenders of nikkeijin in both Canada and the United States worked diligently to construct arguments that would negate the claims of anti-Japanese elements in both countries. Their arguments that Japanese immigrants were capable of responsibly exercising the full rights of citizenship frequently invoked the tremendous effort that Japan had made since 1868 to reconstitute itself as a modern nation modeled after those of the West. In 1897, for example, K. T. Takahashi, self-described as a "Japanese-Canadian," argued against the exclusion of Japanese immigrants from the franchise in British Columbia by pointing to the promulgation of the Meiji Constitution in 1889. Japan's establishment of a modern constitutional government, he contended, proved that Japanese were entirely capable of understanding the significance of voting. The system of government established under the Meiji Constitution, Takahashi added, was more closely modeled after that of Britain than that of any other—conveniently overlooking the ultimate decision of the Meiji oligarchs to use the Prussian constitution as their primary model. "Japan, of all countries in the world," Takahashi declared, "is constitutionally nearest to Great Britain, and her legislative and administrative methods are of the most advanced type ever adopted and experimented upon by mankind." Japan's status as a modern and civilized nation, moreover, was confirmed by the disappearance of a "coolie" or "outcast class" in Japan. The abolition of *eta* and *hinin* as legal categories in 1871 was implicit evidence of the progress that Japan had made, and demonstrated that Japanese people understood responsible citizenship. "This Japan," Takahashi wrote, "has no outcast and no pauper class; and her people in general are as appreciative of democratic principles as are average Canadians, and are law-abiding, industrious and progressive."[8]

Anti-Japanese exclusionists also invoked claims of actual or potential fraud to justify denying the vote to Japanese immigrants in British Columbia who became naturalized British subjects. Eberts's argument against permitting people in this category to vote was based partly on the explicitly racist argument that their votes could easily be bought by unscrupulous candidates because it was not possible to "distinguish one Jap or Chinaman from another."[9] Japanese immigrants, it was also often alleged, applied for citizenship only because it was a prerequisite to obtaining a fishing license.[10] Evidence does exist that Japanese immigrants sometimes shared naturalization certificates and regarded them as valuable commodities precisely because they were key to the ability to earn a livelihood in the fishing industry. The degree of commodification is suggested by a 1922 court case filed by Hakaku Murata against T. Hattaro seeking to recover a naturalization certificate that Hattaro had allegedly refused to return to him. The certificate was of considerable value to Murata, he declared, because it was "required by him to enable him to pursue his calling as a fisherman." If Hattaro failed to return the certificate, Murata sought damages in the amount of $1,000—its designated monetary value in light of the resources to which it would give him access.[11] What B.C. exclusionists overlooked when they criticized Japanese immigrants for resorting to such means or to exaggerating their years in Canada when they applied for citizenship was that migrants of European ancestry who entered British Columbia to participate in the Fraser River fishery on a seasonal basis also avoided the three-year waiting period as a matter of practical economic necessity. If they did not also share naturalization certificates, it was only because certificates were more readily available to the European immigrants whom Canada was trying to attract to its still newly acquired West.[12]

Transience, ironically, was used as an argument both for and against Japanese—to deny citizenship rights by suggesting that Japanese immigrants did not have a genuine stake in Canadian or American society and to argue that there was no danger in allowing them to become citizens because they did not intend to set up permanent homes in North America. As late as 1914, to demonstrate that Japanese immigrants posed no threat to the dominant society, Kawakami adopted exclusionists' arguments that naturalization meant nothing more than access to B.C. fishing licenses to most Japanese. Japanese migrants, he explained to North Americans on both sides of the border, had no intention settling permanently in Canada, and British Columbia was justified in its efforts to find "a way to secure desired labour for the promotion of the salmon industry without at the same time admitting ignorant fishermen into citizenship." Kawakami tried to mitigate the damage done by adopting an exclusionist position by adding that another class of naturalized Japanese were not interested in fishing. Like others among his peers, he conflated status (mibun) with character and intelligence. Men who were not fishermen, he insisted, were "in intelligence and moral character, the equal of the average immigrant from any European country." In contrast, he argued elsewhere, many of the European migrants admitted to citizenship in the United States were "undesirable aliens ill-qualified to assume duties as American citizens."[13]

Other defenders of Japanese immigrants in North America also compared them to the European immigrants who had access to the full rights of citizenship and, like Kawakami, found European immigrants wanting. In 1906, S. K. Kanda had also argued that class and status, rearticulated within a North American framework, should be accorded far more weight than race or national origin in determining who was entitled to citizenship. Even an educated Japanese gentleman who had resided in the United States for twenty years and was a graduate of one of its best universities was denied citizenship when the poorest European immigrants were not. "Why such a well-qualified Japanese is denied the right which undesirable immigrants from South Europe can easily obtain," Kanda mused, "is a matter [deserving] of great consideration."[14] Japanese immigrants characterized as low-class labor migrants by their own diplomatic representatives likewise resented Japanese lack of access to citizenship rights extended even to uneducated Europeans. One such immigrant later reported that Japanese immigrants disparagingly referred to the Slavs who were able to become U.S. citizens after just one year as "X-markers."[15]

Yet another argument put forward by anti-Japanese exclusionists—that the United States was justified in denying access to citizenship to Japanese because Japan did not admit to citizenship those born in other countries, including its own colonial subjects in Korea and Taiwan—won a response from a Japanese newspaper in Seattle, which explained that the problem with the U.S. naturalization policy was that the same standard was not applied to all immigrants: We "want the same treatment accorded to other alien nationals. We want to be admitted to this country on the same basis as a resident of Europe; to have citizenship rights the same as an Italian; to intermarry the same as a Frenchman or Russian with the American people; to intermingle socially the same as an Englishmen; to have the same business rights and protection as a Greek. We want to be treated fairly; the same as you treat other immigrants." If the United States denied citizenship to first-generation immigrants from all nations, the *Taihoku Nippō* argued, that would be acceptable. Granting it to some but not to others was inherently unjust. Japan itself denied Americans and Canadians access to citizenship, but it denied citizenship to people from all countries and did not single out any group.[16]

Another source of concern to anti-exclusionists was the perception that denying citizenship to immigrants from certain nations reflected poorly on those nations. In 1913, Baron Chinda Sutemi, Japan's ambassador to the United States, explained to the U.S. secretary of state that not according the same rights of citizenship to Japanese as to immigrants from other "first-class" nations was "hurtful to their just national susceptibility."[17] Access to citizenship, in other words, was important to the Japanese government primarily because it indicated Japan's status as a nation and only secondarily because it gave its former subjects participatory rights in government. In this sense, the quest for citizenship can also be understood as a quest for mibun in a North American context, not just for the individual but on behalf of Japan as a nation. In 1921, T. Iyenaga and Kensuke Sato made the link between status and citizenship explicit, arguing that the denial of citizenship to issei in the United States was wrong precisely because it thwarted any chances they might otherwise have had to improve their social status in that society. In their words, excluding issei from citizenship prevented them "from becoming well-to-do and refined people, and from getting permanent occupation and homes, all of which are essential if parents are to bring up their sons and daughters to a respectable standard."[18]

LEGAL QUESTS FOR THE FULL RIGHTS OF CITIZENSHIP

When restrictions on access to citizenship persisted despite efforts to address what Japanese immigrants regarded as the underlying concerns that gave rise to anti-Japanese sentiment, a small number of individuals turned to the courts to mount direct challenges to the laws that excluded them. In Canada, the issue came to a head in 1900, some two decades earlier than in the United States, when Tomekichi Homma filed a test case challenging British Columbia's denial of the franchise to British subjects of Japanese ancestry. Although the denial of citizenship to issei was also raised before lower-level U.S. courts around that time, a test case filed by Takao Ozawa in 1914 emerged as the definitive challenge to their exclusion in 1922, when the case was decided.[19] Both Homma and Ozawa regarded access to full citizenship as important not only because it was key to civic participation in both Canada and the United States but also because it was a major indicator of social status and acceptance.[20] Homma's sentiments were reflected in the constitution of the Vancouver Nipponjinkai (Japanese Association), which he helped found in 1901: the purpose of the Nipponjinkai was to enable Japanese to band together to secure the rights denied them under Canadian law and, in that way, to improve their social status and elevate the reputation of Japanese in Canada.[21]

The denial of the franchise to naturalized citizens of Asian ancestry was the keystone of the racial hierarchy established by British Columbia during the late nineteenth and early twentieth centuries. Although its own records showed that there were just 178 naturalized Japanese in the province at the time, the B.C. legislature acted in 1895 to add Japanese to the list of those already excluded from the franchise: people of Chinese and of Native ancestry.[22] Because "Japanese" was defined under the law not just as anyone who was a "native of the Japanese Empire or its dependencies not born of British parents" but also as "any person of the Japanese race, naturalized or not," the legislature's proscription applied both to immigrants born in Japan and to their descendants.[23] B.C. legislation thus established a divide between voters based not just on place of birth—on which the Fourteenth and Fifteenth Amendments forced U.S. legislators to rely—but on race and ancestry. The inability to responsibly exercise the vote, British Columbia legislators appeared to believe, was inherent in an individual's "race" or blood.

On October 19, 1900, Tomekichi Homma, a naturalized British subject born in Japan, applied to have his name added to the voters' list for Vancouver, knowing that his request would be denied because he was acting in defiance of existing law.[24] When the request was indeed denied, Homma filed a test case challenging the discriminatory provisions of the Provincial Voters Act. Within the Japanese immigrant community, reaction to Homma's action was divided. Although he received considerable support from members of the Gyosha Dantai (Fishermen's Association),

Tomekichi Homma and his wife, Matsu, with sons Joseph and Junkichi, in Vancouver, circa 1909. (Japanese Canadian National Museum and Archives, Homma Family Collection. Courtesy of the Homma Family.)

which he had helped found, many other immigrants—a majority of whom had arrived from Japan only recently—questioned the wisdom of mounting a direct challenge to the B.C. government and feared that aggravating provincial authorities would only make them more reluctant to grant the rights denied them.[25] Although the Japanese consul in Vancouver, Shimizu Seizaburo, later protested the denial of the franchise to naturalized Japanese, he initially took steps to distance himself from the case. "Once a Japanese becomes a naturalized British subject," he told a local reporter in Vancouver, "he passes out of my jurisdiction, and I keep track of him no longer." Shimizu conceded, however, that he did take an interest in anything that affected "the Japanese as a race" and would endeavor to ensure that they received all rights to which they were entitled.[26]

Homma argued in the Vancouver County Court that British Columbia lacked the power to exclude any subset of its naturalized male citizens from the franchise because section 91 of the British North America Act, Canada's constitution, clearly stated that naturalization was a subject over which the Dominion government had exclusive control.[27] The Naturalization Act provided in turn that every naturalized alien was entitled to "all political and other rights, powers and privileges to which a natural-born British subject is entitled within Canada."[28] Just one year earlier the Privy Council in London—the final arbiter of legal cases in Canada—had decided Union Colliery v. Bryden, stating that it was the Dominion government that was "invested with exclusive authority in all matters which directly concern the rights, privileges, and disabilities" of aliens resident in Canada, whether naturalized or not. Bryden made clear, Homma argued, that it was beyond the power of the B.C. legislature to pass legislation limiting the rights of any one group of naturalized British subjects residing within its borders. Where Homma insisted that the discriminatory provisions of the Provincial Voters Act were invalid because they were ultra vires, British Columbia argued that the question of who was entitled to vote in provincial elections was an issue of "purely local concern" over which the Dominion government had no authority.[29]

After hearing argument from both sides, Chief Justice Angus McColl, sitting as County Court judge, concluded that—as Homma had argued—the B.C. legislature lacked the power to pass any legislation that did not "apply alike" to all subjects of the queen.[30] Although McColl suggested that he had reached this result reluctantly, he was not insensitive to the ramifications of the legislature's action, expressing concern about B.C.'s attempt to create two separate classes of citizens. "The residence within the Province of large numbers of persons, British subjects in name but doomed to perpetual exclusion from any part in the passage of legislation affecting their property and civil rights would surely not be to the advantage of Canada, and might even become a source of national danger."[31] Some in the community were outraged. Chief Justice McColl's decision, the editors of the *Vancouver Daily Province* declared, had "fully awakened the public to the menace to their liberties which would be given existence should naturalized Chinese or Japanese be permitted to vote."[32]

When B.C.'s appellate court confirmed McColl's decision, the province applied for leave to appeal directly to the Privy Council in London. In June 1901, B.C.'s attorney general wrote to the London barrister who was to argue the province's case to the Privy Council, listing the various points that British Columbia wished to make. Asians numbered about 12,000 in a total provincial population of 125,000. While that might not seem to pose a serious danger to the ability of whites in British Columbia to maintain control of the elective process, Eberts wrote, the threat was greater than it appeared. Because the Asian population in British Columbia was composed almost entirely of adult males and because white women did not vote, Asian males would have a disproportionate impact in any election in which they voted. Also of concern to Eberts was avoiding any possibility of eroding the power to deny the franchise to people identified as Indians under Canada's Indian Act. The bar that the province had erected to exclude B.C. citizens of Asian ancestry from political participation, Eberts seemed to suggest, served not only to exclude them from the franchise but also to reinforce Canada's bar against Native participation in the political process. The issue was more complicated in Canada than in the United States, he explained, because Indians were not citizens in the United States, whereas in Canada, Indians were British subjects. At the same time, he pointed out, there was no constraint in the British North America Act comparable to the Fifteenth Amendment of the U.S. Constitution to prevent Canada from denying the vote to citizens born there based on race or color.[33]

Because B.C. courts had seen the guarantee of political rights in Canada's Naturalization Act as a "stumbling block" to excluding Asian males from the franchise, Eberts instructed the London barrister to base his argument instead on the U.S. legal principles used to justify the denial of political rights to women in that country. Ignoring the irrelevance of the U.S. Constitution to legal questions arising in Canada, Eberts pointed to a discussion of Article IV of the U.S. Constitution in an American legal treatise to argue that the "political rights" referred to in Canada's Naturalization Act did not necessarily include the right to vote. This, Eberts suggested, quoting selectively from the text on which he relied, was "evident from the fact that [the vote is] always withheld from minors, and almost without exception from women." The key to silencing the political voice of Asian males, Eberts argued in effect, was to relegate them to the same political status as women and children.[34]

On December 17, 1901, the Privy Council reversed the decisions of the B.C. courts and upheld the discriminatory provisions of the Provincial Voters Act. Apparently unable to find any precedent in Canada or any other British Commonwealth nation for its conclusion that political rights did not necessarily include the right to vote, the Privy Council turned instead to a source of law it normally would not have considered binding or even persuasive: an edition of a U.S. legal treatise, *Lawrence's Wheaton*, published during the Civil War.[35] Brushing aside the fundamental differences in the constitutional structure of Canada and the United States as Eberts had, the Privy Council extracted a sentence from the outdated American lawbook, taking it out of context and using it as the only direct precedent cited for its conclusion that the reference to political rights in Canada's Naturalization Act did not necessarily entitle naturalized citizens to vote in any given Canadian province: although "(in the United States) the power of naturalization is nominally exclusive in the Federal Government, its operation in the most important particulars, especially as to the right of suffrage, is made to depend on the local constitution and laws."[36]

Not only did the Privy Council fail to explain why Canadian law would follow U.S. law in this regard, but it also ignored the origin of the doctrine it invoked: in the need to accommodate the demands of slave states to preserve local control over the attributes of citizenship in order to maintain racial boundaries.[37] The Privy Council also disregarded the larger point in *Lawrence's Wheaton*: that although individual states retained the practical power to define voter qualifications, any such qualifications "must apply equally to all classes of citizens in the State, whether native or naturalized." If individual states had the power to "disenfranchise naturalized citizens," it was explained in the lawbook, "the federal power of naturalization" would, in effect, be nullified.[38] By failing to qualify the language it adopted as in *Lawrence's Wheaton,* the Privy Council not only grafted onto Canadian law doctrine developed in the context of the slave-based social and economic system of the pre–Civil War United States but expanded on that doctrine. As a result, its decision to uphold the discriminatory provisions of B.C.'s Provincial Voters Act etched into Canadian law a racial divide directly related to, and as deep as, that historically interposed between blacks and whites in the United States.

Notwithstanding Canada's insistence on its own identity as distinct from that of the United States, B.C. citizens readily tolerated the Privy Council's decision because they, too, were ready to assume a mantle of whiteness and establish what Chief Justice McColl recognized as a kind of caste system premised on the existence of two separate tiers of naturalized male citizens divided by race. The extent to which white B.C. residents saw a parallel between the racial divide in the antebellum South and their own efforts to differentiate themselves from Asian immigrants, and to limit Asian males' participation in the political process, is suggested by the publication of an article entitled "Uncle Tom's Cabin Is Now Designated a Criminal Mistake" by the *Vancouver Daily Province* on January 23, 1901, just as Chief Justice McColl's decision was being appealed to the B.C. Supreme Court. Claiming that former slaves were "far happier under slavery" than after the Civil War, the article insisted that those familiar with conditions in the South believed that the "enfranchising of the Negro," in particular, had been a "tremendous blunder."[39] The editors of the *Daily Province* seemed to suggest by publishing the article that Canada should not make a similar mistake by permitting people of Asian ancestry to vote.

Although the Japanese consul in Vancouver had dismissed Homma as undeserving of support because he had turned his back on his status as a Japanese subject, the Meiji government was humiliated by the Privy Council's decision because it marked Japanese as inherently unequal. The significance that the Meiji government assigned to the Privy Council's denial of the franchise to British subjects of Japanese ancestry in British Columbia is suggested by the care taken by the Japanese minister to

Brazil in 1910 to obtain that government's assurance that Japanese who settled in Brazil would have access to the franchise when they were admitted to citizenship. Japan did not allow its nationals to emigrate to Brazil until Brazil agreed.[40] That Japanese Canadians also continued to perceive the denial of the franchise as deeply humiliating during the decades that followed is reflected by the headline chosen half a century later by the *New Canadian*—an English-language newspaper for second-generation Japanese immigrants (*nisei*)—to announce that the franchise had finally been extended to Japanese Canadians in British Columbia. At last, it declared, the "stigma of second class citizenship" had been removed.[41]

DEFINING WHITENESS: THE *OZAWA* CASE

Although the Fourteenth and Fifteenth Amendments guaranteed citizenship and the right to vote to children born in the United States, regardless of race or color, during the early years of the twentieth century a growing number of courts began to hold that first-generation Asian immigrants were excluded from citizenship on the ground that they were not "free white persons" within the intended meaning of the Naturalization Act of 1790. Takao Ozawa, who had been born in Japan in 1875 and who had arrived in the United States in 1894, applied for citizenship in 1914 based on the 1906 version of the Naturalization Act, which appeared to establish a uniform set of criteria for naturalization regardless of race or national origin.[42] Like Homma, Ozawa understood the denial of access to the full rights of citizenship to be a marker of inferior status.

Ozawa and his supporters presented a range of arguments to the various courts before which he appeared, some of which sought to counter the racial divide by urging the courts to distinguish among applicants for citizenship based not on race but on caste.[43] Among the cases submitted to the U.S. District Court and incorporated into the court record in Hawaii, for example, was one that expressly invoked high-caste status as a way to determine whiteness. The case in question was a decision by a Los Angeles Superior Court judge on May 7, 1914, which admitted to citizenship a person born in India based on the court's acceptance of the petitioner's argument that "a Hindu of the Brahman caste is more likely to be pure Caucasian than one of any other caste." Based on this conclusion, the court carved out a caste-based exception to existing

law for those who could show that they were Brahmans, expressly
excluding the remaining castes—the "Kshetriya, Vaisya, Sudra" and
"what are sometimes spoken of as the fifth caste, the outcastes." If an
immigrant from India was unable to convince a court that he was a
Brahman, the judge wrote, his citizenship application should be "unhesi-
tatingly denied." If he was able to prove that he was of the Brahman caste,
however, that was to be taken as evidence that the applicant was "white"
and eligible for naturalization.[44] Also among the cases submitted to the
Hawaiian district court was one in which mibun was expressly raised in
the context of a Japanese immigrant's application for citizenship. In 1905,
Masuji Miyakawa had invoked his formal social status (*shizoku*)—he was
of samurai ancestry—in a citizenship application filed in Indiana, and
indicated his willingness to "expressly renounce such title of nobility" in
Japan if he was admitted to citizenship in the United States. Although the
judge who granted his petition did not make specific reference to his
status, he did conclude that Miyakawa was a man of "good moral character."[45] Ozawa and his supporters argued by implication that high caste
or high status should be a relevant factor in determining whether an individual qualified for naturalization. Ozawa even invoked a founding father:
James Madison, he said, wished to "induce the worthy of mankind to
come" and himself "opposed admitting the *out-cast* of Europe."[46]

In response to prior decisions that had held that "Mongolians" were
inadmissible to citizenship, Ozawa's supporters also tried to problemetize
the way this term was defined, arguing that Japanese qualified for citizenship based on their similarity to Hungarians and Finns. Hungarians and
Finns, they contended, were "as Mongolian as Japanese [and] have been
freely admitted to our citizenship."[47] This argument they may well have
borrowed from Kawakami, who had argued in 1914 that the United States
admitted "Hungarians to citizenship, yet their ancestors were pure
Mongolians, and many of the Russians have far more Mongolian blood
than the Japanese."[48] This similarity, Ozawa's supporters suggested,
meant that Japanese should be permitted to apply for naturalization.

The U.S. District Court in Hawaii, unpersuaded by these or any other
arguments, denied Ozawa's petition for naturalization. Ozawa appealed
its decision to the Ninth Circuit Court of Appeals, writing two of his briefs
himself and adding an appeal based on the role the United States had
played in inducing Japan to open itself to the West. "What will the United

States gain by humiliating Japanese whom our Uncle Sam assisted to become one of the five great Powers?" Why, he asked in effect, would a mentor turn its back on a pupil that had worked so hard to remake itself in the image of that mentor? Ozawa also joined a growing chorus warning against the continued humiliation of Japan on race-based grounds for fear that this would only serve the purposes of those inclined toward war with the United States. Continuing to deny Japanese access to citizenship, Ozawa argued, would "create bitter feeling in the minds of Japanese against the United States [and the] European Race ... transforming a good friend into [an] enemy." If the United States persisted in discriminating against Japanese, "the final result will be the greatest war between the European and Asiatic people."[49]

Only after the Ninth Circuit Court of Appeals certified Ozawa's appeal to the U.S. Supreme Court in 1917 did Japanese immigrant associations in the United States seize on his case to challenge the denial of citizenship to the issei. The wisdom of their decision and the suitability of Ozawa's case as a vehicle for that challenge were vigorously debated in the Japanese immigrant press. As in Homma's case, many within the Japanese immigrant community advised against pursuing a direct challenge to U.S. naturalization policy, fearing to aggravate government officials. Japanese diplomats, concerned that a challenge would also inflame anti-Japanese sentiment and undermine Japan's long-term goal of securing the approval of Western nations, likewise urged Ozawa and his supporters to abandon the case. But Ozawa refused, dismissing such concerns as expressions of cowardice and lack of resolve.[50]

The key issue when the Ozawa case reached the U.S. Supreme Court was whether, in 1790, the reference to "free white person" in the Naturalization Act was meant to be read broadly to exclude only persons of Native and African descent or meant to be read narrowly to include only those who were "white."[51] Ozawa argued, first, that the phrase "free white person" should be broadly construed, but that if it were not broadly construed, Japanese were "white" within the meaning of the act. In arguing the latter point, Ozawa attempted to convince the Supreme Court that Japanese were not Mongolian. Having failed to prevail on the argument that Japanese were akin to Finns or Hungarians before the lower court, Ozawa relied instead on the popular ethnological belief of the time that Japanese were descended in part from the Ainu—categorized as a

Caucasoid race—who had been displaced to Hokkaido by migrants from Southeast Asia during prehistoric times.[52]

When the U.S. Supreme Court handed down its decision in 1922, it conceded that Ozawa was "well qualified by character and education for citizenship," but it rejected both his argument that the reference to "free white person" in the Naturalization Act was intended to be broadly construed and his argument that even if were narrowly construed, Japanese should be included in the category "white."[53] "The provision is not that Negroes and Indians shall be *excluded*," the Court declared, "but it is, in effect, that only free white persons shall be *included*." The Court observed that the applicable standard of review required it to assign the words of the act their "natural significance" in order to give effect to the intent of Congress. It also conceded that it was likely that "these two races were alone thought of as being excluded" by the authors of the act in 1790. But because that reading led to what the Court regarded as an "unreasonable result," it articulated a higher standard, which it declared Ozawa had failed to meet. It did not matter to the Court that the drafters of the act did not "have it in mind" to exclude "the brown or yellow races of Asia" from the right of naturalization. To prevail, Ozawa would have had to show that "had these particular races been suggested, the language of the act would have been so varied as to include them within its privileges." The Court, in other words, imposed an almost impossible burden on Ozawa, requiring him to prove that if the question of whether persons of Asian ancestry were eligible for citizenship had been raised in 1790— unlikely because there were relatively few Asians within the boundaries of the United States at that time—the authors of the act would have revised it to make explicit reference to Asians. If those who drafted the act had intended that only blacks and Natives be excluded from citizenship, the Court added for good measure, that merely demonstrated their general lack of "ethnological knowledge" and "their lack of sufficient information" about Asian races."[54]

The Supreme Court also rejected Ozawa's alternative argument that even if the reference to free white persons was narrowly construed, persons of Japanese ancestry should be treated as "white" for purposes of the act. Here the Court ignored its stated purpose—to discern the intent of those who drafted the act—and instead relied on a series of state and federal cases, most of them decided more than a century after the

Naturalization Act was passed in 1790. Based on those cases, the Court held that a "white person" could only be "a person of what is popularly known as the Caucasian race." Admitting that a "test afforded by mere color of the skin" would result in "a confused overlapping of races and a gradual merging of one into the other, without any practical line of separation," because there was such a broad range of skin color among people of various races, Justice George Sutherland, writing for the majority, believed he had simplified matters by defining "white" as "Caucasian."[55] Like the British Privy Council before it, the U.S. Supreme Court concluded its opinion by denying its own racial bias: "We have no function in the matter other than to ascertain the will of Congress and to declare it. Of course there is not implied—either in the legislation or in our interpretation of it—any suggestion of individual unworthiness or racial inferiority."[56]

In fact, by not only denying to issei the ability to become naturalized citizens but also implicitly condoning the alien land laws passed in California and a number of other western states beginning in 1913 that made it illegal for aliens ineligible for citizenship to own land, the U.S. Supreme Court endorsed the establishment of what Chief Justice McColl would have recognized as a new kind of caste system in the U.S. West based on two separate tiers of noncitizen male residents.[57] What made it impossible for issei to own or lease land under the alien land acts was not their noncitizenship—other noncitizens were allowed to own or lease land even if they chose not to become U.S. citizens—but their ineligibility for citizenship. Japanese, one immigrant in California declared, had been "materially and spiritually ... sentenced to death by the land law."[58] By establishing a direct link between their ineligibility for citizenship and their inability to own or lease land, the states that adopted alien land laws used their status as aliens ineligible for citizenship to shape the urban, agricultural, and industrial landscape in ways intended to ensure that the issei were relegated to the social and economic margins of American society. Ironically, the mechanism paralleled similar practices historically used to maintain caste boundaries in Tokugawa Japan, where, as we saw, members of outcaste communities had often been relegated to lands outside the boundaries of majority communities and the presence of the communities had been erased on official government maps. In much the same way that ordinary Japanese had historically constructed their status as citizens and subjects against that of outcastes in Japan, white North Americans in both the United States and Canada used restrictions on the full rights of citizenship and alien land laws or other legal constraints to establish themselves as full citizens and Japanese and other Asian immigrants as "other."

In the wake of the *Homma* and *Ozawa* decisions, which had etched existing legal barriers more deeply still onto the social, political, and economic landscapes of Canada and the United States, some Japanese immigrants reconsidered their options within an ever more complicated network of constraint and opportunity. Immigrants who had left Japan to escape the still-rigid status constraints of Meiji society moved yet again to avoid the race-based constraints imposed by both nations. In the United States, some moved to other states to avoid the impact of alien land laws. Riichi Satow, for one, left California for Oregon after passage of California's first alien land law in 1913, and Kanichi Tsukamaki, frustrated by the fact that Washington's alien land law prevented him from buying the land he had worked for many years, moved to the Boise Valley in Idaho.[59] Shotaro Shimizu, who had landed in Seattle in 1909, left for Canada when he realized he would never be allowed to become a naturalized citizen in the United States.[60] The same was true of Takeshi Uyeyama's father, who settled in British Columbia because there he was able to become a naturalized British subject; he was denied the ability to vote but was able to own the land he worked. Uyeyama's uncle, in contrast, settled on the U.S. side of the border, where his children would be able to vote.[61] Other Japanese immigrants who had settled in Canada migrated to the United States because there they would be able to acquire a professional education or degrees denied them in British Columbia.[62] Still others returned to Japan permanently in reaction to the passage of exclusionary laws. Hanayo Inouye, for example, reported that the alien land law was a major factor in her father's decision to return to Japan after spending a substantial part of his life in North America.[63]

The need to move elsewhere to achieve their goals produced a new kind of transience that once again made Japanese vulnerable to claims by exclusionists that they did not have the same kind of commitment to settlement as European migrants did. Ignored by exclusionists, however, was the extent to which legal constraints in both nations produced that mobility. Exclusionary laws also reinforced the ties of Japanese

Successful Japanese farmer on his farm in Courtenay, B.C., circa 1918. (Cumberland Museum and Archives, C140.009. Hayashi/Kitamura/Matsubuchi Studio.)

Maikawa fish market, Vancouver, circa 1918. (Japanese Canadian National Museum and Archives, Maikawa Collection.)

immigrants to Japan on both a practical and an emotional level. The fear that their children faced an uncertain future in societies where race defined status encouraged return migration. It also persuaded issei with family in Japan to send at least one of their children to Japan to be educated in order to ensure that the family living abroad could be reintegrated into Japanese society if they were forced to return to Japan.[64] Because issei were denied access to citizenship in the United States, they were acutely aware that as foreign nationals, there was no guarantee that they would be allowed to remain in the United States, no matter how long they lived there. In Canada, in contrast, naturalized issei had some degree of assurance that they would be allowed to remain as long as they wished, but they understood that even though their children were British subjects, being barred from the political process in British Columbia, where most nikkeijin lived, made them vulnerable to the biases of the voting majority.[65]

During the decades after the *Homma* and *Ozawa* decisions, nikkeijin became more and more reluctant to turn to the courts to challenge exclusionary laws either in the United States or in Canada. Both cases ultimately served only to reinforce the racist legislation that Homma and Ozawa had hoped to defeat, and those who had warned against raising such issues in the courts appeared to have been proven right. Japanese immigrants in both countries focused on proving that they were capable of assimilating and that they were deserving of the full rights of citizenship. Demonstrating that Japanese immigrants were as capable as European immigrants of adapting to American and Canadian cultural norms became a key component of the effort to address the issue of the relative status of Japanese immigrants in North America. Japanese consuls repeatedly urged Japanese to adopt the practices of their non-Japanese neighbors in order to avoid attracting negative attention. In 1919, for example, Ukida Goji, the Japanese consul in Vancouver, traveled to Cumberland to speak to Japanese immigrants there about "Good Citizenship." To be good Japanese in Canada, he stated, was "to learn English Canadian laws and customs."[66] The best thing the Japanese can do," one issei told an interviewer in the 1920s, "is to act the part of good citizens, even though [we] may not actually become citizens." Japanese, another suggested, should not try to win the right to become citizens of the United States by challenging their exclusion in the courts but by "showing themselves worthy of citizenship."[67]

The focus of Japanese community leaders increasingly turned to performing citizenship. In Vancouver, a recently arrived immigrant couple, Suzuki Etsu and Tamura Toshiko, made it their goal to help "lower class" women unfamiliar with Western customs and manners by teaching them how to behave in ways that North Americans regarded as higher class; basically, their aim was to help the women rearticulate their status within the framework of North American societies.[68] Their efforts paralleled similar endeavors in the United States, where Japanese community leaders also tried to counter the claim made by exclusionists that the fact that immigrant women worked alongside their husbands was evidence that Japanese were less civilized than whites.[69] In North America, as in modernizing Japan, new kinds of gendered constraints were imposed on women who had assumed responsibility in the family workplace as well as in the home; traditionally they had worked side by side with their husbands in the rice fields or in the shops.[70] A mock advice column in Seattle's Taihoku Nippō wryly parodied the standards imposed on Japanese women by anti-Japanese forces and Japanese consular officials alike, satirizing the stereotyped gender ideal urged on them as part of a larger effort to demonstrate that Japanese were indeed deserving of full citizenship and mocking white women at the same time:

Item: There are telephones for use in ordering what you want from Furuya's or Hirade's. Don't be so foolish as to go in person to market, soiling your shoe soles and wearing out the borders of your skirts.

Item: Division of labor is a law of civilization. Send all of your washing to the laundry; never do any of it yourself. If you have time for such things, spend it in finding fault with Furuya's and Hirade's pickled radish.

Item: Husbands who have brought out brides from Japan must be careful to teach them nothing except walking hand-in-hand.[71]

Japanese immigrants in both the United States and Canada also endeavored to demonstrate their ties to their adopted countries in such public forums as parades and festivals, enacting the dual identities forced upon them by displaying the national flag—Stars and Stripes or Union Jack—as well as the Japanese flag at appropriate events.[72] Because Japanese parents believed that wearing dirty clothes fostered race-based discrimination (haiseki), they told their children to dress neatly in Western clothes and frowned on any behavior that might attract criticism by non-Japanese.[73] Still others turned to Christianity to demonstrate their capacity for assimilation.[74]

The tremendous efforts made by Japanese immigrants to demonstrate their ability to assimilate were responsive not only to criticism directed at them by white exclusionists but also to criticism from those in Japan who continued to blame not North Americans but the immigrants themselves for the existence of anti-Japanese prejudice. A writer for one Japanese newspaper argued in 1915 that "the preponderance of low class Japanese labourers abroad brings the race into bad odour, and this combined with the nationalism and non-assimilability of the Japanese character, provoke the foreign movements for the ostracism of Japanese immigrants."[75] In North America, Stanford professor Yamato Ichihashi concurred, complaining that "our so-called representative Japanese here are far below the accepted social standard, and in my humble opinion many years must be consumed before they can attain that social standard."[76] Restriction on the entry of "low-class" immigrants, some nikkeijin themselves believed, would in time resolve the problem. "As the immigration of the less desirable Japanese is already restricted," one issei in Seattle declared in the 1920s, "after a time there will be here only those Japanese who have been born in this country and the better class of foreign-born Japanese." This, he explained, would result in an improvement in race relations.

In adopting this approach, Japanese immigrants, in effect, accepted the judgment of those who discriminated against them. The strategy reflected the assumptions that had determined attitudes toward members of outcaste groups in Japan for centuries: those discriminated against were responsible for the prejudice directed at them, and they bore the burden of proving that the prejudice was undeserved. As *Ozawa* demonstrated, however, although white exclusionists criticized Japanese immigrants as inassimilable and incapable of responsible citizenship, that was never the real issue. Rather, as California's senator James D. Phelan—to whom B.C. legislators also turned for ideas and advice on how to implement anti-Japanese policy—made clear, the issue was always one of race. It was imperative that a racial divide be maintained, he argued to a U.S. Senate committee in 1924, precisely because Japanese immigrants might well prove to be responsible citizens who used the rights extended to them effectively. The continued denial of access to citizenship to first-generation Japanese immigrants, Phelan insisted, was critical in maintaining that divide. To concede racial equality and allow Japanese immigrants "to enjoy the elective franchise just as the Europeans," he warned, would make it possible for them to defeat "all our protective legislation" through their exercise of the franchise.[77] Race, in short, and not any asserted ability to assimilate, was always the real issue. Consequently, all efforts to prove that Japanese immigrants were worthy of citizenship fell on deaf ears.

CHAPTER EIGHT

Reframing Community and Policing Marriage

IN MAY 1928, the *Japanese-American Courier* in Seattle published a front-page article entitled "Forget Caste and Status According to Occupation."[1] Given the race-based constraints that limited the employment opportunities available to second-generation Japanese (nisei) living in the area, K. Hirade, a local Japanese American merchant, implored issei parents not to insist that their children restrict their studies to preparing for white-collar jobs. He stopped short of urging the issei to allow their children to become shoemakers or shoe repairers, but he did say that Seattle needed workers besides "teachers, engineers, doctors and businessmen." The double burden of race and caste prejudice left the nisei with too few employment options, he believed. As long as nisei did not limit the kinds of jobs they were willing to take based on historical caste associations, however, lucrative opportunities were available to them despite the racist barriers posed to entry into the professions. Given the cultural familiarity of the nisei with North American society, including their ability to converse in English, a carpenter's apprentice could supplement his skills with a technical education that would allow him to become a major contractor. By accepting an entry-level position in a field historically regarded as low in status in Japanese society—as an artisan or a merchant—but building on those skills and developing the business in ways appropriate to the North American context, a young nisei man could not only transform a low-status occupation into a higher-status position but could transcend the restraints on opportunity imposed by white racism. Nikkeijin, Hirade said, would be best served by reframing their perceptions of what specific occupations represented in terms of social status. "Forget the old idea of caste and social position according to occupation," he declared, "and enter upon ventures with an eye to the future."[2]

Hirade's passionate plea for nikkeijin not to allow old associations between craft and mibun to remain barriers to their advancement in North America shows that the historical connection between occupation and social status persisted into the 1920s. The continued resonance of the status categories utilized during the Tokugawa era to explain and identify difference was also reflected in a continuing reluctance to permit family members to marry those whose lineage they thought might taint the family line. Because caste-based differences were thought to inhere in the blood, the question of whether a prospective marriage partner had ancestral ties to an outcaste community in Japan was a matter of particular concern.[3] Sociologists and anthropologists have observed that prohibitions on intermarriage with members of outcaste groups are an important mechanism utilized in caste-based societies to maintain caste boundaries. Even after the Second World War, Hugh Smythe reported in 1952, intermarriage between ordinary Japanese and burakumin remained taboo in Japan.[4] Much the same was true of prewar Japanese immigrant communities in the North American West. It was a "common practice among Issei," Karl Yoneda explained in a 1965 letter, "that the groom's side would always inquire quietly whether the prospective bride came from an Eta family" before allowing a marriage to take place.[5] An elderly nisei woman in Canada likewise described the care with which her father questioned any young man she dated to ensure that his parents did not have ancestral ties to what he also referred to as "eta" communities.[6]

Even an individual willing to violate social taboos by marrying across caste boundaries might be inhibited by the knowledge that the consequences would be visited on his or her entire family. The impact of intermarriage is reflected in the statement of a buraku woman in Japan in 1923: "My husband is a man of the common people. His older brother's son wants to marry. If it becomes known that I am an Eta no girl will wed him. Therefore my husband says I must be separated from him forever."[7] In nikkei communities as well, one scholar concluded, "the breakup of a proposed mixed marriage" remained a typical form of outcaste rejection as late as the 1960s.[8]

In North America, as in Japan, go-betweens (*baishakunin*) played an important role in conducting the inquiries necessary to determine the ancestral ties of potential marriage partners. Because a prospective bride often came from the same area in Japan as the man to whom she was engaged, her status (mibun) was generally already known to the family. Even where that was not the case, Cullen Tadao Hayashida observes, family registration records (koseki) ensured that most intercaste marriages were readily detectable and thus avoidable.[9] Inquiries regarding mibun were also facilitated by the prefectural associations (*kenjinkai*) established after immigrants arrived in Canada and the United States, which assisted in obtaining the information needed to ensure that caste boundaries were not crossed.[10] The requirement that Japanese in North America register with local consular officials, originally imposed in response to a request by the U.S. government to secure compliance with the Gentlemen's Agreement, also proved to be of assistance in determining the status background of potential marriage partners.[11] A practice intended to maintain racial boundaries in the North American West, paradoxically, also helped to maintain historical caste and status barriers specific to Japan.

The persistent concern with ensuring that the family lineage not be tainted by impure blood was reflected not only in a desire to avoid marriage across historical caste and status boundaries but also in a reluctance to marry into families in which any member, however distant, had contracted a disease thought to inhere in the blood, including leprosy, tuberculosis, mental illness, and venereal disease. Families investigated the medical history of prospective marriage partners and their extended families to determine whether such risks were present. Physical deformities were also suspect even when they were known to be the result of accidents. Families with a member who had contracted tuberculosis went to great lengths to avoid the stigma associated with that disease. One nisei woman reported that some families hid those who contracted tuberculosis rather than send them to a hospital in the hope that their illness would not become public knowledge. The failure to seek treatment for the affected family member made it more likely, of course, that the disease would spread to others in the family, reinforcing the belief that a tendency to contract tuberculosis was a product of tainted blood and impure lineage. Even when a disease did not spread, the knowledge that a family was hiding someone ill with tuberculosis or another dread disease made marriage even to a family member who was not ill taboo.[12]

The focus on blood purity that made many issei reluctant to allow marriage across historical caste boundaries or with families thought to be prone to disease was also reflected in a reluctance to allow intermarriage with people of other races. Where marriage to whites (hakujin) was concerned, concerns about blood purity were also sometimes compounded by the resentment that many immigrants felt in response to the racial hostility they encountered in the North American West and the prejudice they feared the children of any such union would face within and without Japanese immigrant communities.[13] It was "unthinkable," Iyenaga and Sato declared in 1921, "that the Japanese should begin wholesale intermarriages with Americans in the near future, to the extent of losing their racial distinction," given the "social stigma" the couples and their children would face on either side of that racial boundary.[14] Although there were exceptions to this general reluctance, from the time Japanese first arrived in North America issei and nisei who married across racial lines ran the risk of being ostracized by Japanese immigrants and others. The young son of a Japanese man and a Mexican woman born in southern California in 1910, for example, was regarded as "practically an outcast" by members of both communities.[15]

To challenge community proscriptions against intercaste or interracial marriages was to put one's own status within the nikkei community at risk. Muriel Kitagawa, a nisei born in Vancouver in 1912, for example, later recalled a marriage "against all old traditions, against family preferences, against social mores." A "hakujin [white] minister" presided over the ceremony, presumably because he was not concerned about or unaware of the taboos being broken. The bride's mother was warned by a "leading member of respectable society" that "to recognize that marriage was to incur the displeasure of decent people." Confronted by Kitagawa about her refusal to recognize the marriage, the bride's mother agreed to send a gift to the groom's parents, but gave it to Kitagawa to deliver so that others would not know and so that she would not be ostracized or made the subject of gossip. Ostracism and gossip were both historically important ways of sanctioning individuals who violated social taboos in Tokugawa- and Meiji-era Japanese society.[16]

The social stigma associated with sanctions for a proscribed marriage or other transgressions extended beyond the transgressor and through time to include his or her entire family and descendants. Maryka Omatsu, a Japanese Canadian lawyer and activist writing in the 1990s, described her mother's anxiety when someone they had hired to do repairs around the house was the subject of rumors that a member of his family had been a thief a century earlier.[17] But in North America the second generation did not always accept the dictates of their elders. A young nisei couple from Cumberland, B.C., eloped after the groom's family forbade the marriage. The reason? The family had purportedly learned that members of the bride's extended family in Japan had tuberculosis.[18] In the recontextualized communities in which Japanese immigrants lived in the North American West, social taboos also sometimes canceled each other out. Roy Kiyooka reports, for example, that a young woman with a family history of tuberculosis in Japan agreed to emigrate and to marry a coal miner in Duncan, B.C., whom she would otherwise never have been allowed to marry, because it was her only hope of finding a husband given her family's medical history.[19]

Historical status distinctions continued to order interpersonal relationships in North America to at least some degree. Based on her anthropological study of one emigrant village in Japan, for example, Audrey Lynn Kobayashi reports that "social networks occurring at the neighborhood level in Japan were extended to Canada, and … these networks were further differentiated according to kinship, age groups, social class within the village hierarchy, and temple affiliation."[20] In North America, however, the goal of maintaining caste boundaries in a far more fluid and complex social and economic environment complicated by race was not always perfectly realized, especially because preexisting status relationships that depended in part on spatial segregation and visible markers could be only imperfectly reproduced. "I heard of the gradual mixing of the ancients' standards of caste until the peasant was elevated to riches and power, while the scion of the aristocracy became submerged into the grey anonymity of his misfortune," Kitagawa wrote. In North America, "family relationships and genealogy became more and more complicated, and there was a distinct tendency for certain families to marry amongst themselves, or to take new marriages unto themselves until the relationships resembled an intricate woven net, and one had to know them all to sort them out."[21] Some nisei eventually realized that their parents had secrets that were a product of historical ways of understanding difference. One such individual, describing the difficulties she encountered in researching her own family history, suspects that "a lot of *issei* women and men have secrets they don't want known, because social stigmas and class values were very strong."[22] Although not all children learned about historical caste divides from their parents, another nisei woman was aware of them because her father was a Meiji traditionalist. He had told her that many people called "eta" who lived in special villages in Japan had emigrated to Canada. To publicly identify such families as "eta," however, came to be considered taboo itself. Implicit in the proscription against publically identifying people in this category—as Hiroshi Ito also suggests in his study of a nikkei community in Florin, California—was the understanding that they had left Japan and immigrated to North America to begin a new life.[23]

Notwithstanding the prohibition against marriage across historical caste boundaries, then, the concurrent need to deal with the ramifications of white racism in the United States and Canada appears to have facilitated the integration of people who were the object of such prejudices into larger nikkei communities on a day-to-day basis. In North America, the conviction that all were entitled to make what they could of themselves had more resonance than in Japan, giving buraku jūmin and other low-status individuals opportunities to define themselves simply as Japanese—a task made easier in societies primarily concerned with race.

In some places high status, self-consciously maintained, could become as isolating a barrier as any other status issue, leading some Japanese immigrants to adopt what they regarded as low-class forms of speech to avoid being relegated to the margins of the communities in which they lived. Kitagawa reports, for example, that although her own family spoke the "refined language of the textbooks and polite society," the equivalent to "Oxford English, the King's English," they were forced "to drop the refinements, the polite phrases, and learn the colloquialisms, the blunt and vulgar speech of lower-class speech forms" in order "to keep from being called down as '*haikara*' [stuck-up] and too good for the neighbourhood."[24] Examples like this suggest that in at least some reconfigured Japanese communities in North America, members of what were historically identified as Japan's lower classes were able to exert a new kind of pressure that made high-status individuals vulnerable to social exclusion if they insisted on maintaining the traditional status divide in daily social interactions by not adopting more common ways of speech. Arguably, then, low-status individuals were able to establish a new framework for belonging in a public sphere. The ability to force those of higher status to conform in this way or to publically disavow knowledge of caste origins did not translate, however, into the private sphere, hence the difficulty that those identified as being of outcaste origin had in finding marriage partners.

Paradoxically, the reluctance to marry across racial lines, rooted though it was in Japanese historical and cultural concerns about the purity of a family's lineage, also served to reinforce the miscegenation laws passed in a number of U.S. states to prohibit marriage between whites and Asians.[25] Although miscegenation laws were never passed in Canada, the matter was periodically raised in the B.C. press and its legislature and represents yet another context in which B.C. legislators looked south for models they could use to maintain racial boundaries. Advocates of miscegenation laws labeled interracial marriages as unnatural, a characterization that would have been doubly offensive to nikkeijin to the extent that it paralleled the historical view of marriage across caste boundaries in Japan. A March 1909 article in the *British Columbian Weekly* declared, for example, that "intermarriage between native Americans and any European race is natural" but that "the union between a Caucasian and an Oriental is unnatural." Quoting from an article first published in California, the *British Columbian Weekly* warned its readers that if the number of Japanese immigrants was allowed to grow, the result would be a "race problem" as great as that faced by the United States. "The time to solve the negro problem was when the first shipload of slaves landed in the United States." And "the time to solve the Japanese problem is before it gets too big or too complex to be solved easily."[26]

At the same time that mechanisms associated with maintaining historical caste boundaries aided in the reinforcement of miscegenation laws, practices used to ascertain the ancestral ties of potential marriage partners were invoked by some defenders of the Japanese immigrant community to challenge the racist assumptions of U.S. immigration officials about Japanese women. As Kawakami explained in 1920, immigration officials who suspected Japanese women of being prostitutes could rest assured that they were not. Before a young woman was accepted into a family, the groom's parents would "spare no pains in inquiring into [her] character, social standing, family relations, genealogy, health and education." Photographs were exchanged, and marriages were arranged only if the "investigation prove[d] satisfactory." The brides arriving in the United States and Canada from Japan were of a status that precluded their becoming prostitutes, Kawakami implied, precisely because of the careful inquiries conducted by future in-laws to maintain caste boundaries and to avoid other taboos.[27]

The constraints imposed on the immigration of Japanese males under the terms of the Gentlemen's Agreements, taken together with provisions permitting immigrants to join family members who had already been admitted, meant that women who were the wives of immigrants already in the United States and Canada remained admissible. After 1908, male immigrants no longer outnumbered female immigrants. According to estimates, women comprised roughly two-thirds of those admitted after 1908.[28] Although the practice of sending for wives from home villages in Japan based on the exchange of letters and photographs was also one in which Europeans engaged, the legal constraints on immigration from Japan rendered Japanese vulnerable to claims that they were using the practice to evade those restrictions. "Picture marriage" (shashin kekkon) was the only option available to laborers who could not afford the time away from their jobs or the cost of passage for what was still a monthlong round trip to Japan.[29] It was also the only option for undocumented immigrants who had entered the United States covertly across the U.S.-Mexico border and were unable to obtain passports to return to Japan to find a bride.[30]

Goaded by anti-Japanese exclusionists, U.S. immigration officials fretted about the validity of shashin kekkon. They imposed a requirement that arriving wives undergo a second marriage ceremony consistent with North American custom and complained that no parallel condition was imposed in Canada.[31] In 1915, the Japanese Association of America in San Francisco hired Barnabas C. Haworth, a former translator for the U.S. Immigration Service who had helped to clarify the link between mibun and the occupation listed on Japanese passports in 1908, to explain Japanese marriage customs to immigration officers who had detained female immigrants. Under Japanese law, Haworth explained, it was not

Photograph sent to the prospective husband by a picture bride admitted into the United States at San Francisco in November 1915. (National Archives and Records Administration, San Francisco, RG 85, File 14835/2–18.)

the presence of a minister or a government official that validated the marriage, as in North America and Europe, but the transfer of the wife's name to the family register (koseki) of the groom.[32] Japan's ambassador also endeavored to persuade the U.S. government of the validity of shashin kekkon under Japanese law, explaining that marriage in Japan was an association between households and not an arrangement between individuals.[33] Because it was the act of registration and not the ceremony that determined the validity of the marriage, Japanese consular officials required each bride to bring with her, in addition to her passport, a certified copy of the family register (koseki tōhon) in which her marriage was recorded.[34]

U.S. immigration officials who believed that Japanese marriage practices were invalid because they did not require that both parties be present at the ceremony insinuated that picture marriages were fraudulent as well as invalid. Some used words such as "alleged husband" and "so-called wife" or—in one instance—"unbridled brides" to describe the parties to these marriages.[35] Others were more direct in voicing their allegations. An Oregon resident sent a handwritten note to U.S. immigration authorities saying that "picture brides, not being legally married, must be shipped back as concubines."[36] To counter such insinuations, the Imperial Embassy of Japan presented a statement to the U.S. Department of State in 1913 delineating the very stringent standards applied before a passport was issued to a picture bride and the care taken by consular officials, in cooperation with local Japanese associations, to ensure that "the characters, occupations and financial standing" of the men who wished to send for a wife were such that the consuls were satisfied that "those men are actually leading a respectable life." Class and status considerations cut both ways, the ambassador suggested. Not just women but prospective grooms were the object of careful investigation. "Laborers who live on wages are not looked upon with favor, irrespective of any high wages which they may receive, inasmuch as they are at any moment liable to be discharged from employment." Any man who tried to send for a picture bride, the ambassador added, was required also "to designate some persons of recognized standing" to "guarantee their capability and readiness of supporting their families."[37]

Some critics of the practice of picture marriage characterized the brides as the pitiable victims of conniving older men, a concern that was

Picture bride admitted into the United States after a hearing in San Francisco, November 1915, shown here with a daughter she was forced to leave behind in Japan. (National Archives and Records Administration, San Francisco, RG 85, File 14776/18–28.)

grounded not in racial animus but in a benevolent concern for the welfare of the young women, or so they insisted. In 1905, the *San Francisco Bulletin* reported that one young picture bride, presumably not met upon arrival by her older, indifferent husband, "sat in the dirty steerage and added her salt tears to the lapping of the salt waters of the bay above her." Only when a "good woman from the Presbyterian Mission found her" did she receive any support.[38] As was often the case with such reports, however, the *Bulletin*'s account was far from accurate. In this instance, U.S. immigration officials themselves conceded that they had refused to allow her to land because they regarded her as unmarried, and she was not permitted to rectify her single status by undergoing a second ceremony under California law because she was a minor unaccompanied by a guardian. Her husband, far from indifferent, had retained an attorney to try to obtain her release.[39] The young woman had been caught in the gap between three separate jurisdictional spaces, created by the U.S. federal government, which required remarriage; the state of California, which regarded her as too young to marry of her own volition; and Japan, which viewed her marriage as entirely valid insofar as it had been properly recorded in her husband's family register.

The remarriage requirement became a subject of considerable debate in nikkei communities in the United States. After the U.S. government withdrew its requirement that picture brides undergo a second marriage ceremony as a condition of entry, the Japanese Association of America, which had earlier expressed strong reservations about the requirement, became an advocate of voluntary remarriage. This, it urged, should be embraced as a "new and beautiful custom" that would demonstrate the couple's high moral standards to Americans, as well as their regard for American manners and customs.[40]

Voluntary remarriage may also have been seen as a way to address the problem of failed picture marriages. Despite the many efforts made by families to ensure that both partners were of similar status, which they assumed would ensure the success of the marriage, sometimes one or the other marriage partner had been misrepresented, and sometimes the newly arrived bride realized that she could not face marriage with the partner selected for her. Some picture brides eloped with men they met after they arrived. Notices offering a reward for the return of eloped couples (*kakeochi*) regularly appeared in local Japanese-language newspapers, adding to the aura of illegitimacy that already surrounded picture marriages in the minds of white North Americans.[41] As Yuji Ichioka explains, the "publication of kakeochi announcements and stories by the immigrant press was also a means of social control," intended to "expose persons who engaged in desertion to public shame." Members of Japanese associations "treated absconding couples as outcasts." "Branded as 'adulteresses' or 'immoral hussies,' " Ichioka wrote, "deserting women were ostracized and invariably forced to move to new locales." Moving away, however, did not always mean that the couple would avoid identification.[42] Determined to enforce moral standards and to eliminate one of the grounds on which Japanese immigrants were subject to criticism by exclusionists, members of local Japanese associations worked determinedly to locate eloped couples, unwilling to allow them simply to disappear.

To give Japanese Americans in Seattle the tools with which to refute the claims of white exclusionists, Ambassador Ishii Kikujirō spoke to them in 1919 about traditional Japanese marriages, describing them as superior to Western marriages and providing arguments his audience could use to respond to criticism of picture marriages. Ishii related marriage practices in Japan to historical status and caste categories, locating those married according to shashin kekkon firmly among Japan's mid-level status categories and equating North American customs with those purportedly practiced by low-status groups. In Japan, the ambassador asserted, "marriage by mutual consent" alone, and without family consent, was "illicit intercourse" and was "practiced only in the lowest class of society." Higher classes in Japan, according to Ishii, considered even the exchange of photographs "vulgar." The ambassador also compared Japanese wives with their American counterparts and found the latter wanting. Whereas Japanese wives were obedient and "chaste, gentle and submissive" in serving their husbands, North American wives were "generally willful and selfish in [their] conduct." Most American men were caught in the throes of "wife-calamity" and passed their lives in "inharmonious homes."[43]

Not all Japanese immigrants subscribed to the views espoused by Ishii. Among those who resisted his view of marriage was the author of a satirical article entitled "What Is an Obedient Woman?" published in Seattle's *Taihoku Nippō* in 1917. The author contested both the characterization of Japan's higher classes as more refined than Japan's lower classes and notions of what was desirable behavior in women, using Japan's pursuit of modernity and Western standards of civilization to invert traditional status and gender hierarchies. At once humorous and deeply sarcastic, the article is best quoted directly:

> The traditional "obedience" of Japanese women is due to "*Bushido*" or *Katsuobushi* [a pun using the word for dried fish flakes] or whatever they call it, with its swashbuckler men swaggering about with their man-killing 3ft. swords stuck in their girdles. The samurai were men of impulse, with underdeveloped mentality, controlling those about them with ... the power of the knife ... The gentleness and compliance of Japanese women is the result of the pride and violence of the men.
>
> By nature human rights and privileges belong to the individual and are equal for all. Hence there should be no such thing as obedience between husband and wife. The relation must be one of mutual agreement. The only conditions in which it is necessary for the woman to obey the man are (1) when the woman is more of a fool than the man (2) when the man is an old-fashioned ignoramus.
>
> Whoever insists today that the woman must obey the man is still swayed by the narrow-minded bigotry of an uncivilized age, applying the standards of the savage man to the modern civilized man. The Japanese man of today, the Japanese man whose head has appeared on the horizon of civilization, who knows that a flying machine can move even without rails, does not desire obedience from the woman. If a woman's attitude towards her husband is that of obedience that woman has disgraced her husband.

The author had little sympathy for those within the community who harshly judged those who abandoned their marriages to elope. "For a man and woman who have never seen each other and do not know each other to marry is like ordering a suit of western clothes without knowing the size. No wonder 99 out of 100 [marriages] are misfits."[44]

Meiji consular officials and local Japanese community leaders had urged male immigrants to obtain wives from Japan as a way of addressing

claims that prostitution was rampant in Japanese immigrant communities, only to find that picture marriages opened their communities to new
lines of attack by anti-Japanese exclusionists. The exclusionists not only
pointed to the immorality of elopements and claimed that picture brides
were prostitutes but also argued that picture marriages were being used
to undermine the limits imposed on immigration from Japan under the
Gentlemen's Agreements. In fact, the relative number of new immigrants from Japan—including picture brides—remained low.[45] Japan's
government nevertheless decided to take the initiative in agreeing to bar
the emigration of picture brides in the hope of forestalling any formal
legislation directed at its nationals. In adopting this strategy, it mirrored
its strategy in agreeing to the Gentlemen's Agreements in the first place.
Before the new Taishō government announced that it would issue no
more passports to picture brides, as it did in February 1920, however,
several Japanese associations in the United States had already acted on
the advice of Japanese consuls to voluntarily ban such marriages. The
Zaibei Nihonjinkai ("All-America" Japanese Association) in San Francisco
issued a voluntary ban in October 1919 after the San Francisco Chamber
of Commerce informed members that Americans regarded the practice
as "unnatural and queer." By using this phrasing, the notice reminded the
recipient association that the practice of shashin kekkon led others to
view Japanese immigrants in much the same way that outcastes had
historically been regarded in Japan.[46] Given the nature of the accusations
made in connection with picture marriages, the Japanese consul in San
Francisco urged that the practice be abandoned voluntarily, arguing that
doing so would significantly reduce anti-Japanese sentiment by undercut-
ting the arguments on which exclusionists relied: "Photograph marriage,
no matter how entirely proper and legal it may be, is looked upon by
Americans as an uncivilized custom, contrary to the good order of society.
Not only so, it is believed that by this strange form of marriage we are
attempting to evade the gentlemen's agreement. Therefore, if we Japanese
were to stop photograph marriage, one of the strongest reasons for the
anti-Japanese movement would be lost in my opinion."[47]

Reaction to the proposed ban within Japanese immigrant communities was far from uniform. The Central Japanese Association of Southern
California and the Tacoma Japanese Association, among others, argued
that Japanese immigrants should not voluntarily relinquish any rights

they retained under the Gentlemen's Agreements. In December 1919, however, the Japanese consul in Seattle issued just such a ban.[48] Kazuo Ito suggests that reaction to the voluntary bans among Japanese in the United States was divided along status lines. Based on the report of an elderly issei interviewed in the 1960s, Ito writes that "high class" Japanese tended to support the voluntary bans whereas "low class" Japanese generally opposed it. One reason for this, Ito suggests, may have been that picture marriage offered the only practical hope of finding a wife for laborers, who, furthermore, were subject to conscription if they returned to Japan for more than one month. The issue of voluntary bans also put local Japanese community leaders, who were dedicated to building permanent, family-based communities, at odds with Taishō consular officials, whose primary concern, like Meiji government authorities before them, continued to be the defense of Japan's status as a modern nation, which the perception that Japanese immigrants engaged in an "unnatural" and "uncivilized" practice necessarily undermined.[49]

By the 1920s, Japanese diplomats had grown more assertive in invoking comparisons between Japanese and Europeans and in mounting direct challenges to the inequitable treatment of Japanese immigrants. Although higher-status Japanese did not abandon the habit of distinguishing between themselves and "low-class" migrants, whom they blamed for anti-Japanese prejudice, the Japanese government itself began to realize that distinguishing among migrants by status was a failed strategy. The result was a shift in emphasis away from criticizing those considered low in status toward defending all its nationals abroad based on their shared identity as Japanese subjects regardless of mibun. To counter accusations that picture marriage was unnatural or unique to Japan, Japanese consular officials pointed out that Europeans also engaged in proxy marriages. In 1921 the Japanese consul in New York demanded that the Ellis Island immigration commissioner provide him with the number and country of origin of European women admitted during prior years as parties to proxy marriages.[50] Although U.S. authorities appear to have avoided any direct response to the consul's request, they admitted in internal correspondence that European women married by proxy had been granted admission to the United States from Spain, Italy, Portugal, and Latin America. By October 1930, the commissioner general of the U.S. Immigration Service was prepared to admit that it was "not inappropriate" to recognize that "Japan is not the only country whose laws permit the contraction of marriages while one of the contracting parties is residing in foreign jurisdiction."[51] Stanford professor Yamato Ichihashi argued passionately in a book released the following year that "'imported wives'" were "not an unknown phenomenon in American colonial history." Readers would be convinced of this, he wrote, if they looked at "The Marriage Mart" chapter in Agnes Repplier's *Mire Marie of the Ursulines,* also published in New York in 1931.[52]

Neither voluntary restrictions on picture marriage nor government concessions that proxy marriage was not unique to Japan satisfied those who criticized the practice. Japanese women, California senator James Phelan insisted, posed a greater danger than men did because they were able to bear children, to whom citizenship and all its attributes, including the ability to buy and lease land, could not be denied. It was by giving birth to a second generation, Phelan declared in a 1919 letter to the U.S. secretary of state, that Japanese immigrants "circumvent[ed] the law."[53] In 1924 he repeated his claims before a U.S. Senate committee. Because the Fourteenth and Fifteenth Amendments guaranteed children born in the United States the full rights of citizenship, he noted bitterly, the children would be able to "own land and enjoy elective franchise and destroy our ideals and institutions."[54] What made Japanese women an object of special concern, in other words, was not their vulnerability to unscrupulous men or any worry that shashin kekkon was an archaic and uncivilized custom but their ability to become wives and mothers. To allow the growth of second and third generations that could not be denied citizenship, Phelan declared, was to "invite a race problem more serious than that in the South."[55] In both the United States and Canada, arguments denouncing the immigration of women based on their ability to bear children were also linked to claims that Japan intended eventually to colonize the Pacific Coast. In 1921, for example, a booklet by V. S. McClatchy, first published in California in 1912, was reprinted and distributed in both California and British Columbia. The sole purpose of Japanese immigrant men in sending for wives, McClatchy declared, was " 'to beget as [sic] many children and secure much land' as the surest means for 'permanently establishing the Yamato race in this country.' "[56]

Notwithstanding the repeated efforts of the Japanese government to forestall comprehensive immigration legislation by the U.S. and

Mitsue Sasaki and Mr. Watanabe, circa 1925. (Japanese Canadian National Museum and Archives, Sasaki Collection.)

Canadian governments, and despite its 1921 agreement to restrict further emigration by picture brides, the U.S. Congress moved forward with plans to implement an immigration act, to take effect in 1924, that would replace previous agreements with Japan. Canada, which had renegotiated its Gentlemen's Agreement with Japan in 1923 to reduce the number of new male immigrants to be admitted to Canada from 400 to 150, moved in 1928 to restrict the number of women admitted each year to 75, and insisted that number was to be included in the 150-person total.[57] Japan's agreement to this proposal effectively put an end to the picture bride system in Canada. Because the Fourteenth and Fifteenth Amendments forced the United States to rearticulate a race-based bar to citizenship in terms of national origin and limited the bar to a single generation, the exclusion of picture brides was arguably all the more critical to sustaining the racialized caste system that it had allowed to develop in the West, the very foundations of which were threatened by the birth of a second generation who could vote and buy land. Canada—not subject to the same kind of constitutional constraints—was arguably willing to tolerate picture marriage to a degree because the birth of a second generation did not threaten the racialized political framework that it had erected: in British Columbia, where nearly 90 percent of Japanese Canadians lived, they, issei or nisei, were denied the vote.

CHAPTER NINE

The Rhetoric of Homogeneity

IN THE FACE OF CONTINUED EXCLUSION from full citizenship and social acceptance in both the United States and Canada, Japanese immigrants increasingly relied on a critique of white racism that involved characterizing their own communities as devoid of race-based divides like those that plagued North American societies. By insisting on the purported homogeneity of nikkei communities, nikkeijin were able to define themselves as morally superior to those who excluded them, even if their position in the racial hierarchies that ordered social relations in the United States and Canada was low. This rebuke of white racism also worked its way into the scholarly literature of the time. In a 1938 monograph entitled "Social Solidarity among the Japanese in Seattle," for example, Shotaro Frank Miyamoto declared that the immigrants had brought with them from Japan "a proud heritage of homogeneous culture."[1] The assertion that there were no divisive prejudices or social cleavages within nikkei communities has been subject to growing criticism in recent decades; still, it has been important in shaping the historiography of Japanese immigration in North America. As recently as 1991, David J. O'Brien and Stephen S. Fugita described Japanese as "among the most homogeneous people in the world, on both physical and cultural dimensions," a quality, they contended, that was also reflected in North American nikkei society.[2]

The rhetoric of homogeneity in North America was heavily reliant on a similar discourse in Japan, where "homogeneous" Japan was contrasted with racist North America. In 1914, for example, Okuma Shigenobu, one of the oligarchs who had guided Japan's successful efforts to modernize during the Meiji period, declared in a "message to America" that unlike the United States, Japan was "fortunately ... free from any racial or religious prejudices."[3] This Japanese critique of the United States was twofold. On the one hand, those who contrasted a racially divided United States with a purportedly homogeneous Japan argued that racism existed in the United States only because it had betrayed its own founding principles. On the other hand, they argued that it was the United States' historical tolerance of both indigenous people and immigrants that had weakened U.S. society and produced a racist reaction. This argument made some Japanese sound sympathetic to U.S. efforts to exclude Japanese immigrants. Terashima Seiichiro explained, for example, that "the strength of a nation is in proportion to the strength of its united forces; and the existence of such diverse races in America tends to constitute a weakness in her national unity." Contrasting a racially and ethnically divided United States with "homogeneous" Japan, he linked the racial and ethnic diversity he regarded as its great failing to its need to rely on immigration and to its short history as a nation: "Well, the Americans are not a homogenious [sic] people ... In 1648, the colonists number[ed] only 21,000. A large influx of immigration began in 1830. Since then, so many immigrants have come that American nationality has undergone a change. By the incoming of these aliens, the homogeneity of the community has been destroyed. America now comprises quite a number of small Italies, small Syrias, small Jerusalems, small—I need not mention any more. Many vortexes of nationality are whirling in the human sea of America."[4]

In North America as in Japan, proponents of the rhetoric of homogeneity used the formal abolition of outcaste status in Japan in 1871 to bolster their claims. As early as 1897, K. T. Takahashi had insisted that the absence of an "outcast" or "pauper" class in Japan demonstrated that the Japanese immigrants did not deserve to be the object of legal constraints like those imposed on the Chinese in Canada.[5] In 1923, Gertrude Haessler reported from Japan that she had heard many people assert that "there are no classes in Japan," although she observed an ongoing prejudice against those descended from former outcastes.[6] The abolition of outcaste status half a century earlier, in short, appears to have allowed those who chose to do so either to ignore caste prejudice or to pretend that because the formal legal category had been abolished, Japan had always been—or at least had become—homogeneous. Frequently repeated assertions that Japan had become a classless and homogeneous society obscured what one observer described as "actual diversity under a mask of uniformity."[7] Decades later, scholars continued to note that Japan "insists on a monoracial ideology and so defines away those who do not fit."[8] The same, in many respects, has been true of nikkei society in both the United States and Canada.

Among those who admitted that homogeneity was not the case was, interestingly, Fujii Chōjiro, a newspaper editor in Seattle who wrote about a series of rice riots he observed on a trip to Japan in 1918.[9] What had motivated the "shinheimin" (new commoners) identified by Japanese government officials as leaders of the revolts in a number of areas, Fujii wrote, was an explosion of pain and frustration resulting from the caste-based oppression that still defined most aspects of their daily lives. Japanese in North America were in a better position than those elsewhere to understand their reaction to being relegated to the margins of the communities in which they lived, he argued, because of their parallel experience with hakujin in the North American West. Although those designated as eta during the Tokugawa period were now officially ranked as commoners in Japan, society failed to treat them like other commoners; moreover, Fujii wrote, their designation as shinheimin meant that they could be readily identified and differentiated from other commoners. Shinheimin were treated as if "their bodies, their minds, their blood, their souls are stained and dirty." In a number of areas to which he had traveled, they were still not permitted to enter "ordinary" homes. No matter how intelligent or talented or warmhearted their sons and daughters were, society did not allow them to become teachers or civil servants. It was no exaggeration, Fujii declared, to say that they were denied all of the essential elements of a decent life: basic human regard, marriage, fame, and honor. Fujii concluded with a cautionary note. Because Japanese immigrants' experience of racial prejudice in North America gave them the capacity to understand the experience of social outcastes in a way that Japanese who had no exposure to white racism could not, Japanese abroad should take it upon themselves to warn Japan that it must reform in order to avoid the dire consequences that would otherwise be sure to follow, even as they warned the United States to reform its own discriminatory attitudes.[10]

Although this remark implied that Japanese immigrants in the United States and Canada might also be driven to revolt, Fujii added a caveat: Japanese had every right to be angry about the race-based discrimination they faced in North America, but if they were treated in a way they regarded as intolerable, they had no need to resort to violence. Instead, Japanese immigrants had the option of returning to Japan, where they not only would have the right to vote and access to the full rights of citizenship but could even aspire to improved status by seeking appointment to high positions. Even if returning to Japan meant the abandonment of the many efforts they had made to build new lives in the North American West, the alternative remained available, which meant, Fujii suggested, that Japanese immigrants did not pose the same kind of threat to the dominant society in the United States and Canada as the shinheimin might pose in Japan. Although racial prejudice might cut as deeply as caste prejudice, shinheimin had nowhere to live free of discrimination, which made their situation even crueler than that of Japanese immigrants contending with white racism in North America.[11]

Fujii was also concerned about the Japanese government's failure to adequately address the problem of continued prejudice against descendants of former outcastes in Japan for another reason. As long as the government tolerated the discriminatory conditions in which shinheimin in Japan continued to live, it lacked the moral authority to "utter one word of complaint about the way those of us here across the sea are persecuted and treated with contempt and discriminated against by these governments, these people, these societies, these laws."[12]

Although Fujii engaged in a vigorous critique of caste-based discrimination in Japan, he ignored the extent to which buraku jūmin were the object of discriminatory practices by other Japanese in North America. The most vocal prewar challenge to the portrayal of Japanese society in Japan or in the North American West as homogeneous came from a group of young men of outcaste ancestry who established an organization called the Suiheisha (Water Levelers Association) in 1922 to find ways to address the social problems that buraku jūmin in Japan continued to face.[13] Suiheisha activists, at the forefront of what they described as a buraku liberation movement, accused the U.S. government of hypocrisy because it endorsed anti-Japanese racism and passed exclusionary laws in violation of its own democratic principles. They also accused Japan's government of precisely the same kind of hypocrisy because of its failure to take meaningful steps to address the issue of caste-based discrimination in Japan. Suiheisha leaders seized on the resentment that all Japanese felt in response to the racially motivated exclusionary laws in North America to try to impress on Japanese both at home and abroad the importance of eliminating caste-based prejudice. Association members' experience of the pain of prejudice in Japan enabled them to understand the experience of racial discrimination, they said, and to challenge it in a way that other non-emigrant Japanese could not.[14]

White racism in North America, in other words, provided the Suiheisha with an ideological tool that they turned against Japanese who continued to discriminate against them. By invoking their dual status as victims of both white racism and caste-based discrimination, Suiheisha members argued for a redefinition of their own role in Japanese society.[15] Japan's ongoing desire to win recognition as a modern nation also allowed Suiheisha leaders to argue that they had a unique role to play on the world stage. The effort to reach a global audience, especially the North Americans and Europeans whose approval Japan had worked so hard to secure, was also reflected in their adoption of a flag displaying a crown of thorns to represent the suffering of their members. Their purpose was less to assert a special tie to Christianity than to invoke a cultural symbol that would be understood in the community of nations to which Japan had turned for approval.[16]

Less than a year after the Suiheisha was established in Japan, a small group of Japanese immigrants living in Los Angeles began publishing a small weekly newspaper which they named the *Suihei Jihō* (Water Levelers Times). An editorial in the introductory issue explained that it was the editors' intention to challenge caste- and race-based discrimination in Japan and North America.[17] As they pointed out, the very establishment of the *Suihei Jihō* highlighted a painful and profound contradiction: that there should be a need for a publication of this kind, given the United States' representation of itself as a beacon of liberty and human rights.[18] The Suiheisha had been established in Japan, the editors explained, to aid in the destruction of archaic customs that should be obsolete in a modernizing nation. And yet the experience of caste-based prejudice was not much different from the racial prejudice in the North American West. The only difference was that in the United States, not just some but all Japanese were treated "as if they were *tokushu burakumin* [special villagers]." Like burakumin, they wrote, Japanese immigrants in the United States were forced to endure insults intended to undermine their pride in themselves as a people. If conditions did not change, nikkeijin in North America would be rendered "unequal, hidden and obscured" by society there, much the way the ancestors of buraku jūmin had been in Japan.[19]

Although Japanese immigrants in the United States sometimes equated their situation with that of African Americans, the denial of the rights of citizenship, the editors of the *Suihei Jihō* argued, meant that they faced even harsher conditions. While blacks (kokujin) were also subject to social and economic discrimination on race-based grounds, they were at least entitled to U.S. citizenship.[20] But the prejudice that Japanese immigrants had to contend with in the United States was still not as harsh or unjust as that faced by buraku jūmin in Japan. After all, from the perspective of North Americans, Japanese immigrants were foreigners and of a different race, whereas burakumin in Japan not only were of the same race but shared place of birth and citizenship with those who discriminated against them.[21] This, the editors of the *Suihei Jihō* argued, made caste-based prejudice even more offensive and deserving of eradication than race-based discrimination. All Japanese living in North America, with their shared experience of racial discrimination, had a basis for understanding the impact of caste-based prejudice that Japanese who had not emigrated could not comprehend. Japanese living in North America were thus in a unique position to rally to the cause of the Suiheisha in Japan and to support its efforts to eradicate once and for all social prejudices rooted in now-obsolete Tokugawa-era status classifications.[22]

Suihei activists in the United States also urged Japanese immigrants living in North America to eradicate caste-based discrimination within their own communities. Reporters sent to investigate conditions in nikkei communities abroad on behalf of the Suiheisha reported that buraku jūmin living in the United States were discriminated against not only by white Americans on race-based grounds but also by other Japanese immigrants on caste-based grounds. One reporter urged Japanese abroad to address prejudices within their own communities even as they reacted with justified anger to white racism. Just to be sympathetic to those who were discriminated against was not enough, however. What was required was the complete eradication of archaic status distinctions—mibun—in all its forms.[23]

During the spring of 1924, the impending passage of a new immigration act by the U.S. Congress to bar further immigration from Japan threatened to undermine once and for all the efforts made by Japanese immigrants and Japanese diplomats alike to address the underlying causes of racial prejudice. In April 1924, while the bill was still under consideration, Ambassador Hanihara Masanao expressed the dismay that his government felt. The proposed legislation, he declared, was "mortifying," and its "manifest object" was nothing less than "to single out Japanese as a nation stigmatizing them as unworthy and undesirable in the eyes of the American people."[24] A cartoon published in one Japanese newspaper showed George Washington weeping as Uncle Sam knocked Japan to the ground; other cartoons urged Uncle Sam to "burn the vicious Bill."[25] Even in the United States, there were those who argued that passage of the bill would only upset the delicate diplomatic relationship with Japan and "defeat its own purpose" by "foster[ing] illegal immigration." "Only to glance at the extent of our Canadian and Mexican boundaries," the New York Post insisted, was enough to realize that barring Japanese would merely drive those who wanted to immigrate underground.[26]

Disregarding all such concerns, the U.S. Congress passed the Immigration Act of 1924. Although it did not expressly single out Japanese, the act effectively prohibited further immigration from Japan by denying admission to any "alien ineligible for citizenship." The restriction excluded all Japanese migrants except those who were temporary visitors, returning residents, or family members of immigrants already living in the United States.[27] The U.S. bar on Japanese immigration led to renewed demands by British Columbia legislators that the Dominion government reduce the number admitted to Canada further still. In 1928, faced with the prospect that Canada might pass exclusionary legislation similar to that of the United States, Tokyo reluctantly agreed to a limit of 150 persons per year, all but cutting off further emigration to Canada.[28] Japan, in its view, had been rendered an outcast nation, excluded from the community of nations that it had so long aspired to join as a member.

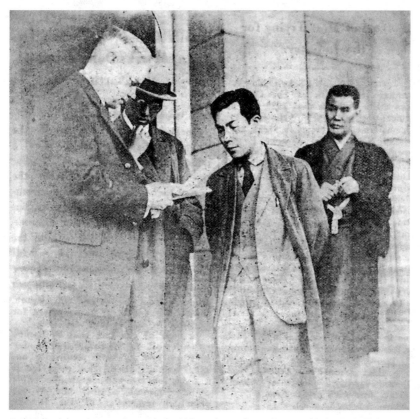

Suiheisha delegates meeting with the U.S. ambassador to Japan at his home in Tokyo, April 25, 1924. (*The Trans-Pacific*, 10 May 1924.)

Suihei activists on both sides of the Pacific responded to the Immigration Act by arguing that their experience of caste-based discrimination gave them the requisite moral authority to challenge its passage. On April 25, 1924, Suiheisha representatives called on the U.S. ambassador at his residence in Japan to request that he urge his government and the American people to reconsider the step they had taken.[29] They left a petition with him urging Americans not to betray their country's history as a leader in embracing liberty and human rights, first by declaring its own independence and later by freeing slaves.[30] Surely, they insisted, the nation that was the birthplace of "Honest Abe" did not really intend to endorse legislation that was the embodiment of "intentional and unreasonable discrimination."[31]

Others in Japan were also outraged by passage of the Immigration Act. The press denoted July 1, 1924, the day it took effect, "National Humiliation Day." So offensive did the Japanese people find the act, one Suiheisha observer wrote, that reaction in Japan to its passage was even more vehement than that which greeted the arrival of Admiral Perry's ships in the mid-nineteenth century, after which Japan was compelled to open its ports to Western nations.[32] In the midst of the "whirlpool" of anger and outrage, the three million Suiheisha members, who knew what it was like "to be treated like beasts," had a special responsibility to make their voices heard.[33] Suiheisha leaders, in other words, saw in the indigna-tion with which all Japanese responded to the act an opportunity to trans-form a history of persecution into a platform from which they could contribute to a cross-Pacific dialogue aimed at eradicating not just caste prejudice but also the racial prejudice directed against all Japanese. The shared need to confront racism in North America provided Suihei activ-ists on both sides of the Pacific with a basis for arguing that it was incum-bent on all Japanese to eradicate caste discrimination in order to effectively resist racist exclusion policies.

Suihei activists living in the United States also responded to the implementation of the Immigration Act with indignation, again accusing the Japanese and the U.S. governments of hypocrisy and noting bitterly that people in their position were outcastes in both countries, albeit on different grounds. As we saw earlier, one immigrant captured the senti-ment in a short poem: "In Japan, I am an outcaste. In America, I am an outcaste called 'Jap.'"[34] One Suihei activist amplified. "In the shallow thinking of commonplace people," he wrote, "America is a Christian country and the land of the free." Instead, although Japanese had long believed that U.S. laws and policies were based on moral principles, that was not the case. Nor, he charged, could Japan claim the moral high ground, because it continued to ignore the difficulties faced by those who were the object of caste-based discrimination.[35] Another Suihei activist argued further that Japanese had not succeeded in their fight against white racism precisely because of their failure to address caste-based prej-udice in their own communities. Only when it was eradicated, he insisted, would they have the moral authority necessary to effectively counter the racial discrimination they faced in the North American West.[36]

Conclusion

IN AUGUST 1965 the Japanese American Research Project asked the Japanese American labor leader Karl Yoneda to comment on a series of questions proposed for the Issei Oral History Survey, intended to capture memories of the prewar period. Yoneda said that several "important and vital" questions had been omitted, including questions about whether the first-generation immigrants had used illegal or extralegal means to enter the United States, such as "Did you have a passport? Did you jump from a ship? Did you enter from Mexico illegally?" Yoneda also urged that "Eta or Shinheimin" be included as the respondents' "social class" options. Although he recognized that every issei "will no doubt say that he was not from the Eta family," he insisted on at least tacit acknowledgment by the nikkei community that buraku jūmin were among those who immigrated to the North American West.[1]

The Japanese American Research Project adopted neither of Yoneda's recommendations. The final set of questions elicited no information about either outcaste ancestry or issues of illegal entry. The failure to include these questions demonstrates the continuing salience of concerns about outcaste status and illegality among Meiji-era Japanese immigrants a half-century after most had first arrived in North America. Descent from outcaste status in itself had the same kind of negative connotations as deliberate participation in illegal activity; knowledge of both was suppressed, erased, as contrary to the image of Japanese in North America that community leaders wished to portray.[2] Yoneda's observation that no issei would admit that he or she was descended from an "Eta" family, moreover, speaks to a perceived need to deny such ancestry in order to avoid the stigma that clearly continued to be associated with it, a stigma evident in Yoneda's own use of the pejorative term "*eta*."[3]

Although the erasures were partly an expression of historical caste bias, they were also always entangled in parallel efforts to respond to exclusionists' claims that Japanese were not deserving of inclusion in their adopted countries. The suppression of such counternarratives did not just spring from relations within immigrant communities but also engaged a series of larger debates about the meaning of modernity and civilization, the significance of race and status, and the place of Japan in an imperial world system. These erasures thus tell us a great deal about the way Japanese believed they had to position themselves within the hierarchies of nation and empire: as fully modern but lacking the flaws that undermined social relations in North America.

The status that Japan had achieved as an imperial nation in its own right allowed it to forestall, for just a few decades, legislation similar to that directed at the Chinese in both the United States and Canada. The Meiji government's vigorous defense of Japan's status as a civilized nation and its commitment to modernization gave it the power during the later decades of the nineteenth century and the early decades of the twentieth to force both countries to frame exclusionary policies in less overtly racist ways—to use more oblique language and more indirect legal forms like the Gentlemen's Agreements to give substance to similar discriminatory policies. Meiji officials pointed to Canada's subordinate status within the British empire in an effort to reach an accommodation regarding the admissibility of Japanese, who were citizens of an imperial nation themselves. At the same time, they invoked shared fears of an expanding U.S. empire to favorably position Japanese subjects in British Columbia. The tension between local concerns and the exigencies of empire was reflected in the province's defiance of both the Dominion government and impe-rial authorities, to the point where its very incorporation into the Canadian nation-state was called into question. That the exclusion of Asian immi-grants was also linked to the subjugation of indigenous peoples is demon-strated by Canadian fears that granting naturalized Canadians of Asian ancestry the vote would undermine the strictures put in place to ensure that indigenous peoples were barred from political participation and relegated to the margins of society.

Local, provincial, national, and imperial spaces in North America were interconnected in myriad ways to one another and to other places around the world. Not only did migrants transit one to reach another, but courts and legislators in Canada and the United States looked to one another, as well as to the far corners of the British empire, for models of exclusionary law. Whether it was British Columbia's reliance on legislation first passed by the colony of Natal, the British Privy Council's willingness to reach south across the Canada-U.S. border and back in time for pre–Civil War legal concepts, or U.S. legislators' practice of citing British Columbia's experience with Asian immigration to justify their own discriminatory actions, the parallel interest of each nation in constructing its own territory as "white" bound the United States and Canada to one another, and to other imperial spaces around the globe, in ways that both nations have at times been reluctant to acknowledge. Canada's willingness, given its common border with the United States, to acquiesce to the development of a coordinated body of exclusionary law and policy, together with its shared interest in constructing itself as "white," helped in turn to concentrate illegal immigration along the U.S.-Mexico border.

Although the efforts of both Canada and the United States to determine their national racial composition was concentrated on the boundaries that defined the limits of their power and their jurisdiction, national borders are also international borders, allowing migrants traveling through international space to access them in unanticipated ways. Migrants were aided in their efforts to evade the barriers that the United States and Canada sought to erect by private entities whose interest in commerce and the free movement of goods and labor across national borders diverged from those of the state. Both countries were further hampered in their efforts to racialize their borders by their wish to maintain economic and diplomatic ties with Japan and their own status as civilized nations. These dual goals forced them to create their borders not as absolute bars but as filters that allowed certain categories of goods and people access even as they excluded others. Only by securing the cooperation of the Meiji government was either government able to balance this set of mutually contradictory objectives.

Meiji officials were willing to accept the idea that the solution to anti-Japanese prejudice in Canada and the United States lay in accommodating the demands of these governments to restrict the movement of its subjects because their major objective was preserving Japan's status as a nation. The Meiji reforms were primarily concerned with creating the social and spatial mobility needed to facilitate industrialization and to win recognition that Japan was a modern nation; dramatic as they were, the reforms did not call into question the basic hierarchical worldview that had informed social relations during the Tokugawa period. Although Meiji diplomats tried to refract—bend to their own view—understandings of race and class, their efforts were undermined by persistent social and cultural biases rooted in Japan's own historical experience, which persuaded them that white racism was best explained by the status and behavior of Japanese emigrants. The worldview that had shaped the Tokugawa status system, as a result, came to be embedded in the diplomatic and legal framework within which Japanese migrants lived and worked, and were rendered legal or illegal, in the North American West. The Meiji government's policy of accommodating and even anticipating the demands of the U.S. and Canadian governments contributed, in turn, to creating the conditions that allowed both Western nations to mark Japanese subjects as excludable in some of the very ways Japan tried to avoid.

The efforts of the Meiji government to mollify anti-Japanese exclusionists by encouraging its subjects to behave in ways that would not attract criticism were undermined not only by the inherent contradictions in its own rhetorical approach but by the determined efforts of its own subjects to act on their own initiative in determining how best to reach their intended destinations. Repeated allegations of clandestine border crossings and fraudulent naturalization, even when not justified by actual numbers, were a powerful factor serving to reinforce underlying stereotypes that treated the Japanese presence in North America as illegitimate and threatened to taint all Japanese as excludable on that basis. Although many immigrants were committed to constructing their communities along lines that they believed would appeal to the dominant societies, others asserted a right to avoid or subvert laws—in Japan and North America—that they believed targeted people of their kind unjustly, whether their kind was defined in terms of race, class, mibun, or national origin. Some saw resorting to extralegal means as a legitimate way to challenge discriminatory legislation even as others feared that their actions would lead North Americans to equate all Japanese with outcastes. Including those too often dismissed as "illegals" in Japanese immigration histories enriches our understanding of the strategies used by immigrants to challenge racist legal barriers and challenges our assumptions about what it means to be "illegal" in the first instance. By analyzing the illegal or extralegal actions of Japanese and other immigrants within a strategic framework that also takes into account the justice or injustice of the laws being violated, a much more complex and dynamic picture emerges of the relationship between immigrants and the state. The suppression of knowledge of these strategies conceals key elements of the complex mix of obstacle and opportunity, vulnerability and power, that national borders represent.

Much as failure to consider the issue of illegality masks a larger and important dynamic, the erasure of buraku jūmin from Japanese immigration histories has obscured narratives—just as significant—that conflicted with those endorsed by Meiji diplomats and nurtured by exclusionists. By allowing exclusionists to focus on economic reasons for migration and endorsing their characterization of Japanese immigrants as less interested in freedom from Old World social constraints than European immigrants were, Meiji officials and others have facilitated the incorporation of a baseless distinction between Asians and Europeans into larger immigration histories. Relatively small though the numbers of buraku jūmin may have been, their presence among migrants illuminates and calls into question the strategies of power brokers in Meiji Japan and in the United States and Canada. Cultural perceptions associated with outcaste status likewise show us why the tactics employed by Meiji diplomats and immigrant community leaders often served to reinforce, rather than undermine, white racism and what the key elements of their rhetorical exchanges signified.

White North Americans used restrictions on the rights of citizenship to create themselves as full citizens as opposed to Japanese and other Asian immigrants in much the same way that higher-status Japanese constructed their own place in society as opposed to that of outcaste groups. Although race was the most prominent axis along which difference was organized in the North American West, mechanisms used to reinforce race-based social and economic barriers in both the United

States and Canada paralleled those used to reinforce caste barriers in Japan during the Tokugawa period, a fact that was not lost on Japanese migrants. In North America and in Japan, those who were the object of discrimination were barred from certain occupations, denied status as complete civic persons, and penalized if they engaged in marriage across race or caste boundaries. At the heart of both social systems as well was a desire to ensure that sufficient labor was available for jobs regarded as undesirable by the dominant societies. Space and movement, freely allowed or subject to constraint, were elements both in producing and marking difference and in breaking down categories of difference dependent on social, economic, and racial divides. Although old relationships dependent in part on spatial organization could not be reproduced in the same way in a new environment, cultural associations that were themselves a product of the Tokugawa status system eroded more slowly, complicating the exchanges that ensued and creating opportunities for inadvertent or expedient misunderstandings.

White racism helped to produce the claims to homogeneity developed to wrest the moral high ground from the dominant societies. On the one hand, the rhetoric of homogeneity helped to obscure from outside view the extent to which buraku jūmin were among those who had emigrated to the United States and Canada. The immigrants' reliance on the discourse of homogeneity as a strategy to counter the impact of white racism within their own communities, however, also forced them to tolerate, at least in public, those historically regarded as "other" in Japan, even as concerns about status and pollution continued to influence decisions related to family. Ironically, it was those who were themselves the object of discrimination in Japanese society who proved best able to see white racism for what it was. Impassioned critics though the buraku jūmin activists were of both caste- and race-based prejudice, however, they were ultimately unable to penetrate the still greater insistence on homogeneity within Japanese immigrant communities.

In the North American West, two distinctive ways of understanding difference intersected, shaping one another and creating multiple levels on which claims about the meaning of race and mibun were refracted both within and without Japanese immigrant communities. Those who participated in what became a cross-Pacific dialogue—Meiji diplomats, immigrants, white exclusionists, business owners, and U.S. and Canadian government representatives—appropriated the formulations of their opponents, as they understood or chose to characterize them, in crafting their own arguments regarding racial boundaries. None relied just on a static set of arguments in refuting others' claims. Instead, concepts rooted in separate ideologies of race and caste were remolded and reworked to respond to the exigencies of the moment. Although major elements of chauvinism and racism informed the arguments of all participants, the terms of the debate were never merely expressions of race or caste bias; they were far more nuanced constructs that endeavored to arrogate and appropriate their opponents' perspectives to render their own positions irrefutable. As a result, the bodies of law and diplomatic agreements that the dialogue produced, and that helped to define race relations in the North American West for the first half of the twentieth century, came to incorporate elements originating in two conceptually distinct cultures of exclusion.

Key Moments in Japanese Immigration History in North America to 1928

JAPAN	UNITED STATES	CANADA
Tokugawa period: 1600–1867 1853: Commodore Perry arrives	1863: Emancipation Proclamation 1865: Civil War ends	
Meiji period: 1868–1912 1868: Meiji Restoration	1868: Fourteenth Amendment 1870: Fifteenth Amendment	1867: Canadian Confederation
1871: Emancipation Edict (outcaste)	1870s: first Japanese immigrants and students arrive in the U.S.	1871: British Columbia joins Confederation

JAPAN	UNITED STATES	CANADA
1876: *samurai* privileges ended		
		1877: first immigrant from Japan arrives in British Columbia
	1882: Chinese Exclusion Act	
1885: bar lifted on labor emigration		1885: Chinese head tax
1890: Meiji Constitution		
1894–1895: Sino-Japanese War		1895: British Columbia Voters Act denies the vote to naturalized *nikkeijin*
1896: Emigrant Protection Law		
		1898: first of British Columbia's Natal Acts
1900: voluntary restriction of number of labor emigrants		
		1901: *Homma v. Cunningham*
1904–1905: Russo-Japanese War	1906: San Francisco school crisis	
	1907: Act of February 20	1907: Vancouver Riot
	1907: Order of March 14	
	1907–1908: Gentlemen's Agreement	1908: Gentlemen's Agreement (Hayashi-Lemieux Agreement)
		1908: *In re Nakane and Okazake* (striking down Natal Act)
1910: annexation of Korea		

(*continued*)

(Continued)

JAPAN	UNITED STATES	CANADA
Taishō period: 1912–1926		
1920: voluntary restriction of picture brides	**1913**: first Alien Land Law passed in California	
1922: Suiheisha established	**1922**: *Ozawa v. United States* upholds denial of citizenship to *issei*	**1923**: Gentlemen's Agreement amended to limit annual number of male labor immigrants to 150
Shōwa period: 1926–1989	**1924**: U.S. Immigration Act bars further immigration to the United States	**1928**: Gentlemen's Agreement amended to include women and children in 150 annual total

NOTES

ABBREVIATIONS

Braun Report, February   Report of Marcus Braun, U.S. Immigrant Inspector, 12 February 1907, RG 85, NARA.

Braun Report, June   Report of Marcus Braun, U.S. Immigrant Inspector, 10 June 1907, RG 85, NARA.

Canada, Sessional Paper No. 74b   Canada, *Sessional Papers 18, Fourth Session of the Tenth Parliament of the Dominion of Canada, Session 1907–1908, 7–8 Edward VII,* Sessional Paper No. 74b, A. 1909.

Comment on Braun Report   Commissioner General, Bureau of Immigration and Naturalization, *Digest of, and Comment Upon, Report of Immigrant Inspector Marcus Braun, Dated September 20, 1907,* 9 October 1907, RG 85, NARA.

Dillingham Commission Reports   *Reports of the Immigration Commission, Committee on Immigration, U.S. Senate, 61st Congress, Presented by Mr. Dillingham* (Washington, D.C.: Government Printing Office, 1911).

NARA   National Archives and Records Administration, Washington, D.C.

Report of the Royal Commission Inquiring into Oriental Labourers   W. L. Mackenzie King, C.M.G., Commissioner, *Report of the Royal Commission Appointed to Inquire into the Methods by Which Oriental Labourers Have Been Induced to Come to Canada* (Ottawa: Government Printing Bureau, 1908).

Report of the Royal Commission on Chinese and Japanese Immigration   *Report of the Royal Commission on Chinese and Japanese Immigration, 1902, 2 Edward VII,* Sessional Paper No. 54, A.1902 (Ottawa: S. E. Dawson, Printer to the King's Most Excellent Majesty, 1902).

RG 76, LAC   Canada, Immigration Branch, Record Group 76, Library and Archives Canada, Ottawa, Ontario.

RG 85, NARA   Record Group 85: Records of the Immigration and Naturalization
  Service, National Archives and Records Administration, Washington, D.C.
Rice Report   *Supplemental Report of W. M. Rice*, U.S. Commissioner on
  Immigration, to Commissioner-General on Immigration, Washington, D.C.,
  dated 2 May 1899, RG 85, NARA.

INTRODUCTION

1. Quoted in Tahara Haruto, "Nijūni haiseki sareru mure yori" (From Those
   Who Are Doubly Discriminated Against), *Dōai* (September 1924). Although
   shinheimin literally means "new citizen," the intended reference here is to
   outcaste status. See Chapter 1.
2. See generally William Robbins, *Colony and Empire: The Capitalist Transformation
   of the American West* (Lawrence: University Press of Kansas, 1994); John Bodnar,
   The Transplanted: A History of Immigrants in Urban America (Bloomington:
   Indiana University Press, 1985).
3. Chitoshi Yanaga, *Japan since Perry* (New York: McGraw-Hill, 1949), 16–19.
4. Studies locating the Japanese migration to the North American West in
   the context of the larger Japanese diaspora include Arthur Jiro Nishimura,
   "Japanese Emigration in the Pre–World War II Era (1868–1937): A
   Reconceptualization of the History" (Ph.D. diss., University of Washington,
   1995); Kazuichiro Ono, "The Problem of Japanese Emigration," *Kyoto
   University Economic Review* 28, no. 1 (April 1958): 40–54; and Lane Ryo
   Hirabayashi et al., eds., *New Worlds, New Lives: Globalization and People of
   Japanese Descent in the Americas and from Latin America in Japan* (Stanford,
   Calif.: Stanford University Press, 2002).
5. These are approximate figures because precise records were not kept until the
   early twentieth century. Yamato Ichihashi, *Japanese in the United States: A Critical
   Study of the Problems of the Japanese Immigrants and Their Children* (Stanford,
   Calif.: Stanford University Press, 1932), 8–9. According to the 1902 census in
   Canada, however, there were just 4,759 Japanese in Canada that year. *Report of
   the Royal Commission on Chinese and Japanese Immigration, 1902*, 2 Edward VII,
   Sessional Paper No. 54, A.1902 [hereafter *Report of the Royal Commission on
   Chinese and Japanese Immigration*] (Ottawa: S. E. Dawson, Printer to the
   King's Most Excellent Majesty, 1902), 389; Consulate-General of Japan,
   Facts about Japanese in Canada and Other Miscellaneous Information (Ottawa:
   Consulate-General of Japan, 1922). See also Yasuo Wakatsuki, "Japanese
   Emigration to the United States, 1866–1924: A Monograph," *Perspectives in
   American History* 12 (1979): 389, noting that the restrictions placed on
   Japanese immigration are partly responsible for the fact that European
   immigration came to be regarded as normative; Sucheng Chan, "European and
   Asian Immigration into the United States in Comparative Perspective, 1820s to
   1920s," in Virginia Yans-McLaughlin, ed., *Immigration Reconsidered:
   History, Sociology, and Politics* (New York: Oxford University Press, 1990),
   61–62.

6. *Buraku* itself simply means "village" or "hamlet," and *min* means "people." Other terms coined over the course of the twentieth century to avoid the pejorative connotations of historical referents included *tokushu buraku* (special hamlets), *kōshin buraku* (underdeveloped hamlets), *saimin buraku* (poverty-stricken hamlets), and *mikaihō buraku* (unliberated hamlets). The Buraku Liberation Research Institute reports that all these terms, including *burakumin*, have acquired discriminatory connotations with use. *White Paper—from the Viewpoint of the Discriminated—on Human Rights in Japan* (Osaka: Buraku Kaihō Kenkyūsho [Buraku Liberation Research Institute], 1984), 49. *Burakumin*, however, remains the term most used by English-language scholars trying to employ a neutral referent.

7. For a discussion of the difficulties associated with accurately translating Japanese into English, see Edward Seidensticker, "On Miner on Translating Japanese Poetry," *Orient/West* 7, no. 1 (January 1962). See also Marleigh Grayer Ryan, "Translating Modern Japanese Literature," *Journal of Japanese Studies* 6, no. 1 (Winter 1980): 49–60. For a discussion of the buraku issue in Japanese literature, see Edward Fowler, "The *Buraku* in Modern Japanese Literature: Texts and Contexts," *Journal of Japanese Studies* 26, no. 1 (Winter 2000): 1–39. John Lie explains that "expressions of Japanese superiority occur indirectly, which effectively masks ethnocentric and even chauvinistic views." John Lie, *Multiethnic Japan* (Cambridge, Mass.: Harvard University Press, 2001), 42.

8. Kazuo Ito, *Issei: A History of Japanese Immigrants in North America,* trans. Shinichiro Nakamura and Jean S. Gerard (Seattle: Executive Committee for Publication of *Issei,* 1973), 557; Kazuo Ito, *Hokubei hyakunen zakura* (Tokyo: Hokubei hyakunen zakura Jikkō Inkai, 1969), 655. See also William Petersen, *Japanese Americans: Oppression and Success* (New York: Random House, 1971), 212 n. 8, noting that most Japanese in North America were unfamiliar with any term other than "*eta.*"

9. Masakazu Iwata noted in 1992 that there were still corporations in Japan at that time that would not employ people it identified as burakumin. Masakazu Iwata, *Planted in Good Soil: The History of the Issei in United States Agriculture,* vol. 1 (Issei Memorial Edition) (New York: Peter Lang, 1992), 92, 106–107 n. 59 (citing "Business Tokyo" report in the Los Angeles newspaper *Rafu Shimpō,* 9 November 1988, p. 4).

10. Because these designations no longer exist as legal categories, "their existence can, therefore, not be officially recognized." Robert B. Hall, Sr., "A Map of 'Buraku' Settlements in Japan," *Papers of the Michigan Academy of Science, Arts, and Letters* 47 (1962): 521. Also see Lie, *Multiethnic Japan,* 139, stating that "the dominant belief was that 'passivity and silence' would eliminate Burakumin discrimination"; Barbara Finkelstein, Anne E. Imamura, and Joseph J. Tobin, eds., *Transcending Stereotypes: Discovering Japanese Culture and Education* (Yarmouth, Maine: Intercultural Press, 1991), 201, referring to calls for censorship of debate regarding the buraku issue by a leading Buddhist in Japan on the grounds that it "constituted a shame" and "called attention to a problem

that did not exist." Some go so far as to regard acknowledgment of the social consequences of the categories historically imposed on outcaste groups as an act of prejudice in itself. Yasuo Wakatsuki, in "Japanese Emigration to the United States," 482, states that merely to mention former outcastes is to open oneself to charges of prejudice and discrimination.

11. Hugh H. Smythe and Chyushiochi Tsuzuki, "The Eta: Japan's Indigenous Minority," *Sociology and Social Research* 37 (November/December 1952): 112–114. Raymond Lamont-Brown notes that the word *burakumin* is rarely listed in Japanese dictionaries and suggests that this may be another example of the silencing of knowledge about people in this category. Raymond Lamont-Brown, "The *Burakumin*: Japan's Underclass," *Contemporary Review* 263, no. 1532 (September 1993): 136–139.

12. See Hugh H. Smythe, "Suiheisha: Japan's NAACP," *The Crisis* (February 1953): 95–97, explaining that "even the few Eta who have attained wealth or some position of prominence ... prefer to remain anonymous so as to escape the onus that would follow their identification"; Susumu Koga, "Etas: The Social Outcasts of Japan," *The Living Age* 319, no. 4139 (November 3, 1923): 224–226, reporting that two army generals in active service who were rumored to be burakumin felt that they had to be very careful to hide that fact and, for that reason, visited their relatives only in civilian dress, in the dark, or in crowded areas where they would not be recognized.

13. While the presence of buraku jūmin in North American nikkei communities and the continued prejudice against them is acknowledged in some historical studies, nearly all such references are quickly passed over. Ken Adachi's book *The Enemy That Never Was*, generally regarded as the most comprehensive study of Japanese Canadian history to date by a nikkeijin in Canada, is a case in point. While Adachi does not entirely ignore the issue of prejudice against those he calls *"eta"* in prewar Japanese immigrant communities in Canada, he devotes just two of 456 pages to the buraku issue. Ken Adachi, *The Enemy That Never Was: A History of the Japanese Canadians* (Toronto: McClelland and Stewart, 1976), 14, 20–21. Others who make brief reference to these issues but do not develop it include Eiichiro Azuma, Eileen Sunada Sarasohn, and Audrey Lynn Kobayashi: see Eiichiro Azuma, *Between Two Empires: Race, History, and Transnationalism in Japanese America* (Oxford: Oxford University Press, 2005), 72; Eileen Sunada Sarasohn, *The Issei: Portrait of a Pioneer, an Oral History* (Palo Alto, Calif.: Pacific Books, 1983), 27; and Audrey Lynn Kobayashi, "Transition and Change: The Culture of the Issei in the Okanagan Valley," in *Inalienable Rice: A Chinese and Japanese Canadian Anthology* (Vancouver, B.C.: Powell Street Revue and the Chinese Canadian Writers Workshop, 1979), 17–20. The Japanese Canadian scientist David Suzuki, writing with the Japanese anthropologist Keibo Oiwa, stated in 1999 that it was "not hard to imagine that many *burakumin* attempted to escape their poverty and oppression during the wave of emigration from Japan to the Americas in the late 1800s and early 1900s." David Suzuki and Keibo Oiwa, *The Other Japan: Voices Beyond the*

Mainstream (Golden, Colo.: Fulcrum, 1999), 141. Again, unfortunately, they do not develop this idea, and neither responded to queries regarding the basis on which they made that assertion. Other scholars simply insist that the records are insufficient to permit including people from buraku communities in the larger story. Toshiji Sasaki, conversation with author, Shiga, Japan, 29 September 2001.

14. Hall, "Map of 'Buraku' Settlements in Japan," 521.

15. Hugh H. Smythe and Yoshimasa Naitoh, "The Eta Caste in Japan," pt. 2, *Phylon* 14, no. 2 (1953): 160; John Donaghue, "Social Persistence of an Outcaste Group," in George De Vos and Hiroshi Wagatsuma, eds., *Japan's Invisible Race: Caste in Culture and Personality* (Berkeley: University of California Press, 1966), 137–138.

16. Hiroshi Ito [pseudonym], "Japan's Outcastes in the United States," in De Vos and Wagatsuma, *Japan's Invisible Race*, 200–221. This essay explores the buraku issue in the context of the Japanese American community in Florin, California.

17. Edward Fowler argued in a recent article exploring the treatment of the buraku issue in modern Japanese literature that "further research needs to be conducted with an eye both to the literary contexts—even if it means doggedly confronting the stench of history—and to the texts themselves, taking care not to be swayed by the stench of tropes." Edward Fowler, "The *Buraku* in Modern Japanese Literature," 38–39, discussing Noma Hiroshi's declaration that "the stench of the *buraku* is not the stench of leather; it is the stench of Japanese history," in Noma Hiroshi, *Seinen no Wa* I (1971): 350–351.

18. Family registration records were closed in 1976 owing to abuses, including ascertaining ancestral ties to places where outcaste communities were historically located. Herman Ooms, *Tokugawa Village Practice: Class, Status, Power, Law* (Berkeley: University of California Press, 1996), 307. See also Cullen Tadao Hayashida, "Identity, Race and the Blood Ideology of Japan" (Ph.D. diss., University of Washington, 1976), 200–202.

19. Yukiko Koshiro, *Trans-Pacific Racisms and the U.S. Occupation of Japan* (New York: Columbia University Press, 1999), 1.

20. In both cases, as Yukiko Koshiro explains, "the historian is confronted with a Sherlock Holmes type challenge. It is the significance of the dog that did not bark in the night, rather than the one that did, that assumes importance ... How is empiricism to be achieved, when the subject is not visible?" Rikki Kersten (University of Leiden), Review of Yukiko Koshiro, *Trans-Pacific Racisms*, in *American Historical Review* 106, no. 2 (April 2001): 542–543, quoting Koshiro, *Trans-Pacific Racisms*, 1.

21. William L. Preston adopts a similar approach in constructing his argument regarding the presence of exotic diseases prior to the arrival of non-indigenous people, in "Portents of Plague from California's Protohistoric Period," *Ethnohistory* 4, no. 1 (2002): 68–105.

22. Richard White, "Race Relations in the American West," *American Quarterly* 38, no. 3 (1986): 396–416.

23. George De Vos, "Essential Elements of Caste: Psychological Determinants in Structural Theory," in De Vos and Wagatsuma, *Japan's Invisible Race*, 329. Gerald D. Berreman offers the following definition of caste: a "system of birth-ascribed groups each of which comprises for its members the maximum limit of status-equal interaction, and between all of which interaction is consistently hierarchical." Gerald D. Berreman, "Stratification, Pluralism and Interaction: A Comparative Analysis of Caste," in Anthony de Reuck and Julie Knight, eds., *Caste and Race: Comparative Approaches* (Boston: Little, Brown, 1967), 51.

24. See Berreman, "Stratification, Pluralism and Interaction," in de Reuck and Knight, *Caste and Race*, 62–63, 68, noting that the "denigration of low caste groups" who are seen as "inferior, tainted and stigmatized" by others may "simply be a rationalization of the deprivations imposed" on the groups in question. See also William H. Newell, "The Comparative Study of Caste in India and Japan," *Asian Survey* 1, no. 10 (December 1961): 3–10.

25. Hugh Smythe, a sociologist at Yamaguchi National University, argued half a century ago that further study of the buraku phenomenon had the potential to make "significant contributions to the study of caste, class, social distance, minority groups, social differentiation, intergroup and race relations, social mobility, and occupation-status relationships." Hugh H. Smythe, "The Eta: A Marginal Japanese Caste," *American Journal of Sociology* 58, no. 2 (September 1952): 194–196. See also Iwata, *Planted in Good Soil*, 107 n. 60, stating that "further study of this aspect [*Burakumin* migration] of Japanese emigration history could be of interest." The sociologist John Lie observes that "ethnic heterogeneity" is "a neglected aspect of the Japanese diaspora," citing as an example the "overrepresentation of Burakumin and Okinawans among Meiji-era emigrants." Lie, *Multiethnic Japan*, 23. Scholars of Japanese emigration have been reluctant to address this gap in the literature. Ken Adachi, however, explains that Okinawans "stood somewhere between the former outcastes, the *eta* of pre-Restoration days, and full-fledged membership in Japanese society" and that their participation in certain kinds of occupations "placed them almost on a level with the despised *eta*, the butchers and tanners and shoemakers of the old days." Adachi, *The Enemy That Never Was*, 20.

26. For a discussion of the long silence in U.S. historiography regarding the issue of slavery, see Michel-Rolph Trouillot, *Silencing the Past: Power and the Production of History* (Boston: Beacon Press, 1995). For an admission that "some upsetting topics were avoided," see Michiko Midge Ayukawa, *Hiroshima Immigrants in Canada, 1891–1941* (Vancouver, B.C.: UBC Press, 2008), 131.

27. It is partly the focus of postwar historians on the internment of people of Japanese ancestry in both Canada and the United States during World War II— important and necessary as it is—that has obscured the divisions that existed in prewar immigrant communities. Understandably intent on demonstrating that internment was unjust and undeserved, historians have tended to focus on the ways in which Japanese immigrants had successfully adapted to North American environments that were often hostile to their presence. The result, as

Eiichiro Azuma points out, is that most Japanese immigrant histories comprise a "discourse on 'tribulations and triumphs' " that have their "ideological roots in their quest to overcome racial subordination." Eiichiro Azuma, "The Politics of Transnational History Making: Japanese Immigrants on the Western 'Frontier,' 1927–1941," *Journal of American History* 89, no. 4 (March 2003): 1401–1430, 1407, 1421. See also Harry Kitano, "Japanese Americans: The Development of a Middleman Minority," *Pacific Historical Review* 63 (November 1974): 500–519.

28. Rolf Knight and Maya Koizumi, *A Man of Our Times: The Life-History of a Japanese-Canadian Fisherman* (Vancouver, B.C.: New Star Books, 1976), 7–8.

29. Chan, "European and Asian Immigration," 38. Europeans are often depicted as emigrating primarily for social and political reasons, whereas Japanese are depicted as emigrating solely for economic reasons. Scholars who have embraced the sojourner thesis in the context of Japanese emigration history include Audrey Lynn Kobayashi, "Regional Backgrounds of Japanese Immigrants and the Development of Japanese-Canadian Community," *McGill Geography Discussion Papers* 1, no. 1 (May 1986): 1-7; and Stefan Akio Tanaka, "The Nikkei on Bainbridge Island, 1883–1942: A Study of Migration and Community Development" (M.A. thesis, University of Washington, 1977), 3. For discussions of the sojourner thesis in the context of the historiography of Chinese immigration, see Anthony B. Chan, "The Myth of the Chinese Sojourner in Canada," in K. Victor Ujimoto and Gordon Hirabayashi, eds., *Visible Minorities and Multiculturalism: Asians in Canada* (Toronto: Butterworth, 1980), 33–42.

30. Donaghue, "Social Persistence of an Outcaste Group," 144–145. As Cole Harris explains, "Among all immigrant groups, cultural attitudes and practices that survived migration were recontextualized" when they built new communities in the North American West. Cole Harris, "Making of an Immigrant Society," in *The Resettlement of British Columbia: Essays on Colonialism and Geographical Change* (Vancouver: University of British Columbia Press, 1997), 250–275. Donaghue notes that emigration to urban centers was itself regarded as a way to obscure outcaste identity although it meant cutting oneself off from family and community.

31. The phrase "geography of status" is used by both David L. Howell and Timothy S. George: David L. Howell, *Geographies of Identity in Nineteenth-Century Japan* (Berkeley: University of California Press, 2005), 3–4, 20–44; Timothy S. George, *Minamata: Pollution and the Struggle for Democracy in Postwar Japan* (Cambridge, Mass.: Harvard University Asia Center, 2001), 28, citing Irokawa Daikichi, *Minamata: Sono sabetsu no fūdo to rekishi*, 1980.

32. Gunther Peck, *Reinventing Free Labor: Padrones and Immigrant Workers in the North American West, 1880–1930* (Cambridge: Cambridge University Press, 2000), 159.

CHAPTER ONE. CASTE, STATUS, *MIBUN*

1. Shimazaki Tōson, *The Broken Commandment,* trans. Kenneth Strong (Tokyo: University of Tokyo Press, 1974), 245; Hugh H. Smythe and Yoshimasa Naitoh, "The Eta Caste in Japan," pt. 1, *Phylon* 14, no. 1 (1953): 24 n. 8 (for a statement that *Hakai* has been a best seller); John Lie, *Multiethnic Japan* (Cambridge, Mass.: Harvard University Press, 2001), 54 (for the comment by Natsume Sōseki).

2. Kenneth Strong, "Introduction," in Shimazaki, *Broken Commandment,* xxi. *Hakai* has also been translated as *The Divorcement* and *The Transgression.* Kenneth Strong explains that the first part of the story, regarding the schoolteacher's expulsion from the school at which he was teaching after it was revealed that he was an *"eta,"* was based on a real occurrence, but that he was unable to determine whether the conclusion was based on a specific event. Ibid., xxi.

3. To ensure that proscriptions against overseas travel were not violated, the Tokugawa government also forbade the construction of oceangoing vessels with a displacement greater than 2,500 bushels. In 1634, it limited European contact with Japan to a handful of Dutch merchants whom it allowed to land on a small island in Nagasaki harbor called Deshima. Together with the restrictions discussed in the text, these provisions were referred to as Japan's *sakoku* or "closed country" policy. Kenneth B. Pyle, *The Making of Modern Japan* (Lexington: D. C. Heath, 1996), 16, 57–59. Cullen Tadao Hayashida, "Identity, Race and the Blood Ideology of Japan" (Ph.D. diss., University of Washington, 1976), 55–56.

4. Samurai were at the pinnacle of this hierarchy of social classes. Farmers, as the class that produced the wealth—rice—on which the Tokugawa economic system depended, were regarded as second highest in status. Artisans occupied the rung immediately below, and at the bottom were the merchants, who were disdained as nonproductive parasites on society. Even merchants, however, were regarded as having an integral place in Japanese society, which was not true of members of "outcaste" groups; they were not considered part of the official class hierarchy to which Japanese "people" belonged. William Lyman Brooks, "Outcaste Society in Early Modern Japan" (Ph.D. diss., Columbia University, 1976), 50–51, 142. See also Gerald Groemer, "The Creation of the Edo Outcaste Order," *Journal of Japanese Studies* 27, no. 2 (2001): 263–293. While David Howell contends that these four categories were not as important as they have been made out to be, he concedes that they were "coherent markers of identity." David L. Howell, *Geographies of Identity in Nineteenth-Century Japan* (Berkeley: University of California Press, 2005), 24–25.

5. Cullen Tadao Hayashida explains that the distinctions between "pure people" (*ryomin*) and "polluted people" (*senmin*) date back to the Heian period (794–1185), when the issue of "ritual pollution" became an important concern for an "unpolluted aristocracy." Hayashida, "Identity, Race and the Blood Ideology of Japan," 48, 143 (describing members of outcaste groups as "people of a different blood").

6. George De Vos and Hiroshi Wagatsuma, eds., *Japan's Invisible Race: Caste in Culture and Personality* (Berkeley: University of California Press, 1966), 4. Other outcaste groups also existed. Robert Hall, Sr., explains that the major outcaste groups included not just *eta* and *hinin* but *kabo*, hunters and trappers such as the *matagi* and *sanka*, some groups of fisherfolk such as the *ie-buni* (boat-dwelling fisherfolk) and "*amah*" (diving fisherfolk), noting that given the range of outcaste groups, it is "ironical that the entire onus of pariahism should, today, be carried by the Eta, and to a lesser extent by the Ie-buni and Mitagi." Robert B. Hall, Sr., "A Map of 'Buraku' Settlements in Japan," *Papers of the Michigan Academy of Science, Arts, and Letters* 47 (1962): 521, 525–526.

7. Shigesaki Ninomiya, "An Inquiry Concerning the Origin, Development, and Present Situation of the 'Eta' in Relation to the History of Social Classes in Japan" (M.A. thesis, University of Washington, 1931), 84; Brooks, "Outcaste Society in Early Modern Japan," 156–157. This may be one reason why outcastes were sometimes popularly assumed to be associated with criminal activity. See Hugh H. Smythe and Yoshimasa Naitoh, "The Eta Caste in Japan," pt. 2, *Phylon* 14, no. 2 (1953): 160.

8. Brooks, "Outcaste Society in Early Modern Japan," 168. Tokugawa law provided legal mechanisms, known as *ashiarai* or *ashinuki*, that allowed some individuals to rise again to their former status. Brooks explains, however, that even after they were reinstated, "stigmatic appellations" were used to refer to them, such as *sato no ko* ("village child") or *iyashii*, meaning "lowly" or "base." Ibid., 162–163; John Price, "A History of the Outcaste: Untouchability in Japan," in De Vos and Wagatsuma, *Japan's Invisible Race*, 21. Some outcaste communities developed hierarchical class structures similar to that of other farming communities. Price, "History of the Outcaste," 119. See also George De Vos, "Discussion: Pariah Castes Compared," in Anthony de Reuck and Julie Knight, eds., *Caste and Race: Comparative Approaches* (Boston: Little, Brown, 1967), 145, noting that "rigid class differentiation exists within the pariah group: there are upper, middle, and lower-class Burakumin."

9. Smythe and Naitoh, "Eta Caste in Japan," pt. 1, 21; Kyohei Yamamoto, "The Pariah People of Japan," *Japan Christian Intelligencer* 1 (5 May 1926): 118–119. Ironically, work with leather, contact with which caused outcaste groups to be disdained by commoners, was highly valued at the start of the Tokugawa period by warriors who depended on leather craftsmen for their armor. Similarly, the fact that people classified as eta were also required to act as executioners meant that those assigned this duty were entitled to wear swords, a privilege generally reserved to samurai alone. Because commoners were strictly forbidden to wear swords, some historians have argued that the conceptual boundary between samurai and outcastes was more ambiguous than has sometimes been recognized. Ibid., 118. See also Price, "History of the Outcaste," 22–23.

10. See Brooks, "Outcaste Society in Early Modern Japan," 56, 62–63, noting that no stigma was associated with the items themselves but only with the making of those items; Smythe and Naitoh, "Eta Caste in Japan," pt. 2, 158.

11. Yamamoto, "Pariah People of Japan," 118; I. Roger Yoshino and Sueo Murakoshi, *The Invisible Visible Minority: Japan's Burakumin* (Osaka: Buraku Kaihō Kenkyūsho, 1977), 40–41. See also Edward Norbeck, "Little-Known Minority Groups of Japan," in De Vos and Wagatsuma, *Japan's Invisible Race,* 193; Herman Ooms, *Tokugawa Village Practice: Class, Status, Power, Law* (Berkeley: University of California Press, 1996), 250, 256. Ironically, although *taiko* drumming has become popular activity in nikkei communities in both Canada and the United States, the role of former outcastes in developing and producing the drums is rarely, if ever, recognized.

12. Regine Mathias, "Female Labor in the Japanese Coal-Mining Industry," in Janet Hunter, ed., *Japanese Women Working* (New York: Routledge, 1993), 98–121; and Mathias, "The Recruitment and the Organization of Labour in the Coal Mining Industry of Northern Kyushu during the Meiji Period," in Ian Nish and Charles Dunn, *European Studies on Japan* (Tenterden, U.K.: Paul Norbury, 1979), 26, noting that a significant percentage of those working in coal mines in northern Kyushu—especially the Chikuhō district—during the second half of the nineteenth century were burakumin. Shigesaki Ninomiya also states that a majority of the miners in the Fukuoka coal mines were "*eta.*" Ninomiya, "Inquiry Concerning the Origin of the 'Eta,' " 106; Brooks, "Outcaste Society in Early Modern Japan," 63.

13. Mary F. Jones, "Japan's Samaritans: The Story and the Problem of the Eta," *Japan Christian Quarterly* (January 1955): 58; Ninomiya, "Inquiry Concerning the Origin of the 'Eta,' " 48.

14. For a debate on whether caste prejudice can be equated with modern racism, see Howell, *Geographies of Identity,* 31 n. 26, arguing against the use of the term "state racism" by Ooms in *Tokugawa Village Practice,* 243, 310.

15. Ninomiya, "Inquiry Concerning the Origin of the 'Eta,' " 9, citing Kikuchi Sanya, *Eta zoku ni kansuru kenkyū* (A Study Concerning the Eta Race) (Tokyo: Sanseisha, 1923), 72–73.

16. Brooks, "Outcaste Society in Early Modern Japan," 22, noting that "what is offered as truth about the Burakumin usually turns out to be a hodge-podge of superstitions someone learned as a child." See also Basil Hall Chamberlain, *Things Japanese: Being Notes on Various Subjects Connected with Japan for the Use of Travellers and Others,* 2nd ed. (London: Kegan Paul; Trench, Trübner, 1891), 147.

17. Ooms, *Tokugawa Village Practice,* 249, 301; Brooks, "Outcaste Society in Early Modern Japan," 63.

18. Smythe and Naitoh, "Eta Caste in Japan," pt. 1, 24; Jones, "Japan's Samaritans," 57–64. Gestures were also used to signal these numbers. Jones, "Japan's Samaritans."

19. Susumu Koga, "Etas: The Social Outcasts of Japan," *The Living Age* 319, no. 4139 (3 November 1923): 224–226.

20. See David L. Howell, "Territoriality and Collective Identity in Tokugawa Japan," *Daedalus* 127, no. 3 (Summer 1998), 105–132, 111.

21. Brooks reports that government officials who found *senmin* ("polluted people") living in towns or farming villages removed them to swampy and other marginal lands on the outskirts of those communities. Brooks, "Outcaste Society in Early Modern Japan," 43, 60, 166. Hugh Smythe notes that outcaste communities rarely occupied entire villages. Even after World War II, "their settlements have remained as peripheral enclaves and the Eta continue to live in isolation as a marginal neighborhood group." Hugh H. Smythe, "The Eta: A Marginal Japanese Caste," *American Journal of Sociology* 58, no. 2 (September 1952): 194–196, 195.

22. Arthur May Knapp, *Feudal and Modern Japan* (Yokohama: Kelly and Walsh, 1906), 207. See also Ooms, *Tokugawa Village Practice*, 287, citing Teraki Nobuaki, *Kinsei buraku no seiritsu to tenkai* (Osaka: Kaihō shuppansha, 1986), 44.

23. Brooks, "Outcaste Society in Early Modern Japan," 168.

24. Even internal status differences were denoted by clothing and hairstyle, both of which were the subject of detailed regulation and made an individual's class and occupation immediately apparent to others. Yoshino and Murakoshi, *Invisible Visible* Minority, 37–40; Ooms, *Tokugawa Village Practice*, 287, 374–376.

25. Smythe and Naitoh, "Eta Caste in Japan," pt. 1, 21; Hayashida, "Identity, Race and the Blood Ideology of Japan," 138.

26. Gertrude Haessler explains, for example, that during the Tokugawa era members of outcaste communities were "obliged to live in houses that [had] no windows or doors facing the street." Gertrude Haessler, "Japan's Untouchables," *The Nation* 117, no. 3035 (5 September 1923): 249–252. Sumptuary laws addressing outcaste appearance in the province of Bizen (part of what is now Okayama prefecture) included the following provision: "[*eta*] should be especially prudent not to aspire to standards of commoner [*heimin*] peasantry in any way ... It is, therefore, required that their clothing shall bear no family crest but shall be of plain dark-brown or indigo color." John B. Cornell, "From Caste Patron to Entrepreneur and Political Ideologue: Transformation in Nineteenth and Twentieth Century Outcaste Leadership Elites," in Bernard S. Silberman and H. D. Harootunian, eds., *Modern Japanese Leadership: Transition and Change* (Tucson: University of Arizona Press, 1966), citing Buraku Kaihō Dōmei Okayama-ken Rengōkai, ed., *Kimpuku shōtan nansoki: Shibuzome ikki shiryō* (Records of a Petition Concerning Regulations Relating to Clothing: Materials on an Insurrection against Shameful Hue) (Okayama, 1958), 3. See also Yamamoto, "Pariah People of Japan," 119; Ooms, *Tokugawa Village Practice*, 267.

27. Smythe and Naitoh, "Eta Caste in Japan," pt. 1, 21–22.

28. Hayashida, "Identity, Race and the Blood Ideology of Japan," 59.

29. As Yukichi Fukuzawa famously observed, "For 360 days out of the year, the work of the clans seemed to be to argue about rank ... this concept of superior and inferior ranks was not confined to humans, but extended to other living creatures, a troublesome system with the ranks set from mammals to insects."

Quoted in Yasuo Wakatsuki, "Japanese Emigration to the United States, 1866–1924: A Monograph," *Perspectives in American History* 12 (1979): 435.

30. Audrey Lynn Kobayashi, "Emigration from Kaideima, Japan, 1885–1950: An Analysis of Community and Landscape Change" (Ph.D. diss., University of California, Los Angeles, 1983), 104. The word *dekasegi* is made up of the characters for *de* (to go out) and *kasegi* (to labor or work for one's living).

31. Mikiso Hane, *Peasants, Rebels and Outcastes: The Underside of Modern Japan* (New York: Pantheon, 1982), 142. Shikoku is the smallest of the four major islands that make up the Japanese archipelago.

32. Smythe and Naitoh, "Eta Caste in Japan," pt. 1, 22, citing Takahashi Sadaki, *A 1000-Year History of the Eta* (Kyoto, 1924), 152–153.

33. Hayashida, "Identity, Race and the Blood Ideology of Japan," 64.

34. See Pyle, *Making of Modern Japan,* 146; Hayashida, "Identity, Race and the Blood Ideology of Japan," 66.

35. Brooks, "Outcaste Society in Early Modern Japan," 284.

36. The feudal system that existed in Japan at the time it was opened to the West was no longer comparable to that which had existed in Europe during the Middle Ages. Feudalism in Japan during the Tokugawa period, scholars have noted, is more aptly described as a system of centralized feudalism. See, for example, Pyle, *Making of Modern Japan,* 26–27.

37. Shotaro Frank Miyamoto, "Social Solidarity among the Japanese in Seattle," *University of Washington Publications in the Social Sciences* II, no. 2 (December 1939): 117.

38. Those from other domains were regarded as *takokumono,* or "outside country persons," as contrasted with *kunimono,* or "country persons" from the same domain. Hayashida, "Identity, Race and the Blood Ideology of Japan," 57. The character pronounced *kuni* or *koku* is also used to denote "country" or "nation."

39. *Ken* (prefectures) were divided into *gun* (districts), which were divided in turn into *mura* (villages). Fred R. Yoder, "The Japanese Rural Community," *Rural Society* 1 (December 1936), cited in Eric Walz, "Japanese Immigration and Community Building in the Interior West, 1882–1945" (Ph.D. diss., Arizona State University, 1998), 22–23. To avoid alienating the daimyō whose families had governed those domains for centuries, the Meiji oligarchs appointed them as the first governors of the new prefectures. Pyle, *Making of Modern Japan,* 116.

40. Kobayashi, "Emigration from Kaideima, Japan," 242.

41. Brooks, "Outcaste Society in Early Modern Japan," 294.

42. Howell argues that those who encouraged the Meiji government to abolish outcaste status saw it as necessary for three reasons: "first, as a matter of fairness in keeping with the principle of the intrinsic equality of the emperor's subjects (*isshi dōjin*); second, as a matter of national pride; and third, as a means to unleash the economic potential of former outcastes in the development of new lands and new industries useful to the state, particularly tanning and animal husbandry." Howell, *Geographies of Identity,* 89.

43. See Ninomiya, "Inquiry Concerning the Origin of the 'Eta,' " 101.

44. As early as 1852, for example, a retainer of the daimyō of Hiji on the island of
    Kyushu had made such a proposal and had also suggested that people in these
    categories then be relocated to the northernmost island of Hokkaido. Brooks,
    "Outcaste Society in Early Modern Japan," 263–264; Smythe and Naitoh,
    "Eta Caste in Japan," pt. 1, 23. For other examples of proposals regarding the
    elimination of outcaste status by Meiji officials, see Howell, *Geographies of
    Identity,* 80–83; Ooms, *Tokugawa Village Practice,* 296–298.
45. Brooks, "Outcaste Society in Early Modern Japan," 267–270.
46. For a detailed description of the debate surrounding outcaste emancipation, see
    Brooks, "Outcaste Society in Early Modern Japan," 255–306; Ninomiya, "Inquiry
    Concerning the Origin of the 'Eta,' " 96, 99.
47. The edict is reprinted in Kyoto Burakushi Kenkyūjo, ed., *Kyoto no burakushi,*
    vol. 6 (Kyoto: Kyoto Burakushi Kenkyūjō, 1984), 47 ("eta hinin nado no shō
    haiseraresoro sōrō jō, jikon mibun shokugyō tomo heimin dōyō taru beki
    koto"). The translation is Howell's in David L. Howell, "Liberating and Killing
    Outcastes in Early Meiji Japan" (Princeton University, Department of East Asian
    Studies, 2001), 5; "former outcastes" is his interpolation; "*heimin*" mine.
48. Howell, "Liberating and Killing Outcastes in Early Meiji Japan," 5. See also
    Brooks, "Outcaste Society in Early Modern Japan," 306. George O. Totten and
    Hiroshi Wagatsuma argue that one of the Meiji government's motivations was
    its interest in incorporating the untaxed land occupied by "eta" into its tax base,
    which it could not do unless it regularized their status. George O. Totten and
    Hiroshi Wagatsuma, "Emancipation: Growth and Transformation of a Political
    Movement," in De Vos and Wagatsuma, *Japan's Invisible Race,* 34.
49. William Elliot Griffis, *The Japanese Nation in Evolution: Steps in the Progress
    of a Great People* (New York: Thomas Y. Crowell, 1907), 109 ("the name of
    Mutsuhito [the Meiji emperor] will go down in history with that of … Abraham
    Lincoln"); William Elliot Griffis, *The Mikado's Empire,* vol. 2: *Personal Experiences,
    Observations, and Studies in Japan, 1870–1874* (New York: Harper and Brothers,
    1908), 566 (making "eta" citizens was an "act as morally grand as the
    emancipation of slaves").
50. Edward Daub, "Respect—Not Pity," *Japan Christian Quarterly* 27 (January 1961):
    38–45; Smythe, "Eta: A Marginal Japanese Caste," 194–196, citing T. Kida,
    "Short History of the Establishment of the Special Community and Discussion
    of Its Abolishment," *Minzoku to rekishi* 2, no. 1 (10 July 1919), 9–77.
51. Hayashida, "Identity, Race and the Blood Ideology of Japan," 193, noting that
    the way the koseki system works makes it difficult to "pass" and to effect a
    permanent change in genseki.
52. Ninomiya, "Inquiry Concerning the Origin of the 'Eta,' " 100. See also Daniel V.
    Botsman, *Punishment and Power in the Making of Modern Japan* (Princeton, N.J.:
    Princeton University Press, 2005), 57.
53. Daub, "Respect—Not Pity," 40, explaining that the tasks that buraku people
    were forced to perform on behalf of the larger community prior to the
    emancipation edict included "driving away beggars, catching criminals, and

disposing of dead animals." According to Smythe and Naitoh, other Japanese began to call former outcastes who demanded to be treated as equals *zōchō*, or "puffed-up people." Smythe and Naitoh, "Eta Caste in Japan," pt. 1, 23.

54. Smythe and Naitoh, "Eta Caste in Japan," pt. 1, 23–24. Edward Daub explains that during the most severe riots that occurred in 1874, twenty-nine buraku jūmin were killed and more than three hundred homes destroyed. Daub, "Respect—Not Pity," 40. For other examples of violent outbursts following the abolition of outcaste status, see Howell, *Geographies of Identity*, 89–95, 106; Ken Adachi, *The Enemy That Never Was: A History of the Japanese Canadians* (Toronto: McClelland and Stewart, 1976), 15. The edict also divided former outcaste communities. Howell notes, for example, that former outcaste communities were themselves "riven by internal discrimination, as Burakumin who gave up traditional outcaste occupations sometimes shunned those who, for economic reasons, did not." Howell, "Liberating and Killing Outcastes in Early Meiji Japan," 6. See also Ninomiya, "Inquiry Concerning the Origin of the 'Eta,' " 101.

55. Totten and Wagatsuma, "Emancipation, " 37, citing *Zenkoku minji kanrei ruisho* (Handbook of Japanese Customs and Folkways).

56. Gotaro Ogawa, *Conscription System in Japan* (New York: Oxford University Press, 1921), 5–6, 11. See also E. Herbert Norman, *Soldier and Peasant in Japan: The Origins of Conscription* (New York: Institute of Pacific Relations, 1943); Kobayashi, "Emigration from Kaideima, Japan," 97–98.

57. Yasuo Wakatsuki, "Japanese Emigration to the United States, 1866–1924: A Monograph," *Perspectives in American History* 12 (1979): 421; Hayashida, "Identity, Race and the Blood Ideology of Japan," 186. The Meiji government itself referred to the conscription law as a "blood tax" in a mandate concerning conscription issued on November 28, 1872. Ogawa, *Conscription System in Japan*, 4. Susumu Koga explains that former outcastes were also subject to conscription, but that was not enough to counter the prejudice they continued to face. In an article published in the December 1923 issue of *Fujin koron* (Tokyo Review for Women), Koga tells of a group of young men who were drafted into the army, two of whom were burakumin. Neither was invited to a farewell party given for those who were drafted, nor were they provided with new uniforms as the others were. Koga quotes the young man shouting from the train as he left: "I shall never return to this village. I have been drafted to defend my country, and yet I have been insulted worse than an alien." Koga, "Etas: The Social Outcasts of Japan," 224.

58. Stefan Akio Tanaka, "The Nikkei on Bainbridge Island, 1883–1942: A Study of Migration and Community Development" (M.A. thesis, University of Washington, 1977), 49; Howell, *Geographies of Identity*, 89–106, describing the dynamics of the "Blood Tax" Rebellion in Mimasaka in 1873, which resulted in a number of deaths and extensive property damage.

59. Paul R. Spickard, *Japanese Americans: The Formations and Transformations of an Ethnic Group* (New York: Twayne, 1996), 2.

60. Wakatsuki, "Japanese Emigration to the United States," 398; John Bodnar, *The Transplanted: A History of Immigrants in Urban America* (Bloomington: Indiana University Press, 1985), 30–31, 34. For a description of secondary handicraft industries in Japan, see Thomas C. Smith, "Farm Family By-Employments in Preindustrial Japan," in Thomas C. Smith, *Native Sources of Japanese Industrialization, 1750–1920* (Berkeley: University of California Press, 1988).

61. Wakatsuki, "Japanese Emigration to the United States," 400, 417; Bodnar, *The Transplanted*, 34–35.

62. Pyle, *Making of Modern Japan*, 106; Wakatsuki, "Japanese Emigration to the United States," 398. For a general discussion of land and taxation in Japan, see Nobutake Ike, "Taxation and Landownership in the Westernization of Japan," *Journal of Economic History* 7, no. 2 (November 1947): 149–182. Also see Kozo Yamamura, "The Meiji Land Tax Reform and Its Effects," in Marius B. Jansen and Gilbert Rozman, eds., *Japan in Transition: From Tokugawa to Meiji* (Princeton, N.J.: Princeton University Press, 1986), 382–399.

63. Yuzo Murayama, "Information and Emigrants: Interprefectural Differences of Japanese Emigration to the Pacific Northwest, 1880–1915," *Journal of Economic History* 51, no. 1 (March 1991): 124–145; Wakatsuki, "Japanese Emigration to the United States," 399. While just "30 percent of the cultivated land was tenanted" at the beginning of the Meiji period, by 1900 nearly half—45 percent—was held by landlords who collected annual rents equal in value to nearly one-quarter of the rice crop. Pyle, *Making of Modern Japan*, 154–155.

64. Wakatsuki, "Japanese Emigration to the United States," 445; Hisashi Tsurutani, *America-Bound: The Japanese and the Opening of the American West*, trans. Betsey Scheiner (Tokyo: Japan Times, 1989), xvi, 29. For a discussion of the development of dekasegi labor patterns during the final decades of the Tokugawa period, see W. Mark Fruin, "A Social Geography of Preindustrial Labour Migration in Japan: Tajima and Kurome Villages in the Century," *Journal of Historical Geography* 4, no. 2 (1978): 105–128. See also Audrey Lynn Kobayashi, "Regional Backgrounds of Japanese Immigrants and the Development of Japanese-Canadian Community," *McGill Geography Discussion Papers* 1, no. 1 (May 1986): 1–7, 1–10; Kobayashi, "Emigration from Kaideima, Japan," 152.

65. Mark Wyman, *Round-Trip to America: The Immigrants Return to Europe* (Ithaca, N.Y.: Cornell University Press, 1993), 17; Bodnar, *The Transplanted*, 43–45. See generally Leslie Page Moch, *Moving Europeans: Migration in Western Europe since 1650* (Bloomington: Indiana University Press, 1992).

66. Approximately 33 percent of Japanese emigrants returned to Japan from 1909 to 1924, as compared to the 30 percent of British immigrants who returned to Britain. Sucheng Chan, "European and Asian Immigration into the United States in Comparative Perspective, 1820s to 1920s," in Virginia Yans-McLaughlin, ed., *Immigration Reconsidered: History, Sociology, and Politics* (New York: Oxford University Press, 1990), 38. Chan bases her figures on Stephan Thurnstrom et al., eds., *Harvard Encyclopedia of American Ethnic Groups*

(Cambridge: Harvard University Press, 1980), 1036–1037; and Yamato Ichihashi, *Japanese in the United States: A Critical Study of the Problems of the Japanese Immigrants and Their Children* (Stanford: Stanford University Press, 1932), 401–408. Cinel states that the return rate for Italian immigrants to the United States between 1908 and 1923 may have been as high as 60 percent. Dino Cinel, *From Italy to San Francisco: The Immigrant Experience* (Stanford: Stanford University Press, 1982), 1. The return rate for Chinese immigrants was as high as 47 percent. Chan, "European and Asian Immigration," 38, citing Mary R. Coolidge, *Chinese Immigration* (New York: Holt, 1909), 498.

67. Chan, "European and Asian Immigration," 38; Bodnar, *The Transplanted*, 53–54. For a discussion of return migration among European migrants, see Wyman, *Round-Trip to America*, 4, 6, 51, 65, 76, 82; and Walter Nugent, *Crossings: The Great Transatlantic Migrations, 1870–1914* (Bloomington: Indiana University Press, 1992), 35.

68. Bodnar, *The Transplanted*, 53; Wakatsuki, "Japanese Emigration to the United States," 447. For use of the term *wataridori* and "birds of passage," see Shimpo Mitsuru, *Ishi o mote owaruru gotoku: Nikkei kanadajin shakaishi* (Like Being Chased by Thrown Stones: A Social History of Japanese Canadians) (Toronto: Tairiku Jihō, 1996); Wyman, *Round-Trip to America*, 82; Michael Piore, *Birds of Passage: Migrant Labor and Industrial Societies* (New York: Cambridge University Press, 1979).

69. Wyman, *Round-Trip to America*, 33, 42 ("dreams of gold"). "America fever" was a term used by both European and Japanese immigrants; the Japanese term was *iminnetsu*. Ibid.; Ito, *Issei*, 26. For a discussion of the ways Chinese migrants envisioned North America, see Susie Lan Cassel, ed., *The Chinese in America: A History from Gold Mountain to the New Millennium* (Walnut Creek, Calif.: AltaMira Press, 2002); Ronald T. Takaki, *Journey to Gold Mountain: The Chinese in Nineteenth Century America* (New York: Chelsea House, 1994).

70. Cinel, *From Italy to San Francisco*, 30–31.

71. My description of the landscape is based on observations I made during a trip to Japan in October 2001. For a description of the collapse of the local fishing industry, see Adachi, *The Enemy That Never Was*, 18. Adachi notes that just 13 percent of the land in this area was suitable for farming. Ibid.

72. Bodnar, *The Transplanted*, 6. The seven prefectures from which the largest number of emigrants went to the mainland United States were Hiroshima, Okayama, Kumamoto, Yamaguchi, Wakayama, Fukuoka, and Kagoshima. Yasuo Wakatsuki, "Emigration of Japanese to the United States," *Pacific Citizen*, 6–13 January 1984, section B, p. 1. A majority of Japanese immigrants in Canada came from seven prefectures: Shiga, Wakayama, Hiroshima, Kumamoto, Fukuoka, Kagoshima, and Okayama. Kobayashi, "Regional Backgrounds of Japanese Immigrants," 1-8. Because of the overlap—Japanese in Shiga and Yamaguchi prefectures mainly went to one country or the other—I have listed a total of eight prefectures for North America. For a chart correlating the number of emigrants from each prefecture with such other factors as the availability of

agricultural land, tenancy rates, and the existence of "pioneer" immigrants, see Murayama, "Information and Emigrants," 130–131.

73. In Bodnar's words, "If immigration was caused largely by the lure of [the American economy], then we would expect that struggling people everywhere would come here in relatively equal numbers with common intentions and, for that matter, backgrounds. But historical reality suggests a different explanation to this process." Bodnar, *The Transplanted*, 3–4, 13.

74. Tanaka, "Nikkei on Bainbridge Island," 20; Murayama, "Information and Emigrants," 141; Kobayashi, "Regional Backgrounds of Japanese Immigrants," 1-4–1-5. Although migration can sometimes be correlated with natural disasters of one kind or another, emigrants from both Europe and Japan tended to wait until conditions began to improve before emigrating. See Wyman, *Round-Trip to America*, 39; Kobayashi, "Regional Backgrounds of Japanese Immigrants," 1-7, 1-8.

75. Kobayashi, "Regional Backgrounds of Japanese Immigrants," 1-4; Kobayashi, "Emigration from Kaideima, Japan," 150; Murayama, "Information and Emigrants," 140. See also Arthur Jiro Nishimura, "Japanese Emigration in the Pre–World War II Era (1868–1937): A Reconceptualization of the History" (Ph.D. diss., University of Washington, 1995), 31, noting that emigration varied even within prefectures.

76. Bodnar, *The Transplanted*, 3, 4; Chan, "European and Asian Immigration," 39.

77. Bodnar, *The Transplanted*, 57–58; Murayama, "Information and Emigrants," 125–126, 138, 141, arguing that the information provided by other migrants was the single most important factor in explaining emigration distribution patterns from Japan. For a discussion of the importance of kinship and information networks in the context of European immigration, see Charles Tilly, "Transplanted Networks," in Virginia Yans-McLaughlin, ed., *Immigration Reconsidered: History, Sociology, and Politics* (New York: Oxford University Press, 1990), 79–95. For a detailed discussion of the role of labor contractors in facilitating the early stages of Japanese emigration, see Alan Takeo Moriyama, *Imingaisha: Japanese Emigration Companies and Hawaii, 1894–1908* (Honolulu: University of Hawaii Press, 1985);Yuji Ichioka, "Japanese Immigrant Labor Contractors and the Northern Pacific and the Great Northern Railroad Companies, 1898–1907," *Labor History* 21, no. 3 (Summer 1980): 325–350.

78. Bodnar, *The Transplanted*, 15–16, 56, noting that British migrants included many who sought to prevent further decline in economic status by emigrating while they still had sufficient resources to exercise that option. Jon Gjerde found that Norwegian emigrants were also motivated by the wish to avoid a decline in social status from one generation to the next, a decline to which they were increasingly more vulnerable at the end of the nineteenth century because local custom—which forbade marriage until a young man acquired sufficient land to support a family—combined with impartible inheritance practices and a decrease in land available for purchase to make it impossible to meet that condition. Jon Gjerde, *From Peasants to Farmers: The Migration from Balestrand,*

Norway, to the Upper Middle West (Cambridge: Cambridge University Press, 1985). Wyman, *Round-Trip to America*, 205–206.

79. Miyamoto, "Social Solidarity among the Japanese in Seattle," 64. For Japanese in Canada, see Adachi, *The Enemy That Never Was*, 18.

80. Josef J. Barton, *Peasants and Strangers: Italians, Rumanians, and Slovaks in an American City, 1890–1950* (Cambridge, Mass.: Harvard University Press, 1975), 1–10, 27–47. Chan thus argues that "where no small parcels were available for sale, few people emigrated across the Atlantic," whereas where land was available, "out-migration was large, and . . . returning migrants . . . often exceeded two-thirds the number" of those who left. Chan, "European and Asian Immigration," 46.

81. See generally Tomoko Makabe, *Picture Brides: Japanese Women in Canada*, trans. Kathleen Chisato Merken (Toronto: Multicultural History Society of Ontario, 1995). See also Roy Kiyooka, *Mothertalk: Life Stories of Mary Kiyoshi Kiyooka*, ed. Daphne Marlatt (Edmonton, Alberta: NeWest Press, 1997), 53.

82. Sydney Greenbie, "A Million Social Outcasts," *World Outlook* (September 1919).

83. See Hiroshi Ito, "Japan's Outcastes in the United States," in De Vos and Wagatsuma, *Japan's Invisible Race*, 205.

84. Kawabata Toshifusa, *Hakai to sono shūhen: Buraku mondai shōsetsu kenkyū* (Kyoto: Bunrikaku, 1984), 73 n. 12 (members of the Kyushu heimin-kai to the shinheimin community elders in Fukuoka prefecture). My translation differs slightly from that of Michael Bourdaghs, who also cites this source. Michael K. Bourdaghs, "Shimazaki Tōson's *Hakai* and Its Bodies," in Helen Hardacre and Adam L. Kern, eds., *New Directions in the Study of Meiji Japan* (Leiden: Brill, 1997), 169–170.

85. Matsu Yasuji, "Suihei yowa" (Suihei Evening Chat), *Jiyū* (September 1926); Tahara Haruto, "Jibun ni iu kotoba" (Words I Say to Myself), *Dōai* (November 1924).

86. Ninomiya, "Inquiry Concerning the Origin of the 'Eta,'" 98, 150. Smythe also cites three million as the population figure for 1952. Smythe, "Eta: A Marginal Japanese Caste," 194–196, citing Hattori Shiso et al., eds., *Kindai hyakunenshi: 1850–1950* (One Hundred Years of Modern [Japanese] History) (Tokyo: Kokusaibunka johosha, 1952) X, 804. Howell explains that although the percentage of outcastes in Japan as a whole was estimated at between 2–3 percent of the population in 1864, their communities were not evenly distributed, so they made up as much as 7 percent of the non-samurai population in some domains. Howell, *Geographies of Identity*, 93 (citing, in particular, the Tsuyama domain).

87. Spickard, *Japanese Americans*, 16; Ito, "Japan's Outcastes in the United States," 204–205; Wakatsuki, "Japanese Emigration to the United States," 484.

88. Hiroshi Ito expressly states that his figure is based on his informants' "guesses." Ito, "Japan's Outcastes in the United States," 204–205.

89. Tahara, "Jibun ni iu kotoba"; Lie, *Multiethnic Japan*, 23.

90. Hall, "Map of 'Buraku' Settlements in Japan," 523; Ian Neary, *Political Protest and Social Control in Pre-war Japan: The Origins of Buraku Liberation* (Manchester,

U.K.: Manchester University Press, 1989), 6; Wakatsuki, "Japanese Emigration to the United States," 483. See also Smythe and Tsuzuki, "Eta: Japan's Indigenous Minority," 112–114, citing Kikuchi, *A Study of the Eta Class* (*Eta zoku ni kansuru kenkyū*). Brooks estimates that 44 percent of buraku jūmin today live in the Kinki region in Osaka, Hyōgo, Kyoto, Nara, Shiga, and Wakayama prefectures; 15 percent in the Chūgoku region in Yamaguchi, Hiroshima, and Okayama prefectures; 12 percent in Shikoku; and 11 percent in northeastern Kyushu. Brooks, "Outcaste Society in Early Modern Japan," 105–106.
91. Bodnar, *The Transplanted*, 32, 118–120.

CHAPTER TWO. EMIGRATION FROM MEIJI JAPAN

1. John H. Sargent, Inspector in Charge, U.S. Immigration Service, Department of Commerce and Labor, Seattle, Washington, to Commissioner-General of Immigration, Washington, D.C., 2 May 1908; Walter E. Carr, Inspector in Charge, U.S. Immigration Service, Department of Commerce and Labor, Port of Winnipeg, Manitoba, to John H. Clark, U.S. Commissioner of Immigration, Montreal, Canada, 17 April 1908, Record Group 85: Records of the Immigration and Naturalization Service [hereafter RG 85], Series A, Subject Correspondence Files, part 1, Asian Immigration and Exclusion, 1906–1913, National Archives and Records Administration, Washington, D.C. [hereafter NARA].
2. U.S. Ambassador O'Brien, Tokyo, Japan, to U.S. Department of State, Washington, D.C., 9 March 1908 (quoting telegram from [U.S. Secretary of State] Root to the U.S. Ambassador in Tokyo, Japan, dated 25 February 1908), RG 85, NARA.
3. U.S. Ambassador O'Brien, Tokyo, Japan, to U.S. Department of State, Washington, D.C., 9 March 1908; notes re conference with Mr. Ishii [Kikujirō], Foreign Office, Tokyo, Japan, by P. A. Jay, U.S. Embassy, Tokyo, Japan, enclosed with Dispatch No. 231 from Ambassador O'Brien, Tokyo, Japan, to U.S. Department of State, Washington, D.C., 10 March 1908, and associated reports.
4. F. P. Sargent, Commissioner-General, Bureau of Immigration and Naturalization, Department of Commerce and Labor, Washington, D.C., to John H. Clark, U.S. Commissioner of Immigration, Montreal, Canada, 17 April 1908, RG 85, NARA.
5. Government officials in both the United States and Canada were aware that Japanese distinguished among themselves based on status. In an 1899 report on Japanese immigration by U.S. Immigration Commissioner W. M. Rice, which was incorporated into the report issued by Canada's Royal Commission on Chinese and Japanese Immigration in 1902, Rice described class attitudes in Japan as follows: "The wealthy class have little or no respect for their own laboring class as individuals, and no sympathy with the toilers in the field and factory. Their condition is regarded as a decree of fate, and hence those who are capable rarely comprehend the dignity and rights of labor as it is regarded in this country." In the same report, Rice explained the Japanese passport system in terms that linked the complicated and localized nature of acquiring one to

attitudes that were a remnant of feudal practices and institutions. *Supplemental Report of W. M. Rice*, U.S. Commissioner on Immigration, to Commissioner-General on Immigration, Washington, D.C., dated 2 May 1899, RG 85, NARA [hereafter Rice Report]; *Report of the Royal Commission on Chinese and Japanese Immigration*, 424–425.

6. Walter E. Carr, Inspector in Charge, U.S. Immigration Service, Department of Commerce and Labor, Port of Winnipeg, Manitoba, to John H. Clark, U.S. Commissioner of Immigration, Montreal, Canada, 17 April 1908, RG 85, NARA.

7. P. L. Prentis, Inspector in Charge, U.S. Immigration Service, Department of Commerce and Labor, Vancouver, B.C., to John H. Clark, U.S. Commissioner of Immigration, Montreal, Canada, 25 April 1908, RG 85, NARA.

8. Ibid.; Barnabas C. Haworth, Japanese Interpreter, to P. L. Prentis, Inspector In Charge, U.S. Immigration Service, Department of Commerce and Labor, Vancouver, B.C., 25 April 1908, file 51930, RG 85, NARA. By noting the existence of an outcaste class, Haworth's explanation also resolved a more puzzling question about the status of those concerned raised by use of the occupational designation "laborer" that U.S. immigration officials had not understood prior to receiving Haworth's account. After carefully studying the various contexts in which the term "laborer" was utilized, U.S. officials had concluded that when the term "laborer" followed the term "emigrant," it was intended to indicate that the bearer was not a member of the "classes known as farmers, artisans, soldiers, etc." Because "outcastes" were the only commoners not encompassed within the other named classes, the observation made by U.S. immigration officials suggests that in at least some cases, "laborer" was a designation used to denote descent from former outcaste groups.

9. Yamato Ichihashi also noted that occupations listed on emigrants' passports were not necessarily those they intended to pursue once they arrived in North America but were intended to "indicate from what classes the Japanese immigrants were drawn." Yamato Ichihashi, *Japanese in the United States: A Critical Study of the Problems of the Japanese Immigrants and Their Children* (Stanford, Calif.: Stanford University Press, 1932), 67. For a breakdown of occupations listed on Japanese passports according to Immigration Commission reports between 1901 and 1909, see H. A. Millis, *The Japanese Problem in the United States* (New York: Macmillan, 1915), 6.

10. John H. Clark, U.S. Commissioner of Immigration to Assistant Secretary of State, 13 May 1908, file 51931, RG 85, NARA.

11. For a detailed description of this episode, see Masaji Marumoto, " 'First Year' Immigrants to Hawaii and Eugene Van Reed," in Hilary F. Conroy and T. Scott Miyakawa, eds., *East Across the Pacific: Historical and Sociological Studies of Japanese Immigration and Assimilation* (Santa Barbara: ABC-Clio Press, 1972), 5–39. After emigration to Hawaii resumed in 1885 and before the territory was annexed by the United States in 1899, more than sixty-five thousand Japanese emigrants went to Hawaii. Ibid., 35.

12. Yasuo Wakatsuki, "Japanese Emigration to the United States, 1866–1924: A Monograph," *Perspectives in American History* 12 (1979): 485; Stefan Akio Tanaka, "The Nikkei on Bainbridge Island, 1883–1942: A Study of Migration and Community Development" (M.A. thesis, University of Washington, 1977), 35, 38.

13. For a detailed discussion of efforts to encourage burakumin to emigrate to Hokkaido during the late Tokugawa and early Meiji eras, see Noah McCormack, "*Buraku* Emigration in the Meiji Era—Other Ways to Become 'Japanese,'" *East Asian History* 23 (June 2002): 90–100. See also John A. Harrison, *Japan's Northern Frontier: A Preliminary Study in Colonization and Expansion with Special Reference to the Relations of Japan and Russia* (Gainesville: University of Florida Press, 1953), 74, noting the presence of settlers of the "poorest class."

14. See Tanaka, "Nikkei on Bainbridge Island," 34, noting that a majority of the 2,261 passports issued between 1868 and 1884 were issued to individuals categorized as students. See also James Thomas Conte, "Overseas Study in the Meiji Period: Japanese Students in America, 1867–1902" (Ph.D. diss.,Princeton University, 1977), 46. Opponents of the Meiji government's policies also went abroad as students. Yuzo Murayama, "Information and Emigrants: Interprefectural Differences of Japanese Emigration to the Pacific Northwest, 1880–1915," *Journal of Economic History* 51, no. 1 (March 1991): 144. Yasuo Wakatsuki observes that many settled in San Francisco, where they established various newspapers and engaged in a lively critique of Japanese government policy. Wakatsuki, "Japanese Emigration to the United States," 419–420.

15. Wakatsuki, "Japanese Emigration to the United States," 400.

16. Mitziko Sawada, "Culprits and Gentlemen: Meiji Japan's Restrictions of Emigrants to the United States, 1891–1909," *Pacific Historical Review* (1991): 340–342. Also see W. L. Mackenzie King, C.M.G., Commissioner, *Report of the Royal Commission Appointed to Inquire into the Methods by Which Oriental Labourers Have Been Induced to Come to Canada* (Ottawa: Government Printing Bureau, 1908), 17 [hereafter *Report of the Royal Commission Inquiring into Oriental Labourers*]. And see Report of W. M. Rice to Commissioner-General of Immigration, 24 April 1899, 2, noting that "under the Japanese law every subject is registered in his native prefecture, which he may not leave without permission of the authorities and from which he, or she, must obtain their passports, when they desire to emigrate."

17. Kazuo Ito, *Issei: A History of Japanese Immigrants in North America*, trans. Shinichiro Nakamura and Jean S. Gerard (Seattle: Executive Committee for Publication of *Issei*, 1973), 62.

18. Ibid.; Kobayashi, "Emigration from Kaideima, Japan," 140; Tanaka, "Nikkei on Bainbridge Island," 42. The original Order Protecting Emigrants was issued in 1894.

19. Ichihashi, *Japanese in the United States*, 85; Ken Adachi, *The Enemy That Never Was: A History of the Japanese Canadians* (Toronto: McClelland and Stewart, 1976), 24. See also Hisatomi Shigenosuke, *Tokō annai: Kanada, nambei,*

hokubei, hawaii (Guide for Travel by Ship: Canada, South America, North America, Hawaii) (Kobe: Bingoya, 1916), 20.

20. Testimony of Alexander R. Milne, C.B., Collector of Customs, Victoria, B.C., in *Report of the Royal Commission on Chinese and Japanese Immigration,* 220. Also see Tatszgoro [*sic*] Nosse to Wilfrid Laurier, 6 February 1903, and J. B. Whitehead, Tokyo, to Marquess of Salisbury, 12 August 1900, in Canada, *Sessional Papers* 18, *Fourth Session of the Tenth Parliament of the Dominion of Canada, Session 1907–1908,* 7–8 Edward VII, Sessional Paper No. 74b, A. 1909 [hereafter Canada, Sessional Paper No. 74b]; F. P. Sargent, Commissioner General of Immigration, Washington, D.C., to President of the United States, 2 January 1907, RG 85, NARA.

21. J. B. Whitehead to Marquess of Salisbury, 19 May 1900, Canada, Sessional Paper No. 74b, enclosing translation entitled "Instructions issued by Foreign Office to Local Governors with regard to the restriction of Emigration to Canada"; S. Shimizu to Wilfred Laurier, Prime Minister, Ottawa, 7 August 1900, Canada, Sessional Paper No. 74b. See also *Report of the Royal Commission on Chinese and Japanese Immigration,* 396; Report of Roland S. Morris on Japanese Immigration and Alleged Discriminatory Legislation against Japanese Residents in the United States (Washington, D.C.: Government Printing Office, 1921), 82; A. E. Buck, U.S. Legation, Tokyo, to Hay, 18 May 1900, RG 85, NARA.

22. Sawada, "Culprits and Gentlemen," 339, citing *Hokubei gasshūkoku ni okeru honpōjin tokōseigen oyobi haiseki ikken,* 2 August 1900.

23. *Report of the Royal Commission on Chinese and Japanese Immigration,* 396.

24. Ito, *Issei,* 31; Tanaka, "Nikkei on Bainbridge Island," 44.

25. Ambassador Hanihara Masanao to U.S. Secretary of State Charles E. Hughes, 10 April 1924, reprinted in Gaimushō, *1924 nen beikoku imin hō seitei oyobi kore ni kan suru nichibei kōshō keika kōbusho eibun fuzoku sho* (Tokyo, 1924). Also see Tanaka, "Nikkei on Bainbridge Island," 44. For Canada, see Charles H. Young and Helen R. Y. Reid, *The Japanese Canadians* (Toronto: University of Toronto Press, 1938), 11.

26. Millis, *Japanese Problem in the United States,* 284.

27. Yuji Ichioka, *The Issei: The World of the First Generation Japanese Immigrants, 1885–1924* (New York: Free Press, 1988), citing *Shin Sekai,* 19 April 1924.

28. Laura Kessler, *Stubborn Twig: Three Generations in the Life of a Japanese American Family* (New York: Random House, 1993), 11.

29. Eileen Sunada Sarasohn, *The Issei: Portrait of a Pioneer, an Oral History* (Palo Alto, Calif.: Pacific Books, 1983), 45–46 (Takae Washizu interview).

30. Ichihashi, *Japanese in the United States,* 81–82, citing T. Okawahira, *Nihon imin ron* (Tokyo, 1905), 41–42, 89. Ichihashi was born into a samurai family in Aichi prefecture on April 15, 1878. Ibid. Gordon Chang notes that Ichihashi's own class consciousness was so acute that he refused to send his only son "to Japanese-language school for fear he would be adversely influenced by youngsters from a lower social position," and he refused ever to see his grandchildren or to have anything to do with his son for two decades after he

married a woman whose family Ichihashi regarded as substantially lower than his own in social class. Gordon H. Chang, *Morning Glory, Evening Shadow: Yamato Ichihashi and His Internment Writings, 1942–1945* (Stanford, Calif.: Stanford University Press, 1997), 74, 252. Although Sucheng Chan notes Ichihashi's strong class bias, she describes his work as the "most scholarly" of his time and "impressive." Sucheng Chan, "Asian American Historiography," *Pacific Historical Review* (1996): 363–399. Paul Spickard, in turn, describes Ichihashi as "foremost" among the sociologists and economists writing during the first few decades of the twentieth century and says that his works "remain the most comprehensive studies of the early years of the Issei generation." Paul R. Spickard, *Japanese Americans: The Formations and Transformations of an Ethnic Group* (New York: Twayne, 1996), 177. Audrey Kobayashi also leans heavily on his work.

31. Yamato Ichihashi, "Emigration from Japan and Japanese Immigration into the State of California" (Ph.D. diss., Harvard University, 1913), 327–328, published as Ichihashi, *Japanese Immigration: Its Status in California* (San Francisco, 1913), 44, part V ("The Social and Political Aspects of Japanese Immigration"), subsection entitled "The Scums of Japan Never Emigrated to America."

32. Brooks notes that the fact that the Meiji government included the names of the former outcastes in the commoner domicile registries canceled exemptions and privileges they had under Tokugawa law and made their lands subject to the new land tax. William Lyman Brooks, "Outcaste Society in Early Modern Japan" (Ph.D. diss., Columbia University, 1976), 305–306; 52. Edward Daub, "Respect—Not Pity," *Japan Christian Quarterly* 27 (January 1961): 38–45.

33. Arthur May Knapp, *Feudal and Modern Japan* (Yokohama: Kelly and Walsh, 1906), 209–210, referring to a visit by Lafcadio Hearn. Knapp does qualify his description by noting this may have been an exceptional community.

34. See, for example, Roger Daniels, *Asian America: Chinese and Japanese in the United States since 1850* (Seattle: University of Washington Press, 1988).

35. Rice Report; *Report of the Royal Commission on Chinese and Japanese Immigration,* 387, 424. For a discussion of the implications of describing laborers as members of a "coolie class," see Moon-ho Jung, *Coolies and Cane: Race, Labor, and Sugar in the Age of Emancipation* (Baltimore, Md.: Johns Hopkins University Press, 2006).

36. Tanaka, "Nikkei on Bainbridge Island," 6; Yosaburo Yoshida, "Sources and Causes of Japanese Emigration," *Annals of the American Academy of Political and Social Sciences* 34 (September 1909): 157–167. For an analysis of the ways in which the field of Asian American history was defined by anti-Asianists, see Gary Y. Okihiro, *Columbia Guide to Asian American History* (New York: Columbia University Press, 2001), 194–226. Azuma also describes ways in which the effort to respond to anti-Asianists shaped nikkei depictions of the history of their own communities. Eiichiro Azuma, "The Politics of Transnational History Making: Japanese Immigrants on the Western 'Frontier,' 1927–1941," *Journal of American History* 89, no. 4 (March 2003): 1401–1430.

37. *Kimin*, written with the characters for *suteru* (discard) and *min* (people), means "discarded people." Tetsuya Fujimoto, *Crime and Delinquency Among the Japanese-Americans* (Tokyo: Institute of Comparative Law in Japan, Chuo University Press, 1978), 50. Also see Yuji Ichioka, "The Early Japanese Immigrant Quest for Citizenship: The Background of the 1922 *Ozawa* Case," originally published in *Amerasia* 4, no. 2 (1977): 1–22, and reprinted in Charles McClain, ed., *Japanese Immigrants and American Law: The Alien Land Laws and Other Issues* (New York: Garland, 1994), 397–426, noting that the word *kimin* was often used by Japanese immigrants to characterize their position and defining it as "an abandoned people." Ichioka explains that *kimin* "refers, on the one hand, to the failure of the Japanese government to come to their aid in times of need ... on the other hand, *kimin* refers to the American repudiation of the immigrants, especially after 1922" (413).

38. Fujimoto, *Crime and Delinquency*, 50; John Price, "A History of the Outcaste: Untouchability in Japan," in George De Vos and Hiroshi Wagatsuma, eds., *Japan's Invisible Race: Caste in Culture and Personality* (Berkeley: University of California Press, 1966), 6, noting that hinin included itinerants; Hisashi Tsurutani, *America-Bound: The Japanese and the Opening of the American West*, trans. Betsey Scheiner (Tokyo: Japan Times, 1989), 39. *Ryūmin* meant "drifting people" or "displaced persons." Andrew N. Nelson, *The Modern Reader's Japanese-English Character Dictionary*, 2nd ed. (Tokyo: Charles E. Tuttle, 1974), 544. The preferred term for imin is *ijūsha*. Although the *i* of *imin* and *ijū* of *ijūsha* are written with the same character, it is not the character but the pronunciation that gives rise to the association between *imin* and *kimin*.

39. Spickard, *Japanese Americans*, 18, noting that attitudes toward emigrants in Japan were largely negative.

40. Michiyo Laing and the Issei Oral History Project, eds., *Issei Christians: Selected Interviews from the Issei Oral History Project* (Sacramento, Calif.: Issei Oral History Project, 1977), 129 (Nisuke Mitsumori interview).

41. Wakatsuki, "Japanese Emigration to the United States," 392, 416. Wakatsuki found that as late as 1961, immigrants included "many who are unable to make a living in Japan" or were "social dropouts," according to 27 percent of the respondents. Ibid, 455.

42. Y. Nakamura, Japan Times employee, Kanda, Japan, to R. S. Miller, United States Legation, Tokio, 21 January 1899, RG 85, NARA.

43. See Ichihashi, *Japanese in the United States*, 89; Inazō Nitobe, *The Intercourse between the United States and Japan: An Historical Sketch* (Baltimore, Md.: Johns Hopkins Press, 1891), 168, 183.

44. Jesse Frederick Steiner, *The Japanese Invasion: A Study in the Psychology of Inter-Racial Contacts* (Chicago: A.C. McClurg, 1917), 103 (originally a Ph.D. diss., University of Chicago), quoting Yoshida Yosaburo.

45. S. K. Kanda, "The Japanese in Washington," *Washington Magazine* (Alaska–Greater Northwest) 1, no. 3 (May 1906): 193–197.

46. Knapp, *Feudal and Modern Japan*, 211. Samurai status was not necessarily inconsistent with outcaste status for the additional reason that "eta" who were assigned to act as executioners were allowed to wear swords, a right that was otherwise strictly limited to members of the samurai class. See Kyohei Yamamoto, "The Pariah People of Japan," *Japan Christian Intelligencer* I (5 May 1926): 118; Price, "History of the Outcaste," 22; David L. Howell, *Geographies of Identity in Nineteenth-Century Japan* (Berkeley: University of California Press, 2005), 31.

47. Sarasohn, *The Issei*, 46.

48. Michael K. Bourdaghs, "Shimazaki Tōson's *Hakai* and Its Bodies," in Helen Hardacre and Adam L. Kern, eds., *New Directions in the Study of Meiji Japan* (Leiden: Brill, 1997), 169–170. See also Price, "History of the Outcaste," 11–12. This is also the explanation that Azuma offers. Eiichiro Azuma, *Between Two Empires: Race, History, and Transnationalism in Japanese America* (Oxford: Oxford University Press, 2005), 72, 229 n. 12, stating without further clarification that outcastes were "considered to be of foreign blood lines, such as Ainu, Chinese, and Koreans." For a discussion of the idea that burakumin were of foreign origin, see Brooks, "Outcaste Society in Early Modern Japan," 22, noting that the belief that burakumin are descended from Koreans or other foreigners "persists even though modern historical studies have shown conclusively that the Burakumin are Japanese in origin."

49. Kiyoshi K. Kawakami, *Asia at the Door: A Study of the Japanese Question in Continental United States, Hawaii and Canada* (New York: Fleming H. Revell, 1914), 101. Kiyoshi Kawakami was born in Tokyo in 1873 and emigrated to the United States after receiving a degree in law from the University of Tokyo. He later adopted the name Karl because he admired Karl Marx. Box 30, "The Anti-Japanese League, Seattle," *Survey on Race Relations*, Hoover Institution on War, Revolution and Peace, Stanford, Calif.

50. Howard Hiroshi Sugimoto, *Japanese Immigration, the Vancouver Riots and Canadian Diplomacy* (New York: Arno Press, 1978), 21–22.

51. Masakazu Iwata, *Planted in Good Soil: The History of the Issei in United States Agriculture*, vol. 1 (Issei Memorial Edition) (New York: Peter Lang, 1992), 106–107 n. 59; Wakatsuki, "Japanese Emigration to the United States," 484.

52. Iwata, *Planted in Good Soil*, 92, 106–107 n. 59. Masukazu Iwata equates the treatment of "*eta*" in Japan with conditions in Nazi Germany in the 1930s and 1940s, noting that during the Hitler era, "Jews were forbidden to marry or have sexual relations with 'Aryans' and restricted in the occupations open to them." Ibid., 107 n. 60.

53. See Richard White, *"It's Your Misfortune and None of My Own": A New History of the American West* (Norman: University of Oklahoma Press, 1993), 181, describing the West as a "world of dramatic possibilities" that offered individuals a chance to transform their lives and to "improve their position in that world."

CHAPTER THREE. NEGOTIATING STATUS AND CONTESTING RACE IN
    NORTH AMERICA

1. Notice from Governor of Fukuoka prefecture to Nakahara Hadataro, Tsuiki-machi, Chikuhō district, 27 November 1906, attached to Report of Marcus Braun, U.S. Immigrant Inspector, 12 February 1907, RG 85, NARA [hereafter Braun Report, February]. After an introductory paragraph the notice offered six prescriptions: "remember that you are a subject of the Japanese Empire and do not leave a shameful impression in a foreign country; control yourself and avoid the temptation to neglect your work or to gamble, drink, etc.; be honest with your employer and avoid any impulse to be rude or aggressive; be friendly with your colleagues and avoid being drawn into any fights or arguments; working hard and saving your money should be your main concerns, do not fritter your money away as soon as you accumulate a little; and be careful about your health and maintain your physical well being" (my translation). Similar notices were issued by other prefectural governors. See, for example, Yukiko Kimura, *Issei: Japanese Immigrants in Hawaii* (Honolulu: University of Hawaii Press, 1988), 5 (notice issued by governor of Hiroshima prefecture). See also Donald Teruo Hata, Jr., " 'Undesirables' ": Unsavory Elements among the Japanese in America Prior to 1893 and Their Influence on the First Anti-Japanese Movement in California" (Ph.D. diss., University of Southern California, 1970), 127, citing Circular from Foreign Ministry to Prefectural Governors of Kanagawa, Hyōgo, Osaka, Nagasaki, and Niigata, 15 September 1891, Nihon Gaimushō, *Nihon gaikō bunsho* (order directing prefectural governors to restrict contract-based labor emigration and to notify emigrants that they should be careful about their appearance in order not to become the object of criticism when they are abroad).

2. K. T. Takahashi, *The Anti-Japanese Petition: Appeal in Protest against a Threatened Persecution* (Montreal: Gazette Printing Co., 1897), 6.

3. "Address of Mr. R. Cassidy, K.C., on Behalf of the Japanese," *Report of the Royal Commission on Chinese and Japanese Immigration*, 402,

4. Official Dispatch No. 14, Takahashi Shinkichi, Consul of Japan, New York City, to Yoshida Kiyonari, Foreign Minister, 13 February 1884, Nihon Gaimushō, *Nihon gaikō bunsho* 18, 104–11, quoted in Hata, "Undesirables," 25, 30–31.

5. *Shokumin kyōkai hōkoku* (Reports of the Colonization Society), No. 14, 1894, as quoted in Patricia E. Roy, J. L. Granatstein, Masako Iino, and Hiroko Takamura, *Mutual Hostages: Canadians and Japanese during the Second World War* (Toronto: University of Toronto Press, 1990), 4.

6. Robert A. Wilson and Bill Hosokawa, *East to America: A History of the Japanese in the United States* (New York: William Morrow, 1980), 114–115; Mitziko Sawada, "Culprits and Gentlemen: Meiji Japan's Restrictions of Emigrants to the United States, 1891–1909," *Pacific Historical Review* (1991): 339, 359, noting the Meiji government's concern that "the character of the Japanese abroad will be taken as an index of the character of the nation at home" and its fear that those emigrating were not " 'the right kind of people.' "

7. Hata, " 'Undesirables,' " 122, quoting a newspaper clipping dated 7 April 1891 marked "San Francisco" enclosed with Official Dispatch No. 6 from Consul Chinda Sutemi to Foreign Minister Aoki Shuzo, 25 April 1891, Nihon Gaimushō, *Nihon gaikō bunsho.*

8. Japanese Consul, San Francisco, to Foreign Ministry, Tokyo, 22 and 25 April 1891, *Hokubei gasshūkoku ni okeru honpōjin tokōseigen oyobi haiseki ikken* (Records Concerning Travel Restriction and Exclusion of Japanese Citizens in the United States) (1891–1912), quoted in Sawada, "Culprits and Gentlemen," 339; Wilson and Hosokawa, *East to America*, 114–115, quoting Official Dispatch No. 6 from Consul Chinda Sutemi to Foreign Minister Aoki Shuzo, 25 April 1891.

9. *Amerika tobei zasshi* 12 (June 1908): 30, as quoted in Sawada, "Culprits and Gentlemen," 344.

10. F. P. Sargent, U.S. Commissioner-General of Immigration, to the President of the United States, 2 January 1907, RG 85, NARA.

11. Baron Rempei Kondo, "Japan Harbors No Ill Feeling toward America," and Hon. Kahei Otani, "America and Japan Always Friends," both in in Naoichi Masaoka, ed., *Japan's Message to America: A Symposium by Representative Japanese on Japan and American-Japanese Relations* (Tokyo, 1914), 39, 62–63. Baron Kondo was president of the Nippon Yusen Kaisha.

12. Roy et al., *Mutual Hostages*, 4, quoting *Shokumin kyokai hokoku* (Reports of the Colonization Society), 1893–1903.

13. Hata, " 'Undesirables,' " 33, quoting Official Dispatch No. 14, Takahashi Shinkichi, Consul of Japan, New York City, to Yoshida Kiyonari, Foreign Minister, 13 February 1884, Nihon Gaimushō, *Nihon gaikō bunsho* 18, 104–111.

14. Initially set at $50, the head tax was subsequently raised to $100 in 1900 and then to $500 in 1903. Patricia Roy, *A White Man's Province: British Columbia Politicians and Chinese and Japanese Immigrants, 1858–1914* (Vancouver: University of British Columbia Press, 1989), 67–68, 97–99, 101–102.

15. *San Francisco Call*, 6 May 1892. Other historians have also noted Meiji diplomats' concerns that North Americans would fail to distinguish Japanese and Chinese in ways they considered significant. Eiichiro Azuma, for example, analyzes arguments to this effect in California. Eiichiro Azuma, *Between Two Empires: Race, History, and Transnationalism in Japanese America* (Oxford: Oxford University Press, 2005), 37–38. Patricia Roy argues that efforts made by Japanese diplomats to convince British Columbians that "Japanese were of a 'different class' than the Chinese" helped to preserve the impression that the two groups should be treated differently under Canadian law. Roy, *White Man's Province*, 98. This chapter builds on these earlier discussions by considering ways in which internally contradictory elements in these and other arguments advanced by Meiji diplomats ultimately undermined their efforts to favorably position Japanese subjects in North America. Another issue explored here is the preoccupation of the Meiji government officials with the historical status differences that they believed existed between themselves and dekasegi laborers.

16. *San Francisco Chronicle*, 23 February 1905.

17. Akira Iriye, "Minds across the Pacific: Japan in American Writing (1853–1883)," *Papers on Japan from Seminars at Harvard University*, vol. I, ed. Albert Craig and J. K. Fairbank (Cambridge, Mass.: Harvard University, East Asian Research Center, 1961), 28, stating that "history was conceived of in terms of progress, and all societies were given status in the scale of civilization in accordance with the degree of progress they had achieved."

18. "Japanese Consul in Cumberland, What He Thinks of the Alien Bill, Our City and Other Things," *The Weekly News* (Cumberland, B.C.), 4 March 1899.

19. Ibid. Regardless of Shimizu's insistence that Canadians generally preferred Japanese to Chinese laborers, newspaper accounts suggest that anti-Asian prejudice cut both ways. In an April 1893 article, for example, Cumberland's *Weekly News* stated that although some Japanese laborers did well, "in the main they are not steady workers like the Chinese." *The Weekly News* (Cumberland, B.C.), 26 April 1893. The Meiji oligarchs established the Ministry of Education in 1871. The Fundamental Code of Education adopted in 1872 initially provided for four years of compulsory education and declared "there shall, in the future, be no community with an illiterate family, or a family with an illiterate person." Kenneth B. Pyle explains that "although the goal was not immediately realized, by the turn of the century more than 90 percent of the children of statutory school age were in school." Kenneth B. Pyle, *The Making of Modern Japan*, 2nd ed. (Lexington, Mass.: D. C. Heath, 1996), 91.

20. Takahashi, *Anti-Japanese Petition*, 7, 14.

21. Ibid., 6. U.S. and Canadian officials both realized just how important the issue of equal status was to Japan. See, for example, testimony of Alexander R. Milne, C.R., Collector of Customs for Victoria, B.C., *Report of the Royal Commission on Chinese and Japanese Immigration*, 220.

22. "Japanese Consul in Cumberland."

23. S. Shimizu, Japanese Consul, Vancouver, B.C., to Sir Wilfrid Laurier, 14 March 1898,Canada, Sessional Paper No. 74b.

24. "Nosse in Montreal: Japanese Consul Gives His Opinion on British Columbia and Oriental Immigration," *Victoria Daily Colonist*, 28 March 1897. For a general description of the head tax imposed on Chinese immigrants, see *Report of the Royal Commission Inquiring into Oriental Labourers*, 61. For a description of the way Chinese immigration was organized, see Wilson and Hosokawa, *East to America*, 103–105.

25. "Nosse in Montreal." Although some Japanese immigrants converted to Christianity, especially later, Nosse appears to have been exaggerating the percentage of such conversions in 1897 for rhetorical effect.

26. Tatszgoro [*sic*] Nosse, Japanese Consul, to Wilfrid Laurier, 3 February 1903, 97, Canada, Sessional Paper No. 74b.

27. "Nosse in Montreal."

28. Ibid.

29. "Address of Mr. R. Cassidy, K.C., on Behalf of the Japanese," *Report of the Royal Commission on Chinese and Japanese Immigration*, 409. Cassidy's argument

that there was no racial divide in Canada ignored, of course, Canada's
marginalization of its indigenous peoples on racial grounds.

30. For a general discussion of Canadian fears of U.S. expansionism, see Doug
Owram, *Promise of Eden: The Canadian Expansionist Movement and the Idea of the
West, 1856–1900* (Toronto: University of Toronto Press, 1980).

31. "Nosse in Montreal."

32. Takahashi, *Anti-Japanese Petition*, 13.

33. Ibid., 15.

34. Yasuo Wakatsuki, "Japanese Emigration to the United States, 1866–1924: A
Monograph," *Perspectives in American History* 12 (1979): 421.

35. For a description of the coal-mining industry in B.C, see *Report of the Royal
Commission on Chinese and Japanese Immigration*, 71–90. See also Gayel A.
Horsfall, "Ethnic Conflict in Context: Cumberland, B.C., 1880–1940" (paper
presented at the Sixth B.C. Studies Conference, November 1990, Vancouver,
B.C., November 1990, copy on file in University of British Columbia, Special
Collections and Archives, SPAM 21521), 2, explaining that Japanese miners
were paid the same tonnage rates for coal as Europeans, but other sources of
payment, such as yardage rates, were lower," and there was no "guaranteed
. . . daily wage minimum," citing *Report of the Royal Commission Inquiring into
Oriental Labourers*, 48. Similar wage differentials were also a factor in other
industries to which Japanese laborers turned when they first arrived, including
lumber mills, railroad construction, and fish canneries. H. A. Millis, *The
Japanese Problem in the United States* (New York: Macmillan, 1915), 37–40.

36. Kazuo Ito, *Issei: A History of Japanese Immigrants in North America*, trans.
Shinichiro Nakamura and Jean S. Gerard (Seattle: Executive Committee for
Publication of *Issei*, 1973), 293.

37. See, for example, Shigesaki Ninomiya, "An Inquiry Concerning the Origin,
Development, and Present Situation of the 'Eta' in Relation to the History of
Social Classes in Japan" (M.A. thesis, University of Washington, 1931), 106. For
contemporary attitudes toward mining in Japan, see also Baroness Shidzué
Ishimoto, "Are Miners Human Beings?" in her autobiography, *Facing Two
Ways: The Story of My Life* (Stanford, Calif.: Stanford University Press, 1984),
158–164 (originally published in 1935). Shidzué Ishimoto, herself a convert to
Christianity, provides a compassionate account of the conditions she observed
in a coal mine in southern Japan during the early twentieth century, one that
highlights the harsh and dehumanizing conditions in which coal miners, male
and female, worked. Ishimoto notes that the miners competed for work with
groups of chained prisoners (315). Although Ishimoto recognizes the essential
humanity of the miners, she nevertheless invokes the same kind of animal
imagery historically associated with outcaste status to describe their daily lives.
Ishimoto says, for example, that "it would be hard to tell the difference between
the life of pigs and the life of these miners. Certainly the human beings were
living like animals in barns" (316). Emiko Ohnuki-Tierney makes reference to
Natsume Sōseki's book, *Kōfu* (The Miners) in the following terms: "To ask if

there is an occupation more inferior (*katō*) than mining is like asking if there are any days in the year after December 31." She also describes a conversation in which "an educated miner, who had also fallen," tells the young man, "If you are a Japanese, get out of the mine and find an occupation that is good for Japan." Emiko Ohnuki-Tierney, *Rice as Self: Japanese Identities through Time*, trans. Megan Backus (Princeton, N.J.: Princeton University Press, 1993), 104–105. See also Edward Norbeck, "Little-Known Minority Groups of Japan," in George De Vos and Hiroshi Wagatsuma, eds., *Japan's Invisible Race: Caste in Culture and Personality* (Berkeley: University of California Press, 1966), 193, describing mine workers as a low-status group only slightly less inferior than "eta."

38. Michiko Midge Ayukawa, "Creating and Recreating Community" (Ph.D. diss., University of Victoria, 1996), 51, 60–64. See also Cheryl Maeva Thomas, "The Japanese Communities of Cumberland, British Columbia, 1885–1942: Portrait of a Past" (M.A. thesis, University of Victoria, 1992), 48, 53, citing interview 260:89.08.27 with the daughter of a miner who told her "her father had come from Kumamoto in 1910 to be a miner with about sixty other men."

39. *Report of the Royal Commission on Chinese and Japanese Immigration*, 372.

40. Ito, *Issei*, 557.

41. *The Weekly News* (Cumberland, B.C.), 26 April 1893.

42. According to Shigesaki Ninomiya, a majority of miners in the Fukuoka coal mines were "*eta*." Ninomiya, "Inquiry Concerning the Origin of the 'Eta,' " 106. See also Regine Mathias, "Female Labor in the Japanese Coal-Mining Industry," in Janet Hunter, ed., *Japanese Women Working* (New York: Routledge, 1993), 98–121, stating that a significant percentage of those working in the coal mines in northern Kyushu during the second half of the nineteenth century were burakumin. And see Ayukawa, "Creating and Recreating Community," 55–57, 63, 68, citing Sasaki Toshiji, "Yunion Tanko: Dainiji Keiyaku Imin," *Pan* 7 (December 1987). Mikiso Hane reports that even some mining companies in Japan refused to employ "*eta*" until well into the Meiji period because they believed they would pollute the mines; others forced them to wash in water that was first used to wash horses. Mikiso Hane, *Peasants, Rebels and Outcastes: The Underside of Modern Japan* (New York: Pantheon, 1982), 242.

43. *The Weekly News* (Cumberland, B.C.), 8 February 1893, reporting that six Japanese miners who had deserted the Union mine were arrested in Nanaimo as vagrants.

44. *Report of the Royal Commission Inquiring into Oriental Labourers*, 42, 48, comprising records provided to the Japanese consul in Vancouver, B.C., by the Canadian Nippon Supply Company in 1907. Notations in the records indicating occupation also singled out miners for identification.

45. Nihon Gaimushō, *Nihon gaikō bunsho* 23, 650; Wakatsuki, "Japanese Emigration to the United States," 409.

46. Ito, *Issei*, 296–297, 562–563.

47. Thomas, "Japanese Communities of Cumberland, B.C.," 53, 114–115 (interview 260:89.08.27).

48. Ito, *Issei*, 57.
49. Roy Kiyooka, *Mothertalk: Life Stories of Mary Kiyoshi Kiyooka*, ed. Daphne Marlatt (Edmonton, Alberta: NeWest Press, 1997), 73.
50. Ito, *Issei*, 57, 75.
51. Hisashi Tsurutani, *America-Bound: The Japanese and the Opening of the American West*, trans. Betsey Scheiner (Tokyo: Japan Times, 1989), 159.
52. Ito, *Issei*, 75. The admiral's name was in fact Tōgō Heihachirō.
53. Osamu Kasahara, conversation with author, Burnaby, B.C., 21 August 2003. See also Robert Guest, "A Tale of Two Sisters: Japanese Untouchables Emerging from Centuries of Scorn," *Far Eastern Economic Review* 155, no. 27 (9 July 1992): 28–29, describing the decision made by one of two sisters in late-twentieth-century Japan to change her name in order to try to avoid the impact of the prejudice they had to contend with because of their descent from outcaste groups.
54. "First Certificate: Japanese Complies with the Provisions of the Immigration Act," *Victoria Daily Colonist*, 15 January 1901. Also see "Reports of the Immigration Officer for the Island District," W. H. Ellis, Victoria B.C., 14 January 1901, *Reports of Immigration Officers Under Act of 1900*, 2 Ed. 7 (1902), 849. Edward Norbeck states that blacksmiths also constituted a "despised occupational class" during the Tokugawa era. Norbeck, "Little-Known Minority Groups of Japan," in De Vos and Wagatsuma, *Japan's Invisible Race*, 188.
55. Canada, Immigration Records, Victoria, B.C., RG 76, LAC. The real names of the immigrants in question, and those they would have provided had there been any question about their legal status, may have been Kajikawa and Hirasawa, but this is difficult to know from the records that exist.

CHAPTER FOUR. CONFRONTING WHITE RACISM

1. Kazuo Ito, *Issei: A History of Japanese Immigrants in North America*, trans. Shinichiro Nakamura and Jean S. Gerard (Seattle: Executive Committee for Publication of *Issei*, 1973), 37–38. See also, Yasuo Wakatsuki, "Japanese Emigration to the United States, 1866–1924: A Monograph," *Perspectives in American History* 12 (1979): 439, explaining that motion pictures first reached Japan in 1897.
2. Nagai Kafū, *American Stories*, trans. Mitsuko Iriye (New York: Columbia University Press, 1992), 179. Kafū, the eldest son of a high-ranking diplomat, left for the United States on September 24, 1903, and spent four years in Tacoma, making occasional visits to Seattle, before going on to live in New York, Washington, D.C., and France. Mitsuko Iriye, "Introduction," in ibid., vii, x, xii–xiii.
3. Osada Shohei, comp., *Kanada no Makutsu* (Brothels of Canada) (Vancouver, B.C.: Tairiku Nippō-sha, 1909), 4–5 (my translation). See also Masue Tagashira, interviewed by Joanne Wood and Eric Sokugawa, Vancouver, B.C., 6 July 1983, Japanese Canadian Oral History Collection, National Nikkei Museum and Heritage Centre, Burnaby, B.C.; Eileen Sunada Sarasohn, *The Issei: Portrait of a*

Pioneer, an Oral History (Palo Alto, Calif.: Pacific Books, 1983), 44 (Ai Miyasaki interview explaining that she "wanted to go to a big country where it was free").

4. See Andrea Geiger, "Cross-Pacific Dimensions of Race, Caste and Class: Meiji-Era Japanese Immigrants in the North American West" (Ph.D. diss., University of Washington, 2006), 137.

5. Katharine Jane Lentz, "Japanese American Relations in Seattle" (Ph.D. diss., University of Washington, 1924), 79.

6. Kotaro Mochizuki, former Member of Parliament and Barrister at Law, ed., *Japan and America: In Commemoration of the Visit of Japanese Representative Businessmen to America at the Invitation of the American Chambers of Commerce on the Pacific Slope* (Tokyo: Liberal News, 1909), 21. See also Shibusawa Eiichi, "Japanese-American Relations and Myself," in Naoichi Masaoka, ed., *Japan's Message to America: A Symposium by Representative Japanese on Japan and American-Japanese Relations* (Tokyo, 1914), 20. And see Wakatsuki, "Japanese Emigration to the United States," 432–433, noting the image of the United States as a "benefactor who had opened up their country."

7. Lentz, "Japanese American Relations in Seattle," 87.

8. Wakatsuki, "Japanese Emigration to the United States," 437, citing Yokoyama Gennosuke, *Kaigaikatsudo no nihonjin* (Japanese Active Overseas) (Tokyo, 1906), 8.

9. Yone Noguchi, *Japan and America* (Tokyo: Keio University Press, 1921), 51.

10. Roy Kiyooka, *Mothertalk: Life Stories of Mary Kiyoshi Kiyooka*, ed. Daphne Marlatt (Edmonton, Alberta: NeWest Press, 1997), 70, 128.

11. Ken Adachi, *The Enemy That Never Was: A History of the Japanese Canadians* (Toronto: McClelland and Stewart, 1976), 90.

12. Kiyooka, *Mothertalk*, 26–27, 44–47.

13. Tomoko Yamazaki, *The Story of Yamada Waka: From Prostitute to Feminist Pioneer*, trans. Wakako Hironaka and Ann Kostant (Tokyo: Kodansha International, 1985), 54.

14. Sarasohn, *The Issei*, 25 (Sadame Inouye interview). See also "Life History of a Forty-Five Year Old Japan Man at Santa Paula," trans, M. Doda, Folder 323 (17), Box 31, circa 1922, *Survey on Race Relations*, Hoover Institution on War, Revolution and Peace, Stanford, Calif.

15. Wakatsuki, "Japanese Emigration to the United States," 433.

16. Kiyoshi K. Kawakami, *Asia at the Door: A Study of the Japanese Question in Continental United States, Hawaii and Canada* (London: Fleming H. Revell, 1914), 78–79.

17. Sarasohn, *The Issei*, 21 (Shoichi Fukuda interview), 62–63 (Ai Miyasaki interview).

18. T. Yasuda, "Leathermaking in Japan," *The Japan Magazine* 6 (January 1916): 547–548. Even butcher shops established in Yokohama by foreigners during the early years of the Meiji period were relegated to the edge of town. Julia Meech-Pekarik, *The World of the Meiji Print: Impressions of a New Civilization* (New York: Weatherhill, 1986), 50.

19. In a short story written in 1871 and entitled "The Beefeater," intended as a parody of the unthinking embrace of Western ways, the main character at one point says to his dinner companion: "Beef is certainly a most delicious thing, isn't it? For over 1,620—or is it 1,630—years people in the West have eaten huge quantities of beef ... We really should be grateful that even people like ourselves can now eat beef, thanks to the fact that Japan is steadily becoming a truly civilized country." Kanagaki Robun, "The Beefeater," in Donald Keene, ed., *Modern Japanese Literature* (New York: Grove Press, 1956), 32. See also Naomichi Ishige, *The History and Culture of Japanese Food* (London: Kegan Paul, 2001), 150–151, stating that "meat eating was held up as a symbol of modern civilization ... in the early Meiji period people absorbed civilization in part through their stomachs."

20. George O. Totten and Hiroshi Wagatsuma, "Emancipation: Growth and Transformation of a Political Movement," in George De Vos and Hiroshi Wagatsuma, eds., *Japan's Invisible Race: Caste in Culture and Personality* (Berkeley: University of California Press, 1966), 34, citing Buraku Mondai Kenkyūjo (Buraku Issue Research Institute), ed., *Buraku no rekishi to kaihō undō* (1955), 129.

21. Wakatsuki, "Japanese Emigration to the United States," 405.

22. Akemi Kikumura, *Through Harsh Winters: The Life of a Japanese Immigrant Woman* (Novato, Calif.: Chandler and Sharp, 1981), 27, 112.

23. Sakuya Nishimura and Susan Michi Sirovyak, "A Guidebook to Living in Canada—1906 Style!" *Nikkei Images* 6, no. 2 (Summer 2001), citing J. S. Watanabe, *An English-Japanese Conversational Guide and Cook Book* (1906).

24. During the early decades of the Meiji period, the phrase used to express that reaction—still recognizable today—was *batā kusai*, or "reeking of butter." In a short story, Nagai Kafū also refers to the "smell of sweat characteristic of a meat-eating race." Nagai Kafū, "Rude Awakening," in *American Stories*, 108. When Americans and Europeans first arrived in Japan, Japanese were also repulsed by the smell of tobacco smoke. See Kinya Tsuruta, ed., *The Walls Within: Images of Westerners in Japan and Images of the Japanese Abroad: Selected Proceedings* (Vancouver: University of British Columbia, 1989), 84.

25. *New York Daily Tribune*, 1 July 1906.

26. Lydia Minatoya, *Talking to High Monks in the Snow: An Asian American Odyssey* (New York: HarperCollins, 1992), 16.

27. Sasabune [Sasaki Chuichi], *Amerika seikatsu* (Life in America) (Los Angeles: Taishūsha, 1937), 136–137 (my translation). The phrase the author uses instead of *hakujin* is *ketō no fujin*—roughly, "hairy Tang woman." "Tang," a reference to a Chinese dynasty, here means "Chinese [i.e., foreign]."

28. Tsuruta, "Introduction," in Tsuruta, *Walls Within*, ii. See also Steve Rabson, " 'Occidentalism' and Self-Reflection: Western Personae in the Work of Modern Japanese Poets," in Tsuruta, *Walls Within*, 83–84, citing additional examples, including comparisons of Caucasians to pigs, cats, bears, and orangutans. And see Marilyn Ivy, *Discourses of the Vanishing: Modernity, Phantasm, Japan*

(Chicago: University of Chicago Press, 1995), 23, describing *burakumin* and *gaijin* (foreigners) as categories where difference is recognized as such in a Japan that otherwise insists on homogeneity. Maryka Omatsu notes that even after the war Japanese Canadians still thought of their Caucasian neighbors as gaijin. Maryka Omatsu, *Bittersweet Passage: Redress and the Japanese-Canadian Experience* (Toronto: Between the Lines, 1992), 151. Herman Ooms argues that the equation between gaijin and outcastes is also reflected in the use of the term *jingai* to refer to outcaste groups in certain areas. *Jingai* is written with the same characters as *gaijin*, but reversed. Herman Ooms, *Tokugawa Village Practice: Class, Status, Power, Law* (Berkeley: University of California Press, 1996), 288.

29. See John Price, "A History of the Outcaste: Untouchability in Japan," in De Vos and Wagatsuma, *Japan's Invisible Race*, 37–38, citing *Zenkoku minji kanrei ruishu* (Handbook of Japanese Customs and Folkways).

30. Michiyo Laing and the Issei Oral History Project, eds., *Issei Christians: Selected Interviews from the Issei Oral History Project* (Sacramento, Calif.: Issei Oral History Project, 1977), 161.

31. Sarasohn, *The Issei,* 67 (Juhei Kono interview).

32. Inazo Nitobe, *The Intercourse between the United States and Japan* (1891), 190.

33. Sarasohn, *The Issei,* 61 (Minejiro Shibata interview). Another immigrant later used the words of a character in an autobiographical novel to express a similar sentiment: "These hakujin think we are animals. They treat us like animals." Tooru J. Kanazawa, *Sushi and Sourdough: A Novel* (Seattle: University of Washington Press, 1989), 87. Audrey Lynn Kobayashi recounts a similar experience: "When, in 1981, I interviewed an elderly woman in Japan who had spent some years working as a domestic servant in Canada, she rapidly became upset, expressing anger and contempt for the woman who had treated her 'like an animal.' " Audrey Kobayashi, "For the Sake of the Children: Japanese/ Canadian Workers/Mothers," in Audrey Lynn Kobayashi, ed., *Women, Work, and Place* (Montreal: McGill-Queen's University Press, 1994), 63.

34. *Shin Sekai,* 20 November 1923, as quoted in and translated by Eiichiro Azuma, "Interstitial Lives: Race, Community, and History among Japanese Immigrants Caught between Japan and the United States, 1885–1941" (Ph.D. diss., University of California, Los Angeles, 2000), 165. In the book based on the dissertation, however, Azuma skims over this point, summarizing this quotation by stating only that "one editorial compared Issei to *burakumin*, Japan's outcast group that was often thought to be of alien origin." Eiichiro Azuma, *Between Two Empires: Race, History, and Transnationalism in Japanese America* (Oxford: Oxford University Press, 2005), 72.

35. Kafū, "Chronicle of Chinatown," in *American Stories,* 199.

36. Andrew N. Nelson, *The Modern Reader's Japanese-English Character Dictionary,* 2nd ed. (Tokyo: Charles E. Tuttle, 1974), 366, 528. Tooru Kanazawa records the use of the word *ketō,* translating it as "dirty, hairy foreigner," as well as *chikushō,* translating it as "a beast" and "like a wild animal," to refer to white men,

particularly those who discriminated against Japanese. Kanazawa, *Sushi and Sourdough*, 76, 83.

37. Wolfgang Hadamitzky and Mark Spahn, *Kanji and Kana: A Handbook and Dictionary of the Japanese Writing System* (Tokyo: Charles E. Tuttle, 1981), 313.

38. "Taro's Notebook: Suggestions to Resident Japanese," *Taihoku Nippō* (Great Northern Daily News; Seattle) (early twentieth century), translation found in RG 85, NARA. The author's reference to a "Nagasaki period" is probably a reference to late sixteenth-century and early seventeenth-century Japan, when Europeans first arrived in Japan and when Deshima, a small island in Nagasaki Bay, was designated the only place where Europeans—specifically, the Dutch—were permitted to land.

39. David Starr Jordan, "The Japanese Problem in California," *Out West: A Magazine of the Old Pacific and the New* (March 1907): 224. Other newspapers had also noted that Southern sympathy for exclusionists on the West Coast was based on their equating the "problem" posed by Asian immigrants with their own "Negro problem." Eleanor Tupper and George E. McReynolds, *Japan in American Public Opinion* (New York: Macmillan, 1937), 29–30, 47, citing the *New Orleans Times-Democrat*, 17 March 1910; *The Atlantic Journal*, 14 February 1909; and the *Charleston News and Courier* and the *Louisville Courier-Journal*.

40. Cullen Tadao Hayashida, "Identity, Race and the Blood Ideology of Japan" (Ph.D. diss., University of Washington, 1976), 119. See also Kei Tanaka, "Japanese Picture Marriage in 1900–1924: California Construction of Japanese Race and Gender" (Ph.D. diss., Rutgers University, 2002), 75, noting that "Japanese immigrants degraded African Americans" and citing the example of one immigrant who complained that a black maid "treated me—Japanese race—as if I were of her own kind. Whenever she did that, well, because I am Japanese, I felt frustrated." And see Kathianne Hingwan, "Identity, Otherness and Migrant Labour in Japan," in Roger Goodman and Ian Neary, eds., *Case Studies on Human Rights in Japan* (Richmond, England: Japan Library, 1996), 51.

41. William Elliot Griffis, *The Japanese Nation in Evolution: Steps in the Progress of a Great People* (New York: Thomas Y. Crowell, 1907), 111. Griffis noted that this explanation is unsupported by any evidence. In his words, "There are no scientific grounds for supposing that the Eta or hi-nin were 'curly-haired negroids,' or 'offskins' of any kind, or that they were extra-ethnic in origin." Ibid.

42. Kafū, "The Inebriated Beauty," in *American Stories*, 43.

43. Sarasohn, *The Issei*, 67 (Osuke Takizawa interview).

44. Ito, *Issei*, 134 (Dr. Sakigake Hideyoshi interview).

45. Hugh H. Smythe and Mabel M. Smythe, "Race, Culture, and Politics in Japan," *Phylon* 13, no. 3 (1956): 198; emphasis in original.

46. Shunkichi Akimoto, "Thoughts in America: American Race Problems—The 'Eta' of Chicago—Japanese Reactions to Exclusion—Visit America and See," *The Trans-Pacific*, 21 March 1929.

47. John Donoghue, "The Social Persistence of Outcaste Groups," in De Vos and Wagatsuma, *Japan's Invisible Race*, 147, 166.

48. See generally Osada, *Kanada no Makutsu*.

49. Nihon Gaimushō, *Nihon gaikō bunsho* 24, 460, as quoted in Robert A. Wilson and Bill Hosokawa, *East to America: A History of the Japanese in the United States* (New York: William Morrow, 1980), 32.

50. Wilson and Hosokawa, *East to America*, 32. According to the report prepared for the Meiji government by Fujita Yoshiro in July 1891, of the 250 Japanese in Seattle at that time, just 40 were proprietors or employees of groceries or restaurants; approximately 200 were either directly involved in prostitution or were gamblers or pimps; and 10 were employed in other areas. Ibid., 33.

51. Nitobe, *Intercourse between the United States and Japan*, 184. Although fears about the way in which North Americans viewed Japanese was the predominant concern, it is worth noting that some prostitutes were historically categorized as hinin in Tokugawa-era society. Ooms, *Tokugawa Village Practice*, 301; Price, "History of the Outcaste," 22.

52. Hata " 'Undesirables,' " 91 n. 18, quoting *San Francisco Bulletin*, 4 May 1892. Articles of this kind also appeared in other U.S. cities and in Canada. See, for example, "Bad Character from Japan," *Victoria Times*, 22 May 1907 (about the alleged attempt of Keijiro Suzuki to smuggle five women into Canada); "Six Little Maids All Unwary," *Victoria Colonist*, 1 July 1904.

53. In 1907, the United States passed legislation excluding "women or girls coming into the United States for the purpose of prostitution or for any other immoral purpose" and "persons who procure or attempt to bring in" women for that reason. Amendments to this legislation in 1910 provided for the "punishment and deportation of aliens who in any way profit or derive benefit from the proceeds of prostitution." "Abstract of the Report on Importation and Harboring of Women for Immoral Purposes," in *Reports of the Immigration Commission, Committee on Immigration, U.S. Senate, 61st Congress, Presented by Mr. Dillingham* (Washington, D.C.: Government Printing Office, 1911), vol. 2, p. 327. The reports are hereafter cited as the Dillingham Commission Reports.

54. Lentz, "Japanese American Relations in Seattle," 85.

55. Hisashi Tsurutani, *America-Bound: The Japanese and the Opening of the American West*, trans. Betsey Scheiner (Tokyo: Japan Times, 1989), 167; Adachi, *The Enemy That Never Was*, 33.

56. Osada, *Kanada no Makutsu*, 91.

57. "Traffic in Japanese Girls," *The Literary Digest*, 28 July 1894, quoting *The Japan Mail*.

58. Yamazaki, *Yamada Waka*, 16.

59. "Traffic in Japanese Girls," *The Literary Digest*, 28 July 1894, quoting *The Japan Mail* and *The Japan Gazette*.

60. Osada, *Kanada no Makutsu*, 6–7. According to Mikiso Hane, young girls from the named prefectures were particularly vulnerable to the practice of selling young girls to brothels in Japan as a way to forestall financial ruin for the rest of the family. Mikiso Hane, *Peasants, Rebels and Outcastes: The Underside of Modern Japan* (New York: Pantheon, 1982), 207. Women in Europe were also vulnerable

to deception. See Dillingham Commission Reports, vol. 2, p. 335, describing a case where "a girl left her home in Europe with the consent of her parents to act as maid to the woman procurer" but without knowing the nature of the work she would be expected to do after arriving in the United States. In a short story Nagai Kafū describes the moment he realized that there were pimps in America who tricked women into prostitution and that Western women were also vulnerable to such trickery. Kafū, "Lodging on a Snowy Night," in *American Stories*, 71.

61. Osada, *Kanada no Makutsu*, 90. Another well-known example is that of Yamada Waka. Persuaded to go abroad by a woman who befriended her after her father's death, she believed the woman's assurances that she would be able to earn far more as a seamstress in the United States than in Japan and would thus be better able to help her family. Instead, Yamada was handed over to a brothel owner as soon as she landed in Seattle. Yamazaki, *Yamada Waka*, 53–54.

62. Osada, *Kanada no Makutsu*, 90, 97.

63. In Yamazaki's words, prostitutes were "unhappy women who suffered as outcasts." Yamazaki, *Yamada Waka*, 112, 146.

64. Hane, *Peasants, Rebels and Outcastes*, 215. Hane explains that although city dwellers were somewhat more sophisticated, "in the rural areas ... prostitutes were considered less than human." Ibid., 207.

65. Yamazaki, *Yamada Waka*, 62.

66. Osada, *Kanada no Makutsu*, n.p.

67. Yamazaki, *Yamada Waka*, 69.

68. Osada, *Kanada no Makutsu*, 3. See also Ooms, *Tokugawa Village Practice*, 197, 216; Laurence Caillet, *The House of Yamazaki: The Life of a Daughter of Japan*, trans. Megan Backus (Tokyo: Kodansha International, 1994), 86; Robert J. Smith and Ella Lury Wiswell, *The Women of Suye Mura* (Chicago: University of Chicago Press, 1982), xix, noting that those who violated social taboos in Japanese village society "were subjected to the intensely powerful sanction of gossip."

69. Osada, *Kanada no Makutsu*, 2–3. Seizo Oka, Director, Japanese American History Archives, San Francisco, translates *Kanada no Makutsu* as "Canadian Dens of Whores" in his unpublished translation of *Zaibei nihonjinshi* (1940).

70. *Revelstoke Herald and Railway Men's Journal*, 20 April 1905, 27 April 1905.

71. Osada, *Kanada no Makutsu*, 151. Jennie's name was written Jonnie in the *katakana* used by the editors, but other sources make clear that the English name she used was actually Jennie. Her last name was Kiohara (also pronounced "Kiobara"). Jennie had clearly been subjected to violence on other occasions. According to Osada Shohei, Jennie had a scar on her forehead in the shape of the Japanese character for "10"—which resembles a cross—that stemmed from an altercation with her "owner" in which he had cut her with a knife. Ibid., 149. Local criminal records also reflect that in May 1903 a man named Alex Millet was found guilty of assault and fined for dragging her by

the hair and kicking her. Revelstoke Museum and Archives, Revelstoke, B.C., Criminal Records, 12 May 1903, 34–35. Millet had attacked another woman in a similar manner in Nakusp a year earlier but had avoided arrest. *Revelstoke Herald and Railway Men's Journal*, 28 May 1905.

72. *Kootenay Mail* (Revelstoke, B.C.), 22 April 1905 ("Shocking Murder—Woman Killed on Front Street"). The motive of at least one of the two Japanese, the *Kootenay Mail* reported, based on a love letter reportedly found in Jennie's room, was jealousy. Ibid. On April 29, the *Kootenay Mail* reported that the two Japanese men were innocent and that the crime may have involved theft, noting that many in Revelstoke had known that Jennie had accumulated as much as $10,000 and that she was preparing to leave that city to return to Japan. On May 6, the *Kootenay Mail* reported that a question had been raised about the involvement of certain Chinese but no definitive conclusion had been reached. *Kootenay Mail*, 29 April 1905, 6 May 1905. Revelstoke police reports reflect that approximately eighteen Japanese women were arrested for prostitution during the first decade of the twentieth century. Revelstoke Museum and Archives, Revelstoke, B.C., *Police Reports, 1899–1910*.

73. Osada, *Kanada no Makutsu*, 151.

74. Ibid., 5 (reference to kurombo); ibid., 149, stating that when someone visited the "earnest Fanny" and questioned her about her faith, she said she believed that good people go to heaven, bad people go to hell, and those who are neither good nor bad are reborn right away.

75. The chief constable, R. G. Chamberlain, provided the following patronizing statement for publication: "I regret to say some Japanese women are following the life of shame in this country, and hope this effort will prove a benefit to their fellow-countrymen and prevent the importation of Japanese women for immoral purpose, and restore those already leading an immoral [life] to a higher calling, and I am sure will be most useful to the Japanese in their own country." Osada, *Kanada no Makutsu*, frontispiece.

76. Ibid., 149.

77. Katsuyoshi Morita reported that many of the articles and the book were the result of a conversation with a man named Kashiwa who was the original publisher of the *Tairiku Nippō*, in which the various chapters of *Kanada no Makutsu* first appeared as serialized articles, and that he was later ostracized for his role in drawing attention to the role of Japanese in prostitution. Katsuyoshi Morita, *Powell Street Monogatari*, trans. Eric Sokugawa (Burnaby, B.C.: Live Canada Publishing, 1988), 78–79.

78. Ito, *Issei*, 134; Wilson and Hosokawa, *East to America*, 106.

79. *Japanese-American Commercial Weekly*, 2 June 1906, as quoted in Mitziko Sawada, *Tokyo Life, New York Dreams: Urban Japanese Visions of America, 1890–1924* (Berkeley: University of California Press, 1996), 19.

80. Kenji Ōshima, "On the Hardships Leading to the Founding of Our Shoemakers League," *Kakō dōmeikai kaihō*, 1 January 1911, 9–14; Hata, " 'Undesirables,' "

106, citing Yamato Ichihashi, *Japanese in the United States: A Critical Study of the Problems of the Japanese Immigrants and Their Children* (Stanford, Calif.: Stanford University Press, 1932), 229.

81. Ichihashi, *Japanese in the United States*,88; Urakawa Sei, "On the Future of Our League," *Kakō dōmeikai kaihō*, 1 January 1911, 5–9.

82. Kenji Ōshima, "On Hardships," 9–14. See also membership lists, *Nihonjin kakō dōmei kiyaku oyobi saisoku* (Constitution and Bylaws of the Japanese Shoemakers Association), Japanese American History Archives, San Francisco (JAHA). And see Price, "History of the Outcaste"; and Totten and Wagatsuma, "Emancipation," 22–23, 35 (shoemaking and leatherwork were occupations reserved to eta under Tokugawa law). Emiko Ohnuki-Tierney explains that "it is the lower parts of the body, including the feet, that are seen to be most defiling. Therefore, things representing that area—footgear, floor, and ground—are all dirty, and require no contact or immediate healing." Emiko Ohnuki-Tierney, *Illness and Culture in Contemporary Japan: An Anthropological View* (Cambridge: Cambridge University Press, 1984), 31.

83. Minutes of Meetings, Nihonjin Kakō Dōmeikai, 14 January 1908, JAHA.

84. The notion of a unique Japanese race (Yamato *minzoku*) infused with a spirit that is essentially Japanese (Yamato *damashii*), one that invokes Japan's ancient roots, was reconstituted and redefined during the Meiji period to facilitate the development of a strong sense of national identity. See, for example, Baron Shimpei Goto, "The Real Character of the Japanese Race," in Masaoka, *Japan's Message to America*, 12–13; T. Iyenaga and Kenoske Sato, *Japanese and the California Problem* (New York: G. P. Putnam's Sons, 1921), 16–19. See also Carol Gluck, *Japan's Modern Myths: Ideology in the Late Meiji Period* (Princeton, N.J.: Princeton University Press, 1985), 136.

85. *Nihonjin kakō dōmei kiyaku oyobi saisokui* (Constitution and Bylaws of the Japanese Shoemakers Association), article 6, JAHA; and *Kakō dōmei setsuritsu no shui* (Establishment Manifesto of the Japanese Shoemakers Association), 1893, JAHA.

86. That Jō Tsunetarō was only the public face of the organization is suggested by the appearance of his name in fifth place among the twenty names listed as the founders of the Nihonjin Kakō Dōmeikai in its original constitution and bylaws. The original membership lists of the Nihonjin Kakō Dōmeikai include some who appear—based on their names—to have been former samurai. Membership lists, *Nihonjin kakō dōmei kiyaku oyobi saisoku*, JAHA. But see Tsurutani, *America-Bound*, 199, identifying Jō Tsunetarō of Kumamoto prefecture as the primary founder of the Nihonjin Kakō Dōmeikai.

87. William Griffis reported in 1907 that the development of a Western-style army and the adoption of other Western practices and customs had boded well for butchers and shoe manufacturers, who had profited from the increasing demand for boots and other meat and leather products. Griffis,

Japanese Nation in Evolution, 109, 116. See also Price, "History of the
Outcaste," 35, noting that after the Meiji Restoration, a growing number of
majority Japanese invested in the "burgeoning leather goods industry," taking
"advantage of skills of former Eta." Ohnuki-Tierney explains that "money
represents spiritual dirt; it symbolizes worldly concerns that are impure in at
least the ideal Japanese value system." Ohnuki-Tierney, *Illness and Culture in
Contemporary Japan,* 29.

88. See, e.g., Nakano Buei, "In Rome Do as the Romans Do," in Masaoka, ed.,
Japan's Message to America, 38.

89. A former samurai who had sided with the Tokugawa during the battles
leading up to the Meiji Restoration, Nishimura Katsuzō later became
interested in the new kinds of military techniques and equipment being
imported from France. In 1869, he joined forces with a merchant from
Niigata prefecture to supply military uniforms to the new conscript army.
Nishimura's contract with the Meiji government also required him to supply
leather boots to replace the *zori* (straw sandals) that many of the newly
conscripted soldiers wore. Initially reluctant to manufacture leather boots
because it was an occupation historically restricted to members of outcaste
communities, he and his partner tried importing the boots. It quickly became
apparent, however, that this was far too expensive, so Nishimura resigned
himself to manufacturing the boots in Japan. In time, Nishimura became
president of Sakura-gumi, a large shoe factory in Tokyo, and helped to
found the Japanese Shoemakers Association, which served as a model for
the establishment of the Nihonjin Kakō Dōmeikai in San Francisco in 1893.
Japanese Leatherware Journal, nos. 1–3 (25 October 1902; 10 December 1902;
25 January 1903). According to information provided by Seizo Oka of the
Japanese American History Archives in San Francisco, Nishimura
was a high-ranking samurai who was a brother of the privy councilor
Nishimura Shigeki. Seizo Oka, conversation with author, San Francisco, 23
July 2002.

90. John B. Cornell, "Buraku Relations and Attitudes in a Progressive Farming
Community," in De Vos and Wagatsuma, *Japan's Invisible Race,* 167 n. 30, noting
one man's perception as late as 1951 that "because I am a shoemaker, everyone
would know of my Buraku origin."

91. The Japanese word for "shoe repairer" is *shūrikō,* not *kakō.* Nelson, *Japanese-
English Character Dictionary,* 952. Seizo Oka of the Japanese American
National History Archives in San Francisco noted that "shoe repairers" and
not "shoemakers" was still the preferred translation for *kakō.* Seizo Oka,
conversation with author, San Francisco, 23 July 2002.

92. Tsurutani, *America-Bound,* 199.

93. "Japs in the Shoe Trade," *San Francisco Chronicle,* 12 March 1905, reprinted in
a pamphlet entitled *The Japanese Invasion: The Movement against the Dominant
Influence of the Little Brown Men in American Trades* (San Francisco: Allied
Printing, 1905).

94. Nihonjin kakō dōmeikai kiyaku oyobi saisoku, 1893, article 10. To become a member of the organization, it was necessary to provide the names of five guarantors. Ibid., article 20. New members were first recognized at a meeting of the board of directors and then introduced to the entire membership at the general meeting. Ibid., article 30. Membership fees were fifty cents for business owners and thirty-five cents for craftsmen and apprentices. All were also required to deposit fifty cents a month to a reserve fund to be used for emergencies or capital investments, up to a total of $50 which would be returned if a member withdrew from the organization or returned to Japan. Ibid., articles 33 and 34. The organization employed one clerk to handle the related paperwork. Ibid., article 40.

95. "Japs in the Shoe Trade," quoting a 1903 statement by Mr. Gallagher of the Boot and Shoe Repairers' Union.

96. "Japs in the Shoe Trade."

97. Wilson and Hosokawa, *East to America*, 59.

98. S. K. Kanda, "The Japanese in Washington," *Washington Magazine (Alaska–Greater Northwest)* 1, no. 3 (May 1906): 196. Kanda also lists two meat and fish markets and twenty barber shops, bathhouses, and laundries.

99. H. A. Millis, *The Japanese Problem in the United States* (New York: Macmillan, 1915), 63 (citing *Japanese and Other Immigrant Races in the Pacific Coast and Rocky Mountain States, Presented by Mr. Dillingham,* part 25 of the Dillingham Commission Reports, vol. 23, p. 100 [table]). According to Ichihashi, there were approximately 105 shoe and cobbler shops in West Coast cities early in the twentieth century. Ichihashi, *Japanese in the United States*. The Los Angeles branch of the Nihonjin Kakō Dōmeikai appears to have had more difficulties retaining members than the San Francisco branch. Minutes of Meetings, Nihonjin Kakō Dōmeikai, 14 January 1908.

100. Kenji Ōshima et al., "Message upon Publication," *Kakō dōmeikai kaihō,* 1 January 1911, 2.

101. Millis, *Japanese Problem in the United States,* 68 (citing Dillingham Commission Reports, vol. 23, pp. 119–121); Nihonjin kakō dōmeikai kiyaku oyobi saisoku.

102. Urakawa Sei, "On the Future of Our League," 5–9.

103. *Kakō dōmeikai kaihō,* 1 January 1911, 9–15, 59–60, 67. Bashō's famous haiku reads: "furu ikeya, kaeru tobikomu, mizu no oto" (old pond, a frog jumps in, the sound of water). *Kyōgen* are humorous skits performed in conjunction with far more serious *noh* plays. The author added tongue-in-cheek that once the hidden talents of these individuals were revealed, the response they got was so unenthusiastic that they discontinued their efforts.

104. Ibid., 10.

105. Ibid. See also Nihonjin kakō dōmeikai kiyaku oyobi saisoku, article 6; and *Kakō dōmei setsuritsu no shui.*

106. Ichihashi, *Japanese in the United States,* 135.

107. Seizo Oka, conversation with author, San Francisco, 23 July 2002.

108. Ibid.

CHAPTER FIVE. THE U.S.-CANADA BORDER

1. See, for example, letter complaining about "Oriental labor, including the Japs," who "are constantly giving us trouble in the courts over imaginary wrongs, while we have no such trouble with the 'white labor.' " Geo. H. Webster to Dr. A. S. Monro, Medical Inspector and Immigration Agent, Vancouver, B.C., 12 August 1907. Canada, Immigration Branch, Record Group 76, Library and Archives Canada, Ottawa, Ontario [hereafter RG 76, LAC].

2. Kazuo Ito, *Issei: A History of Japanese Immigrants in North America,* trans. Shinichiro Nakamura and Jean S. Gerard (Seattle: Executive Committee for Publication of *Issei,* 1973), 36.

3. Charles Earl, Solicitor, Memorandum, 28 March 1907, Records of the Immigration and Naturalization Service, Series A, Subject Correspondence Files, part 2, Mexican Immigration, 1906–1930, File 1869–5, RG 85, NARA.

4. "Japs Turned Away, Three Orientals Unable to Pass Educational Test, First Fair Test of the New British Columbia Act," *The Province,* Vancouver, B.C., 23 January 1901; "Stop Issue of Passports, No More Japanese Immigrants to Be Allowed to Come to Canada, This Action Taken on Account of Enforcement of Provincial Act," *The Province,* 26 January 1901. The U.S. House of Representatives first considered legislation that would have required immigrants to demonstrate their literacy in 1902. Morris Report, 83, RG 85, NARA. The literacy test adopted in the United States in 1917 required immigrants only to read a passage in "some language" to demonstrate that they were literate. Ian R. H. Rockett, "American Immigration Policy and Ethnic Selection: An Overview," *Journal of Ethnic Studies* 10, no. 4 (Winter 1983): 7.

5. Abraham E. Smith, U.S. Consul, Victoria, B.C., to Assistant Secretary of State, Washington, D.C., 19 September 1907, RG 85, NARA. Australia had also imposed a literacy test similar to that adopted in British Columbia. T. Iyenaga and Kenoske Sato, *Japanese and the California Problem* (New York: G. P. Putnam's Sons, 1921), 65–66; B.C. Legislature, *Papers, Re Labour Regulation Act, 1898,* 63 Vict. 497–498. British Columbia's Natal Acts provided for a penalty of up to $500 or twelve months in jail. Ito, *Issei,* 108. B.C. legislators ignored the more stringent requirements for literacy in Japanese than in English—Japanese required mastery of a far more complex written language—and the education standards established by the new Meiji government: a majority of the migrants arriving from Japan had at least four years of schooling in Japanese.

6. J. Chamberlain, Downing Street, London, England, to Earl of Aberdeen, Governor General, Canada, 20 July 1898, enclosing copy of Immigration Restriction Act, 1897, of the Colony of Natal, requiring a test to be conducted in "any language of Europe." Canada, Sessional Paper No. 74b.

7. *Report of the Committee of the Privy Council, Approved by His Excellency the Governor General,* 21 September 1900, Canada, Sessional Paper No. 74b.

8. Kato [Takaaki, Japanese Minister to the Court of St. James] to Marquis of Salisbury, London, England, 3 August 1898, Canada, Sessional Paper No. 74b.

9. S. Shimizu, Vancouver, B.C., to Governor General, 1 September 1900, Canada, Sessional Paper No. 74b.

10. Tatszgoro [*sic*] Nosse to Governor General, 25 June 1902, Canada, Sessional Paper No. 74b.

11. David Mills, Minister of Justice, to Governor General, Ottawa, 8 November 1898, Canada, Sessional Paper No. 74b.

12. *Report of the Committee of the Privy Council.*

13. *Report of the Royal Commission on Chinese and Japanese Immigration*, 398–399; Joseph Chamberlain, Colonial Secretary, London, England, to Earl of Aberdeen, 20 July 1898, and to Earl of Minto, 23 March 1899; Chamberlain to Governor General, Canada, 19 April 1899, Canada, Sessional Paper No. 74b.

14. "That Jap," *Rosland Courier*, 11 June 1903, copy in Canada, Immigration Branch, vol. 83, file 9309, RG 76, LAC. See also Abraham E. Smith, U.S. Consul, Victoria, B.C., to Assistant Secretary of State, Washington, D.C., 19 September 1907.

15. *Victoria Daily Colonist*, 25 April 1905.

16. "Japs Arrested Tuesday Near Blaine Have Been Remanded Till Tomorrow," *Victoria Daily Colonist*, 18 December 1902.

17. "Defunct Law Was Invoked in Arrest of Japanese," *Vancouver Daily Province* (Vancouver, B.C.), 12 January 1903.

18. "Reports of the Immigration Officer for the Island District," W. H. Ellis, Victoria B.C., 14 January 1901, *Reports of Immigration Officers under Act of 1900*, 2 Ed. 7 (1902), 849; "Stop Issue of Passports"; later versions of the Natal Act in British Columbia required "any person who when asked to do so by an officer [to] write out a dictation in the character of some language of Europe and sign in the presence of the officer a passage of fifty words." C. Fitzpatrick, Minister of Justice, to Governor General, 16 November 1904; Japanese Consulate General to Lord Minto, 3 January 1901, Canada, Sessional Paper No. 74b.

19. "Reports of the Immigration Officer for the Island District," W. H. Ellis, Victoria B.C., 14 January 1901, *Reports of Immigration Officers under Act of 1900*, 2 Ed. 7 (1902), 856.

20. "Natal Act Said to Be Worthless, Farcical in Application," *Vancouver Daily Province*, 12 January 1903.

21. Clipping from *The Evening Journal*, 17 February 1908, copy in vol. 83, file no. 9309, RG 76, Canada. See also *The Vancouver Daily Province*, 20 February 1908.

22. Joseph Chamberlain to Lord Minto, 22 January 1901, Canada, Sessional Paper No. 74b.

23. In re Nakane and Okazake, 21 February 1908 (Hunter, C.J.), 13 B.C.R. 370, 28 February 1908 (Full Court), 9 Ed. 7.

24. Dorothy Ochiai Hazama and Jane Okamoto Komeiji, *Okage sama de: The Japanese in Hawai'i, 1885–1895* (Honolulu: Bess Press, 1986), 26, 42; Dennis M. Ogawa, *Kodomo no tame ni: For the Sake of the Children (The Japanese American Experience in Hawaii)* (Honolulu: University Press of Hawaii, 1978), 78. See

also Fukuda Moritoshi, *Legal Problems of Japanese-Americans: Their History and Development in the United States* (Tokyo: Keio Tsushin, 1980), 24.

25. Ogawa, *Kodomo no tame ni*, 78; Fukuda, *Legal Problems of Japanese-Americans*, 31–32, 39. Canadian government records show that 5,571 Japanese immigrants arrived in B.C. ports in 1907. See *Report of the Royal Commission Inquiring into Oriental Labourers*, 54–63.

26. *Report of the Royal Commission on Chinese and Japanese Immigration*, 389; Ogawa, *Kodomo no tame ni*, 62–63; Hazama and Komeiji, *Okage sama de*, 27–30. See also *Report of the Royal Commission Inquiring into Oriental Labourers*, 54–63.

27. See generally, Morris Report.

28. H. A. Millis, *The Japanese Problem in the United States* (New York: Macmillan, 1920), 16–17.

29. Braun Report, February, 3–4. Marcus Braun was appointed a special commissioner by the U.S. Immigration Service in the fall of 1906 to study conditions affecting Japanese immigration to the United States, including opportunities to cross covertly into the country along its borders with both Canada and Mexico. Marcus Braun submitted his report to Congress on 12 February 1907. E. Manchester Boddy, *Japanese in America* (repr., San Francisco: R & E Research Associates, 1970), 35, 38. See also Act of February 20, 1907, c.1134, 34 Stat. 898.

30. Braun Report, February, 3–4. Braun concluded his report by declaring, "We are not harsh, we are not cruel, we are not unjust, when we say to the Alien, 'You came here clandestinely, you cheated our Government when you came here without subjecting yourself to our enacted law; therefore, back you go.'" Ibid., 41–42.

31. Millis, *Japanese Problem in the United States*, 14. Korean immigrants were included in the Executive Order because Japan's annexation of Korea had made them Japanese imperial subjects. Ibid., 15; Hyung-chan Kim, *A Legal History of Asian Americans, 1790–1990* (Westport, Conn.: Greenwood Press, 1994), 114.

32. R. L. Pruett, Immigration Service Interpreter, El Paso, Texas, to Marcus Braun, Immigration Service, New York, 18 June 1907, RG 85, NARA, reporting remarks made by Kamada Sannosuke, sent by the Meiji government to investigate conditions in Japanese labor camps in Mexico.

33. Commissioner General, Bureau of Immigration and Naturalization, *Digest of, and Comment Upon, Report of Immigrant Inspector Marcus Braun, Dated September 20, 1907*, 9 October 1907, RG 85, NARA [hereafter *Comment on Braun Report*].

34. Yamato Ichihashi, *Japanese in the United States: A Critical Study of the Problems of the Japanese Immigrants and Their Children* (Stanford, Calif.: Stanford University Press, 1932), 69 n. 9; Mitziko Sawada, "Culprits and Gentlemen: Meiji Japan's Restrictions of Emigrants to the United States, 1891–1909," *Pacific Historical Review* (1991): 342.

35. Contract Labor Act, U.S. Statutes at Large (1885, amended 1891): c.164, 23 stat. 332 (26 February 1885). Canada had yet to bar contract labor two decades later. Dillingham Commission Reports, vol. 2, p. 621.

36. *Report of the Royal Commission Inquiring into Oriental Labourers,* 55; Abraham E. Smith, U.S. Consul, Victoria, B.C., to Assistant Secretary of State, Washington, D.C., 19 September 1907. See also G. L. Milne, Medical Inspector and Immigration Agent, Victoria, B.C., to W. D. Scott, Superintendent of Immigration, 31 October 1907, reporting that "the United States have decreed not to allow Japanese immigrants from the Hawaiian Islands to land on the mainland of the United States." Canada, Immigration Branch, vol. 83, file 9309, RG 76, LAC.

37. *Ottawa Free Press,* 5 July 1907.

38. Abraham E. Smith, U.S. Consul, Victoria, B.C., to Assistant Secretary of State, Washington, D.C., 19 September 1907; P. L. Prentis, Inspector in Charge, U.S. Immigration Service, Vancouver, B.C., to Commissioner of Immigration, Montreal, Quebec, 23 August 1907, RG 85, NARA. Also see *Report of the Royal Commission Inquiring into Oriental Labourers,* 55–63.

39. Letter dated 19 December 1907 (probably from G. L. Milne), Victoria, B.C., Canada, Immigration Branch, vol. 83, file 9309, RG 76, LAC; Act of February 20, 1907, c.1134, 34 Stat. 898, section 2, as amended by Act of March 26, 1910.

40. Nayan Shah, *Contagious Divides: Epidemics and Race in San Francisco's Chinatown* (Berkeley: University of California Press, 2001), 2, 133 n. 46; Alan M. Kraut, *Silent Travelers: Germs, Genes, and the "Immigrant Menace"* (Baltimore, Md.: Johns Hopkins University Press, 1994), 97. Also see petition describing Chinese and Japanese as "a menace to health." Canada, Sessional Paper No. 74b.

41. Abraham E. Smith, U.S. Consul, Victoria, B.C., to Assistant Secretary of State, Washington, D.C., 19 September 1907. Nayan Shah makes a similar observation based on a separate body of evidence: "It was possible in managing national borders to mobilize bacteriological expertise to screen particular migrants." Shah, *Contagious Divides,* 202.

42. Kraut, *Silent Travelers,* 55, describing reactions of European immigrants to the medical examinations.

43. Ibid. Trachoma and other eye diseases were a primary focus of the medical examinations in both Canada and the United States. In 1903, quarantinable diseases included cholera, yellow fever, smallpox, typhus fever, leprosy, and plague. Walter Wyman, Surgeon General, Bureau of Public Health and Marine Hospital Service, Washington, D.C., to D. A. Chambers, Attorney, Pacific Mail Steamship Company et al., 11 June 1903, RG 85, NARA. Excludable contagious diseases included flavus (a fungal disease). Lloyd C. Griscom, United States Legation, Tokyo, Japan, to John Hay, Secretary of State, Washington, D.C., 28 September 1903, RG 85, NARA. After 1910, immigrants arriving in the United States were also required to undergo an examination for hookworm, which involved providing a stool sample. No hookworm examination was required in

Canada. Hisatomi Shigenosuke, *Tokō annai: Kanada, nambei, hokubei, hawaii* (Guide for Travel by Ship: Canada, South America, North America, Hawaii) (Kobe: Bingoya, 1916), 8. Immigrants were also subject to examination for whipworm, roundworm, and threadworm, or filariasis, after 1910, and liver fluke or clonorchiasis after 1917. Shah, *Contagious Divides,* 190, 193.

44. Daniel J. Keefe, Commissioner General, Bureau of Immigration and Naturalization, to Secretary of Commerce and Labor, Washington, D.C., 26 July 1909, RG 85, NARA.

45. Shah, *Contagious Divides,* 202.

46. Ohnuki-Tierney emphasizes the "close association between the notion of purity as it applies to the body and the general health of Japanese, and that of moral purity," and explains that a link was historically perceived to exist between illness, impurity, and tasks relegated to outcastes. Emiko Ohnuki-Tierney, *Illness and Culture in Contemporary Japan: An Anthropological View* (Cambridge: Cambridge University Press, 1984), 31, 36. Michael Bourdaghs also explores associations between disease and outcaste status in Japanese culture. See Michael K. Bourdaghs, "Shimazaki Tōson's *Hakai* and Its Bodies," in Helen Hardacre and Adam L. Kern, eds., *New Directions in the Study of Meiji Japan* (Leiden: Brill, 1997), 163–168.

47. Karatani Kōjin describes medical science and hygiene as an "agent of modernization in Japan." Karatani Kōjin, "Sickness as Meaning," in *Origins of Modern Japanese Literature,* trans. Brett de Bary (Durham, N.C.: Duke University Press, 1993), 97–113, quoted in Bourdaghs, "Shimazaki Tōson's *Hakai* and its Bodies," 163. Also see Shah, *Contagious Divides,* 3, noting that in Europe and North America, "heightened standards of sanitation, vaccination and treatment were regarded in and of themselves as markers of modern progress, integral to a nation's identity as modern and civilized," and as the "ultimate expression of scientific progress."

48. Hisashi Tsurutani, *America-Bound: The Japanese and the Opening of the American West,* trans. Betsey Scheiner (Tokyo: Japan Times, 1989), 68; B. C. Howard, Agent, Yokohama, Japan, to Messrs. H. Hackfeld and Co., Ltd., Agents, Honolulu; K. Matsui, Imperial Japanese Embassy, Washington, D.C., to Ransford S. Miller, U.S. State Department, 18 January 1910, RG 85, NARA, noting that migrants who did not undergo medical examination in Japan would "suffer no small embarrassment" when required to undergo examination on their arrival in the United States. See also Morris Report, 88, E. C. Bellows, U.S. Consul General, Yokohama, Japan, to Hineta, 9 November 1903, RG 85, NARA. Steamship companies, anxious to minimize the costs associated with transporting those denied entry back to Japan at their own expense, were more than willing to cooperate with this arrangement. Tatszgoro [*sic*] Nosse, Imperial Consul General of Japan, Montreal, to Sir Wilfrid Laurier, 6 February 1903, Canada, Sessional Paper No. 74b.

49. Translation of *Kobe tokō goshi kaisha,* "How we can emigrate to foreign countries? And some cares for emigrants to be taken [*sic*]," 1897, RG 85, NARA.

50. Hisatomi, *Tokō annai*, 3, 5.

51. U.S. Public Health and Marine Hospital Service of the United States, Medical Officer in Command, Yokohama, Japan, to Surgeon General, Washington, D.C., expressing concern that "the operation of eversion of eyelids, essential for the diagnosis of trachoma, would, if practiced upon cabin passengers, be likely to embarrass the work of the Service here." RG 85, NARA.

52. Hisatomi, *Tokō annai* 3, 5, 7–8.

53. See Andrea Geiger, "Cross-Pacific Dimensions of Race, Caste and Class: Meiji-Era Japanese Immigrants in the North American West" (Ph.D. diss., University of Washington, 2006), 208.

54. Morris Report, 105–106, 118–119; Percival Dodge, American Embassy, Tokyo, Japan, to Elihu Root, Secretary of State, 11 October 1907; Thomas J. O'Brien, U.S. Ambassador, Tokyo, to Elihu Root, Secretary of State, 29 November 1907, noting that Count Hayashi agreed that sending "young adventurous men" to Manchuria, Formosa (Taiwan), and Korea was a logical policy as conditions in those countries became inviting. RG 85, NARA. See also Kazuichiro Ono, "The Problem of Japanese Emigration," *Kyoto University Economic Review* 28, no. 1 (April 1958): 40–54.

55. Tsurutani, *America-Bound*, 68.

56. See, for example, U.S. Immigration Bureau, letters dated 7 May 1907 and 19 June 1907 referring to a migrant deported from San Francisco who bore a passport in the name of Nishioka Niichi and who admitted to immigration officials that this was not his real name. RG 85, NARA. For an example in Canada, see Canada, Certificate of Naturalization, Gainich [*sic*] Kadoya (copy in the possession of the Japanese Canadian National Museum and Archives). For European examples, see Mark Wyman, *Round-Trip to America: The Immigrants Return to Europe* (Ithaca, N.Y.: Cornell University Press, 1993), 9, citing Reino Kero, "The Return of Emigrants from America to Finland," in *University of Institute of General History, Publications*, no. 4 (1972): 11–13; and Gunther Moltmann, "American-German Return Migration in the Nineteenth and Early Twentieth Centuries," *Central European History* 13 (December 1980): 378.

57. Ooms notes that fugitives often sought refuge in outcaste communities because they were "set apart from society," a practice that contributed to this association. Herman Ooms, *Tokugawa Village Practice: Class, Status, Power, Law* (Berkeley: University of California Press, 1996), 291.

58. Ito, *Issei*, 69.

59. Dillingham Commision Reports, vol. 2, citing *Immigration Laws and Regulations of July 1, 1907*, 2nd ed.

60. Onodera Kannichi, ed., *Kanada e wattatta tōhoku no mura: Imin hyakunen to kokusai kōryū* (Miyagi: Kōfusha, 1996), 107, 116, 288, 358, 372 (quoting *Kanada dōhō hatten taikan*); Canada, Immigration Branch, W. D. Scott, Superintendent of Immigration, Department of the Interior, Ottawa, Canada, to Mr. Mitchell, 26 July 1913; *Victoria Daily Colonist*, 21 October 1906. Passport requirements were not as rigid as they are today. See generally John Torpey, *The Invention*

of the Passport: Surveillance, Citizenship and the State (Cambridge: Cambridge University Press, 2000.)

61. Onodera, *Kanada e wattatta tōhoku no mura*, 358; Nitta Jiro, *Phantom Immigrants,* trans. David Sulz (n.p., 1998), a translation of *Mikkōsen suian maru* (Tokyo: Kodansha, 1979).

62. Onodera, *Kanada e wattatta tōhoku no mura*, 360; David Sulz, "Japanese Entrepreneur on the Fraser River: Oikawa Jinsaburo and the Illegal Immigrants of the *Suian Maru*" (M.A. thesis, University of Victoria, 2003), 47. My analysis is based on my own original research as described in "Enforcing Discrimination: the RCMP's Investigation of Japanese Immigrants in Canada, 1931–34," a paper presented at the Western History Association Meeting, Colorado Springs, Colorado, October 2002. See Geiger, "Cross-Pacific Dimensions of Race, Caste and Class," 325. An article based on a parallel set of primary sources is James D. Cameron, "Canada's Struggle with Illegal Entry on Its West Coast: The Case of Fred Yoshy and Japanese Migrants before the Second World War," *BC Studies* 146 (Summer 2005): 37–62. Cameron dismisses Yoshie as simply a "bad apple" motivated by greed and describes him as "odious, shameful, embarrassing, and dangerous." Cameron, "Canada's Struggle," 54, citing a conversation with Midge Ayukawa, 28 May 2005. I argue that Yoshie's motivations were more complex than Cameron suggests, and that the government's case was not without its weaknesses. See also Norman Amor and Tsuneharu Gohnami, *Kanada iminshi shiryō: Bessatsu* (Historical Materials of Japanese Immigration to Canada: Supplement) (Vancouver: University of British Columbia Library, 2000), 47.

63. F. C. T. O'Hara, Superintendent of Commercial Agencies, Department of Trade and Commerce, Ottawa, to Superintendent of Immigration, Interior Department, Ottawa, 21 September 1907, RG 76, LAC.

64. See, for example, *Comment on Braun Report.*

65. P. L. Prentis, Inspector in Charge, U.S. Immigration Service, Vancouver, B.C., to John H. Clark, Commissioner, U.S. Immigration Service, Montreal, Quebec, 27 July 1907, RG 85, NARA.

66. *Comment on Braun Report.*

67. J. H. Clark, Commissioner, U.S. Immigration Service, Montreal, Quebec, to T. Nosse, Consul General of Japan, Ottawa, Canada, 13 December 1907; J. H. Clark, Commissioner, U.S. Immigration Service, Montreal, Quebec, to U.S. Inspector of Immigration, Montreal, Quebec, 13 December 1907, RG 85, NARA.

68. Canada, Immigration Branch, W. D. Scott, Superintendent of Immigration, Department of the Interior, Ottawa, Canada, to Mr. Oliver, 27 November 1907, RG 85, NARA. See also U.S. Immigration Bureau, John H. Clark, Commissioner, U.S. Immigration Service, Montreal, to F. P. Sargent, Commissioner General of Immigration, 18 November 1907, RG 85, NARA.

69. *Comment on Braun Report.* Also see Gunther Peck, *Reinventing Free Labor: Padrones and Immigrant Workers in the North American West, 1880–1930* (Cambridge: Cambridge University Press, 2000), 72, 88, 210, describing the

padrone system as it existed among Japanese. For a detailed discussion of Japanese labor contractors in the Pacific Northwest, see Yuji Ichioka, "Japanese Immigrant Labor Contractors and the Northern Pacific and the Great Northern Railroad Companies, 1898–1907," *Labor History* 80, no. 3 (Summer 1980): 325–350.

70. U.S. Immigration Bureau, File 1869–5, Charles Earl, Solicitor, Memorandum, 28 March 1907, RG 85, NARA.

71. A. Stewart, Manager, Dodwell and Co., Ltd., to John H. Clark, Commissioner, U.S. Immigration Service, Montreal, 31 July 1907, RG 85, NARA.

72. *Reasons Given by Japanese for Disembarking at Victoria, B.C., Instead of Proceeding to U.S. Points, June 15 to December 31, 1907,* RG 85, NARA.

73. *Comment on Braun Report;* Oscar S. Straus, Secretary of Commerce and Labor, to Elihu Root, Secretary of State, 30 December 1907, RG 85, NARA.

74. T. Nosse to Sir Wilfrid Laurier, 18 January 1907, Canada, Sessional Paper No. 74b. See also P. L. Prentis, Inspector in Charge, U.S. Immigration Service, Vancouver, B.C., to John H. Clark, Commissioner, U.S. Immigration Service, Montreal, Quebec, 23 July 1908, RG 85, NARA.

75. *Report of the Royal Commission Inquiring into Oriental Labourers,* 64–65.

76. *Comment on Braun Report.* See also Canada, Immigration Branch, John H. Clark, Commissioner, U.S. Immigration Service, Montreal, Quebec, to W. D. Scott, Superintendent of Immigration, Department of the Interior, Ottawa, Ontario, to Mr. Oliver, 23 December 1907; Canada, Parliament, *Report of the Royal Commission Inquiring into Oriental Labourers,* 64–65, stating that "Japanese prefer to debark in Canada as when rejected by U.S. authorities they need not return to Japan which they must do at Tacoma, Seattle." See also *Report of the Royal Commission on Chinese and Japanese Immigration,* 337.

77. B. A. Hunter, Acting Inspector in Charge, to Commissioner, U.S. Immigration Service, Montreal, Quebec, 20 December 1907, RG 85, NARA.

78. *Comment on Braun Report.*

79. John H. Clark, Commissioner, U.S. Immigration Service, Montreal, to F. P. Sargent, Commissioner General of Immigration, 26 June 1907, insisting that Japanese immigrants turned back at the U.S. border would "endeavor to effect surreptitious entry along the Washington boundary" whether or not they received treatment in Canada. RG 85, NARA.

80. Charles L. Babcock, Immigrant Inspector, U.S. Immigration Service, Vancouver, B.C., to F. P. Sargent, Commissioner General of Immigration, Washington, D.C., 7 October 1907, RG 85, NARA.

81. Braun Report, February.

82. Charles L. Babcock, Immigrant Inspector, Port of Vancouver, B.C., to F. P. Sargent, Commissioner General, U.S. Immigration Service, 7 October 1907; John H. Clark, Commissioner, U.S. Immigration Service, Montreal, to F. P. Sargent, Commissioner General of Immigration, 26 June 1907, RG 85, NARA.

83. John H. Sargent, Inspector in Charge, Seattle, Washington, to F. P. Sargent, Commissioner General, U.S. Immigration Service, 19 September 1907; Charles

L. Babcock, Immigrant Inspector, Port of Vancouver, B.C., to F. P. Sargent, Commissioner General, U.S. Immigration Service, 7 October 1907, reporting that Japanese immigrants were seen crossing the Great Northern Railway bridge at the point at which the railway line crossed the Nooksack River. RG 85, NARA. See also Ito, *Issei*, 87, explaining that Japanese immigrants sometimes walked backwards across the bridge so if they were spotted, they could run in the direction they really intended to go.

84. P. L. Prentis, Inspector in Charge, U.S. Immigration Service, Vancouver, B.C., to John H. Clark, Commissioner, U.S. Immigration Service, Montreal, Quebec, 27 July 1907; *Comment on Braun Report*. Local immigration officials requested a "launch of such dimensions as to make it of practical use in rough seas, and with power and speed sufficient to enable it to overtake the large sail boats ... largely used by aliens, when ... gaining suriptitious [*sic*] entry to the United States." Charles L. Babcock, Immigrant Inspector, Seattle, Washington, to F. P. Sargent, Commissioner General of Immigration, 5 November 1907, RG 85, NARA.

85. Charles L. Babcock, Inspector, U.S. Immigration Service, Vancouver, B.C., to F. P. Sargent, Commissioner General of Immigration, Washington, D.C., 28 September 1907, RG 85, NARA. U.S. immigration officials were not concerned only about Japanese migrants who were crossing the border clandestinely but also about Chinese, East Indian, and European migrants who took advantage of conditions along the border to do the same. Among those who crossed the border illegally on the day Babcock prepared his report, for example, were Italians and Finns. Ibid.

86. "Customs Fraud at Boundary," *Vancouver Daily Province*, 17 October 1900. The *Daily Province* reported that Chilliwack residents charged $25 per person to guide migrants into the United States alone or in pairs, and $10 to $15 per person for a larger group. Ibid.

87. T. Nosse, Consul General of Japan, Ottawa, Canada, to U.S. Inspector of Immigration, Montreal, Quebec, 10 December 1907; John H. Clark, Commissioner, U.S. Immigration Service, Montreal, to F. P. Sargent, Commissioner General of Immigration, 9 December 1907; H.I.J.M's Consul at Vancouver, B.C., to Viscount Aoki, Imperial Japanese Embassy, Washington, D.C., 23 December 1907, RG 85, NARA.

88. S. Morikawa, Consul of Japan, Vancouver, B.C., 27 November 1907 to W. D. Scott, Superintendent of Immigration, Department of the Interior, Ottawa, Canada, dated 28 November 1907 (handwritten note stating that "Mr. Nosse called about this"), Canada, Immigration Branch, vol. 83, file 9309, RG 76, LAC; John H. Clark, Commissioner, U.S. Immigration Service, Montreal, to F. P. Sargent, Commissioner General of Immigration, 18 November 1907; John H. Clark to T. Nosse, Consul General of Japan, Ottawa, 13 December 1907, RG 85, NARA.

89. Morris Report, Exhibit B, Thomas J. O'Brien, U.S. Ambassador, Tokyo, Dispatch No. 54, 19 November 1907, noting that Lemieux had arrived in Japan and

reporting that Britain's ambassador had told him Britain had "considerable interest ... in the way of sympathy for the Canadian people in their objection to further emigration" from Japan and that Canada was also interested in imposing restrictions on Japanese immigration similar to those of the United States. See also "Oriental Question Becomes Grave," *The British Columbian*, 7 January 1908.

90. For a description of the Vancouver Riot, see, for example, William Hemmingway, "A Japanese Hornet's Nest for John Bull," *Harper's Weekly* (issue entitled " 'White Canada': The Slogan of Vancouver"), 5 October 1907.

91. John H. Clark, Commissioner, U.S. Immigration Service, Montreal, to F. P. Sargent, Commissioner General of Immigration, 6 August 1907, 17 November 1907, postscript to letter of 16 November 1907, 18 November 1907, and 9 December 1907, RG 85, NARA.

92. *Report of the Royal Commission Appointed Inquiring into Oriental Labourers*, 66.

93. The Japanese government, one contemporary observer of Japanese relations with the United States observed, "was unwilling to be discriminated against in the matter of immigration." Boddy, *Japanese in America*, 27.

94. Under the terms of the Gentlemen's Agreement between Japan and the United States, immigration was limited to "(1) returning immigrants, being in possession of certificates of residence, issued by competent Japanese consuls; (2) the parents, wives, or children of actual residents in America, also in possession of [residence] certificates; and (3) a small number of settled agriculturalists, who had obtained special sanction from the Foreign Office." Memorandum from Vice Minister of Foreign Affairs [Ishii Kikujirō], Tokyo, Japan, 1 July 1908, RG 85, NARA. Also see *Annual Report of the Commissioner General of Immigration for the Fiscal Year Ended June 30, 1908*, 125–126, cited in Millis, *Japanese Problem in the United States*, 109.

95. Under the terms of the agreement negotiated by Lemieux, the Meiji government agreed to limit passports for Canada only to (1) merchants, officers, students, and travelers; (2) former residents of Canada; (3) relatives or friends of Japanese immigrants in Canada in cases where the local consul certified that they were wanted and that a home or immediate employment was waiting for them; and (4) after April 1908, contract laborers approved by the Canadian government. *Report of the Royal Commission Inquiring into Oriental Labourers*, 66. See also Ken Adachi, *The Enemy That Never Was: A History of the Japanese Canadians* (Toronto: McClelland and Stewart, 1976), 81; Patricia E. Roy, J. L. Granatstein, Masako Iino, and Hiroko Takamura, *Mutual Hostages: Canadians and Japanese during the Second World War* (Toronto: University of Toronto Press, 1990), 11.

96. Canada, House of Commons, *Debates, 1912–1913*, p. 6971, cited in Charles H. Young and Helen R. Y. Reid, *The Japanese Canadians* (Toronto: University of Toronto Press, 1938), 11.

97. A. Warner Parker, Chief, Law Division, U.S. Immigration Service, to Commissioner General, Bureau of Immigration and Naturalization, 14 July 1908; Commissioner A. H. Worth to Commissioner General of Immigration, 16 August 1909, RG 85, NARA.

98. S. Kuroda to Hon. C. Yada, Japanese Consul, Vancouver, B.C., 6 October 1909, RG 76, LAC.

99. T. Nakamura, Consul General for Japan, Imperial Consulate General of Japan for the Dominion of Canada, to Frank Oliver, Minister of the Interior, Ottawa, Canada, 28 October 1909, RG 76, LAC.

100. Superintendent of Immigration, Ottawa, Canada, to G. L. Milne, Medical Inspector and Immigration Agent, Victoria, B.C., 24 December 1909, RG 76, LAC.

101. Everett Wallace, Acting Commissioner, U.S. Immigration Service, Montreal, Quebec, to Commissioner General of Immigration, U.S. Immigration Service, Washington, D.C., 3 February 1909, RG 85, NARA.

102. Robert A. Wilson and Bill Hosokawa, *East to America: A History of the Japanese in the United States* (New York: William Morrow, 1980), 125.

103. Memorandum from the Foreign Office, Tokyo, Japan, 1 July 1908, RG 85, NARA.

104. Wilson and Hosokawa, *East to America*, 125; Millis, *Japanese Problem in the United States*, 18.

105. "Japs Play Clever Game with Passports," *Vancouver Daily Province*, 3 April 1909.

106. Tatszgoro [*sic*] Nosse to Sir Wilfrid Laurier, Montreal, 18 July 1903, Canada, Sessional Paper No. 74b.

107. Tatszgoro [*sic*] Nosse to Wilfrid Laurier, 6 February 1903, *Sessional Papers, Canada*, vol. 42, no. 18, 1907–1908.

108. Eileen Sunada Sarasohn, *The Issei: Portrait of a Pioneer, an Oral History* (Palo Alto, Calif.: Pacific Books, 1983), 101 (interview with Osuke Takizawa explaining that he traveled to Victoria, even though his ultimate destination was San Francisco, because he feared he might not pass the more rigorous medical examination required by U.S. medical authorities, and he knew that if he did not pass, he would be able to stay in Canada). See also P. L. Prentis, Inspector in Charge, U.S. Immigration Service, Vancouver, B.C., to John H. Clark, Commissioner, U.S. Immigration Service, Montreal, Quebec, to 23 July 1908, RG 85, NARA. And see Gordon G. Nakayama, *Issei: Stories of Japanese Canadian Pioneers* (Toronto: Britannia Printers, 1983), 101, explaining that Maeda Rokusuke, born in Okayama prefecture in 1888, settled in Canada in 1907 after being refused entry into the United States and being returned to Canada.

109. Audrey Lynn Kobayashi, "Regional Backgrounds of Japanese Immigrants and the Development of Japanese-Canadian Community," *McGill Geography Discussion Papers* 1, no. 1 (May 1986): 1-17–1-18 n. 5. The emphasis on prior residence also placed a premium on the ability to demonstrate this, which created new kinds of problems for immigration officials regarding the kind of proof that was required given the laxer admission requirements of earlier years.

CHAPTER SIX. THE U.S.-MEXICO BORDER

1. Emil Engelcke, Inspector in Charge, San Diego, California, to William H. Chadney, Chinese Inspector, Calexico, California, 23 April 1907, file 10192, RG 85, NARA.

2. Braun Report, February; Report of Marcus Braun, U.S. Immigrant Inspector, 10 June 1907, RG 85, NARA [hereafter Braun Report, June]. For a discussion of ways in which Greek, Italian, and Mexican labor contractors used the international border to facilitate their own goals, see generally Gunther Peck, *Reinventing Free Labor: Padrones and Immigrant Workers in the North American West, 1880–1930* (Cambridge: Cambridge University Press, 2000),

3. Interview with Kawamoto Shinji, 30 April 1908, County Jail, El Paso, Texas, U.S. Immigration Service, RG 85, NARA.

4. Braun Report, June. U.S. immigration officers along the U.S.-Mexico border did not focus only on Japanese migrants. Also of concern were "Greeks, Italians, Southern Slavs from the Balcan [*sic*], Russian Jews and some Italians from South America, or 'maidens' from France, Belgium and Spain, who probably have tried to enter via Atlantic ports," as well as Chinese. Braun Report, February. For a discussion of Chinese immigration along the U.S.-Mexico border, see Erika Lee, *At America's Gates: Chinese Immigration during the Exclusion Era, 1882–1943* (Chapel Hill: University of North Carolina Press, 2003), 151–188.

5. James T. Gardiner, President, Mexican Coal and Coke Co., to President Theodore Roosevelt, 27 March 1907, RG 85, NARA.

6. Yada to Hayashi, 20 October 1906, cited in Jerry Garcia, "Japanese Immigration and Community Development in Mexico, 1897–1940" (Ph.D. diss., Washington State University, 1999), 112.

7. "Flock to Border," *Ottawa Free Press,* 5 July 1907, copy in Canada, Immigration Branch, vol. 83, file 9309, RG 76, LAC. See also "Japs Try to Rush Landing—One Man Is Drowned," *The British Columbian,* 4 February 1908.

8. Braun Report, February. For discussions of Japanese immigration to Mexico, see Kenneth B. McCullough, "America's Back Door: Indirect International Immigration via Mexico to the United States from 1875 to 1940" (Ph.D. diss., Texas A&M University, 1994); and Garcia, "Japanese Immigration and Community Development in Mexico." Both rely heavily on Maria Elena Ota Mishima, *Siete Migraciones Japonesas en México, 1890–1978* (México: El Colegio De México, 1982), which McCullough describes as the best historical overview of Japanese emigration to Mexico. Also see Josai Inshi, "Japanese in Mexico," *The Japan Magazine* (December 1914).

9. Garcia, *Japanese Immigration and Community Development in Mexico,* 90, 100. Fujita Miyoji, who eventually settled in Spokane, Washington, was recruited by the Tairiku Imin Gaisha to go to Mexico in 1906 at the age of sixteen to work on the railroad. He had no intention of breaking his contract; he had bought a Spanish dictionary in Kobe and studied it diligently on board ship. He was one of a group of migrants, however, who abandoned their contracts

after concluding that the conditions in which they were expected to live were unbearable and appropriate only for cattle. Although he was able to reach the border and enter the United States legally, he paid a forty-yen penalty in Japan. Kazuo Ito, *Issei: A History of Japanese Immigrants in North America*, trans. Shinichiro Nakamura and Jean S. Gerard (Seattle: Executive Committee for Publication of *Issei*, 1973), 68–69.

10. Baron Takahira Kotaro to Foreign Minister, Count Komura Jutaro, 24 November 1908, quoted in Ito, *Issei*, 65. For the association of Mannen-cho with individuals classified as outcastes, see, for example, Miyake Akimasa, *Technology Change and Female Labor in Japan* (Tokyo: United Nations University Press, 1994), chapter 3.

11. Baron Takahira Kotaro to Foreign Minister, Count Komura Jutaro, 24 November 1908, quoted in Ito, *Issei*, 65. A year earlier, the *Mexican Herald* had reprinted a report originally published in Spofford, Texas, which reported that Japanese migrants working in the coal mines were forced to contend with "unhealthy conditions, poor pay, bad food, acts of cruelty and violence." It was because they experienced "a state of conditions worse than that of slaves that they escaped to the United States seeking refuge." *Mexican Herald*, 4 December 1906, quoted in Garcia, *Japanese Immigration and Community Development in Mexico*, 98, 100.

12. W. J. Maher, Inspector in Charge, Eagle Pass, Texas, to Commissioner General of Immigration, Washington, D.C., 15 March 1907, RG 85, NARA.

13. *Chūō Shimbun*, 9 December 1909, translation enclosed in letter from T. J. O'Brien, U.S. Ambassador, Tokyo, Japan, to Secretary of State, Washington, D.C., 10 December 1909, RG 85, NARA.

14. Ito, *Issei*, 70–73.

15. W. J. Maher, Inspector in Charge, Eagle Pass, Texas, to Commissioner General of Immigration, Washington, D.C., 15 March 1907. RG 85, NARA.

16. Braun Report, February, 13, 20.

17. Braun Report, June.

18. Ibid.

19. F. H. Larned, Acting Commissioner General, Bureau of Immigration and Naturalization, to Assistant Secretary of Commerce and Labor, 30 July 1908, file 51938, RG 85, NARA.

20. R. L. Pruett, Immigration Service Interpreter, El Paso, Texas, to Marcus Braun, Immigration Service, New York, 18 June 1907, RG 85, NARA.

21. Braun Report, February, 15–17. See also Mishima, *Siete Migraciones Japonesas en México*, cited in McCullough, "America's Back Door," 218.

22. Ito, *Issei*, 66.

23. Braun Report, February.

24. Braun Report, June, 17–18.

25. Robert E. Park and Wm. C. Smith, "Life History of Paul Hiratzaka [*sic*]," circa 1922, Box 30, *Survey on Race Relations*, Hoover Institution on War, Revolution and Peace, Stanford, Calif.; U.S. Immigration Service, "Memorandum [re Japanese Immigrants in Texas]," circa 1907, RG 85, NARA.

26. Robert A. Wilson and Bill Hosokawa, *East to America: A History of the Japanese in the United States* (New York: William Morrow, 1980), 97.

27. Interview of Mrs. Terasawa, Matron and Interpreter for Oriental Women at Angel Island [San Francisco], by Mrs. R. E. Park, circa 1922, Box 30, *Survey on Race Relations,* Hoover Institution. For a general discussion of immigration to Texas, see Thomas K. Walls, *The Japanese Texans* (San Antonio: University of Texas Institute of Texan Cultures at San Antonio, 1987).

28. Braun Report, June.

29. H. Sterling, Acting Inspector in Charge, Denver, Colorado, to Commissioner General of Immigration, Washington, D.C., 19 March 1908, and [signature illegible] Adamsen, Inspector in Charge, Denver, to Commissioner General of Immigration, 1 April 1908, RG 85, NARA.

30. Braun Report, June. Although immigration inspectors were permitted to refuse transit to those who were excludable as immigrants even if the migrants did not intend to remain in the United States, the United States did not have the power to deny the transit privilege in cases where a migrant was not otherwise excludable without violating its obligations under its treaties with Japan. Charles Earl, Solicitor, Memorandum, 28 March 1907, file 1869–5, RG 85, NARA.

31. Charles Earl, Solicitor, Memorandum, 28 March 1907 file 1869–5, RG 85, NARA.

32. Attorney, Southern Pacific Company, to F. P. Sargent, Commissioner General of Immigration, Washington, D.C., 18 March 1908, file 51931, RG 85, NARA.

33. F. P. Sargent, Commissioner General of Immigration to All Immigration Officials re Enforcement of Department Circular No. 147, 14 May 1907; Secretary of Commerce and Labor, Washington, D.C., to All Immigration Officials, 13 May 1907, file 51564/6. RG 85, NARA.

34. F. P. Sargent, Commissioner General of Immigration to All Immigration Officials re Enforcement of Department Circular No. 147, 14 May 1907; Secretary of Commerce and Labor, Washington, D.C., to All Immigration Officials, 13 May 1907, file 51564/6, RG 85, NARA.

35. Oscar S. Straus, Secretary of Commerce and Labor, Bureau of Immigration and Naturalization, Washington, D.C., to T. F. Schmucker, Inspector in Charge, El Paso, Texas, 12 April, 1907, RG 85, NARA.

36. Francis W. McFarland, Acting Inspector in Charge, to General Commissioner of Immigration, Washington, D.C., 20 May 1907 (enclosing article in unnamed San Francisco newspaper dated 3 May 1907 and translated by Yoneshima, immigration interpreter at El Paso), RG 85, NARA.

37. R. L. Pruett, Immigration Service Interpreter, El Paso, to F. P. Sargent, Commissioner General of Immigration, Washington, D.C., 11 June, 1907, and to Marcus Braun, Immigration Service, New York, 18 June 1907, RG 85, NARA.

38. Marcus Braun, Immigrant Inspector, Eagle Pass, Texas, to Commissioner General of Immigration, Washington, D.C., 13 April 1907, RG 85, NARA.

39. Luther C. Steward, Supervising Inspector, U.S. Immigration Service, San Antonio, Texas, to General Commissioner of Immigration, Washington, D.C., 16 March 1909, RG 85, NARA.

40. Braun Report, June.

41. Braun Report, February, Exhibit B (Report of R. L. Pruett). One Japanese guidebook urged migrants to study English en route to North America: if they memorized five words each day, it would be possible to learn seventy words during the two weeks it took to travel to North America. Those seventy words, the author added, would have given them the tools to communicate about basic issues when they arrived. See Hisatomi Shigenosuke, *Tokō annai: Kanada, nambei, hokubei, hawaii* (Guide for Travel by Ship: Canada, South America, North America, Hawaii) (Kobe: Bingoya, 1916).

42. The name of the pamphlet, *Hokubei mekishikokoku tankō yuki imin ōbo annai*, the revised edition of which was published in Meiji 39 (1906), is more correctly translated as "Guidebook for Immigrants Recruited to Work in Mexico's Coal Mines." *Comment on Braun Report*, Exhibit K. Although the single map shows railroad routes in Mexico, it does not show connections beyond Mexico's northern border.

43. U.S. Immigration Bureau, *Japanese Aliens Arrested Prior to June 1, 1907, as Being in the United States in Violation of Executive Order of March 14, 1907*, RG 85, NARA. Of the thirty-one who were arrested, one was deported to Mexico, twenty-nine were deported to Japan, and one escaped. Ibid.

44. Morris Report, Exhibit B, Thomas J. O'Brien, U.S. Ambassador, Tokyo, Dispatch No. 120, 2 January 1908, Enclosure No. 1, Memorandum from Foreign Office dated 30 December 1907.

45. R. L. Pruett, Immigration Service Interpreter, El Paso, Texas, to Marcus Braun, Immigration Service, New York, 18 June 1907. Pruett himself was accused the following year of being too sympathetic to Japanese migrants and dismissed from the Immigration Service on suspicion of having aided Japanese to enter the United States illegally. Richard H. Taylor, Immigrant Inspector, U.S. Immigration Service, El Paso, Texas, to Frank P. Sargent, Commissioner General of Immigration, Washington, D.C., 18 March 1908, RG 85, NARA.

46. Department of Commerce and Labor, Bureau of Immigration and Naturalization, *Regulations Relating to the Transit of Japanese and Korean Laborers through the Continental Territory of the United States*, 31 October 1907, RG 85, NARA.

47. M. Berkohing, Supervising Inspector, Immigration Service, San Antonio, Texas, to F. H. Larned, Acting Commissioner General, Bureau of Immigration and Naturalization, Washington, D.C., 14 May 1908, file 51931, RG 85, NARA.

48. Patricia E. Roy, J. L. Granatstein, Masako Iino, and Hiroko Takamura, *Mutual Hostages: Canadians and Japanese during the Second World War* (Toronto: University of Toronto Press, 1990), 11. The continuous passage rule was also intended as a bar against immigration from India, something that had been difficult to accomplish because Indian immigrants were also British subjects.

Canadian authorities were aware, however, that no vessels traveled directly from India to North America and that it was necessary for immigrants from India to change ships at one port or another along the way, which made them vulnerable to a continuous passage rule. See, for example, Hugh Johnston, *The Voyage of the Komagata Maru: The Sikh Challenge to Canada's Colour Bar* (Vancouver, B.C.: UBC Press, 1989).

49. Superintendent of Immigration, Department of the Interior, Ottawa, Canada to John H. Clark, U.S. Immigration Commissioner, Montreal, Canada, 25 April 1908, file 51931, RG 85, NARA. U.S. officials were advised of the continuous passage rule on 15 January 1908. See note appended to letter from Emmett J. Wallace, Acting Commissioner of Immigration, U.S. Immigration Service, Montreal, Canada, to F. P. Sargent, Commissioner General of Immigration, Washington, D.C., dated 18 March 1908, RG 85, NARA.

50. Luther C. Steward, Acting Supervising Inspector, U.S. Immigration Service, San Antonio, Texas, to F. P. Sargent, Commissioner General of Immigration, Washington, D.C., 13 April 1908, file 51931, RG 85, NARA. Also see H. A. Millis, *The Japanese Problem in the United States* (New York: Macmillan, 1920), 16–17.

51. Emmett J. Wallace, Acting Commissioner of Immigration, U.S. Immigration Service, Montreal, Canada, to F. P. Sargent, Commissioner General of Immigration, Washington, D.C., 18 March 1908, file 51931, RG 85, NARA.

52. W. Haggard, Petropolis, Brazil, to H.M.'s Government, 12 November 1907, RG 76, LAC.

53. Irving B. Dudley, American Embassy, Petropolis, Brazil, to Elihu Root, Secretary of State, Washington, D.C., 2 December 1907, RG 85, NARA.

54. *Notes of Articles from the "Taiyo" on the Expansion of Japan* (quoting T. Uchida, Japanese Minister to Brazil circa 1910), RG 76, LAC. Japanese traveling to South America were not required to undergo medical examinations when they arrived, but Chile, Peru, Mexico, and Brazil each required immigrants to obtain a health certificate in Japan. Hisatomi, *Tokō annai,* 28.

55. Millis, *Japanese Problem in the United States,* 10–11.

56. "New Outlets for Japanese," *The British Columbia Weekly,* 23 February 1909.

57. *Notes of Articles from the "Taiyo."* Also see T. Iyenaga and Kenoske Sato, *Japanese and the California Problem* (New York: G.P. Putnam's Sons, 1921), 69. For the history of Japanese immigration to Brazil, see Teiiti Suzuki, *The Japanese Immigrant in Brazil* (Tokyo: University of Tokyo Press, 1969); J. F. Normano and Antonello Gerbi, *The Japanese in South America: An Introductory Survey with Special Reference to Peru* (New York: Institute of Pacific Relations, 1943).

CHAPTER SEVEN. DEBATING THE CONTOURS OF CITIZENSHIP

1. *Japanese Immigration: Hearings before the Committee on Immigration and Naturalization, House of Representatives,* 66th Cong., 2nd Sess., July 12 to August 3, 1920, 25. In Seattle, the *Taihoku Nippō* characterized Phelan's proposal that the U.S. Constitution be amended to deny citizenship to people of Asian

ancestry, including those born in the United States, as clear evidence of racial prejudice on his part. Ibid., 33.

2. Canada's status as a dominion of Great Britain, which retained constitutional authority over its foreign affairs in particular, limited the ability of the Canadian Parliament to pass exclusionary laws that contravened treaties between Great Britain and Japan. See Peter W. Ward, *White Canada Forever: Popular Attitudes and Public Policy toward Orientals in British Columbia* (Montreal: McGill-Queen's University Press, 1978), 57–58. Canadian government officials noted that Australia did not allow Asians to become naturalized citizens. James Baker, Clerk, Executive Council, British Columbia, to Secretary of State, Ottawa, 6 May 1897, Canada, Sessional Paper No. 74b.

3. D. M. Eberts, B.C. Attorney General, to Christopher Robinson, Esq., K.C., London, 29 June 1901, published in the *Victoria Daily Colonist*, 3 January 1903. Although the Fourteenth and Fifteenth Amendments were passed soon after the end of the U.S. Civil War, U.S. courts soon acted to limit their scope. Kenneth L. Karst, *Belonging to America: Equal Citizenship and the Constitution* (New Haven: Yale University Press, 1989), 56–61.

4. *Victoria Daily Colonist*, 25 April 1905.

5. *Vancouver Daily Province*, 1 December 1900.

6. D. M. Eberts, B.C. Attorney General, to Christopher Robinson, Esq., K.C., London, 29 June 1901. An essay published by the *Vancouver Daily Province* on May 4, 1901, described the Hon. David McEwen Eberts as "a man's man every inch of him, charming companion and prince of gentlemanly good fellows, a sportsman true at heart in every game of wits or field, a man born to command and to be popular, a warhorse in the strife of politics when once he discards the mantle of his indolence, a keen and accurate reader of men and motives," and "the ablest man in British Columbia's government."

7. *Report of the Royal Commission on Chinese and Japanese Immigration*, 240, 389.

8. K. T. Takahashi, *The Anti-Japanese Petition: Appeal in Protest against a Threatened Persecution* (Montreal: Gazette Printing Co., 1897), 12. The argument that Japan had a parliamentary system similar to that of Great Britain and that Japanese citizens were fully capable of understanding the meaning and responsibilities of citizenship in the United States was also made before the U.S. Congress in 1920. *Japanese Immigration, Hearings before the Committee on Immigration and Naturalization, House of Representatives*, 66th Cong., 2nd Sess., July 12 to August 3, 1920, 747. See also Kenneth B. Pyle, *The Making of Modern Japan* (Lexington: D. C. Heath, 1996), 122 (for the Meiji oligarchs' decision use the Prussian Constitution as a model for the Meiji Constitution).

9. D. M. Eberts, B.C. Attorney General, to Christopher Robinson, Esq., K.C., London, 29 June 1901.

10. See, for example, *Vancouver Daily Province*, 1 December 1900; *Victoria Daily Colonist*, 27 July 1900 ("Fraudulent Naturalization"); and *Victoria Daily Colonist*, 1 December 1900. Also see D. M. Eberts, Attorney General, *Return of*

Correspondence Relating to Fraudulent Naturalization of Japanese, 1 Ed. 7, 531, 14 March 1901.

11. *Summons* and *Plaint, Hakaku Murata v. T. Hattaro,* Vancouver County Court, case no. B746/22, filed 21 March 1922.

12. For a discussion of efforts made by the Canadian government to attract European immigrants, see generally Doug Owram, *Promise of Eden: The Canadian Expansionist Movement and the Idea of the West, 1856–1900* (Toronto: University of Toronto Press, 1980); Ninette Kelley and Michael Trebilcock, *The Making of the Mosaic: A History of Canadian Immigration Policy* (Toronto: University of Toronto Press, 2000).

13. Kiyoshi K. Kawakami, *Asia at the Door: A Study of the Japanese Question in Continental United States, Hawaii and Canada* (London: Fleming H. Revell, 1914), 248–250; Kiyoshi K. Kawakami, *The Real Japanese Question* (New York: MacMillan, 1921), 222. H. A. Millis relied on Kawakami for his conclusion that "In British Columbia and the neighboring provinces a few thousand Japanese have become naturalized, the majority of them incidental to obtaining licenses as fishermen." Millis, *The Japanese Problem in the United States* (New York: Macmillan, 1915), 47, citing Kawakami, *Asia at the Door,* 68–69. See also *Report of the Royal Commission on Chinese and Japanese Immigration,* 351 (fraudulent naturalization issue).

14. S. K. Kanda, "The Japanese in Washington," *Washington Magazine (Alaska–Greater Northwest)* 1, no. 3 (May 1906): 193–197.

15. Kazuo Ito, *Issei: A History of Japanese Immigrants in North America,* trans. Shinichiro Nakamura and Jean S. Gerard (Seattle: Executive Committee for Publication of *Issei,* 1973), 127.

16. *Japanese Immigration Legislation: Hearings before the Committee on Immigration, United States Senate, 68th Cong., 1st Sess. on S. 2576, A Bill to Limit the Immigration of Aliens into the United States, March 11–15, 1924* (Washington, D.C.: Government Printing Office, 1924), 134 (quoting *Taihoku Nippō*). See also U.S. Immigration Bureau, file 52424–13, postcard from P. W. Ebersoll, Portland, Oregon, stating that "Japanese, by excluding Koreans and Chinese because of their lower standard of living, gives us so much more right to exclude the Japs." RG 85, NARA. And see "Japanese Invasion the Problem of the Hour for United States," *San Francisco Chronicle,* 23 February 1905. For a general discussion of the Japanese law of citizenship during the Meiji and Taishō periods, see Tsunejiro Miyaoka, "The Japanese Law of Nationality and the Rights of Foreigners in Land under the Laws of Japan," *International Conciliation,* no. 206 (January 1925).

17. Millis, *Japanese Problem in the United States,* 305 (quoting communication by Baron Chinda to U.S. secretary of state dated 4 June 1913).

18. T. Iyenaga and Kenoske Sato, *Japanese and the California Problem* (New York: G. P. Putnam's Sons, 1921), 173.

19. *Cunningham v. Homma* [1903] A.C. 151 (P.C.); *Ozawa v. United States,* 260 U.S. 178 (1922). Although the *Ozawa* case was not finally decided until 1922, the issue had been before the courts since before the turn of the century.

20. Homma's biographer, Koyama Shigeharu, argues that Homma was also motivated in part by a deep sense of responsibility stemming from his status as a samurai, which impelled him to assume a leadership role in challenging the racist legal barriers that Japanese immigrants encountered in British Columbia. Koyama Shigeharu, *Nikkei kanada imin no chichi, Homma Tomekichi: Ō no shōgai* (The Father of Japanese Immigrants in Canada, Tomekichi Homma: An Honorable Life) (Mihama, Japan, 1995), 8, 60. Homma was the third son of a former samurai family that traced its ancestry back to retainers of the Ashikaga shoguns in the 1400s. Ibid. A tribute published in 1922 described Homma as a man of great courage, who was both strong-minded and generous of spirit. Nakayama Jinshiro, ed., *Kanada dōhō hatten taikan* (Encyclopedia of Japanese in Canada) (Vancouver, B.C., 1929), 111.

21. Other reasons cited by the founders of the Vancouver Nipponjinkai included upholding the national dignity of Japan and enhancing the profitability of Japanese-run businesses. Nakayama Jinshiro, ed., *Kanada no hōko* (Treasures of Canada) (Tokyo, 1929), 646.

22. *Return of Correspondence Relating to Fraudulent Naturalization of Japanese,* 1 Ed. 7 (14 March 1901), 537, Walter J. Thicke to A. E. Beck, Vancouver, B.C., 22 September 1900. As amended, B.C.'s Provincial Voters Act provided that "no Chinaman, Japanese, or Indian shall have his name placed on the Register of Voters for any Electoral District." An Act to Amend the "Provincial Voters Act," S.B.C. 1895, c. 20; *Vancouver Daily Province,* 1 December 1900 (citing numbers provided by Thomas Cunningham, collector of voters for Vancouver, B.C.). The B.C. legislature amended British Columbia's Voters Act to bar Chinese and Native residents of B.C. from voting in provincial elections in 1875. *An Act Relating to an Act to Make Better Provision for the Qualification and Registration of Voters,* 38 Vic. 1875, no. 2, s.1 (B.C.). Canada's Royal Commission on Chinese and Japanese Immigration found that a majority of the 4,578 Japanese immigrants in B.C. in 1902 (out of a total population of 177,272) arrived after July 1, 1899, some four years after the 1895 amendment was passed. *Report of the Royal Commission on Chinese and Japanese Immigration.* For a detailed discussion of the *Homma* case, see Andrea Geiger, "Writing Racial Barriers into Law: Upholding B.C.'s Denial of the Vote to Its Japanese Canadian Citizens, *Homma v. Cunningham,* 1902," in Louis Fiset and Gail M. Nomura, eds., *Nikkei in the Pacific Northwest: Japanese Americans and Japanese Canadians in the Twentieth Century* (Seattle: University of Washington Press, 2005), 20–43.

23. Provincial Voters Act, S.B.C. 1897, c.67, s.3. The B.C. Legislature imposed a $50 fine and up to one month's imprisonment on any collector of voters who violated the act by adding the name of someone of Asian descent to the voters list. Ibid.

24. *Vancouver Daily Province,* 27 October 1900; 1 December 1900.

25. Koyama, *Nikkei kanadajin no chichi,* 66.

26. *Vancouver Daily Province,* 1 December 1900. Shimizu later lodged several protests on behalf of the Japanese government against legislation directed at

Japanese immigrants in B.C. *Victoria Daily Colonist*, 3 January 1903. Also see
Patricia E. Roy, J. L. Granatstein, Masako Iino, and Hiroko Takamura, *Mutual
Hostages: Canadians and Japanese during the Second World War* (Toronto:
University of Toronto Press, 1990), 7, noting that because denial of franchise
affected only naturalized British subjects, the government of Japan did not
"protest the denial of these basic civil rights to its former subjects."

27. *Victoria Daily Colonist*, 30 November 1900. Homma was represented in that
action by a local barrister, R. W. Harris of the law firm Harris and Bull. The
Constitution Act, 1867 (the *British North America Act*), ss. 91 and 92, provided
that the Canadian Parliament had exclusive legislative authority over the
subjects of "naturalization and aliens," and that the provincial governments'
authority was generally limited to "all Matters of a merely local or private
Nature in the Province." The quintessential question in Canadian constitutional
law prior to the adoption of the Charter of Rights and Freedoms in 1982 was
whether a matter "in pith and substance" came within section 91 or 92, it being
assumed that all matters came within one or the other. Herbert Arthur Smith,
*Federalism in North America: A Comparative Study of Institutions in the United
States and Canada* (Boston: Chipman Law Publishing Co., 1923), 108–109.

28. *Naturalization Act*, R.S.C. c. 113, s. 15.

29. *In re the Provincial Voters Act and re Homma* (1900) 7 B.C.R. 368 (Co. Ct.), B.C.'s
argument was based on the language in section 92 of the British North America
Act, which gave the provincial Legislature exclusive jurisdiction with regard to
"the amendment from time to time, notwithstanding anything in the Act, of
the constitution of the Province, except in respect of the office of Lieutenant-
Governor." In *Union Colliery Company v. Bryden,* the Privy Council overturned
B.C. legislation that barred Chinese miners from working underground. Union
Colliery Company of British Columbia, Limited v. Bryden [1899], A.C. 580, 587
(P.C.)

30. *In re Provincial Voters Act and re Homma,* 7 B.C.R. 372 (Co. Ct.); *Victoria Daily
Colonist*, 30 November 1900. Chief Justice McColl's conclusion that the province
lacked the power to pass legislation that did not "apply alike" to all subjects of
the queen was based on the language of the Naturalization Act itself. In the
Constitution Act of 1867 (British North America Act), there was no equivalent
to the Equal Protection Clause of the U.S. Constitution. Canada incorporated
a Charter of Rights into its Constitution in 1982, after the British Parliament
granted it the power to amend its own constitution. Charles Arnold-Baker,
The Companion to British History, 2nd ed. (London: Routledge, 2001), 189. The
Charter of Rights includes a provision guaranteeing the right to vote.

31. *In re Provincial Voters Act and re Homma,* 7 B.C.R. 372 (Co. Ct.).

32. *Vancouver Daily Province,* 1 December 1900.

33. D. M. Eberts, B.C. Attorney General, to Christopher Robinson, Esq., K.C.,
London, 29 June 1901, quoting *Gibb v. White,* 5 Ont. Practice Reports, 315,
affirmed in *Johnson v. Jones,* 26 Ontario Reports 109. Although the
Provincial Voters Act did not provide for a direct appeal to the Privy Council,

the province requested a waiver that would allow it to file such an appeal. The B.C. Supreme Court granted its request, assuming correctly that the Privy Council would accept it, and the Dominion government intervened on Homma's side of the dispute.

34. D. M. Eberts, B.C. Attorney General, to Christopher Robinson, Esq., K.C., 29 June 1901. Vancouver newspapers also frequently invoked the idea that the denial of the vote to women justified denial of the vote to Asian men. See, for example, the *Victoria Daily Colonist,* 25 April 1905, arguing that the exclusion of people of Asian ancestry from the franchise was justified on the ground that "not even all British subjects were entitled to vote" and citing the fact that women were not allowed to vote as a telling example. The work being quoted by Eberts is *The Constitutional Law of the United States of America,* originally written in German by Dr. H. von Holst, a professor at the University of Freiburg. An English edition, translated by Alfred Bishop Mason, was published in 1887 by Callaghan and Company in Chicago, Illinois. Frederick Jackson Turner referred to von Holst's work on slavery in his essay "The Significance of the Frontier in American History," *Annual Report of the American Historical Association for the Year 1893* (Washington, D.C., 1894), 200.

35. Henry Wheaton, *Elements of International Law,* 2nd annotated ed., ed. William Beach Lawrence (1863; London, 1864) ("*Lawrence's Wheaton*"). In the context of Aboriginal law cases, Canadian courts have sometimes turned to decisions of U.S. courts for precedent, reasoning that federal Indian law doctrine in both Canada and the United States has its origins in pre–Revolutionary War British colonial Indian policy, and particularly the Royal Proclamation of 1763, which established the basic tenets of what later became federal Indian law in both the United States and Canada. No similar rationale exists, however, for invoking U.S. law in this context, particularly because the language in question arises out of a discussion of an article of the U.S. Constitution, which, by definition, has no application in Canada.

36. *Cunningham v. Homma, supra,* A.C. 156, quoting *Lawrence's Wheaton,* 903. The phrase "in the United States" is in the original. Thus, there can be no question that the Privy Council was aware that the phrase it extracted occurred within the context of a discussion of U.S. law and policy. The Privy Council also made the general observation that the franchise had sometimes been withheld from British subjects in England, "conspicuously upon grounds of religious faith," suggesting that the historical toleration in British law of the denial of civil rights on religious grounds somehow justified the denial of civil rights on race-based grounds. The Privy Council again failed to explain how withholding the franchise in England justified its conclusion as to the scope of political rights in Canada.

37. See, for example, *Lawrence's Wheaton,* 904; von Holst, "Significance of the Frontier," 19. For a detailed discussion of the historical debates regarding the scope of the franchise in the United States, see Alexander Keyssar, *The Right to*

Vote: The Contested History of Democracy in the United States (New York: Basic Books, 2000).

38. *Lawrence's Wheaton,* 909–910. The Privy Council also avoided any acknowledgment that, even assuming the clause it extracted was good law in 1863, it was no longer good law even in the United States at the time the Privy Council made its decision in 1902. The flaw in—or perhaps even the reason for—its choice of the 1863 edition of *Lawrence's Wheaton,* and not a more current summary of the law, becomes quickly apparent when one examines later editions of the treatise. Not just the language quoted by the Privy Council to support its decision, but the entire chapter of which it was a part, was completely cut from all post-1864 editions.

39. *Vancouver Daily Province,* 23 January 1901 (reprint of an article from a recent edition of the *New York Herald* reporting the opinion of a Mr. Smith, a Southerner living in New York).

40. Canada, Immigration Branch. *Notes of Articles from the "Taiyo" on the Expansion of Japan,* quoting T. Uchida, Japanese Minister to Brazil.

41. *The New Canadian,* 12 March 1949.

42. Act of June 29, 1906, 34 Stat. 596, chap. 3592; Yuji Ichioka, "The Early Japanese Immigrant Quest for Citizenship: The Background of the 1922 *Ozawa* Case," in Charles McClain, ed., *Japanese Immigrants and American Law: The Alien Land Laws and Other Issues* (New York: Garland, 1994), 406–407.

43. My focus here is particularly on arguments made by Ozawa and his supporters that invoked caste to argue for racial inclusion. For other race-based arguments not discussed here, see Mae Ngai, *Impossible Subjects: Illegal Aliens and the Making of Modern America* (Princeton, N.J.: Princeton University Press, 2003), 41–45; and John S. W. Park, *Elusive Citizenship: Immigration, Asian Americans, and the Paradox of Civil Rights* (New York: New York University Press, 2006), 121–124.

44. *In the Matter of the Petition for Naturalization of Sakharam Ganesh Pandit,* Los Angeles County Superior Court, 7 May 1914 (Judge Willis I. Morrison), U.S. District Court, District of Hawaii, Honolulu, Naturalization Case Files, 1927–1959, Ozawa Case File, RG 21, NARA. The inclusion of the case in the file maintained by the court is a strong indication that it was considered by that court in reaching a decision in Ozawa's case. The briefs submitted to the U.S. Supreme Court are reprinted in Consulate-General of Japan, comp., *Documental History of Law Cases Affecting Japanese in the United States, 1916–1924,* vol. 1: *Naturalization Cases and Cases Affecting Constitutional and Treaty Rights* (San Francisco, 1925), 17. The U.S. Supreme Court formally rejected this argument in *Thind v. United States,* 261 U.S. 204 (1923).

45. U.S. District Court, District of Hawaii, Ozawa Case File, RG 21, NARA, copy of letter from Masuji Miyakawa, Associate Editor, Comparative Law Bureau of the American Bar Association, to President Woodrow Wilson, 22 April 1913, enclosing application for citizenship and court order dated 9 October 1905. Some American citizens also saw the issue primarily as a matter of class or

status rather than race. In 1907, for example, U.S. Ambassador to Japan Luke E. Wright, informed the U.S. State Department that he could see "no objection to giving better class Japanese the right of naturalization." Morris Report, 96.

46. *In the Matter of the Application of Takao Ozawa for Admission to Citizenship,* U.S. District Court for the Territory of Hawaii, 4–5 June 1914; emphasis in original.

47. Letter from Doremus Scudder, Minister, Central Union Church, Honolulu, Hawaii, 13 April 1915. U.S. District Court, District of Hawaii, Ozawa Case File, RG 21, NARA.

48. Kawakami, *Asia at the Door,* 15. Kawakami also argued that it was "absurd" that citizenship was extended to "many non-Caucasians, such as Tartars, Finns and Hungarians; Turks, Syrians, Persians and Hindus; Mexicans and South Americans; Zulus, Hottentots, Kaffirs and men from any tribe in Africa; but it denies the same privilege to Japanese and Chinese, however well qualified they may be." Kawakami, *Real Japanese Question,* 222.

49. U.S. District Court, District of Hawaii, Ozawa Case File, RG 21, NARA. The briefs were handwritten by Ozawa in notebooks in a strong, clear, fluent hand with only minor grammatical errors and were retyped for submission to the court.

50. Taro Iwata, "Race and Citizenship as American Geopolitics: Japanese and Native Hawaiians in Hawai'i, 1900–1941" (Ph.D. diss., University of Oregon, 2003), 38; Ichioka, "Early Japanese Immigrant Quest for Citizenship," 397–426, 406.

51. The Naturalization Act of 1790 states that "[a]ny alien, being a free white person, ... may be admitted to become a citizen[.]" *Ozawa,* 260 U.S. at 192, quoting An Act to Establish an Uniform Rule of Naturalization, 26 March 1790, c.3 (1 Stat. 103). Because the Naturalization Act of 1790 was amended after the U.S. Civil War to include "aliens of African nativity and persons of African descent," there was no dispute that people in these categories were eligible to become naturalized citizens of the United States. Act of July 14, 1870, 16 Stat., chap. 254. The phrase "free white persons" was omitted from the Revised Statutes of 1873, sec. 2165–2169, suggesting that it applied to all immigrants regardless of race or national origin. In February 1875, Congress passed the Act of February 18, 1875 (18 Stat. 318), "to correct errors and supply omissions in the Revised statutes." The Naturalization Act was amended at that time to limit the right of naturalization to "aliens being free white persons and to aliens of African nativity, and to persons of African descent." *In the Matter of the Petition for Naturalization of Sakharam Ganesh Pandit,* Los Angeles County Superior Court, 7 May 1914 (Judge Willis I. Morrison).

52. Iwata, "Race and Citizenship as American Geopolitics," 29. Iwata notes that some of Ozawa's supporters felt uncomfortable with his argument that Japanese were white. Iwata quotes Ototaka Yamaoka of the Pacific Coast Japanese Association Deliberative Council as saying, for example, "We might be unlearned, but we never made an argument that Japanese are of the white race, which is akin to child's play [*jigi*]." Ibid., 30.

53. *Ozawa v. United States*, 260 U.S. 178, 189 (1922). The Court noted that after graduating from high school in Berkeley, California, Ozawa studied for three years at the University of California and worked for many years for a U.S. company. It also noted that his children had been educated in American schools, that the family spoke only English at home, and that they attended "American" churches. *Ozawa*, 260 U.S. at 189.

54. *Ozawa*, 260 U.S. at 194–195, setting out the standard of review but explaining that if such a reading led to an "unreasonable" result, it was appropriate for the Court to consider the legislative history of the statute. The Court agreed with Ozawa that the reference to "free" in the phrase "free white person" was intended to distinguish those who were in bondage.

55. *Ozawa*, 260 U.S. at 198. Justice Sutherland was forced to acknowledge, however, that a "zone of more or less debatable ground" would remain, into which individuals in "borderline cases" would fall. Those cases, he noted, could be decided as they arose pursuant to "a gradual process of judicial inclusion and exclusion." Sutherland characterized the applicable standard as "a racial and not an individual test." For a general discussion of the law of citizenship and race, see Charles Gordon, "The Racial Barrier to American Citizenship," *University of Pennsylvania Law Review* 93, no. 3 (March 1945): 237–257.

56. *Ozawa*, 260 U.S. at 198.

57. See *Japanese Immigration Legislation, Hearings on S. 2576; Japanese Immigration: Hearings before the Committee on Immigration and Naturalization, House of Representatives*, 66th Cong., 2nd Sess., July 12 to August 3, 1920,, 1266. California was the first state to pass an alien land law, on May 19, 1913; a more comprehensive version was passed on November 2, 1920. See Iyenaga and Sato, *Japanese and the California Problem*, 204–215. By April 1921, Washington, Nebraska, Arizona, and Texas had passed alien land laws, and Colorado and New Mexico had scheduled votes on constitutional amendments that would have the same effect. Oregon, Idaho, Montana, Utah, and Nevada had considered such measures and rejected them. Kawakami, *Real Japanese Question*, 109. Japanese immigrants were sometimes able to avoid the impact of the law in part by placing land in the name of an American-born child, setting up corporations with Caucasians in which they owned most of the stock, or relying on Caucasian friends to buy land for them. See, for example, Ann Koto Hayashi, *Face of the Enemy, Heart of a Patriot: Japanese-American Internment Narratives* (New York: Garland, 1995). Iyenaga and Sato suggest that Australia provided a model for the alien land laws, noting that several Australian states did not allow Asian immigrants to own or lease land, "under the pretext that they are not eligible to citizenship." Iyenaga and Sato, *Japanese and the California Problem*, 67. According to Ayukawa, legislation similar to the alien land laws that would have referred to "persons ineligible for the franchise" was proposed but not implemented in British Columbia. Michiko Midge Ayukawa, "Creating and Recreating Community" (Ph.D. diss., University of Victoria, 1996), 158. Adachi explains that "the province wanted an amendment to the British

North America Act that would enable it to prohibit Orientals from acquiring proprietary interests in farming, timber and mining lands or in fishing and other industries." Ken Adachi, *The Enemy That Never Was: A History of the Japanese Canadians* (Toronto: McClelland and Stewart, 1976), 133.

58. "Life History of a Japanese Man at Santa Paula," trans. M. Dodo, 29 December 1924, folder 323–18, *Survey on Race Relations,* Hoover Institution on War, Revolution and Peace, Stanford, Calif.

59. Michiyo Laing and the Issei Oral History Project, eds., *Issei Christians: Selected Interviews from the Issei Oral History Project* (Sacramento, Calif.: Issei Oral History Project, 1977), 27; Ito, *Issei,* 478 (Kanichi Tsukamaki interview).

60. Gordon G. Nakayama, *Issei: Stories of Japanese Canadian Pioneers* (Toronto: Britannia Printers, 1983), 127.

61. Takeshi Uyeyama, interview by Kirsten McAllister, Nanaimo, B.C., 12 May 1990, Japanese Canadian Oral History Collection (JCOHC), Japanese Canadian National Museum and Archives, Burnaby, B.C.

62. Muriel Kitagawa, for example, remembers that her mother supported the family by sewing while her father attended dental college in Oregon because students of Japanese ancestry were denied entry to medical school in British Columbia. Muriel Kitagawa, *This Is My Own: Letters to Wes and Other Writings on Japanese Canadians, 1941–1948,* ed. Roy Miki (Vancouver, B.C.: Talonbooks, 1985), 274–275. See also Mary Takeyasu, interview by Minnie Hattori, Vancouver, B.C., 5 June 1997, JCOHC. Takeyasu explains that her grandmother sent her only son to Tacoma, Washington, to learn dentistry because he was barred from studying dentistry or medicine in British Columbia; Takeyasu also states that doctors and dentists were able to work among "their own people" but that public school teachers, lawyers, and accountants were not allowed to do so, which meant that sawmill workers in British Columbia included some with university degrees who were barred from the professions for which they had been trained.

63. Eileen Sunada Sarasohn, *The Issei: Portrait of a Pioneer, An Oral History* (Palo Alto, Calif.: Pacific Books, 1983), 35 n. 9.

64. These children sent to Japan were called *kika nisei* in Canada and *kibei nisei* in the United States (referring to their return either to Canada or the United States). See, for example, Adachi, *Enemy That Never Was,* 174–175; Roger Daniels, *Asian America: Chinese and Japanese in the United States since 1850* (Seattle: University of Washington Press, 1988), 176–177. See also Katharine Jane Lentz, "Japanese American Relations in Seattle" (Ph.D. diss., University of Washington, 1924), 79, noting that anti-Japanese laws functioned as "the greatest hindrance to complete Americanization of the Japanese" since they made "Japanese feel that as they may have to get out some time there is no use to plan for permanent residence."

65. See, for example, *Japanese-American Courier,* 15 September 1928, observing that that the second generation was "not permitted to participate as citizens," which meant that they did "not look to the future with as much hope and confidence as ... their cousins in the United States."

66. *The Islander,* 23 August 1919. For discussion of the *beika,* or Americanization movement, see Sarasohn, *The Issei,* 68 (Juhei Kono interview).

67. Lentz, "Japanese-American Relations in Seattle," 82.

68. Rolf Knight and Maya Koizumi, *A Man of Our Times: The Life-History of a Japanese-Canadian Fisherman* (Vancouver, B.C.: New Star Books, 1976), 38, 50. See also Miyoko Kudō, *Vankuvā no Ai: Tamura Toshiko to Suzuki Etsu* (Tokyo: Domesu Shuppan, 1982).

69. U.S. Immigration officials sought assurances during immigration interviews that wives would keep house and not work with their husbands in the fields. See, for example, U.S. Immigration Bureau, Special Inquiry, *In re Haruki Teramura—Japanese, Ex. SS. Mongolia, 6 December 1913, for Admission to the United States,* RG 85, NARA.

70. See, for example, Sharon H. Nolte and Sally Ann Hastings, "The Meiji State's Policy toward Women, 1890–1910," in Gail Lee Bernstein, ed., *Recreating Japanese Women, 1600–1945* (Berkeley: University of California Press, 1991), 17–41; and Kathleen S. Uno, "Women and Changes in the Household Division of Labor," in Bernstein, *Recreating Japanese Women,* 151–174.

71. "Taro's Notebook: Suggestions to Resident Japanese," *Taihoku Nippō,* translation found in RG 85, NARA.

72. See, for example, *The Islander,* 26 January 1918.

73. Mary Takeyasu, interview by Minnie Hattori, Vancouver, B.C., 5 June 1997, JCOHC, also stating that "you have to melt with the pot"; Paul R. Spickard, *Japanese Americans: The Formations and Transformations of an Ethnic Group* (New York: Twayne, 1996), 70. See also H. S. Hayashi, "My Advice to the Japanese Immigrant Laborers by the Feared, [1893]," in Jiro Nakano, ed., *Kona Echo: A Biography of Dr. Harvey Saburo Hayashi* (Kona, Hawaii: Kona Historical Society, 1990), stating his belief that Japanese could prevent white racist attitudes by dressing neatly.

74. See, e.g., Adachi, *The Enemy That Never Was,* 111.

75. Conyngham Greene, British Embassy, Tokio, to The Right Honourable Sir E. Grey, Bart., K.C., M.P., 20 April 1915, RG 76, LAC.

76. Yuji Ichioka, " 'Attorney for the Defense,' " *Pacific Historical Review* 55, no. 2 (May 1986): 192–225, 213.

77. *Japanese Immigration Legislation: Hearings before the Committee on Immigration, United States Senate, 68th Cong., 1st Sess. on 2576* (1924), 120.

CHAPTER EIGHT. REFRAMING COMMUNITY AND POLICING MARRIAGE

1. "Forget Caste and Status According to Occupation Says Local Business Man," *Japanese-American Courier,* 12 May 1928.

2. Ibid. For employment difficulties faced by nisei in the United States, also see Forrest E. LaViolette, *Americans of Japanese Ancestry: A Study of Assimilation in the American Community* (Toronto: Canadian Institute of International Affairs, 1945), 72–83. Audrey Lynn Kobayashi states that questions yet to be fully addressed include the "extent to which occupational differences result in

class differences within the [nikkei] community, as well as the extent to which such differences are reproduced or restructured in relation to differences that may have existed formerly in Japan." Audrey Lynn Kobayashi, "Regional Backgrounds of Japanese Immigrants and the Development of Japanese-Canadian Community," *McGill Geography Discussion Papers* I, no. 1 (May 1986): 1-14.

3. Karl Yoneda to Joe Grant Masaoka, 21 August 1965, Japanese American Research Project (JARP), University of California, Los Angeles. See also Yukiko Kimura, *Issei: Japanese Immigrants in Hawaii* (Honolulu: University of Hawaii Press, 1988), 69; Cullen Tadao Hayashida, "Identity, Race and the Blood Ideology of Japan" (Ph.D. diss., University of Washington, 1976), 138, noting that the "emphasis on blood" in assessing family lineage "has been considerably affected by traditional notions of purity and pollution" and that "the entrance of those of pariah status has always been considered a way of staining a family's *ketto* (blood lineage)." See also Ken Adachi, *The Enemy That Never Was: A History of the Japanese Canadians* (Toronto: McClelland and Stewart, 1976), 89.

4. Hugh H. Smythe and Yoshimasa Naitoh, "The Eta Caste in Japan," pt. 1, *Phylon* 14, no. 1 (1953): 24. Hayashida notes that investigative agencies have been used in Japan during recent decades to avoid hiring or marriage to burakumin. Hayashida, "Identity, Race and the Blood Ideology of Japan," 186, 196–197, 235, including a translation of a "pedigree report" prepared by an investigative agency in 1973 tracing family lineage. See also Gerald D. Berreman, "Concomitants of Caste Organization," in George De Vos and Hiroshi Wagatsuma, eds., *Japan's Invisible Race: Caste in Culture and Personality* (Berkeley: University of California Press, 1966), 316; Gerald D. Berreman, "Stratification, Pluralism and Interaction: A Comparative Analysis of Caste," in Anthony de Reuck and Julie Knight, eds., *Caste and Race: Comparative Approaches* (Boston: Little, Brown, 1967), 65.

5. Karl Yoneda to Joe Grant Masaoka, 7 August 1967, JARP.

6. See Andrea Geiger, "Cross-Pacific Dimensions of Race, Caste & and Class: Meiji-Era Japanese Immigrants in the North American West" (Ph.D. diss., University of Washington, 2006), 255. William Petersen concluded that most North American nikkeijin were unfamiliar with any term except *eta*, so there was no neutral designation to describe former outcastes. William Petersen, *Japanese Americans: Oppression and Success* (New York: Random House, 1971), 212 n. 8.

7. Susumu Koga, "Etas: The Social Outcasts of Japan," *The Living Age* 319, no. 4139 (3 November 1923): 225–226. Koga explains that discovering that one's spouse was of buraku origin was treated, even in the 1920s Japan, as legitimate grounds for granting an immediate divorce.

8. Hiroshi Ito, "Japan's Outcastes in the United States," in De Vos and Wagatsuma, *Japan's Invisible Race,* 201, 221, citing the "breakup of a proposed mixed marriage" as a typical form of outcaste rejection among Japanese Americans in California.

9. Hayashida, "Identity, Race and the Blood Ideology of Japan," 193. See also Taimie L. Bryant, "For the Sake of the Country, For the Sake of the Family: The Oppressive Impact of Family Registration on Women and Minorities in Japan," *UCLA Law Review* 39 (1991): 109–168.

10. Adachi, *The Enemy That Never Was,* 119, noting the important role played by kenjinkai in investigating the family background of potential marriage partners to ensure that the family had no connections to former outcaste communities. For a general description of the role of kenjinkai, see Robert A. Wilson and Bill Hosokawa, *East to America: A History of the Japanese in the United States* (New York: William Morrow, 1980), 110–111.

11. See Yuji Ichioka, "Japanese Associations and the Japanese Government: A Special Relationship, 1909–1926," *Pacific Historical Review* 46, no. 3 (August 1977): 409–437, 421.

12. See Hayashida, "Identity, Race and the Blood Ideology of Japan," 138, stating that " 'abnormalities' like mental illness, physical deformity, leprosy, criminality, suicide, epilepsy, color-blindness, hemophilia, feeble-mindedness, history of alcoholism, 'women trouble,' and any other assumed hereditary ailment are frequently believed to be inherent in the blood"; Cheryl Maeva Thomas, "The Japanese Communities of Cumberland, British Columbia, 1885–1942: Portrait of a Past" (M.A. thesis, University of Victoria, 1992), 95, explaining that she had been told by people she interviewed in Cumberland, B.C., that "family backgrounds [were] scrutinized and if conditions like tuberculosis and insanity [were] found, the marriage [was] discouraged." These practices were also common in Japan. Emiko Ohnuki-Tierney, *Illness and Culture in Contemporary Japan: An Anthropological View* (Cambridge: Cambridge University Press, 1984), 60–62.

13. See Paul R. Spickard, *Japanese Americans: The Formations and Transformations of an Ethnic Group* (New York: Twayne Publishers, 1996), 33, noting that social pressure from within nikkei society discouraged Japanese from marrying whites and other non-Japanese.

14. T. Iyenaga and Kenoske Sato, *Japanese and the California Problem* (New York: G. P. Putnam's Sons, 1921), 155. Iyenaga and Sato also state that the "strong race prejudice [of the Japanese] has been exemplified by their attitude toward … the outcast class of their fellow countrymen, called *Eta*, which has been nothing short of prejudicial discrimination." Ibid., 18.

15. "Life History of Peter," prepared by Wm. C. Smith, box 29, document No. 251–1, circa 1924, *Survey on Race Relations,* Hoover Institution on War, Revolution and Peace, Stanford, Calif. Marriages across racial boundaries were often the subject of comment in local English-language newspapers. See, for example, *The Weekly News* (Cumberland, B.C.), 15 February 1898, reporting that "a Jap by the name of Fugie Kakutoro and a Mrs. Annie Turner were united in marriage by the Rev. Mr. Hicks Feb. 27th."

16. Muriel Kitagawa, *This Is My Own: Letters to Wes and Other Writings on Japanese Canadians, 1941–1948,* ed. Roy Miki (Vancouver, B.C.: Talonbooks, 1985),

220–221. For the use of gossip as a sanction in Japanese village society, see Herman Ooms, *Tokugawa Village Practice: Class, Status, Power, Law* (Berkeley: University of California Press, 1996), 197, 216–21; Robert J. Smith and Ella Lury Wiswell, *The Women of Suye Mura* (Chicago: University of Chicago Press, 1982), xix.

17. Maryka Omatsu, *Bittersweet Passage: Redress and the Japanese-Canadian Experience* (Toronto: Between the Lines, 1992), 99.

18. Thomas, "Japanese Communities of Cumberland, B.C.," 95.

19. Roy Kiyooka, *Mothertalk: Life Stories of Mary Kiyoshi Kiyooka,* ed. Daphne Marlatt (Edmonton, Alberta: NeWest Press, 1997), 53.

20. Kobayashi, "Regional Backgrounds of Japanese Immigrants," 1–10.

21. Kitagawa, *This Is My Own,* 219–220.

22. Malve von Hassell, "*Issei* Women: Silences and Fields of Power," *Feminist Studies* 19, no. 3 (Fall 1993): 563.

23. See Geiger, "Cross-Pacific Dimensions of Race, Caste and Class," 255; Hiroshi Ito, "Japan's Outcastes in the United States," in De Vos and Wagatsuma, *Japan's Invisible Race,* 200–221. According to Miyamoto, rumors that certain families were "*eta*" were not necessarily based on knowledge of ancestry. Shotaro Frank Miyamoto, conversation with author, Seattle, Washington, Spring 2000.

24. Kitagawa, *This Is My Own,* 283, reporting that her family was living on Lulu Island in the midst of the Fraser River Delta in Vancouver, B.C., at the time. See also Kiyooka, *Mothertalk,* 150; Smith and Wiswell, *Women of Suye Mura,* 233 (*haikara ni naru* means "become very fancy"). Meiji linguistic patterns persisted among the immigrants who had settled in North America long after they had been modified and replaced with new expressions in Japan, leading to diverging patterns of speech in Japan and North America. Spickard, *Japanese Americans,* 64.

25. By the end of the 1920s, a number of U.S. states had passed or considered miscegenation laws. The earliest miscegenation law was passed in California in 1905 and forbade marriage between white women and Japanese. Spickard, *Japanese Americans,* 33; Hisashi Tsurutani, *America-Bound: The Japanese and the Opening of the American West,* trans. Betsey Scheiner (Tokyo: Japan Times, 1989), 178. See generally John N. Tinker, "Intermarriage and Ethnic Boundaries: The Japanese American Case," *Journal of Social Issues* 29, no. 2 (1973), stating that "intermarriage is an especially sensitive indicator of the permeability of ethnic boundaries"; and Peggy Pascoe, "Race, Gender, and Intercultural Relations: The Case of Interracial Marriage," *Frontiers: A Journal of Women Studies* 12, no. 1 (1991): 5, arguing that the study of intermarriage in the U.S. West provides a useful lens for seeing the "making and remaking of notions of race, gender, and culture in individual lives."

26. "Why Japs Are Unwelcome," *The British Columbian Weekly,* 2 March 1909, quoting an article by a "newspaperman of Fresno, Cal., who contributed recently to Collier's Magazine."

27. See Kiyoshi K. Kawakami, *The Real Japanese Question* (New York: MacMillan, 1921), 258. Passport regulations were extremely strict in Japan by this time. See Hisatomi Shigenosuke, *Tokō annai: Kanada, nambei, hokubei, hawaii* (Guide for Travel by Ship: Canada, South America, North America, Hawaii) (Kobe: Bingoya, 1916), 11.

28. Wilson and Hosokawa, *East to America*, 125–126.

29. Kazuo Ito, *Issei: A History of Japanese Immigrants in North America*, trans. Shinichiro Nakamura and Jean S. Gerard (Seattle: Executive Committee for Publication of *Issei*, 1973), 200; Confidential Memorandum from Office of Naval Intelligence, 10 March 1920, RG 85, NARA.

30. Statement by Reverend K. S. Itow, Long Beach, California, 2 August 1924, box 33, *Survey on Race Relations*, Hoover Institution.

31. John H. Clark, U.S. Immigration Commissioner, Montreal, Canada, to F. P. Sargent, Commissioner General of Immigration, Washington, D.C., 11 June 1908 and 9 July 1908, RG 85, NARA, proposing that "uniformity as to a marriage ceremony under Washington or British Columbia laws, should be enforced." See also U.S. Senator James D. Phelan, to Secretary of State, 24 July 1919; Daniel C. Murphy, President, San Francisco Labor Council, to President Woodrow Wilson, 16 May 1916, RG 85, NARA.

32. See, for example, U.S. Immigration Records, file no. 14776, Chiyoe Sakaguchi, 5 November 1915, RG 85, NARA, San Bruno.

33. Secretary of State Robert Lansing to Secretary of Labor, 30 April 1917, enclosing note of 28 April 1917 from Japanese Ambassador Aimaro Sato and *Extracts from the Civil Code of Japan*, translated by Dr. L. H. Loenholm, RG 85, NARA. According to *Extracts*, 9, under section 775 of the Japanese Civil Code, a marriage took effect when the bride's name was transferred from her own family register (koseki) to that of the groom.

34. T. Tanaka, Imperial Japanese Embassy, Washington, D.C., to Frank P. Lockhart, Bureau of Far Eastern Affairs, Department of State, 17 April 1917, RG 85, NARA.

35. See, for example, John H. Clark, U.S. Immigration Commissioner, Montreal, Canada, to F. P. Sargent, Commissioner General of Immigration, Washington, D.C., 11 June 1908; Richard L. Halsey, Inspector in Charge, U.S. Immigration Service, Honolulu, Hawaii, to Secretary of Labor, Washington, D.C., file 4285, 21 October 1921, RG 85, NARA.

36. Handwritten note from P. W. Ebersoll, Portland, Oregon, file 52424-13, RG 85, NARA.

37. Memorandum issued by Imperial Japanese Embassy, Washington, D.C., May 1913, RG 85, NARA.

38. *The San Francisco Bulletin*, 21 January 1905.

39. U.S. Immigration Commissioner, San Francisco, to F. P. Sargent, Commissioner General of Immigration, Washington, D.C., 8 February 1905, RG 85, NARA. In evaluating the accuracy of the newspaper report, also worth noting is another error: the young woman was turned over not to a woman from

the Presbyterian Mission but to a Miss Lake of the Japanese Methodist Mission. Ibid.

40. Confidential Memorando, Office of Naval Intelligence to State Department and Department of Labor, Bureau of Immigration, 20 and 22 September 1917, RG 85, NARA.

41. Yuji Ichioka, "*Amerika Nadeshiko:* Japanese Immigrant Women In the United States, 1900–1924," *Pacific Historical Review* 49 (1980): 350–354; Eileen Sunada Sarasohn, *The Issei: Portrait of a Pioneer, Aan Oral History* (Palo Alto, Calif.: Pacific Books, 1983), 130, stating that the reward for catching eloped couples was $25. For a recent dissertation on picture marriage in California that addresses elopement, see Kei Tanaka, "Japanese Picture Marriage in 1900–1924 California: Construction of Japanese Race and Gender" (Ph.D. diss., Rutgers University, 2002), 162–176. For a general discussion of the historical experiences of issei women in the United States between 1875 and 1985, see Malve von Hassell, "Issei Women between Two Worlds: 1875–1985" (Ph.D. diss., New School for Social Research, New York, 1987).

42. Ichioka, "*Amerika Nadeshiko,*" 352–353.

43. Confidential Memorandum from Director of Naval Intelligence, 1 November 1919, RG 85, NARA.

44. Office of Naval Intelligence, translation dated 24 May 1917 of San Yo Sei [pen name], "What Is an Obedient Woman," *Taihoku Nippō* (Seattle), 18 May 1917, RG 85, NARA.

45. Audrey Lynn Kobayashi, "For the Sake of the Children: Japanese/Canadian Workers/Mothers," in Audrey Lynn Kobayashi, ed., *Women, Work, and Place* (Montreal: McGill-Queen's University Press, 1994), 55, observing that "the ratio of men to women, which had been 30:1 in 1893, dropped to 5:1 by 1910 and dropped ... to 2:1 by 1920." But the overall number of migrants continued to remain relatively small. See, for example, Ito, *Issei*, 188, explaining that the number of picture brides who arrived in Seattle from 1915 through 1919 was 1,048—the number was 150 in 1915, peaked at 281 in 1918, and dropped to 267 in 1919 before picture brides were banned in 1920. The impact of this demographic shift was also reflected in guidebooks written for emigrants traveling to North America. By 1916, for example, one guidebook provided specific instructions to migrants on how to cable their husbands from on board ship to ensure that they would be there when the ship docked. Hisatomi, *Tokō annai*, 10.

46. Ito, *Issei*, 197.

47. Confidential Memorandum from Office of Naval Intelligence to War College, 17 October 1919, attaching translation of article entitled " 'Stop Photograph Marriage and Anti-Japanese Party Will Lose Most Effective Argument,' Conversation of Consul-General Ota of San Francisco: Problem Difficult Because Americans Don't Understand," *Japanese-American* (probably a reference to the *Nichibei Shimbun*), 9 October 1919, RG 85, NARA.

48. Ito, *Issei*, 195. Ito reports that the *Nichibei Shimbun* in San Francisco opposed picture marriages, while the *Shin Sekai* supported them.

49. Ibid., 197, 200; Ichioka, *"Amerika Nadeshiko,"* 355.

50. H. Nishi, Vice Consul, Consulate General of Japan, New York, to Frederick A. Wallis, Commissioner of Immigration, Ellis Island, New York, 4 May 1921; Assistant Commissioner General to Commissioner of Immigration, Ellis Island, N.Y.H., 12 May 1921, RG 85, NARA.

51. Harry E. Hull, Commissioner General, U.S. Immigration Service, 8 October 1930, RG 85, NARA.

52. Ichihashi, *Japanese in the United States*, 295 n. 15. For a discussion of European marriage practices see Suzanne M. Sinke, "The International Marriage Market: Theoretical and Historical Perspectives," in Dirk Hoerder and Jörg Nagler, eds., *People in Transit: German Migrations in Comparative Perspective, 1820–1930* (Cambridge: Cambridge University Press, 1995), 227–248.

53. U.S. Senator James D. Phelan, to Secretary of State, 24 July 1919, RG 85, NARA. See also "Japanese Picture Brides Are Swarming Here" and "White or Jap— Which? Shall the Pacific Coast Be Japanized?" both in *The Seattle Star*, 30 July 1919; Ichioka, *"Amerika Nadeshiko,"* 355.

54. *Japanese Immigration Legislation: Hearings before the Committee on Immigration, United States Senate, 68th Cong., 1st Sess. on S. 2576, A Bill to Limit the Immigration of Aliens into the United States, March 11–15, 1924* (Washington, D.C.: Government Printing Office, 1924), 120, 137. See also *Japanese Immigration: Hearings before the Committee on Immigration and Naturalization, House of Representatives*, 66th Cong., 2nd Sess., July 12 to August 3, 1920, 172, stating in a section entitled "Future Voters" that "California bears in mind that there are now 21,611 Japanese minor children born in California, all of whom will shortly become full-fledged voters, having already acquired the right to vote."

55. U.S. Senator James D. Phelan, to Secretary of State, 24 July 1919.

56. V. S. McClatchy, " 'Picture Brides' and Their Successors: Japanese Ingenuity in Forcing Peaceful Penetration under the 'Gentlemen's Agreement,' " *The Sacramento Bee*, 28 November 1921 (reprinted as a pamphlet by News Printing and Publishing Co., Sacramento).

57. Patricia E. Roy, J. L. Granatstein, Masako Iino, and Hiroko Takamura, *Mutual Hostages: Canadians and Japanese during the Second World War* (Toronto: University of Toronto Press, 1990), 16–17.

CHAPTER NINE. THE RHETORIC OF HOMOGENEITY

1. Shotaro Frank Miyamoto, "Social Solidarity among the Japanese in Seattle," *University of Washington Publications in the Social Sciences* II, no. 2 (December 1939): 57. Miyamoto also argued that "a conspicuous characteristic of [their] communities [was] their powerful internal solidarity." Ibid., 59. Miyamoto explains, however, that he has since modified his thesis. Shotaro Frank Miyamoto, conversation with the author, Seattle, Washington, February 2000.

2. David J. O'Brien and Stephen S. Fugita, *The Japanese American Experience* (Bloomington: Indiana University Press, 1991), 3. See also Edna Bonacich and John Modell, *The Economic Basis of Ethnic Solidarity: Small Business in the Japanese American Community* (Berkeley: University of California Press, 1980). Those who have criticized this approach include John Lie, *Multiethnic Japan* (Cambridge, Mass.: Harvard University Press, 2001), 1–2, citing numerous examples; Stefan Akio Tanaka, "The Nikkei on Bainbridge Island, 1883–1942: A Study of Migration and Community Development" (M.A. thesis, University of Washington, 1977), 129 (referring to the "myth of cohesion"); Malve von Hassell, "*Issei* Women: Silences and Fields of Power," *Feminist Studies* 19, no. 3 (Fall 1993); and Eiichiro Azuma, "The Politics of Transnational History Making: Japanese Immigrants on the Western 'Frontier,' 1927–1941," *Journal of American History* 89, no. 4 (March 2003): 1410, arguing that "the homogenized memory fabricated certain forms of intraethnic unity among Japanese in America."

3. Okuma, "Our National Mission," in Naoichi Masaoka, ed., *Japan's Message to America: A Symposium by Representative Japanese on Japan and American-Japanese Relations* (Tokyo, 1914), 4–5.

4. Terashima Seiichiro, "Exclusionists Not True to the Principles of America's Founders," in Masaoka, *Japan's Message to America*, 73–78.

5. K. T. Takahashi, *The Anti-Japanese Petition: Appeal in Protest against a Threatened Persecution* (Montreal: Gazette Printing Co., 1897), 12.

6. Gertrude Haessler, "Japan's Untouchables," *The Nation* 117, no. 3035 (5 September 1923): 249–252.

7. Frederick S. Hulse, "Status and Function as Factors in the Structure of Organizations among the Japanese," *American Anthropologist* 49 (1947): 157. Considered as a strategy, the insistence on homogeneity despite the distinctions made among nikkei themselves was consistent with the distinction made in Japan between *tatemae* and *honne* (formal appearances and inner feelings), *uchi* and *soto* (private and public), or *omote* and *ura* (face/front and rear). See Barbara Finkelstein, Anne E. Imamura, and Joseph J. Tobin, eds., *Transcending Stereotypes: Discovering Japanese Culture and Education* (Yarmouth, Maine: Intercultural Press, 1991), 17. See also Joy Hendry, *Wrapping Culture: Politeness, Presentation, and Power in Japan and Other Societies* (Oxford: Clarendon Press, 1993), 145, discussing honne and tatemae.

8. As David M. Potter and Paul Kneppner observed in 1996, koseki (family registration records) have essentially defined who is Japanese since the early Meiji period. David M. Potter and Paul Knepper, "Comparing Official Definitions of Race in Japan and the United States," *Southeast Review of Asian Studies* 18 (1996): 105, 107.

9. According to Shigesaki Ninomiya, the Rice Riot arrests and Japan's proposal for racial equality, which it made at the Versailles Conference, were "two of the greatest influences in the awakening of the masses of the 'Eta' people," because they highlighted the "great inconsistency in Japan's advocating race equality when discrimination in existence within the country came into the minds of

the leaders of the 'Eta' people." Shigesaki Ninomiya, "An Inquiry Concerning the Origin, Development, and Present Situation of the 'Eta' in Relation to the History of Social Classes in Japan" (M.A. thesis, University of Washington, 1931), 127. See also "To Redeem Japan's Pariahs," *The Literary Digest*, 4 September 1926, stating that only after the First World War did the "race and class consciousness that came in [its] wake [inspire] the eta to demand a position of equality with the rest of the nation."

10. Fujii Chojiro, "Eta mondai to nihon no shōrai," *Taihoku Nippō*, 1 January 1919 (my translation).

11. Ibid.

12. Ibid. (my translation).

13. The Suiheisha was established on March 3, 1922. Hugh H. Smythe, "Suiheisha: Japan's NAACP," *The Crisis* (February 1953). The organization was repressed during World War II but was revived after the war under the name Buraku Kaihō Zenkoku Iinkai. Ibid. See also Haessler, "Japan's Untouchables," 249–252. The organization comprised several branches, one of which was heavily influenced by Marxist thought.

14. Shimosaka Masahide, "Seigi o sakebi uru mono" (People Who Are Able to Cry Out for Justice), *Aikoku Shimbun* (11 June 1924): 4.

15. The founders of the Suiheisha quickly extended their vision beyond Japan and conceived of their association as a worldwide movement, relevant not only to Japan but also to the United States and Canada. See "Sekai no suihei undō" (The Worldwide Suihei Movement), *Seisen* 3 (c. 1924): 3. What was at stake, in their view, was not just their own welfare but the welfare of all human beings. Matsu Yasuji, "Suihei yowa," *Jiyū* (September 1926); Hirano Shoken, "Kisha mosu," *Suihei Jihō* (1923). The Suiheisha also established ties with Korean activists who had established a *Kohei,* or Korean equality movement, in 1923, and also urged an end to anti-Chinese prejudice in Japan. See "Sekai no suihei undō," 3; "Shinajin haiseki mondai" (The Issue of Anti-Chinese Prejudice), from "Nōto Kara," *Aikoku Shimbun*, 11 May 1924; Shimosato, "Seigi o sakebi uru mono." Because Koreans were Japanese subjects, the 1924 Immigration Act also applied to them. Mary Paik Lee, *Quiet Odyssey: A Pioneer Korean Woman in America* (Seattle: University of Washington Press, 1990), xlvii–xlix, 136.

16. Ninomiya, "Inquiry Concerning the Origin of the 'Eta,' " 3. The flag, designed by Saiko Mankichi, is on display at Liberty Museum, Osaka.

17. "Sekai no suihei undō," 3.

18. Ibid.; Hirano Shoken, "Beikoku taishi o hōmon no hi" (The Day on Which We Called on the U.S. Ambassador), *Aikoku Shimbun*, 1 June 1924. Scholars have noted that the emphasis on national social solidarity in Japan was itself a product of an effort to deal with the social disruption in the wake of the Meiji Restoration. See, for example, Kenneth B. Pyle, "The Technology of Japanese Nationalism: The Local Improvement Movement, 1900–1918," *Journal of Asian Studies* 33, no. 1 (November 1973): 55. Also see Harumi Befu, *Hegemony of Homogeneity: An Anthropological Analysis of Nihonjinron* (Melbourne: Trans

Pacific Press, 2001); Kosaku Yoshino, "The *Nihonjinron:* Thinking Elites' Ideas of Japanese Uniqueness," in Michael Weiner, ed., *Race, Ethnicity and Migration in Modern Japan,* vol. 1 (London: Routledge Curzon, 2004), 253–255.

19. "Sekai no suihei undō," 3–4. *Tokushu burakumin* (special villagers) was a euphemism used to denote former outcastes in Japan during the early twentieth century.

20. Ibid., 5.

21. Ibid.; Shimosato, "Seigi o sakebi uru mono," 4.

22. "Sekai no suihei undō," 3.

23. Matsu, "Suihei yowa."

24. Letter from Hanihara Masanao, Ambassador to the United States, to Charles E. Hughes, 10 April 1924, reprinted in Gaimushō, *1924 nen beikoku iminhō seitei oyobi kore ni kansuru nichi-bei kōshō keika kōbunsho; eibun fuzokusho* (Tokyo: Gaimushō, 1924), 198. After passage of the 1924 Immigration Act, the Japanese government issued a statement that section 13(c) was "manifestly intended to apply to Japanese." Ibid., 254. The act was signed by Calvin Coolidge on May 26, 1924, and was to go into effect on July 1 of that year. Ibid., 252.

25. See *The Trans-Pacific,* 15 March and 10 May 1924.

26. *The Trans-Pacific,* 22 March 1924 (reprinting *New York Post* article). The possibility that tension between the United States and Japan over the issue of immigration might lead to war had been raised as early as 1909. *The British Columbian,* 26 January 1909: "Japanese Are Still Friendly; Officials Think That Anti-Japanese Acts Are to Stir Up Hostile Feelings ... Press of Island Kingdom Mostly Expresses Confidence That Peace Will Exist with U.S.A."

27. An Act to Limit the Immigration of Aliens into the United States, and for Other Purposes (Immigration Act of 1924), 43 Stat. 153, section 13(c). For a detailed discussion of the reasoning underlying the act, see Mae Ngai, *Impossible Subjects: Illegal Aliens and the Making of Modern America* (Princeton, N.J.: Princeton University Press, 2003), chapter 1.

28. Patricia E. Roy, J. L. Granatstein, Masako Iino, and Hiroko Takamura, *Mutual Hostages: Canadians and Japanese during the Second World War* (Toronto: University of Toronto Press, 1990), 16–17.

29. *The Trans-Pacific,* 10 May 1924. The three men who visited the U.S. Ambassador were Sakamoto Seiichiro, Yoneda Tomiichiro, and Hirano Shoken.

30. Hirano, "Beikoku taishi o hōmon no hi."

31. Ibid. Members of the right wing of the Suiheisha were extremely critical of the visit to the U.S. ambassador, describing it as "crazy." They argued that the Suiheisha should focus its criticism on the "weak policy" of the Japanese government, which continued to try to accommodate the "shameful foreign policy" of the United States. "Dai-ajia no meimō" (Greater Asia Confusion), *Senmin* (15 May 1924).

32. Hirano, "Beikoku taishi o hōmon no hi." For a description of the range of reaction to the Immigration Act by groups other than the Suiheisha in Japan, see Izumi Hirobe, *Japanese Pride, American Prejudice: Modifying the Exclusion*

Clause of the 1924 Immigration Act (Stanford, Calif.: Stanford University Press, 2001), 21–47; Izumi Hirobe, " 'Grave Consequences': The Movements to Modify the Japanese Exclusion Clause in the Immigration Law of 1924" (Ph.D. diss., Harvard University, 1995), 6–31. See also Ken Adachi, *The Enemy That Never Was: A History of the Japanese Canadians* (Toronto: McClelland and Stewart, 1976), 133, describing the reaction of Japanese press to the act: it was as "spiteful as vipers and snakes." Because Korea was a colony of Japan at the time, Koreans were also treated as Japanese subjects under the act. Hyung-chan Kim, *A Legal History of Asian Americans, 1790–1990* (Westport, Conn.: Greenwood Press, 1994), 114.

33. Hirano, "Beikoku taishi o hōmon no hi." Interestingly, David Suzuki and Keibo Oiwa make a similar argument with regard to buraku jūmin in Japan. "As victims of discrimination," they argue, buraku jūmin have an opportunity to educate other Japanese "by reminding them of the pain and irrationality of bigotry." David Suzuki and Keibo Oiwa, *The Japan We Never Knew: A Journey of Discovery* (Toronto: Stoddart, 1996), 145, republished in the United States as *The Other Japan: Voices Beyond the Mainstream* (Golden, Colo.: Fulcrum, 1999).

34. Quoted in Tahara Haruto, "Nijū ni haiseki sareru mure yori" (From Those Who Are Doubly Discriminated Against), *Dōai* (September 1924).

35. Tahara, "Nijū ni haiseki sareru mure yori."

36. Matsu, "Suihei yowa."

CONCLUSION: REFRACTING DIFFERENCE

1. Karl Yoneda to Joe Grant Masaoka, 21 August 1965, referring to pages 4 and 5 of the *Issei Oral History Survey*, Japanese American Research Project, University of California, Los Angeles. Karl Yoneda, also known as Karl Hama, was a labor activist and an editor of the *Rōdō* [Labor] *Shimbun*. Yoneda, a *kibei nisei,* was born in Glendale, California, in 1906. He was sent to Japan to study at the age of seven and returned to the United States at the age of twenty in order to—in his words—"escape the Japanese Imperial Army" into which he had been drafted. Karl Yoneda, "100 Years of Japanese Labor History in the USA," in Amy Tachiki, Franklin S. Odo, Eddie Wong, and Buck Wong, eds., *Roots: An Asian American Reader* (Los Angeles: Continental Graphics, 1971), 150.

2. Yoneda's suggestion that historical caste categories still retained considerable significance among the issei decades after the end of the Second World War is supported by others who have spoken frankly of their experiences. In 1992, for example, Maryka Omatsu, a nisei lawyer and activist, observed that women of her mother's generation could "still 'place' most [nikkei] families ... across" Canada in terms of both status and geographical origin. Maryka Omatsu, *Bittersweet Passage: Redress and the Japanese-Canadian Experience* (Toronto: Between the Lines, 1992), 99. Similarly, in the context of discussing the extent to which traditional status categories important during the Meiji era continued to be a factor among Japanese Canadians, the mother of the well-known Japanese Canadian poet Roy Kiyooka mused, "I know

class doesn't seem to count for much nowadays when all sorts of people mix but I think class persists. People like to tout their differences." Roy Kiyooka, *Mothertalk: Life Stories of Mary Kiyoshi Kiyooka,* ed. Daphne Marlatt (Edmonton, Alberta: NeWest Press, 1997), 26.

3. Ooms notes that people classified as outcastes resisted being called *eta* even during historical times. Herman Ooms, *Tokugawa Village Practice: Class, Status, Power, Law* (Berkeley: University of California Press, 1996), 248–249, 306. The term *shinheimin* is also problematic in that it emphasizes the recent nature of their inclusion as commoners in Japan and became "a marker of continuing discrimination." David L. Howell, *Geographies of Identity in Nineteenth-Century Japan* (Berkeley: University of California Press, 2005), 85.

GLOSSARY OF SELECTED TERMS

burakumin	term used today to refer to descendants of former outcastes; literally, "village persons"
buraku jūmin	term used today to refer to descendants of former outcastes; literally, "village residents"
dekasegi	temporary labor migrants
eta	derogatory term historically used to refer to a particular outcaste group
genrō	Meiji oligarchs
hakujin	Caucasian; literally, "white person"
heimin	commoner or citizen
hi-imin	historical term used to describe Japanese emigrants other than labor emigrants (*imin*)
hinin	derogatory term historically used to refer to a particular outcaste group
ijūsha	term preferred today to refer to Japanese immigrants
imin	term historically used to refer to Japanese labor immigrants
issei	first-generation Japanese immigrants; immigrants born in Japan and residing elsewhere
kokujin	African American; literally, "black person"
koseki	family registration record

mibun   social status or rank, especially within the Tokugawa status system

nikkeijin   people of Japanese ancestry; literally, "Japan," "thread," and "people"

nisei   second-generation Japanese immigrants, the first generation born abroad

samurai   the highest of the four official Tokugawa-era status groups: samurai, farmers, artisans, merchants

shashin kekkon   marriage based on exchange of letters and photographs; literally, "picture marriage"

shinheimin   term meaning "new commoner," used to identify former outcastes after outcaste status was formally abolished in 1871; now obsolete

INDEX

Page numbers in *italics* refer to illustrations.